Writing the Modern Research Paper

SECOND EDITION

Robert Dees
Orange Coast College

Allyn and Bacon
Boston ■ London ■ Toronto ■ Sydney ■ Tokyo ■ Singapore

Vice President, Humanities: Joseph Opiela
Editorial Assistant: Kate Tolini
Marketing Manager: Lisa Kimball
Production Administrator: Rowena Dores
Editorial-Production Service: Susan Freese, Communicáto, Ltd.
Text Design and Electronic Composition: Denise Hoffman, Glenview Studios
Composition/Prepress Buyer: Linda Cox
Manufacturing Buyer: Suzanne Lareau
Cover Administrator: Linda Knowles

Copyright © 1997, 1993 by Allyn & Bacon
A Viacom Company
160 Gould Street
Needham Heights, MA 02194

Internet: www.abacon.com
America Online: keyword:College Online

Library of Congress Cataloging-in-Publication Data

Dees, Robert.
    Writing the modern research paper, 2nd ed. / Robert Dees.
        p.   cm.
    Includes bibliographical references and index.
    ISBN 0-205-26142-6 (alk. paper)
    1. Report writing.   2. Research.   I. Title.
    LB2369.D44 1997   96-32294
    808'.02—dc20   CIP

Printed in the United States of America

10 9 8 7 6 5   01 00 99

C O N T E N T S

Preface   x

1 *Critical Thinking and the Research Paper*   1

Research Teaches Thinking   2
What Is a Research Paper?   2
   The Research Topic 3 ■ *Length* 3 ■ *Organization* 3
Doing Research for Your Paper   4
   Finding Sources 4 ■ *Documenting Sources* 5
Organizing Your Research   5
   Planning a Research Schedule 6 ■ *Patterns of Research
   Progress* 8 ■ *Keeping a Research Notebook* 8
Including Your Own Ideas in the Research Paper   13
Working with Others   13

2 *Using a Library for Research*   15

Understanding Academic and Public Libraries   15
   Academic Libraries 16 ■ *Public Libraries* 17
How Libraries Are Organized   18
   The Reference Area 18 ■ *The Book Area* 19
   The Periodicals Room 19 ■ *Other Specialized Areas* 19
Library Classification Systems   19
   The Dewey Decimal System 20 ■ *The Library of
   Congress System* 21
Working with the Library Catalog   22
   Using the Card Catalog 22 ■ *Using the Online Catalog* 24
   Using Other Types of Library Catalogs 26

Library Services and Resources   27
Librarian Assistance 27 ■ *Information Service* 27
Search Assistance 28 ■ *Interlibrary Loan* 28
Reserve and Recall 28 ■ *Nonprint Sources* 28
Photocopying 28 ■ *Computer Facilities* 29
Working with Others   29

3 Planning the Focus of Your Research   30

Understanding a Subject and Topic   31
Finding a Research Subject and Topic   31
Selecting an Appropriate Research Subject   32
Assigned Subjects 32 ■ *Free-Choice Subjects* 32
Reviewing Your Interests 33 ■ *Recording Subject Ideas* 33
Using Library Sources to Find a Research Subject   34
Encyclopedias 34 ■ *Current Books* 35 ■ *The* Reader's
Guide 37 ■ *The* Social Issues Resources Series (SIRS) 38
Moving from a Subject to a Research Topic   38
Focusing Your Efforts 39 ■ *Going Online to Find
a Topic* 40 ■ *Recording Potential Topics* 42
Using Discovery Techniques to Focus on a Topic   43
Freewriting 43 ■ *Clustering* 45 ■ *Relating a Subject
to Your Interests* 46
Narrowing the Focus of the Research Topic   46
Working with a Back-Up Topic in Mind   47
A Checklist for Topic Selection   48
Formulating a Research Question   49
Recording Research Questions   50
Using Critical Thinking Techniques to Focus on Research   50
Considering Your Audience   52
Defining the Paper's Purpose   52
The Argumentative Paper 53 ■ *The Informative Paper* 54
Working with a Preliminary Thesis   55
Working with Others   55

4 Researching Library Sources   57

Preparing the Working Bibliography   57
Listing Sources on Cards or in a Computer File 58
Gauging the Topic's Feasibility 61

Using Bibliographies to Locate Sources   61
  Becoming Familiar with General Bibliographies   62
  Searching Trade Bibliographies for Sources   64

Using Indexes to Locate Sources   66
  Periodical Indexes   66 ■ *Newspaper Indexes*   77
  Newspapers Online   79 ■ *Periodical Files or Serials Lists*   80
  Indexes to Literature in Collections   80 ■ *Pamphlet
  Indexes*   83 ■ *Indexes to U.S. Government Publications and
  Documents*   84 ■ *Locating Government Sources Online*   87

Reviewing Your Library Search   89

Working with Others   89

5 *Researching beyond
    the Campus Library*   **91**

Using Primary and Secondary Sources   91

Observing Onsite   92

Researching Society and Museum Libraries   94
  Society Libraries   94 ■ *Museum Libraries*   95 ■ *Finding
  Special Libraries and Museums*   95

Finding Other Sources of Research   96

Interviews   97
  Determining the Purpose   97 ■ *Selecting the Right Person*   98
  Scheduling the Appointment   98 ■ *Preparing for the
  Interview*   99 ■ *Conducting the Interview*   99
  Interview Structures   99 ■ *Quoting from the Interview*   100
  Interview Length   100 ■ *Using Telephone or Mail
  Interviews*   100 ■ *Documenting the Interview*   103

Surveys   104
  Using Published Surveys   104 ■ *Conducting Your Own
  Survey*   105 ■ *Documenting the Survey*   109

Speeches and Lectures   110
  Listening to Community Speakers   110 ■ *Attending Campus
  Lectures*   111 ■ *Documenting Speeches and Lectures*   111

Radio and Television   112
  Investigating the Past   112 ■ *Researching Current News*   113
  Documenting Radio and Television Programs   114

Public Print Sources   115
  Finding Materials   115 ■ *Documenting Public
  Print Sources*   116

Working with Others   116

6 *Researching Online and through the Internet* 118

Using a Database for Research 118

Researching through the Internet 120
Internet Addresses 120

Using Online/Internet Search Tools 121
The World Wide Web 121 ■ *Telnet* 122 ■ *FTP* 122
Gopher 123 ■ *Archie and Veronica* 123 ■ *WAIS* 124
Other Resources 125

Working with Others 129

7 *Reading and Recording Information* 131

Planning Your Reading 131

Types of Reading 132
Skimming 132 ■ *Close Reading* 135

Taking Effective Notes 136
What to Take Notes About 136 ■ *Note Format* 137
Note Content 137 ■ *Where to Record Notes* 141
Types of Notes 144 ■ *Plagiarism* 150

Critically Evaluating Sources 153
Developing Critical Judgment 154 ■ *Consulting Other Opinions* 154 ■ *Evaluation Criteria* 156

Working with Others 157

8 *Planning Your Paper* 158

Using Your Research Notes 158
Arranging and Studying Your Notes 158 ■ *Reviewing the Research Question* 159 ■ *Reviewing the Preliminary Thesis Statement* 159

Devising a Final Thesis Statement 160
Writing an Effective Thesis Statement 160
Reviewing Your Paper's Purpose 162 ■ *Comparing the Purposes of Sample Papers* 163 ■ *Using Your Paper's Purpose for Planning* 164

Working with an Outline 164
An Informal Outline 165 ■ *A Formal Outline* 165

Types of Outlines 168 ■ *Creating Your Own Outline* 170
Guidelines for the Formal Outline 172

A Review of Basic Patterns of Development 174
Argumentation 174 ■ *Comparison-and-Contrast* 175
Classification 176 ■ *Cause-and-Effect* 176 ■ *APA and
Scientific Patterns* 177

Creating a Title 177

Working with Others 178

9 Writing Your Paper 180

Reviewing Your Preparation for Writing 180

Preparing to Write 180
Progressing in Stages 180 ■ *Determining an
Appropriate Style* 181 ■ *Considering the Audience* 182

Writing the Paper 184
The Introduction 184 ■ *The Body* 187
The Conclusion 196 ■ *Other Backmatter* 199

Preparing a Final Draft 200
Revising 200 ■ *Editing* 201 ■ *Proofreading* 202

Working with Others 203

**10 Acknowledging Sources:
Intext Citation and Content Notes
(MLA Style) 205**

Following a Standard Documentation Format 205

MLA Documentation 206
Using Intext Citation 206 ■ *Using Content Notes* 213

Working with Others 217

Appendix 218

**11 Documenting Sources:
The Works Cited List (MLA Style) 238**

What to Include 238

Works Cited Entries 239
Listing Works Cited Entries 239 ■ *Formatting the Works
Cited Page* 239 ■ *General Guidelines* 239

Index to Works Cited Forms   246
  Books   246   ■   *Magazines and Journals*   247
  Newspapers   247   ■   *Other Sources*   247
Works Cited Forms   248
  Books   248   ■   *Magazines and Journals*   261
  Newspapers   265   ■   *Other Sources*   267
Working with Others   278

12 *Alternative Documentation Styles: Author-Date (APA and* Chicago*), Number-System, and CBE*   279

Understanding Various Styles   280
Author-Date Documentation   281
APA Style   281
  Abstracts   281   ■   *Headings*   282   ■   *Intext Citation*   282
  References   289   ■   *Sample References List: Psychology*   299
  Discipline Practices: APA Variations   299
Number-System Documentation   301
  Intext Citation   301   ■   *References*   302
  Other Features   304
CBE Style   305
  Name-Year Intext Citation Form   305   ■   *Citation-Sequence Intext Citation Form*   306   ■   *References Forms*   307
  Discipline Practices: CBE Variations   310
Chicago-Style Documentation   312
  Intext Citation   312   ■   *Notes*   314   ■   *References*   314
Discipline Style Manuals   314
Working with Others   317

13 *Preparing the Final Manuscript*   318

Reviewing and Strengthening the Final Draft   318
Revising   318
  How to Revise   319   ■   *What to Revise*   319
Editing   320
  How to Edit   320   ■   *What to Edit*   320   ■   *Technical Editing Guidelines*   322
Producing the Final Manuscript   341
Working with Others   344

APPENDIX A
Sample Research Papers: APA (Author-Date) and CBE (Citation-Sequence System) Documentation Styles   345

Sample Paper 1: APA (Author-Date) Documentation Style   345

Sample Paper 2: CBE (Citation-Sequence System) Documentation Style   366

APPENDIX B
Reference Sources for Selected Subjects   375

Index to Subjects   375

Reference Sources by Subject   376
   Anthropology and Archaeology 376 ■ *Art and Architecture* 376 ■ *Biological Sciences* 377
   Business 378 ■ *Chemistry and Chemical Engineering* 379
   Computer Science 380 ■ *Ecology* 380 ■ *Education* 381
   Ethnic Studies 382 ■ *Film* 384 ■ *Geography* 384
   Geology 385 ■ *Health and Physical Education* 385
   History 386 ■ *Journalism and Mass Communications* 387
   Language 387 ■ *Literature* 388 ■ *Mathematics* 390
   Medical Sciences 390 ■ *Music* 391 ■ *Philosophy and Religion* 391 ■ *Physics* 392 ■ *Political Science* 393
   Psychology 394 ■ *Sociology and Social Work* 394
   Speech 395 ■ *Women's Studies* 395

Index   397

PREFACE

Like its predecessor, the second edition of *Writing the Modern Research Paper* continues to provide college students in all disciplines with an up-to-date, step-by-step guide to doing enjoyable, effective research and to writing thorough, well-documented papers. This edition, however, also includes much new material intended to increase the text's usefulness and currency:

■ *Critical thinking:* Chapter 1 introduces critical thinking—including summary, evaluation, analysis, and synthesis—as an integral part of any successful research project. Later chapters echo the need for students to react thoughtfully to the sources they discover and encourage students to use those sources discerningly to support their research conclusions.

■ *Electronic resources and the Internet:* The nature of research processes and opportunities has been changed significantly by the proliferation of information available on compact disc (CD–ROM) and online and by the accessibility of worldwide databases. This second edition discusses these and other new aspects of research with attention to what they mean for students writing college or university research papers. A new Chapter 6, "Researching Online and through the Internet," has been added to introduce students to more recent opportunities for using databases and the Internet, in particular. This chapter discusses accessing Internet addresses, the World Wide Web, and the very latest computer search tools, such as Gopher, Telnet, ftp, and others that make doing online research both valuable and exciting.

■ *Current documentation styles:* Most academic discipline authorities have changed their recommended documentation styles within the past few years to address the use of electronic resources and to streamline traditional practices. In keeping with these changes, Chapters 10 through 12 have been revised to present the most recent documentation forms (including those for electronic sources) recommended by the Modern Language Association (MLA), the American Psychological Association (APA), the Council of Biology Editors (CBE), and *The Chicago Manual of Style*.

■ *Suggestions for writing on computer:* Since it is likely that many students will write their papers on computer, this edition offers specific suggestions for using computer technology effectively at various stages of the research process—from organizing notes and sources through writing, proofreading, and editing the first draft and printing the final paper. Examples within the text follow current MLA and APA preferences for using underlining, rather than italics, especially for titles of published works. The text also explains, however, that either option is acceptable for research papers and advises students to consult with their instructors regarding which option they prefer.

Plan for the Text

My own years of teaching about the research paper have shown me that in order to think critically and creatively during the research process, students need to understand the range of possibilities for conducting research and know how to use those possibilities to their advantage. Chapter 1, "Critical Thinking and the Research Paper," introduces students to critical thinking and the importance of summary, evaluation, analysis, and synthesis in using researched sources to reach logical and supportable conclusions. The chapter also provides an overview of the research paper and explains the value of framing a research question, planning a research schedule, and keeping a research notebook.

Chapter 2, "Using a Library for Research," continues the introduction to research by discussing the use of libraries and the wealth of resources they have to offer, including computer catalogs, reference sources, online accessibility, and experienced support staff. Techniques for using such resources and ways of narrowing a research topic are covered in Chapter 3, "Planning the Focus of Your Research." Chapter 4, "Researching Library Resources," discusses bibliographies and indexes and explains how to prepare a working bibliography.

Since not everything students need to know about their research topics will necessarily be found in college libraries, Chapter 5, "Researching beyond the Campus Library," leads students past traditional library sources and out into their communities. In addition to encouraging research using primary and secondary materials from public sources, this chapter also explains how to gather information by observing onsite, conducting personal interviews, taking surveys, and utilizing such media as radio and television. Chapter 6, "Researching Online and through the Internet," continues to expand students' awareness of and ability to research independently by discussing how to use databases, access the Internet and World Wide Web, and employ search tools like ftp, Telnet, Gopher, and others.

Chapter 7, "Reading and Recording Information," discusses the importance of careful reading and notetaking—practical, time-saving skills that can ensure accurate content and source citation later. This chapter presents critical thinking techniques to evaluate sources and discusses how and when to use summary, paraphrase, and quotation in research papers. The importance of citing sources to avoid the problem of plagiarism is addressed, as well.

Once students have begun to assemble a quantity of research data, they are often confused about how to begin organizing it and writing their papers. Because of the importance of these activities, they are discussed in two separate but related chapters. Chapter 8, "Planning Your Paper," explains how to formulate and use preliminary and final thesis statements to focus the paper's discussion as well as how to devise an appropriate outline to organize the content. Basic written patterns of development are also reviewed. Chapter 9, "Writing Your Paper," explains a variety of ways to write the introduction, body, and conclusion and discusses how to revise, edit, and proofread the final draft.

Three chapters are devoted to explaining and differentiating among the most common documentation styles used for research papers. Chapters 10 and 11 demonstrate correct forms for intext citations and the Works Cited section of a research paper using the MLA style of documentation. A sample MLA-style research paper is included in Chapter 10. Chapter 12 discusses alternative documentation styles, including the author-date styles followed by the APA and *Chicago* and name-year and citation-sequence styles followed by the CBE.

Chapter 13, "Preparing the Final Manuscript," addresses the many technical and stylistic matters that often confront students writing research papers. MLA conventions for handling abbreviations, numbers, illustrations, titles, and so forth are explained, as is the meaning of *fair use* according to current copyright law.

To assist writers using documentation styles other than MLA, Appendix A presents two additional sample research papers: the first using APA author-date style and the second using CBE citation-sequence style. Appendix B provides a guide to selected subject reference sources.

Like those in the first edition, each chapter in this new edition of *Writing the Modern Research Paper* concludes with a special Working with Others section, which promotes collaboration among students and takes the loneliness out of the research process. These sections may be used by groups of students working on their own, or they may be assigned by instructors as part of structured classroom activities.

Acknowledgments

As always, I am very grateful to Joe Opiela, Vice President, Humanities, at Allyn and Bacon, for his encouragement and advice on this and the previous edition, as well as to his assistant, Kathryn Tolini, who worked diligently to get this new edition ready for production. I also wish to thank those individuals who reviewed this book for Allyn and Bacon and offered useful suggestions for preparing the second edition: Janice Coleman, University of Mississippi; Carol Golliher, Victor Valley Community College District; Li Huo, Concordia College; and Jean A. Weber, Walla Walla Community College.

I am also grateful for the assistance of Bill Stevenson of Orange Coast College for his help in researching and writing one of the sample research papers. And of course, my deepest thanks go to my wife, Van, for her patience and love during a tough year.

CHAPTER 1

Critical Thinking and the Research Paper

Writing a research paper provides an opportunity for some of the most integrated thinking and learning you can accomplish as a writer. Whether you investigate the topic of interstellar travel or the plight of people who are homeless, your research efforts will result in your knowing a subject thoroughly as well as understanding how others regard it and why. Ultimately, your research will bring you to formulate your own opinion and to explain it in writing. The finished product—a thoughtfully researched and written research paper—will represent thinking that reflects your careful evaluation of evidence and your analysis and synthesis of a number of different sources.

Such thinking, even when performed unconsciously, is known as *critical thinking*. We can define *critical thinking* as the careful questioning and consideration of evidence, leading to a reasoned, bias-free conclusion. An effective research effort and the paper that results from it usually employ critical thinking throughout the research/writing process in the form of four basic techniques:

1. *Summary:* briefly and objectively restating the main ideas of a text or relating the major episodes of an event
2. *Evaluation:* judging the claims of others to determine the significance of their evidence
3. *Analysis:* applying a set of principles to an idea or situation to reveal its nature
4. *Synthesis:* incorporating facts and opinions from others into your own thinking to support your conclusions

Such techniques of critical thinking are integral to conducting successful research, beginning with selecting a topic and continuing through examining sources and writing the final report. Take, for example, the question Is intelligence environmentally induced or genetically inherited? Thinking critically about the question should raise a number of additional questions:

> Who says so and in what source?
>
> What is his or her authority on this subject?
>
> What kinds of claims are made in this source, and what type of evidence is offered to support those claims?
>
> What do other sources say?
>
> What conclusions can I draw, based on the material I have examined?

Thinking critically about these and similar questions regarding a research topic will involve you in an ongoing process in which you will learn according to your own ways of thinking.

Research Teaches Thinking

In fact, you should regard writing a research paper as learning how to think on your own about significant issues. None of your professors will simply hand you information in the form of a lecture or notes, nor will a textbook or other single source sum up all you need to know and understand about a subject. Your efforts in producing a research paper will educate you in ways of acquiring information and give you practice in thinking critically about what you discover. You will come to see that doing research is learning to think in its most fundamental form: the independent acquisition, evaluation, and synthesis of new information.

What Is a Research Paper?

The research paper you write will be a documented report resulting from your thinking critically about the information you examine. Its content will focus upon a topic that your own intellectual curiosity brings you to study. The primary purpose of such a paper is to inform the reader about the research topic and to demonstrate the validity or reasonableness of your conclusions about it. Although it is more objective than a personal essay, keep in mind that a research paper is also an expression of your own understanding of the topic. Your personal values, insights, and experiences will shape your responses throughout the research process, eventually finding expression in what you conclude and how you write about the topic.

The Research Topic

The information you collect for a research paper relates to a research subject or, more accurately, to a particular aspect of it called the *topic*. If you were interested, for example, in researching the subject of space exploration, a possible topic might be the benefits of long-range space probes like *Explorer I* or *Galileo*. Another topic for a paper on space exploration might be the physiological effects upon humans of spending prolonged periods of time in outer space.

Once you have selected a suitable topic for research, you can begin to frame a *research question,* which will become the focus of your research and your paper's discussion. How beneficial are long-range space probes? might be one question to investigate. Should we continue sending long-range probes into space? would shift the focus to a different aspect of the same subject. A topic concerning the effects upon humans of prolonged time in space could generate a research question such as Are prolonged flights in space too dangerous for humans?

Questions like these direct the investigation of sources and focus your notetaking. They ensure that your paper will raise a significant issue and provide thoughtful discussion about the topic.

Length

The amount of discussion needed to support your main point about the research topic will determine your paper's length. In general, you will probably want to select a research topic that can be adequately discussed in 10 to 12 typewritten pages (5,000–6,000 words), the assigned length for most college research papers. Depending upon your topic, the length of time you have for research, and the expectations of your instructor, your paper may be somewhat shorter or longer.

Organization

A completed research paper includes several major parts, usually arranged in this order:

Title page
Outline (optional)
Text
Notes (optional)
Works Cited/References
Appendix (optional)

The largest part of the paper—the *text,* or content, portion—generally consists of three major sections:

Introduction	Introduction of the topic leads to a statement of the paper's thesis.
Body	Several paragraphs that illustrate and support the thesis through discussion, analysis, and examples; acknowledgment of sources as appropriate.
Conclusion	A summary of major arguments or a final statement and example.
Works Cited or References	A list of sources acknowledged in the paper.

FIGURE 1.1   Simplified diagram of a research paper

1. The *introduction,* which sets forth the paper's *thesis,* or main point
2. The *body,* which illustrates and supports the main point with paragraphs of information and discussion
3. The *conclusion,* which states a final idea or summarizes the paper's major arguments

A research paper also includes *documentation,* the citing of sources in the text of the paper as well as their listing at the end of the paper in a section titled Works Cited or References. Figure 1.1 presents a simplified diagram of a typical research paper.

Doing Research for Your Paper

To "re-search" a subject is literally to see it another way: You gather original information of your own or study the work of others and evaluate it from your own point of view and experience.

Finding Sources

The investigation you do for a research paper may draw upon several kinds of sources. *Primary sources* include original material from such sources as the following:

■ Your own experiences
■ Field observations
■ Interviews
■ Laboratory reports
■ Diaries
■ Letters
■ Literary works

Or you may be involved in research that uses information written by others about your subject. These *secondary sources* are those found in most libraries and include materials like these:

■ Encyclopedias
■ Magazines
■ Journals
■ Books
■ Newspapers
■ Pamphlets
■ Indexes
■ Computer databases
■ Government reports

In order to give your paper both depth and breadth in its discussion of the research topic, use both primary and secondary sources as much as possible (see Chapters 4 and 5). You will find the critical thinking techniques of summary, evaluation, analysis, and synthesis helpful in assessing and taking useful notes from each kind of source (see Chapter 5).

Documenting Sources

Regardless of which kinds of sources you use, your paper will include *documentation,* a method of acknowledging where you found your information and giving credit for any ideas that are not your own. Depending upon the kind of paper you write and for which discipline, the documentation may appear within the text of the paper itself in footnotes or at the end of the paper in endnotes. As described earlier, your paper will also include a list of all the works cited as documentation in the paper. (See Chapter 11 and Appendix A on documentation forms for various academic disciplines.)

Organizing Your Research

A successful research paper reflects careful planning, not only of the research activities themselves but also of the time involved to accomplish them. The due date for your paper limits the time available for research and writing, and it puts pressure on you to finish the paper by a specified date. In order to complete the research process fully and to make sure the paper is finished on time, you will need to plan a reasonable research schedule and do all you can to keep to it.

Planning a Research Schedule

A *research schedule* is a calendar of all the steps necessary for completing a successful research paper on time. Obviously, your schedule will list the paper's due date, but you should also include the major research steps that are described in this text:

1. Investigating one or more potential research subjects
2. Selecting a topic and framing a research question
3. Establishing a preliminary bibliography
4. Reading and taking notes on the topic
5. Devising an outline and tentative thesis statement
6. Writing the paper
7. Listing the works cited
8. Revising and editing

In addition, you should add any steps that are unique to your individual research methods and necessary for your particular topic.

Your planning for a successful research paper should begin early. In fact, you ought to start thinking about your subject, available resources, and your time for researching and writing the paper the first day you know about the assignment. Starting early like this will save time later and allow you to collect ideas and resources throughout the term.

Once you actually begin your research assignment in earnest, expect to spend at least four to five weeks of ongoing thinking, researching, and writing. If you are not familiar with using a computer to research online materials, give yourself additional time to learn about and practice using such a valuable research tool. Since writing a good research paper requires allowing enough time to complete all the activities mentioned, you should devise a research schedule that identifies the date for accomplishing each task as well as the turn-in date for your paper.

Figure 1.2 presents student Mark Stevenson's research schedule for his paper about television talk shows. The finished paper—titled Talk Television: Can "Trash TV" Survive?—is one of the sample research papers included in Appendix A. Note that Mark's research schedule includes the major steps given in this text as well as several activities required by his topic and his individual way of approaching it. Mark also decided to use asterisks to mark any due dates for various steps in the research process.

Mark became interested in the topic of talk shows shortly after watching a segment of *Montel Williams* titled "Should Parents Do Time for Their

Mark Stevenson
English 101

RESEARCH PAPER SCHEDULE

		Completed
September 22	Begin thinking about research subject. Start research notebook.	[ ]
October 15	Select research subject.	[ ]
November 14	Read encyclopedia, and review general sources on possible research topics.	[ ]
*November 17	Make topic decision. Get OK from Professor Curry.	[ ]
November 18	Start preliminary reading and notetaking.	[ ]
*November 21	Turn in preliminary bibliography.	[ ]
November 22–December 2	Research in library.	[ ]
November 24	Locate newsgroups, conferences, or chat groups discussing talk shows on the Internet or other online sources.	[ ]
November 28	Meet with psychology professor Robert James. Ask about talk show guests' motives and consequences of "self-disclosure."	[ ]
December 3–4	Analyze research notes. Make up outline and preliminary thesis statement.	[ ]
December 5–8	Write first draft of paper.	[ ]
*December 8	First draft due to Professor Curry for advice.	[ ]
December 8–10	Write final draft.	[ ]
December 11–12	Revise and edit final draft.	[ ]
December 14	Finish Works Cited list.	[ ]
*December 16	Final research paper due!	[ ]

FIGURE 1.2   Student Mark Stevenson's research paper schedule

Kids' Crimes?" Mark was impressed by the extent to which the program's audience both criticized and offered advice to the show's parents and their troublesome children. Given that, he began with the idea of writing about the positive effects television talk shows could have upon individuals and even society in general. But when his early research did not yield much material to support the claim that the shows were especially beneficial, Mark changed his mind. He decided to shift the focus of his research to the criticism given to talk shows and what impact it has upon them.

Patterns of Research Progress

The shift in direction that Mark made is not at all unusual for someone who is starting work on a research paper. His research schedule may look complete, but the fact is that Mark's planning, like his topic, actually changed several times during the assignment period. Even though this book will introduce you to the steps every research paper writer must complete, bear in mind that these steps do not necessarily occur in order or only once during the research effort. Your analysis of what you discover one day about your topic (say, the validity of IQ tests) may lead to new discoveries the next day, then a revision of your first analysis, and so on throughout your research. The book you thought would be of no help when you began your research may suddenly become essential at some later stage.

As Mark Stevenson discovered after he changed his research focus, research proceeds more in loops and zigzags than in a direct line. Keep your research efforts on track, but try not to become discouraged by this irregular pattern of progress: Looping and zigzagging is the nature of productive research.

The format for your own research schedule may vary from Mark's, but do not overlook this important planning step in preparing to write a research paper. Your schedule will change along with your research; it will also serve as your planning guide and a source of reassurance about the timeliness of your efforts. As you move progressively further into the research process, you will also find that checking off each completed task provides satisfaction and encouragement as you work to complete the paper.

Keeping a Research Notebook

Most of the thinking for your research paper will occur during times that you have specifically set aside for research and writing. Unfortunately, however, the best ideas and sudden insights do not always occur on schedule. Many useful thoughts will spring up spontaneously, often coming only half formed at unexpected times. Seeing a neighbor who works for the city housing agency, for example, may suddenly remind you that he or she would be an excellent interview source for a paper on people who are homeless. While crossing campus on your way to a morning class, you might recall the magazine article you read yesterday on the cost of space exploration. At that moment, you may start to think about how your paper might use some of those statistics.

To make sure useful ideas like these are not lost, you should write them down in a research notebook. A *research notebook* is any handy-size, spiral-bound notebook that you can literally carry with you everywhere and make a habit of using throughout the research process. You will find such a notebook a useful place to record valuable information, especially the spontaneous, mental pondering that occurs both during and between your planned research activities. The research notebook is also a good place to jot down titles you want to look for later, to pose questions you need answered, or to record your progress.

A research notebook will be most useful to you if you give some thought ahead of time to a few practical considerations. Follow these suggestions as you begin to set up your research notebook:

1. Keep a particular notebook reserved especially for your research notes and writing. Mixing your research material with other kinds of writing or class assignments defeats the purpose of the research notebook, which is to record and organize all of your thinking for the research paper in one easily accessible place.

2. Use pencil or ink to record ideas and information. While you do not need to worry about neatness, write legibly and make complete entries. Nothing is more frustrating than having to retrace your steps to find omitted information or not being able to decipher a hastily written note later.

3. Record names, titles, and other bibliographic data accurately and fully to avoid errors in your final paper. Make a point of later copying all such information about sources onto 3″ × 5″ notecards for easier use.

4. Use as many headings or subtitles in the notebook as necessary to keep your entries organized. Headings like Notes and Ideas, Research Subjects, Topic Choices, Sources to Find, and Questions to Answer will keep your entries accessible and encourage your thinking for each section.

5. Date each entry in the research notebook. This will help you see a pattern to the research as well as provide an occasional nudge when you have ignored something for too long.

The pages in Figure 1.3 are from student Nancy Prado's research notebook and show entries she made while preparing a paper on the need to

Nancy Prado

English 101

Research Notebook

Notes and Ideas

September 22: Professor Benfey described our research paper assignment today. Ten to fifteen pages on an issue related to the O. J. Simpson trial and our discussions in class about it. Start thinking of what I want to write about.

October 11: The jury selection process interests me. Who shows up for jury selection and who does not must have an impact on decisions. How do attorneys get to decide who stays on a jury and who doesn't? How much does jury selection affect the outcome of a trial? What did it mean in the Simpson case?

October 20: Library research on juries. Check online resources in the library and through America Online at home.

November 13: There have been a lot of cases recently in which juries have made controversial decisions—the Menendez brothers' case and the Marion Barry trial, for example. Attorneys use juror consultants, experts who analyze cases and recommend the kind of people to keep on a jury. What do they look for? I need to investigate this more.

November 17: Library hours for weekends: 8–5 Sat. & Sun.

November 19: Went online to Lexus, a database for legal resources. Excellent material for my paper.

November 24: Interview with Professor Robert Jamieson at the law school. This was a good idea. He is opposed to <u>peremptory challenges,</u> the kind that let attorneys dismiss potential jurors during the jury selection phase of a trial.

FIGURE 1.3 Student Nancy Prado's research notebook

Research Topics

1. The case for mandatory jury duty for all citizens over 18
2. Jury sequestering—a necessary evil?
3. The use of jury consultants
4. Jury nullification—ignoring the law to preserve justice
5. Ways to increase jury diversity

Research Questions

✓1. What are the laws in different states about who serves on a jury?
✓2. What are <u>peremptory challenges</u>, and what is their purpose?
3. Why are people losing faith in the jury system in the U.S.?
4. How much historical information about the jury system should I include in the paper?
5. How many of my own ideas go in the paper, and how many sources do I need to include?

Sources to Find

✓<u>November 5:</u> Check library for Lexus and Dialog databases. Research <u>TimeOnline</u> through America Online at home.

✓<u>November 10:</u> Find <u>Anatomy of a Jury</u> by Seymour Wishman, 1986.

<u>November 23:</u> Look for <u>Journal of Criminal Justice</u> in campus law library.

FIGURE 1.3 Continued

reform the American system of jury selection. Nancy became interested in this topic shortly after the conclusion of the O. J. Simpson trial. Her freshman English class had followed the trial and written several short essays about it. So for their research paper assignment in the course, Nancy's instructor asked students to select topics related to some aspect of the Simpson trial. Nancy had closely observed the jury selection period and was interested in the strategies that attorneys on both sides used to select jurors. Once she began reading more about jury selection in general, Nancy decided that she would write her research paper about the need for reforming the American jury selection system. She eventually completed the sample research paper in Chapter 10, titled Flawed Justice: Why and How the American Jury System Must Be Reformed. The entries in Figure 1.3 demonstrate how she used the research notebook to record and organize work on her paper.

As these entries show, a research notebook may contain many kinds of information, from short reminders about library hours to extended thinking about sources. You may decide to use your notebook as a place to record all your research notes and do extensive writing for the research paper, or you may want to use it only as a place to try out ideas in very brief forms.

Notice that Nancy Prado dated each entry. She also made a checkmark next to each task as she completed it (see p. 11). You may want to devise your own way of keeping track of what you accomplish, and you may even prefer using a different format than Nancy's for your notebook entries. The most important thing is to utilize your research notebook in a way that is genuinely helpful for preparing your research paper.

While there are no set requirements for what goes into a research notebook, the following kinds of entries are typically the most useful:

■ *Your research schedule:* Having your research schedule readily available will keep your efforts organized and give you direction. Make it the first item you put in your notebook.

■ *Ideas about your research topic:* Jot down spontaneous insights before you forget them. If you find yourself writing a lot, keep going. What you write could become valuable material for the final paper.

■ *Research questions:* Keep track of questions you need to answer for yourself about the paper's topic (What are my city's educational requirements for police personnel?) as well as those questions you will need to ask others (Do I hand in my research notebook with my final paper?).

■ *Sources to follow up on:* Record authors' names, source titles, libraries, data services, and other information you may need for your paper.

Since you never know when an idea or useful information may suddenly become available, make a habit of carrying your notebook with you wherever you go, not just to the library or during research times. Once you start using a research notebook regularly, you will find it an essential aid in researching and writing your paper.

Including Your Own Ideas
in the Research Paper

Unfortunately, too many beginning writers make the mistake of letting research content alone dominate their papers. Anxious to demonstrate the hours of research they have devoted to their papers or simply overwhelmed by the amount of material discovered, they end up writing summarizing reports instead of the thoughtful, creative responses to research that their instructors had expected. A work that only summarizes sources, instead of using them to illuminate ideas or support an argument, is not a research paper.

Make sure your paper analyzes, compares, and evaluates information and sources to support your position and clarify your thoughts for the reader. As you go about writing, remember that your own ideas are not only valuable but actually are, in one sense, what the paper is about. If you are writing a paper on the subject of homeless people in the United States, for example, your reader will not only want to know about these people but also what the information you present adds up to. Your presentation and interpretation of the facts, your analysis and comparison of other writers' opinions, and your conclusions about all of these constitute the heart of your research content.

W O R K I N G   W I T H   O T H E R S

Make a habit of talking over your research assignment with friends or classmates as early in the term as possible. Begin by discussing the following questions together to get a broad view of research and to be sure you understand the class assignment clearly.

- Discuss a recent film or television program you have seen that required someone to do research for its content or production. What kind of research was done? How was it done and by whom? How important to the success of the production was the research? Cite examples of how research or its results are being carried out in other areas of society.

- Review any previous experience you have had researching information, and discuss the major steps or tasks involved. How did that kind of research differ from that involved in doing the research paper for your current assignment?

- What kinds of research have you done on a computer? Discuss your knowledge and experience with those of one or more of classmates. Find out what computer resources for conducting research are available at your campus. What resources do you have at home?

- Regardless of whether you have had previous experience doing some kind of research, what questions do you now have about research and research papers generally?

- Discuss your current research paper assignment. Do you foresee any major obstacles to your successful completion of the assignment? If so, how will you overcome these obstacles?

- Exchange ideas about potential local resources for research. What primary or secondary resources are available?

- Have you used anything like a research notebook or made up something like a research schedule in the past? Why or why not? How helpful do you feel either of these will be to your completing the current research paper assignment?

- Share any ideas you have for a research subject or topic. What interests you about these issues? How do they fit your current research paper assignment?

Each of the chapters in this book concludes with suggestions for Working with Others on a research paper assignment. Also check with your instructor about any guidelines he or she may have for working together, and take advantage of any opportunities you have to share your ideas and progress. You will find that time spent discussing your research and writing with others is one of the best resources available.

CHAPTER **2**

Using a Library for Research

Before you can think clearly and critically about a subject, you must have a good understanding of it and know what others have said or written about it. Thus, whether writing a library-based research paper or one developed fully from your own field or laboratory studies, you will need the resources of a good library. You should use the library to discover what is already known about the research topic, what issues need to be addressed, and what sources exist for you to consider. Most campus libraries and large community libraries can provide the information you will need, first to establish the direction of your research and later to investigate a specific research question in depth.

This chapter will introduce you to academic and public libraries and how to use them, including newer types of library resources like computer catalogs, citation indexes, and database searches. You will need to understand such libraries and resources in order to make your research both efficient and comprehensive.

Understanding Academic and Public Libraries

It is best to begin your research at the largest library available. Access to numerous resources will ensure success in getting started and give you insight to the limitations and possibilities of the research topic. Once you have a topic and can focus on a potential research question, your goal will be to locate appropriate numbers and types of sources to investigate. Both academic and public libraries will be useful to your research for the different emphases and variety of sources they provide.

Academic Libraries

College and university libraries are created primarily to serve the study and research needs of students, faculty, and scholars. For this reason, academic libraries are your best resource for general as well as scarce or highly specialized materials. The sheer quantity of books, periodicals, microfilms, and other resources at most academic libraries makes them especially essential to competent research. (The combined libraries at Harvard University, for example, house over 11,000,000 books alone.) Since they are intended to serve research, the reference sections as well as the research support services of most academic libraries are also more extensive than those of community or private libraries.

Special Emphasis Libraries.   Most colleges and universities also maintain separate libraries for such professional areas as law, medicine, business, and technology. Such discipline libraries often contain specialized resources that you would not readily find in other libraries or at least not in such quantity. If you were researching a topic like *AIDS,* for example, you would most likely find a reference source such as *AIDS: A Multimedia Sourcebook,* by John J. Miletich (Greenwood Press, 1993), only at a college or university medical library. Similarly, you would go to a campus law library for *Index to Legal Periodicals* to locate the numerous legal journals not ordinarily found at the main college or university library. You will find that community college libraries are good resources for general research and especially for trade and vocational subjects.

The general emphasis of a college or university is often a reliable clue to its library's resources. Because of its focus on art and design, the Massachusetts College of Art, for example, has an extensive collection of slides, films, videos, and recordings in addition to a large general library. The library at Northrop University, a private California college emphasizing technology and business, houses over 65,000 books, many of them engineering and airframe maintenance sources that would be unavailable at most other academic or public libraries.

To work in the library at a school you do not attend, you may be restricted to using materials right in the library or checking them out on a community-use basis. You may also be able to check out resources through the interlibrary loan services on your own campus. Access to the libraries of private colleges and universities may be available for a small fee. And if you do visit another school's library, do not overlook the campus bookstore as an additional place to find very recent material on your subject.

Assessing What Is Available.   You should thoroughly investigate your own campus or another academic library and its resources before starting research. Though you may feel that you can research effectively at a nearby community library, you never know what research ideas might be better developed through the facilities of a larger library. Ask your instructor or a librarian what subjects the libraries of nearby universities and colleges emphasize.

Thanks to the Internet, you can access the catalogs of many university libraries just by going online. Use *Telnet* (medlib@gumedlib.georgetown. edu), for example, to get the catalog of library holdings at Georgetown University Medical Center, or use *Gopher* (yaleinfo.yale.edu) to get a list of all current library catalogs accessible on the Internet. (See Chapter 6 for a discussion of Telnet, Gopher, and other computer search systems.)

Also consult the following print references for information about major focuses, programs, and libraries at any college or university:

American Library Directory: 1994–95. New York: Bowker, 1994.
McKinley Internet Directory, Ed. Christine Maxwell. Indianapolis, IN: New Riders, 1995.
New Riders' Official Internet Yellow Pages. Indianapolis, IN: 1994.
The Right College: 1990. New York: ARCO, 1989.

Public Libraries

If your research steers you toward topics of community, county, or state importance, you may profit by investigating the holdings of one or more public libraries in your area. Public libraries do not usually offer the extensive general holdings or scholarly reference materials found in academic libraries. Most all public libraries, however, carry major encyclopedias; dictionaries; subject bibliographies; indexes to magazine, journal, and newspaper articles; and other standard reference works, which can be of help when you are first starting to research.

Special Focus Materials. Local libraries also offer resource materials not available at most academic or private libraries. News that has particular local importance—say, the closing of a nearby nuclear atomic power plant or the life and career of a famous area resident—may be more thoroughly covered by the small community newspapers kept on file at the local public library.

In addition, county and city libraries are often the only resources for local or regional historical documents. Because of a particular librarian's personal interest or a patron's donation of items, local city or county libraries may have special collections of materials (such as diaries, letters, scrapbooks, and antiques) not commonly included in academic library holdings. Your local public library may also maintain small informal files of pamphlets, handbills, political advertisements, theater announcements, and other items of community interest. Check with the librarian to see what kinds of special collections may be available and useful for your research.

Locating Public Libraries.   Remember that public libraries vary as much as the communities they serve. Sometimes a brief phone call can tell you whether visiting a city or county library would be worth your time. You can probably locate the nearest public libraries just by looking in the telephone book. For more comprehensive information about the location and particular collection emphases of any academic, public, or private library, consult the *American Library Directory: 1996–97* (2 vols.) (New York: Bowker, 1994).

Do not overlook the value of using public libraries at some stage of your research. Their different emphases may provide ideas about what to research, or if you already have a topic, they may suggest a local angle for the paper to make it more representative of your individual approach. The campus library may be the best place to research the general topic of *teenage gangs;* however, the local library may help you research a paper focusing on efforts to eliminate a widespread gang problem in your own community.

How Libraries Are Organized

You can save time and avoid a lot of frustration doing research by understanding the general arrangement of materials in a library. Although libraries are not alike in the ways they organize information, the reference, book, and periodical sections are the ones you should be most familiar with in doing your research.

The Reference Area

A library's reference area houses its encyclopedias, dictionaries, bibliographies, directories, atlases, indexes, and almanacs. Information is usually available at a reference desk from which a librarian provides assistance by answering questions or locating items that are difficult to find. The reference desk is also where you can request a librarian-assisted database search for your topic.

Since reference books are generally not allowed to circulate outside the library, plan to complete most of your working bibliography in the reference room itself. To save time and get ideas about what resources are available in the reference area, it is always wise to browse awhile in this section before settling into your research. Many libraries provide printed guides that show the general layout of the reference section and other parts of the library.

The Book Area

Also called *the stacks,* this is the area containing books and the bound volumes of periodicals, including magazines and journals. Depending on the library, the stacks may range in size from many rows of shelved books to several floors of them. Some libraries have a separate *oversize* section for all books that exceed normal height or width.

Access to the stacks varies among libraries. In those with open stacks, you can go among the aisles of books yourself to find what you need. In a library with closed stacks, a staff person brings books to you after you make out a request form.

The Periodicals Room

Unbound issues of current magazines, journals, and newspapers are kept in the library's periodical room. Practice varies, but most libraries keep several back issues of a periodical on the shelf until they are ready to be bound into volumes. Some libraries provide only the current issue of a periodical, making past issues available by request.

Academic libraries seldom allow recently published, unbound periodicals to circulate, and they may not always subscribe to certain popular periodicals. In these cases, public libraries may serve your needs much better, since they subscribe more heavily to popular periodicals and frequently allow recent and unbound issues to circulate.

Other Specialized Areas

In addition to the reference, book, and periodicals areas, your library may also maintain a separate microform section, a government documents desk, a media library, or a special collections library. Make a point of exploring your library and finding out which of these or other specialized areas are available.

Library Classification Systems

Libraries organize their holdings by classifying them into groups and storing items of the same groups together in one place. Each item in a group is marked with a *call number,* a series of numbers and/or letters identifying it and the group to which it belongs. The call number also accompanies the item's description in the library catalog system to indicate where it is located.

Two of the most common methods used to classify a library's holdings in this way are the Dewey Decimal (DD) and the Library of Congress (LC) subject-classification systems. Small libraries favor the DD system because it is simpler and thus fulfills their needs. The LC system is used by large libraries because it is almost infinitely expandable and has more main divisions. Most libraries use either one system or the other, though some may be in transition between the older DD system and the newer LC system. Knowing something about how each system works can make your research more effective in any library.

The Dewey Decimal System

The Dewey Decimal classification system assigns a library book or other resource a call number according to the 10 major subject categories shown in Figure 2.1. By the DD system, a book with any call number in the *300s,* for example, has a subject in the *social sciences,* a major category that includes *group dynamics, law, government, education,* and *economics* as subdivisions. A book with a call number beginning with *342* addresses *constitutional and administrative law,* while one with a call number beginning with *345* treats *criminal law.* Successive numbers and decimal points further classify such books more precisely:

340	Law
34.	Criminal law
345.ᴄ	Criminal courts
345.05	General criminal procedure
345.052	Criminal investigation and law enforcement
345.056	Rights of suspects
345.06	Evidence

CALL NUMBER	MAIN DIVISION
000–99	General works
100–199	Philosophy
200–299	Religion
300–399	Social sciences
400–499	Languages
500–599	Natural sciences
600–699	Technology and applied sciences
700–799	Fine arts
800–899	Literature
900–999	History and geography

FIGURE 2.1 The Dewey Decimal subject-classification system

The Library of Congress System

The most obvious difference between the Library of Congress and Dewey Decimal systems is that the LC system uses letters instead of numbers to identify subject classifications, as identified in Figure 2.2. Like the DD system, the LC system provides subcategories within each of the main divisions. In the LC system, subdivisions are made by adding a second letter and numbers. For the main division of technology (*T*), for example, works about *motor vehicles, aeronautics,* and *astronautics* are classified under the subdivision *TL*. All books classified under *TL670-723* are about *airplanes*. The call letters *TL721* indicate that a book is about *commercial airplanes,* while *TL723* shows it is about *government airplanes.*

As with the Dewey Decimal system, paying attention to the subject designators of the Library of Congress system can save you valuable time during your research. If you were investigating the *safety of private planes,* for example, you would want to spend your time tracking down books

CALL LETTER	MAIN DIVISION
A	General works
B	Philosophy and religion
C	History—Auxiliary sciences
D	History—Topography
E–F	American history—Topography
G	Geography—Anthropology
H	Social sciences
J	Political sciences
K	Law
L	Education
M	Music
N	Fine arts
P	Language—Literature (nonfiction)
Q	Sciences
R	Medicine
S	Agriculture
T	Technology
U	Military science
V	Naval science
Z	Bibliography and library science
P–Z	Literature (fiction)

FIGURE 2.2 The Library of Congress subject-classification system

with a *TL685.1* designation, *private airplanes*, rather than *TL685.3, military airplanes*. Careful attention to the LC designator would also keep you from spending time trying to locate a work listed in the library catalog under "airplanes" but designated *QA930, airplane aerodynamics*.

Working with the Library Catalog

Without the catalog, the collection of materials in any library would be practically inaccessible. Arranged alphabetically by author, title, and subject or a combination of the three, the library catalog tells what books and other materials the library has and where they are located.

While the basic information a library catalog provides is generally standard, the kind of catalog a library uses can vary. Card catalogs, in which information about each item in the library is printed on a small card, are still used in some local library systems, though they are rapidly being replaced by more modern and more efficient online computer catalogs. Book catalogs, microform catalogs, and CD–ROM (Compact Disc–Read-Only Memory) catalogs have their own special uses and are found most often at academic or large public research libraries. Most libraries today use one or more of these kinds of catalogs. You will need to understand how to use each to do effective research in any library.

Using the Card Catalog

A *card catalog* consists of hundreds—or in a large library, possibly thousands—of alphabetized cards, usually filed in rows of small drawers, that list every item in the library. Separate author, title, and subject cards are stored in alphabetical order according to the first important word. The words *a, an,* and *the,* for instance, are dropped from the beginnings of titles and subjects when you want to locate a work. An author's name is reversed, putting the last name first. Thus, if you were looking for a book titled *The Life of a Forest,* you would find it in the "L" section of the card catalog under "Life of a Forest, The." If you looked the book up under its author's name, *William R. Owens,* you would look under "O" in the card catalog until you came to "Owens, William R." The DD or LC call number on the card would tell you where the book is shelved in the library.

The information in most library card catalogs is stored in triplicate, with every resource listed on separate subject, title, and author cards. This system allows you to find any book or other work, regardless of whether you know very much about it.

Subject Cards.   Use the subject card catalog to begin compiling the preliminary bibliography or any time you need to know what books are available on any particular subject. Begin by looking in the catalog under the subject or topic you are researching. The subject heading appears at the top of each card, with full information about each book and its location in the library (see Figure 2.3, "Subject Card").

If you cannot locate subject cards for your research subject, you may need to look under a different subject heading. For instance, you may have looked under "Macintosh" and need instead to look under "computers." *"See also" cards* may direct you to other headings in the catalog. If not, you can find alternative headings by consulting the library's two-volume copy of *Library of Congress Subject Headings,* a list of subject headings and related terms used for all library card catalogs.

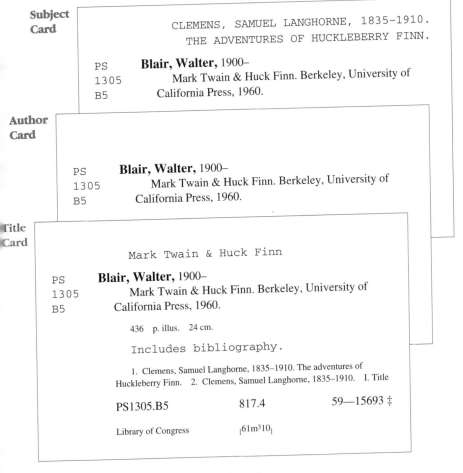

Subject Card

CLEMENS, SAMUEL LANGHORNE, 1835–1910.
THE ADVENTURES OF HUCKLEBERRY FINN.

PS   **Blair, Walter,** 1900–
1305   Mark Twain & Huck Finn. Berkeley, University of
B5   California Press, 1960.

Author Card

PS   **Blair, Walter,** 1900–
1305   Mark Twain & Huck Finn. Berkeley, University of
B5   California Press, 1960.

Title Card

Mark Twain & Huck Finn

PS   **Blair, Walter,** 1900–
1305   Mark Twain & Huck Finn. Berkeley, University of
B5   California Press, 1960.

436   p. illus.   24 cm.

Includes bibliography.

1. Clemens, Samuel Langhorne, 1835–1910. The adventures of Huckleberry Finn.   2. Clemens, Samuel Langhorne, 1835–1910.   I. Title

PS1305.B5   817.4   59—15693 ‡

Library of Congress   [61m³10]

FIGURE 2.3   Subject, author, and title cards

Author and Title Cards.   Another way to find sources for your research is to consult the author and title cards of the library catalog. If you
know the author of a book or if you want to find the titles of works by a
particular authority, consult the author card index. You will find a card for
each book by that author filed alphabetically by title under the author's last
name (see Figure 2.3, "Author Card").

If you know precisely which book you want, you can locate it most
quickly by going right to the title card catalog. Author and title cards give
the same information as subject cards. Title cards, however, also have the
book's title printed at the top (see Figure 2.3, "Title Card").

Using the Online Catalog

An *online catalog* uses a computer terminal to provide a complete listing of all the items in a library. Such a catalog provides a great deal more
than a computerized version of its predecessor, the traditional library card
catalog. With an online catalog, you cannot only locate books by subject,
author, and title, but many systems will also tell you which local libraries
have a book if yours does not. Because they can be more easily updated,
can provide more information than traditional card catalogs, and can be
made available at several locations throughout the library, online catalogs
have generally replaced or subordinated other catalog systems.

Locating a Subject.   The tremendous amount of and number of
types of information in a modern online catalog system have made research easier as well as more thorough than ever before. For example,
many online systems have a browse feature that allows you to begin with a
subject like *birds* and alphabetically scan the system's subject catalog in a
matter of minutes:

Birds
Birds—Behavior
Birds—Habitats
Birds—History
Birds—Physical characteristics

As the system displays a list of subjects, you simply select the one you
want to investigate. The online screen will then display a list of all the
available books in the library on your selected subject.

Using an online catalog, you do not even need all the information that
would be required if you were using the card catalog to locate a book. You
can enter a single term—let's say "college"—and the system will display all
titles, subject and author entries, and bibliographic notes in which the term

college appears. To save time, you can also enter a title code and have the system display only titles with a particular word or combination of words in them. For example, if you know only the first word or two of a title, like *College Entrance Examinations,* you can enter any one or a combination of main words—"college," "entrance examinations," "college entrance," and so on. The online screen will display a list of all books with the words you enter in their titles.

Locating an Author. You can also enter an author's last name and get a display of all authors with that name. Selecting one author from the displayed list will produce a second display listing all available works by that particular author. Or suppose you are unsure of how to spell an author's last name—like that of *Ernest Hemingway,* for example. Just enter an online code, plus "HEM". The system will display the names of all authors whose names begin with *HEM:*

Hembree, Ron
Hemenway, Joan M.
Heming, William
Hemingway, Ernest
Hemker, H. C.
Hemlon, Marie
Hemmingway, Charles A.

Other Features. Some online catalog systems allow you to print the information on the display screen as you view it, thereby saving you the work of copying down the information you find. One particular library's online catalog may even be accessible through the system at a neighboring library or on your own home computer through the use of a modem (a device that connects two computers via a telephone line) and payment of a small fee. Since all online catalog systems are not alike in their capabilities or operations, consult a librarian or follow available directions for using the system in your own library.

A word of caution: While online catalogs are wonderful aids to research, they are not everything you need to write a good research paper. As you use your library's computerized online catalog, be careful not to rely on its systems so much that you eliminate your own creative thinking about your research. Browse the bookshelves of the library yourself. Remember that some valuable sources may even be too old to have been entered into the online system. Think of connections between sources and subjects that the system's technology may not have included. Use the online catalog all you can, but remember to approach your research subject with your own individual thinking about it, too.

Using Other Types of Library Catalogs

The most commonly used library catalogs are the card and online computer types, just discussed. Many libraries, however, also use other types of catalogs either as the main cataloging system or as a supplement. You will want to know something about each of these catalogs in order to take advantage of the assistance they can also offer the researcher.

Book Catalogs.   Available in the library reference section, a *book catalog* is, as the name suggests, a book listing all the library's holdings. The pages of a book catalog may be composed of photographed and reduced copies of all the cards in the library's card catalog, or they may contain bound, computer-generated lists of all the items in the library collection. Many libraries use a book catalog as a back-up to their online catalog.

Though most online catalogs have information only about local libraries, book catalogs from out-of-area libraries are additionally valuable for researching long distance. A researcher in Tampa, Florida, for example, can use the book catalog from the University of California at Los Angeles to find out what books are at UCLA, to get bibliographic information about resources there, or to obtain a book through interlibrary loan services.

Book-form card catalogs also allow you to scan whole pages of entries at once. Seeing multiple entries allows you to compare several items on the page: publication date, bibliography, number of pages, and so on. If the library allows it, book catalogs also make it possible for you to photocopy the pages themselves as a quick way to record data for several entries at once.

Microform Catalogs.   Library catalogs in microform—or COMCATS (Computer Output Microfilm Catalogs)—are copied at greatly reduced size on cards or sheets of microfilm that must be read at special machines available in the library. Because of the reduced size of its print, a single microform card, for example, can hold up to a thousand pages of regularly printed material. Microfilm, microcards, microfiche, and microprint are all varieties of microforms that differ only in their format (card or sheet) and the amount of reduction they provide.

Because of the small print and the necessity of reading them at a machine, microform catalogs are not as easy to work with as other types of catalogs. Some libraries have machines that can give you a print-out of a microform, but the practice can be time consuming and expensive. In most cases, doing your research through the library's card catalog or online computer catalog will prove more satisfying.

Compact Disc Catalogs.   Rather than working as an online catalog, the CD–ROM (Compact Disc–Read-Only Memory) provides a fixed catalog that library computer terminals read off a single imprinted disc. Similar in size and appearance to a common music compact disc, a CD–ROM disc can store well over a half million words. You read a CD–ROM catalog at a library computer terminal equipped with a monitor, keyboard, and (usually) a printer.

CD–ROM catalog information is generally the same as that given by other catalogs, although information stored on an individual disc cannot be added to or otherwise changed. The catalog is kept current by the addition of new discs as they become available. For this reason, always note the date on the CD–ROM catalog disc you are working with. If it is not current, you may need to go to the online catalog or elsewhere for more recent information.

Library Services and Resources

In order to use any library efficiently, you need to know what assistance it can provide. The services that make life easier for researchers vary with the size and purpose of a library. Naturally, larger libraries can generally give more support than smaller ones, but most libraries can offer more help than you may realize.

Librarian Assistance

Probably the most valuable assistance you can get in the library will come from a librarian. Trained in the resources of a library and the process of research, librarians are also experienced in assisting students with research papers. It is likely that your librarian has helped another student with a topic similar to yours and can tell you what resources to consult or avoid. He or she knows what is available and where to find it in the library as well as how to access materials located elsewhere. Do not underestimate the help a librarian can give you at any stage of your research. You cannot find a better resource.

Information Service

Larger libraries often staff a telephone information service just to answer questions that can be handled with a few minutes of searching by the librarian. Most libraries will gladly answer questions over the telephone, whether you need to know what resources are available or just forgot to write down an author's name. Find out at the start of your research if your library has such an information service.

Search Assistance

A library's search service can locate books or other materials that were not on the shelf when you looked for them. Someone else may have been using a book when you were looking, it may have been at the bindery, or it may have been misshelved. If you cannot locate a book where the catalog says it should be, ask a librarian for a library search request form. You can usually get a search report on the book's status in one or two days.

Interlibrary Loan

You can obtain books and other materials that are unavailable in your own library through interlibrary loan. Your library's online catalog may tell you when a book is located at another local library, or the librarian can use a national library computer network called *OCLC* (Online Computer Library Center) to find where any book is available. Once a work is located, your librarian can arrange to have it sent to you at the library. Be aware that material requested through interlibrary loan may take three to ten days to arrive.

Reserve and Recall

Do not give up on library books or other items you need just because they have been checked out. The library can reserve materials for you, placing a hold on their circulation and notifying you as soon as they have been returned. At academic libraries, where books are often checked out for long periods of time, you can recall items that the original borrower has had out for over two or three weeks.

Nonprint Sources

Many libraries maintain collections of nonprint materials, including audio cassettes, phonograph records, video cassettes, and films. The forms for including such sources in your working bibliography and Works Cited list are addressed in Chapter 11.

Photocopying

Since photocopying has proven so necessary to modern research, most libraries today provide machines for that purpose. A good system of notetaking (see Chapter 7) can reduce the expense of photocopying, but such an aid can be valuable when you need to study noncirculating, lengthy, or complex materials outside the library. Read the copyright restrictions posted on most machines, and avoid plagiarism (discussed in Chapter 7) by crediting any sources from which you borrow.

Computer Facilities

Your library's online catalog and database systems will allow you to search for hundreds of sources in your own and other libraries. If you have a personal computer and a modem, paying a small fee will enable you to link up with your library's catalogs and other databases right at home. For those who prefer to write with a library's resources at hand, most large academic libraries also have computers and word-processing programs available in the library.

WORKING WITH OTHERS

Use the following suggestions to evaluate local academic and public libraries as well as to gauge your understanding of library resources discussed in this chapter.

- Find out whether your campus library offers orientation tours or special classes for students engaged in research projects. Sign up with a classmate to go on such a tour or to take part in a library research class. If these options are not available, ask a librarian to provide a short orientation for you and a few classmates.

- Discuss your campus library with another student to review what you know of its reference, book, and periodicals collections. If your college has more than one library, also discuss how the others might be useful to your research assignment.

- What local public libraries are available to you, and what kinds of resources might they offer? Consider state, county, and city libraries in your area and how they might differ in the services and resources they provide.

- Compare your own campus library's services with those discussed in this chapter. Which campus library services may be particularly helpful in working on your research project? If you have used any special library services in the past, describe them and their usefulness.

- Find out what kinds of computer research facilities and services are available at your own campus library, and discuss them with a classmate. Also discuss any other library computer resources you are acquainted with and how they may be useful to your research.

CHAPTER 3

Planning the Focus of Your Research

Getting started on a research paper begins with selecting a suitable topic to investigate and write about in depth. Your goal in selecting such a topic, as well as throughout your research, is continually to refine and narrow the area of investigation in order to make the research and resulting paper significantly specific.

In general, you should start by considering a broad subject of interest to research and then move to a more particular topic within that subject. Preliminary investigation of sources should next lead you to formulate a research question that states what you want to know about the topic. Figure 3.1 illustrates the continual narrowing process of focusing your research in this way. Once you have defined a research question, use it to focus your later investigation of sources and direct notetaking toward a tentative answer, or preliminary thesis, about the topic.

General subject	Topic	Research question
Advertising	Subliminal messages in advertising	Should subliminal messages in advertising be banned?

FIGURE 3.1   Focusing your research

Understanding a Subject and Topic

You will be better able to focus your research efforts if you understand the concepts of a research subject and topic at the beginning of your assignment. A research *subject* is any general area of experience, knowledge, or events that can be studied for more understanding. A *topic* is a more focused area of ideas included within a broader research subject. *AIDS* and *acid rain,* for example, are each research subjects. *AIDS on the college campus* and *the effects of acid rain on human health* are topics included within the subjects *AIDS* and *acid rain,* respectively. A subject is always more general than the topic or topics included within it. Notice how the following subjects for college research papers contain one or several more specific topics:

Subject	*Topics*
Euthanasia	1. Mercy killing and people with AIDS
	2. Euthanasia in Holland
Native Americans	1. Fishing rights of Native Americans
	2. Threats to ancestral burial grounds
	3. Native language use in the classroom
Alcoholism	1. College students and drinking
	2. Pregnancy and alcohol
	3. Television beer commercials
Popular music	1. Sexual violence in popular music
	2. The social power of rap music

Understanding the distinction between a subject and a topic can help you to plan your research sooner and more effectively. If you begin the assignment by planning at the subject level, you can compare several potential areas of interest to research before committing to a particular topic. On the other hand, if you begin with a topic already in mind, a sense of its relationship to a broader subject can help you to gauge your progress in focusing the research.

Finding a Research Subject and Topic

Several steps described in this chapter for discovering a research subject or topic can work equally well for finding both. Which purpose any of the steps fulfills for you will depend upon how far you have progressed in your planning or actual research. Although the steps are presented sequentially here, they may overlap or occur in different order in actual practice. The *Reader's Guide,* for example, is recommended for first discovering a subject; however, you will likely return to it again later for narrowing a subject to a particular topic or to find specific sources to investigate in depth. As you proceed in following the suggestions given here about a subject or topic, keep the overlapping nature of these two elements in mind.

Selecting an Appropriate Research Subject

Unfortunately, many beginning writers have had the frustrating experience of wasting valuable time on subjects or topics that they decided upon too quickly. You can avoid dead-end topics—those that are unsuitable for your interest or resources—with careful planning. The best approach is to consider several possible subjects initially and then to move systematically toward a more particular topic and relevant research question.

Assigned Subjects

If your paper's subject is assigned by your instructor, he or she has already considered its suitability for research as well as your probable level of interest and understanding. It will be your responsibility in an assigned-subject paper to demonstrate a grasp of basic concepts through independent research and thinking. With assigned subjects that are closely related to the course focus, you have the benefit of your class notes, textbook reading, and your instructor's own expertise to draw upon, though you will of course need to do your own research work, as well.

You will find that an assigned subject requires as much original thinking as one you might have chosen for yourself. Try to find an approach that makes your paper different from others on the same subject. This is what Nancy Prado did when her instructor required that all students' research papers relate to issues regarding the O. J. Simpson trial. Nancy's paper, titled Flawed Justice: Why and How the American Jury System Must Be Reformed, grew out of her own independent thinking and individual interest in the subject's focus. (See Nancy's paper in Chapter 10.)

Free-Choice Subjects

If you are like most students facing a research paper assignment, you will need to select what to write about. This means you may not have the benefit of lectures or class discussions to help you get to know and understand a subject, as you would if it were assigned. When responsible for finding your own research subject, you will need as much time as possible to select the right one.

For this reason, you should start thinking about an appropriate research paper subject from the day you first learn about the assignment. Use the class in which the paper is assigned or other courses you are taking as resources. As you listen to lectures, study your textbooks, or join in class discussions throughout the term, be alert to potential areas for research. The following suggestions will help you discover a research subject that interests you and is appropriate for your assignment.

Reviewing Your Interests

If there were one simple rule for selecting the right research subject, it would be this: *Work with your interests.* As you begin working with a research subject or topic, think critically about those you may be willing to spend time researching. You will recognize more potential topics in a subject you care about than in one you select because it seems impressive or easy to research. In addition to the information you gather from other sources, remember that your research paper should reflect your own insights and opinions.

You will write best on a subject you care about and already have a feeling for. Avoid any that are not part of your general field of interest or that you may be drawn to for the wrong reasons. Though a subject like *uniform commercial code laws* may sound impressive, you will not go very far with it unless you are genuinely interested in laws governing various kinds of commercial transactions. Similarly, *microwave cooking* may sound like an easy subject to write about. Unless you care enough to research and think critically about it, however, such a subject may generate only a tiring exercise for you and a dull paper for your instructor.

Recording Subject Ideas

Begin discovering the right research subject for yourself by using a research notebook (see Chapter 1) to record and later review your general interests. Title a section of the notebook Research Subjects, and use it to explore potential areas of research:

■ Take time to think about your hobbies or any clubs and organizations to which you belong. Use your research notebook to discuss events that you want to know more about. What controversies need greater examination?

■ Consider the subjects of magazines or particular sections of the newspaper you read regularly. What is happening that you have a strong position on? What issues need clarification or updating for an interested and even generally informed audience? Record these subjects in your research notebook.

■ Think about your favorite college course, your prospective career, or even the latest book or movie you enjoyed. What subjects do these areas of interest cover? What famous persons or events in these areas intrigue you? List these in the Subjects section of your research notebook.

■ Review the entries of possible subjects you have been keeping in your research notebook. Which subjects seem to interest you most? Which would match your interests and the requirements of your assignment best? Which do you want to learn more about?

Subdividing your interests with questions in this way will put you on the track of potential subjects. Just remember to take your time. Start with a variety of possibilities, and gradually narrow the list to the three or four most suited to your interests and the assignment. Find out more about each of these subjects to select the most promising one for extensive study and research.

Using Library Sources to Find a Research Subject

A library's reference section or book collection contains excellent sources for discovering a potential subject or topic for your paper. Use these sources to discover a research focus or to gauge the potential of possible subjects already listed in your research notebook. Before settling upon any single subject for research, be sure to consult as many such sources as possible. Preliminary investigation of standard library materials will provide important general information as well as specific sources essential to your later research.

Encyclopedias

The articles found in encyclopedias offer excellent, authoritative discussions on nearly every subject known. Written by well-chosen experts who provide reliable facts and informed insights, encyclopedia articles are vital to effective research and writing on any issue. No matter what subject or topic you decide upon, it is wise to begin all your research with a study of relevant encyclopedia articles. You can use what you learn from them to investigate and better understand other sources.

You are probably already familiar with multivolume, comprehensive encyclopedias like *Encyclopedia Americana, Encyclopaedia Britannica,* or *Collier's Encyclopedia.* These references cover hundreds of subjects and include maps, illustrations, and highly useful bibliographies. Entries appear alphabetically by subject, and discussions vary in length from a single paragraph to a dozen or more pages. Most public or campus libraries carry one or more complete editions of such encyclopedias as well as the yearbook supplements intended to keep them up to date. Many encyclopedias, such as *Encyclopedia Britannica* and the *Academic American Encyclopedia,* are available online at most libraries or through the Internet.

When using encyclopedia articles, keep in mind that they provide intentionally broad introductions to a given subject. More frequently published sources, such as books and periodicals, usually give more detailed or current information. Use encyclopedias to acquaint yourself with fundamental facts about a subject and to understand it in broad terms. It is also wise to consult more than one encyclopedia to begin your research in order to find the most useful information or the most instructive organization of your research subject.

Current Books

Whether written for popular or academic audiences, books are excellent resources in which to discover a direction for your research. Simply browsing through a book's introduction or sampling a few of its chapters can tell you a lot about whether its subject will prove appropriate to your research interests and abilities. Your own textbook for a course may be a good source to begin with, or you can go to the library section for a particular subject and consult several books at one sitting.

A book whose scope is broad and introductory is best for an overview of a possible research subject. (More highly focused books will prove useful when you decide about a specific topic for your research.) As you examine books to investigate possible subjects, keep in mind that your purpose is not to read the books but to get an overview of your potential focus for research.

Using the Table of Contents. The subject a book covers is outlined by the headings found in its table of contents (see Figure 3.2). You can study the contents to find the major categories of interest for your subject or to see under what headings it might be discussed. If it helps, skim a particular chapter in order to learn more about the subject. (See Chapter 7 on skimming and close-reading techniques.)

CONTENTS

Preface
ix

1   The Nature of Persuasion
1

2   Measuring Attitudes: Scales, Polls, and Samples
21

3   How Attitudes Influence Behavior
43

4   How Actions Influence Attitudes
59

5   Personality and Persuasion
79

6   Social Influence and Group Decision Making
101

7   Persuasion and Political Issues
119

8   Persuasion and Health/Safety Issues
139

9   Persuasion and the Mass Media
159

References
189

Index
195

FIGURE 3.2   A table of contents from a book

Using the Index.   The index at the end of a book can also be useful for discovering research subjects and their specific subtopics (see Figure 3.3). As you skim the indicated pages for an index entry, take note of addi-

ABC. *See* American Broadcasting Corporation (ABC)
absolutist state, 68–69
Adams, Gordon, 122
administration (as element of state), 59–60
Africa, 88, 126, 159, 228. *See also names of specific countries*
African Americans
    Civil Rights Movement and, 55, 106, 188
    nationalism by, 212–213
    political participation by, 63, 136, 148, 150, 200
    representation in Congress by, 139
agenda setting (by mass media), 107–109
Alford, Robert R., 60, 73, 135
American Academy of Arts and Sciences, 94
American Broadcasting Corporation (ABC), 103, 105–106
American Dilemma, An (Myrdal, 1944), 11
American Federation of Labor, 72
American Medical Association, 163
antiestablishment movement (of the 1960s). *See also* Civil
        Rights Movement; Vietnam War
    effect on political sociology, 23–24
    events/issues behind, 52, 149, 181
    political participation and, 149, 150, 152, 181
Argentina, 128, 188, 217
aristocracy, 61, 65, 68
Aristotle, 3, 21, 50, 60–61, 88–89, 136, 218, 220, 221, 225

FIGURE 3.3   An excerpt from an index, showing main topics and subtopics

tional subjects or topics that you may want to pursue for your research. You may find it useful to compare two or more books' index entries to recognize important concepts or compare discussions of the same subject.

The Reader's Guide

Nearly all popular magazine articles are cataloged in one or another of several available indexes. The most well-known of such indexes is the *Reader's Guide to Periodical Literature*, which covers articles and book reviews appearing in nearly 200 popular magazines. (Other magazine indexes are discussed in Chapter 4.)

You can use the *Reader's Guide* to get an overview of a subject as well as to get ideas about major topics within a subject. Figure 3.4 shows a *Reader's Guide* entry for "jury selection."

As this sample entry illustrates, the *Reader's Guide* has its own system of listing information. As in other periodical indexes, information about the magazine's title, date of publication, number of pages, and other useful data are presented. When using the *Reader's Guide* or any periodical index, refer to the front of the volume for an explanation of the symbols and abbreviations used to describe an article entry.

NOTE: When you are recording source information on your research bibliography cards, remember that the form and data given in the *Reader's Guide* and other indexes are not the same as you will use later in the Works Cited list of your research paper.

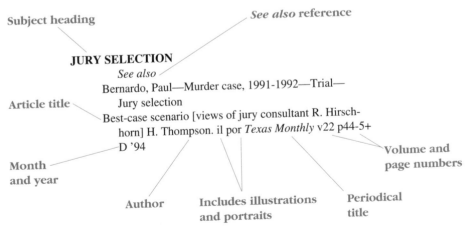

FIGURE 3.4 An entry from the *Reader's Guide to Periodical Literature*

Source: Entry from *Reader's Guide to Periodical Literature*, November 1995, p. 480. Copyright © 1995 by The H. W. Wilson Company. Reprinted by permission.

The Social Issues
Resources Series (SIRS)

Your library's reference section will no doubt carry several volumes of the *Social Issues Resources Series,* or *SIRS.* With over 30 different subjects titled and numbered on the spine, these large, three-ring binders contain hundreds of short, up-to-date articles on dozens of interesting subjects. A Quick Reference Guide lists the subject volumes and indicates which ones contain articles on various major topics. *SIRS* is also available online in many public and university libraries. Those that have *SIRS* online also usually keep the printed and bound copies available on shelves, as well. If your library has both, use the most up-to-date version.

You can use the *SIRS* to find a subject or to learn about a potential topic. Looking over the Quick Reference Guide, for example, may start you thinking about the relationship of *aging* and *divorce,* or you might begin to wonder about *aging* and *civil rights* as possible research interests. A brief search through the subject volume on drugs will turn up such articles as "Addicted Doctors," "The Drug Gangs," "Should Hard Drugs Be Legalized?" and "Cocaine's Children." You can also use the *Index of SIRS Critical Issues* to find out about major issues of national and international importance. Figure 3.5, for example, shows some of the topics listed in the SIRS *Atmosphere Crisis* index. After reading some of these articles, you could decide if one of the topics interested you enough to research it further, or you could turn to a different volume to get ideas about another subject.

Moving from a Subject
to a Research Topic

Since you cannot read or write meaningfully about everything relevant to the research subject, you will need to narrow your investigation to a more particular topic within it. Because they represent general areas of interest, subjects contain several topics suitable for research (see also Chapter 1). A broad subject like *AIDS,* for example, includes many potential topics:

Subject:	AIDS
Topic:	The problem of AIDS on college campuses
Topic:	AIDS education in high schools
Topic:	Mandating AIDS testing for expectant mothers
Topic:	Potential cures for AIDS
Topic:	Support groups for people with AIDS
Topic:	Children with AIDS

E

Earth, Chemical composition
  See Geochemistry
Earth, Orbit, 2
Earth-friendly products
  See Green products
Earth Summit
  See United Nations Conference
  on Environment and Devel-
  opment
Earthwatch, 18
Ecology
  See Coastal ecology: Food
  chains (Ecology)
Education, Environmental
  See Environmental education
El Nino Current, 7, 8
**Electric apparatus and appli-
  ances,** 5
Emission reduction credits, 9
**Emission standards, Automo-
  bile**
  See Automobiles, Environmen-
  tal aspects
Energy efficiency, 16
Environment, Effect of man on
  See Man, Influence on nature
Environmental degradation,
  20
Environmental education, 20
Environmental health, 17, 20
  See also Health risk assess-
  ment
**Environmental impact
  analysis,** 8
Environmental policy, 11
Environmental technology, 4
EPA
  See U.S. Environmental
  Protection Agency (EPA)
Extinct amphibians, 10
Extinction (Biology), 20

FIGURE 3.5   Listing from the Index of *SIRS Critical Issues: The Atmosphere Crisis*
Source: Listing from the Index of *SIRS Critical Issues: The Atmosphere Crisis,* Vol. 3, Articles
1–20. Copyright © 1994 SIRS, Inc., The Knowledge Source. Reprinted with permission.

Focusing Your Efforts

While considering several possible topics like these during the early research phase may be a good idea (in case one or more prove uninteresting or impractical), you must nevertheless also focus your efforts. A paper attempting to cover all of these topics would be shallow in content, just skimming the surface of each in order to discuss them all. Or it would arbitrarily treat two or three areas and ignore other equally important ones. To avoid producing a scattered, superficial research paper, you will eventually need to select a single topic to investigate at length.

Going Online to Find a Topic

Information available through the Internet or other online resources is highly organized, usually listed by topic and categorized in successively narrower, increasingly focused menus. Once online, you can use these organizational features to discover subjects of interest to you or to help find a related topic for research.

Many of the documents you can read online contain *hypertext,* which is colored or highlighted text, as shown in Figure 3.6. Selecting one of these hypertext words or phrases will take you to an area providing more information or discussion of that particular subject. For instance, if you chose *peremptory challenge* in the hypertext example in Figure 3.6, you would automatically jump to an area discussing this subject and related topics within it. These related topics may also be listed as hypertext, in which case you could then select them and find still more topics to investigate. Using hypertext, you can identify possible topics to investigate and, at the same time, become aware of important concepts that may be relevant to your later research and discussion.

A petit jury, which decides criminal or civil cases, has a maximum of twelve members, which is often fewer than the number of jurors on a grand jury. Although practices vary within each state, the most common method of jury selection is through voir dire examination, which includes questioning by the attorneys, the judge, or both, as to background and possible bias of prospective jurors. Attorneys can dismiss a potential jurist "for cause" or through a peremptory challenge. This latter method of excusing a juror requires no reason to be given to the court . . .

FIGURE 3.6   An excerpt from a hypertext document

Another useful way to search online for a research topic is to use *Gopher,* an Internet search program that allows you to choose among successively narrower menus of information or related resources at its own or another site. Gopher searches are available through most college and university library computer systems, or you may be able to make such a search at home through a commercial provider, such as NETCOM or America Online.

Suppose you were interested in researching an ecological topic but did not know for sure what might interest you. You could begin by accessing the Gopher server at the University of California at Santa Cruz ("gopher://scilibx.ucsc.edu"). By selecting "The Researcher" and then "Science & Engineering," followed by "Environmental Science" from the menu, you could jump to the Gopher server at the University of Minnesota's College of Natural Resources. Once at this university's Gopher menu, you would be able to select from successively narrower menus to eventually arrive at the one similar to that shown in Figure 3.7. This particular menu lists several options for exploring ecological issues related to *water,* including *conser-*

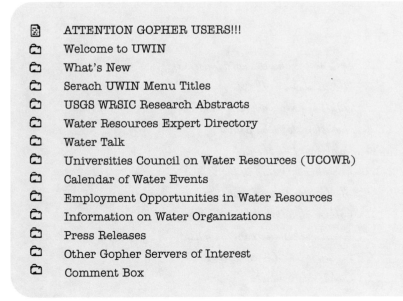

FIGURE 3.7   A Gopher menu showing options for topic exploration

Source: Reprinted with permission of NETCOM On-Line Communication Services, Inc.

vation, pollution, desalinization, and other topics for research. (See Chapter 6 for further discussion of Gopher and other search tools that are useful for discovering and refining research topics.)

Recording Potential Topics

Under a heading like Research Topics, keep an ongoing list of ideas in your research notebook. Jot down facts, questions, or potential sources as they occur to you. Mark those topics that appear most promising or that you want to discuss with your instructor. You will find that certain entries eventually dominate the list and your interest. These preliminary topics will provide a core of possibilities as you decide which ones to investigate further. The list of potential research topics that Mark Stevenson kept in his notebook included the entries shown in Figure 3.8. Notice that some topics are more general than others, but all identify topics of inquiry for research.

Mark did preliminary reading about most of these topics, and he discussed those marked with asterisks with his instructor and a few friends. Although he began with the idea of discussing the benefits that television

---

Research Topics

* 1. *SAT scores and college admissions*
  2. *Illegal aliens in the U.S.*
* 3. *Rights of people who are homeless*
* 4. *The use of force by police*
* 5. *Television talk shows*
* 6. *Foreign ownership in the U.S.*
  7. *The Galileo space discoveries*
  8. *College athletic programs*
  9. *Social criticism in popular music*
*10. *Japanese vs. U.S. education*
 11. *Global peace efforts*
 12. *The war against drugs*

FIGURE 3.8 Notebook entries for research topics

talk shows provide their guests and society in general, he later decided to focus on the issues that were fostering criticism of the shows. Eventually, Mark chose to write about the criticism that talk shows receive and how it would eventually force changes in the numbers of such shows on television and what content they covered. In making this choice, he moved from a broad research subject to a more focused topic for writing. Moreover, thinking about the other topics on his list gave Mark useful back-up options, in case he later decided that *television talk shows* was not a good topic for his paper.

Using Discovery Techniques to Focus on a Topic

A practical method of deciding what you want to research about any topic is to explore your own understanding of it. You need not follow all the methods described here; rather, use those that will help you focus on a topic that matches your interests with your resources and your assignment.

Freewriting

Freewriting allows you to discuss a subject or topic as freely as necessary to start ideas flowing to a conscious level. You begin by simply writing (with a pen or pencil or at a computer) all your thoughts on a subject, as they occur to you. Do not worry about organization, punctuation, or spelling. The important goal in freewriting is to get your ideas down. Write for about 10 minutes at a time, longer if you suddenly find yourself deeply involved in a discussion on a particular topic.

Figure 3.9 shows the freewriting Mark Stevenson did in his research notebook for his paper on television talk shows. Notice that this exercise allowed him to identify more clearly the topic he eventually chose for his research and to discover several ideas he would later develop in the paper.

If you have trouble getting started with freewriting, try focusing with introductory phrases that will launch you directly into a discussion of your research subject. Start freewriting with introductory phrases like the following:

One unsettled question about (subject) is . . .

(Subject) is important today because . . .

(Subject) should (or should not) be . . .

I am interested in (subject) because . . .

Freewriting
November 16

People are arguing about what good or what harm TV talk shows like <u>Donahue</u>, <u>Jerry Springer</u>, <u>Ricki Lake</u>, and others do. It's hard to say. They seem to be doing some good in giving people with problems an opportunity to come on stage and talk about them or to confront the people who are the source of those problems. Like the woman yesterday who surprised her husband with the fact that she knew he was having an affair. But my reading tells me that such confrontations are not always healthy, that the problems dealt with on these shows are really too sensitive to just get thrown out on TV and shared publicly. Can a psychologist or other expert really give good advice after just fifteen or twenty minutes of hearing people talk about their problems? What about the audience—are they being hardened by daily exposure to adultery, child abuse, and the like? People argue about weird behavior like shooting a neighbor's cat or children beating up their parents like it was a matter of what color socks you want to wear or something! Most of the shows are about sex. Some get out of control—like when a guest shot and killed another guest after the show. The shows may be getting out of control. Their ratings are down. It's likely all the criticism will cause them to deal with less controversial material in the future.

FIGURE 3.9   Freewriting to examine issues

After you finish freewriting, look over the results. Pick out recurring ideas or phrases that indicate a potential topic to discuss at greater length. Use such ideas or phrases as the focus of a second freewriting session. You will gradually recognize that you have a lot to say about one or two particular aspects of your subject. These particular aspects are most likely the research topics you have been seeking.

Clustering

Clustering is another useful way to discover a research topic. Begin by writing your research subject in the center of a piece of paper and drawing a circle around it; then jot down any ideas you associate with the circled subject and connect them to it with lines. Circle each new idea and connect it to other associated concepts, grouping them as you proceed. When you have run out of ideas for one line of thinking, start at the subject circle and begin again with a new connection. Figure 3.10 shows the clustering Nancy Prado did when considering topics for her paper about reforming the American jury selection process.

As with freewriting, do not worry about which ideas or associations come to mind as you cluster. Get your ideas down in any order or grouping, as they occur. Review and organize your thinking after recording your thoughts.

FIGURE 3.10   Clustering to examine issues

Relating a Subject to Your Interests

Your own interests should play a major role in your selection of a research topic. Once you have decided upon a research subject, relate it to your personal interests by listing them opposite each other. You can tell what they add up to by following this formula, in which X equals your paper's topic focus:

My interest + Subject = X

Nancy Prado's use of this technique in her research notebook produced several possible research topics to consider. Since she intends to study law, Nancy began by considering how she felt about attorneys serving on juries:

1. Attorneys on juries + jury selection procedures = discussing the pros and cons of attorneys serving as jurors
2. Women jurors + jury selection procedures = questioning whether female and male jurors interpret evidence differently
3. College students + jury selection = examining how the jury selection process deals with students' needs to attend classes and study while serving on juries
4. Race + jury selection procedures = looking at how race affects jury selection and jury decisions

Narrowing the Focus
of the Research Topic

Make any topic you select as specific as possible. Remember that nearly every topic may become increasingly focused as you learn more about it through research. Figure 3.11 demonstrates how continual narrowing of the subject *environmental hazards,* for example, can lead to the general topic of the *decreasing ozone layer,* which, in turn, can be continually narrowed toward even more specific aspects of the original subject.

A different emphasis or interest on your part, of course, will determine the direction of your narrowing and the choice of topics with which you will work. In the above example, the topic of the ozone layer's general *effects on human health* could also lead to entirely different subtopics, such as *cataracts and cancers.* Whether you would decide to pursue the broader topic of the *decreasing ozone layer* or research its relationship to *skin cancer,* for example, would ultimately depend upon your interests or the availability of resources for one or the other topic.

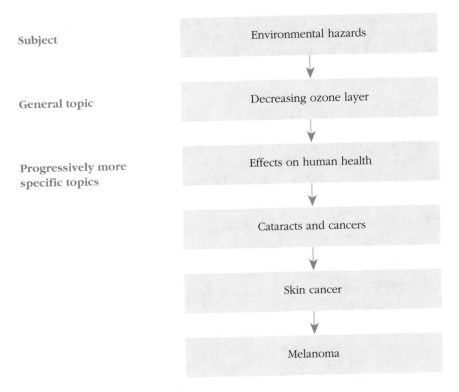

Subject — Environmental hazards

General topic — Decreasing ozone layer

Progressively more specific topics — Effects on human health

Cataracts and cancers

Skin cancer

Melanoma

FIGURE 3.11   Narrowing a topic

Working with a Back-Up Topic in Mind

As you explore particular areas for your research paper, consider more than one potential topic, in case your first choice later proves impractical. The unavailability of resources or a lack of time to investigate your first topic thoroughly may make another choice more feasible, or you may later learn enough about an alternate topic to make it a more appealing option. If that happens, you will find that any broad, preliminary thinking about the general subject for the first topic can provide useful background for selecting a related second topic.

For example, you might begin with a general subject like *alternative automobile fuels* and then progress to a narrower topic such as *electric power as an alternative to gasoline*. Preliminary investigation, however, may not uncover enough sources discussing recent developments in electrically powered automobiles. In this case, you could move to a back-up topic such as *gasahol as an alternative to gasoline* and still make use of your earlier research. Keeping a back-up topic in mind as you research will require some mental juggling and a little extra time; however, the precaution will be worthwhile, should an original topic prove unuseful.

A Checklist for Topic Selection

The topic you finally select to research and write about will need to meet a number of criteria. As you narrow your general subject to one or two possible topics, check each of your most promising choices against the following guidelines:

☐ 1. Be sure the topic meets the requirements of your research assignment.

☐ 2. Focus on a topic that you want to learn more about.

☐ 3. Pick a topic for which you can meet an audience's needs and expectations.

☐ 4. Check to see that sufficient resources are available. Depending upon the materials involved, using interlibrary loan or trusting the mail may take more time than you have.

☐ 5. Avoid philosophical topics or those based on personal belief. Topics like *the value of the family* and *why you play sports* rely upon personal opinion and values, rather than objective research and discussion.

☐ 6. Avoid strictly biographical topics—*Abraham Lincoln as a father*—that are already discussed fully in book-length studies.

☐ 7. Avoid describing processes such as *how cocaine is sold on the street* or *why getting a suntan may be dangerous.* Such information will not allow for original insight and judgment on your part.

☐ 8. Avoid topics too narrow or too recent for discussion. A paper on *local airport conditions* or *last week's international event* will not allow for adequate use of research materials.

☐ 9. Avoid standard, popular topics commonly chosen for student research papers. Unless recent developments have added new information or conditions, it may be difficult to impress your instructor with yet another paper on the *death penalty* or *animal intelligence.* Besides, all the resources on these topics will be checked out by others when you need them. Pick a topic that shows your individual abilities and interests.

☐ 10. Cease consideration of any topic that you cannot get very far with in terms of an approach or finding resources. If you seem to be meeting a dead end with a topic, ask your instructor or a librarian for help, but recognize that some topics may just not be right for you and your circumstances.

As you approach selecting a research topic, consider yourself part of the paper's audience, someone who will also benefit from its discussion. Through researching and writing, you will discover what you know or do not know about your topic. Writing will allow you to test your ideas and to analyze and evaluate your research data to a far greater extent than before. The topic you select should be one you want to help others, as well as yourself, understand better.

Formulating a Research Question

Even a well-defined research topic presents too broad an area to research and write about by itself. A topic like *women in the Olympics,* for example, needs a more specific focus for the research to promise more than an accumulation of facts. To make your research more effective, formulate a research question about the topic. Questions like the following focus on the topics and the research required for them:

Topic	*Television and race*
Research questions	1. Does television present stereotypes of racial minorities?
	2. Do minority actors have equal opportunities on television?
	3. What does television teach us about race relations?
Topic	*Fan violence and sports*
Research questions	1. What should be done to curb fan violence?
	2. Does the alcohol sold at games contribute to fan violence?
Topic	*Women in magazine advertisements*
Research questions	1. What image of women is conveyed by advertisements in leading national magazines?
	2. Do magazine advertisements over the last 10 years reflect any changes in the way women are presented?
	3. How do women's groups respond to current advertisements for women and women's products?

Remember to regard the answer to any research question as a working hypothesis that your research may confirm or alter significantly. Just asking whether minority actors have equal opportunities in television, for example, implies that they may not. It will be your responsibility to research the question objectively and to demonstrate the validity of your answer in the paper you write.

Recording Research Questions

Which questions you decide to pursue in your research will depend upon several factors, including your own interests, the requirements of your assignment, the available resources, and the needs of your audience. As you begin preliminary research for a topic, keep a section in your research notebook for recording ideas and potential questions about that topic. A section titled Topics and Questions in Mark Stevenson's research notebook (see Figure 3.12) contained five entries for various topics he was interested in pursuing.

Mark went on to develop the third topic and research question shown here, changing both slightly as his research and further thinking led him to do so. Mark's notebook entry enabled him to identify his own central concerns and led to a research question that could answer them. The other notebook entries gave him useful alternative topic choices and a means of judging what seemed the most interesting and challenging issues to research.

Using Critical Thinking Techniques to Focus on Research

After examining preliminary sources about your subject, you may find that one or more critical thinking approaches will help you identify issues and arrive at a research question or more focused approach to it. If you were investigating the subject of *subliminal advertising*, for example, the following approaches might be helpful:

1. *Summarize* your preliminary sources to identify unresolved issues and define points of view regarding the subject. For example, your sources may each describe several common uses of subliminal advertising but each have a different opinion about whether these uses are harmful.

2. *Evaluate* the sources in terms of their evidence and the extent to which it may be useful in supporting your own research conclusion. A

Topics and Questions

1. *College admissions and SAT scores.* Are SAT scores and other test scores used to screen and select applicants for college fair? Are they accurate at predicting student success in college?

2. *Affirmative action.* What exactly is it? Does it really favor minorities unfairly, as some people say? Who is affected by it now, and what will be the consequences of eliminating or reducing it?

3. *Talk television.* Is it as bad as people say it is? Why do people go on the programs? What do they gain from them? One issue is whether or not the shows are harming their audiences—especially children. Are we becoming too liberal about the kind of topics on these shows? Is "Trash TV" harming us?

4. *Rights of people who are homeless.* Do the homeless have any rights? In many cities they are being kicked out of where they live because they trespass or are seen as being a nuisance. What about hospital care? Do they have a right to it? Do they pay taxes? Work? Why are these people homeless? Whose fault is it?

5. *Japanese vs. American education.* Which is really better? There is a lot of talk about how poor American schools are and how great the Japanese system of education is. But is it? What accounts for the apparent differences?

FIGURE 3.12 Entries from a research notebook

source that gives weak evidence about the dangers of subliminal advertising may convince you of just the opposite conclusion, or you may think of ways that you could introduce stronger evidence from other sources to better support the same argument.

3. *Analyze* the subject and unresolved issues to examine underlying principles and apply them to specific cases or issues. For instance, is it right to allow people, including children, to be unknowingly targeted by such advertising?

4. *Synthesize* the ideas provided by sources to clarify what questions or issues are left unresolved or how they could be incorporated to support your own conclusion. You may find that while most sources claim there is little real evidence of the abuse of subliminal advertising, what evidence exists supports the argument that the use of subliminal ads is unethical and dangerous.

Considering Your Audience

Part of selecting a topic and research question to investigate also involves considering your paper's audience. Naturally, the instructor who assigned the paper is your most immediate audience, though he or she is not the only one you want to think of as you consider a focus for your research.

While your instructor may be your paper's primary reader, his or her reading will have the same criteria that you would want to meet for other readers. When planning the research for your paper, you should assume that the audience is generally knowledgeable about the subject but needs additional information to understand and be convinced of your paper's main point, or thesis. This is the audience you should write for and whom you want to consider when thinking of your research paper.

When considering any topic and research question, assess your readers' needs. Ask yourself what they need to know or what you can discuss to enlighten them further about the topic. What questions do people need to have answered about *organically grown foods,* for example? What would an audience of chemists want to know? What would a mother of young children want to know? What questions do you need to ask and which audience's needs can your research fulfill?

Because the audience you assume will be generally informed already, avoid topics and research questions that will be so familiar they will offer nothing new. The question of whether cigarette smoking endangers people's health is not likely to interest an already informed audience. Likewise, such an audience is unlikely to find much interest in a paper simply arguing against drug addiction: Why listen to an argument most informed people have already accepted? A good topic and research question stimulates your readers' thinking, drawing upon an assumed interest in the subject to present new perspectives.

Defining the Paper's Purpose

As you determine the focus of your research, you will also need to define your paper's *purpose,* which includes answering the research question and planning your strategy for presenting information. The kind of paper you write and the investigation you do for it will reflect the research question and the paper's purpose.

The Argumentative Paper

Research papers that aim primarily at interpreting information are *argumentative* papers. When you write an argumentative paper, the intention is to lead readers to understand and agree with your analysis of the research topic and your conclusion about the research question.

Argumentative papers are meant to persuade an audience that the writer's perceptions are correct. Such a paper states the author's argument (or *thesis*) and then presents evidence to support it. Argumentative research papers also appear in the form of scholarly articles, scientific essays, legal briefs, business reports, historical studies, and government analyses. In short, writers use an argumentative approach whenever they feel their audience needs or expects comprehensive discussion and reasoned conclusions about a topic.

Because it seeks to persuade readers of her research conclusions, Nancy Prado's paper on the need to reform the American jury system has an argumentative purpose. After selecting the jury selection system as the focus of her research, Nancy formulated a research question that addressed her further interest and insight about the topic: To what extent does the current system of jury selection work effectively? The resulting thesis statement in Nancy's paper explains her answer: In order to restore the public's confidence in jury decisions and in the justice system as a whole, the United States must begin by reforming the system by which jurors are selected. After stating this thesis in her introduction, Nancy went on to discuss the thesis argument and support it with her own research and analysis of the subject (see Chapter 10).

Similarly, Mark Stevenson's paper on television talk shows argues that such shows have likely gone too far in their pursuit of ratings to survive the backlash from criticism by those who find them offensive and detrimental. Mark's argument is an answer to his research question: What are the criticisms of talk shows, and what consequences are they likely to have? (see Appendix A).

Both Nancy and Mark recognized early in their investigations that their topics provided enough questions or controversy to call for further discussion and reasoned conclusions from them. While investigating your research topic, keep similarly alert to obvious—as well as implicit—questions that readers want answered.

An effective argumentative research paper should demonstrate your ability to gather information and assess it accurately. In discussing any topic, especially a controversial one, present all sides of an issue, not just those that favor your argument. You should acknowledge any facts and opinions that seem to oppose your position, offering counter-arguments or qualifying discussions as you do so. In this way, you are being fair to your audience and to your own understanding of the topic.

The Informative Paper

Informative research is primarily intended to present information for the reader's benefit. In one sense, of course, all research papers inform their audiences: They offer information to illustrate the writer's ideas and to show how the various parts of the topic relate. Informative research studies, however, minimize expression of the author's viewpoint. Topics for informative research papers are those about which readers need information more than anything else. The research questions for informative papers usually emphasize description, measurable results, or processes, as in these examples:

1. What effect has deforestation in the Amazon had upon already threatened species of wildlife?
2. How are colleges across the United States dealing with the problem of violence on campus?
3. Do students from private schools get better SAT scores than those from public schools?
4. How are other countries coping with the growing problem of waste disposal?

You inform readers when you explain, summarize, report, chart, list, or otherwise make information itself the primary focus of your presentation. Your major role in writing an informative paper is to gather data and organize it in a more clear manner than your readers would otherwise have it. The information you gather to describe may range from entirely new data, such as a report analyzing the impact of an oil spill on local fishing grounds, to a review of the current literature in a field, as was done in Daniel Nguyen's paper on AIDS research (see Appendix A). If you foresee the need to write an informative paper, remember that it should not be merely a summary of sources or string of quotations from various authorities. Your ability to formulate and answer a significant research question is vital to an effective paper.

Knowing whether you want to write an argumentative or informative research paper will help you decide what to write about and how to shape your ideas for research. As you plan the focus of your research, keep in mind these two major kinds of purposes. You may need to check with your instructor about which kind of paper is required or may be most appropriate for your research assignment.

Working with a Preliminary Thesis

At some point in the initial stages of your investigation, you will undoubtedly begin to perceive a potential answer to the research question you have formulated about the topic. For some writers, such an answer is formed early in the research process. For others, it develops slowly or changes as the focus of the research question itself shifts in response to more information about the topic. Some writers resist forming even a potential answer to the research question until their investigation of sources has been completed.

Guided by a research question, however, most writers find it also helpful to have in mind a preliminary thesis as they work. The *preliminary thesis* is a statement in one or two sentences that summarizes your tentative response to the research question at a particular point in your investigation. Along with the research question, such a thesis statement will direct your research activities toward relevant material, helping you decide what to give close attention to in examining sources.

For example, suppose your research topic is *the effectiveness of antiyouth gang programs in large cities.* An appropriate research question would be: What is required for a successful antigang program? Drawing upon what you know of the topic from your beginning investigation, you might formulate a potential preliminary thesis such as this: The most effective antigang programs include community-based education and employment assistance. Key concepts such as *community-based education* and *employment assistance* can focus your reading. Defining what your paper will mean by *effective* (and its opposite, *ineffective*) can strengthen its content and add breadth to your discussion.

Remember that a preliminary thesis is not intended to be your final opinion on the topic. As you investigate the topic more thoroughly, you will most likely modify the thesis or change it entirely in response to your increased knowledge. You might begin with something like this: The average American's diet is certain suicide. Later, you may decide that the following statement more suitably expresses your ideas: Americans can choose to eat better and live longer. If a preliminary thesis seems helpful at the planning stage, use it with the research question as a way of furthering the focus of your research.

W O R K I N G   W I T H   O T H E R S

Discussing your research ideas with others will promote and clarify your own thinking. A five-minute conversation can sometimes eliminate an inappropriate subject from further consideration or make you suddenly enthusiastic over a topic you might not have thought of alone. Use the following suggestions to help you work with others in planning the focus of your research. You will find sharing your ideas and progress acts as a stimulus to your perseverance and thinking for the research paper.

- Meet with a classmate or friend to review the potential subjects listed in your research notebook. What makes each subject particularly appealing to you? Does your friend or classmate have a preference for one subject over another? Why? Discuss each subject and the kinds of resources that might be available for it. What other subjects can you suggest to each other?

- Work with another person to narrow a potential subject toward a particular topic. Try brainstorming together to come up with as many related topics for the subject as you can. What are the major concerns regarding this subject? What questions need to be answered about these concerns? What important research steps might some of these topics require?

- If you used freewriting or clustering to arrive at a topic, share the results. What pattern of ideas or interest is apparent? Does your approach seem to favor an argumentative or informative approach to the discussion? Take turns completing introductory phrases about potential topics, such as "Water conservation is important today because . . ."

- If you are not familiar with using a computer or search tools such as Gopher to find information, ask a classmate or friend to give you a demonstration. Discuss possible topics for research, and explore them together on the Internet or other online resources.

- Once you have some specific topics in mind, use the topic checklist presented earlier (see pp. 48–49) to discuss their merits. Discuss whether each topic seems suitable for the assignment and available resources. Does any particular topic seem too philosophical or too narrow? Will it result in little more than a restatement of well-known and accepted ideas?

- After selecting a suitable topic, your next step will be to investigate specific sources and to take notes. Discuss your general plans with your collaborator, and make arrangements to review your progress together again. If you are working with a classmate, use your research schedules to plan times to meet and begin thoroughly researching sources together.

Researching
Library Sources

Having determined an appropriate topic and research question, you will next need to think about locating the information on which to base your research. A large, general library, such as that found at most colleges or universities, will provide the greatest number and variety of resources for you to begin your research.

Organize your search for information by first establishing a *working bibliography*, a list of sources on the research topic. The working bibliography will serve as an ongoing, developing pool of sources to consult throughout your research. You will want to use the full range of standard library resources and reference materials to ensure that the working bibliography, and therefore your research on the topic, is as comprehensive as possible.

Preparing the Working Bibliography

The working bibliography is a *preliminary* list of sources for your paper, one that will change as you add or delete sources uncovered throughout the research process. The list is a *bibliography* because it names and provides information about sources on a particular topic. It is a *working* bibliography because it is tentative: You use the working bibliography to record information about available sources, to determine whether there are enough and the right kinds of sources for your research needs, and to locate and work with such sources as you research and write the paper. Sources included in the working bibliography—books, magazines, newspapers, journal articles, interviews, and others—lay the groundwork for the notetaking and organization of data that will come later in your research. Information for all or most of the sources in the Works Cited section of the final paper will also come from your working bibliography.

Listing Sources on Cards
or in a Computer File

You will need to devise a consistent means of storing the information you accumulate as you build the working bibliography for your paper. Although researchers vary in how they prefer to do this, storing the working bibliography on index cards, in a computer file, or both is most practical.

Bibliography Cards.   Many library researchers carry packets of *bibliography cards,* usually 3″ × 5″ (or larger) index cards, on which they record information about all their sources as they find them. Such cards offer several advantages for researchers:

1. Cards allow for quick organization and sorting of bibliographic sources.
2. Unwanted cards can be easily discarded or new ones conveniently added.
3. Information from the cards can be easily transferred to a computer file and then serve as a back-up to the file.
4. Because they can be easily shuffled and arranged alphabetically, the cards will later provide bibliographic information in the order needed for preparing the Works Cited list.

Keep a stock of blank bibliography cards handy as you do research in the library, bookstore, or other places that may contain useful sources. Make a habit of jotting down the title and author's name on separate cards every time you come across a possible resource for the paper. If you keep your working bibliography in a computer file, transfer the information from the cards to the file on a regular basis to save time later.

A Computer File.   Another efficient way to list sources for the working bibliography is to enter information about each item into a computer file. Doing so lets you organize the information in different ways—for instance, in categories like *books* and *periodicals* or *primary* and *secondary sources.* Keeping the working bibliography in a computer file also allows you to copy the information to other files or to insert it handily into the draft of the paper once you begin to write. However, since it is unlikely that you will always have a computer on hand for research in libraries or elsewhere, you may still need to use bibliography cards, as well.

It may seem as though transferring the information from your bibliography cards to a computer file creates unnecessary work, but taking this extra step is worth it. Once you begin transferring data from the cards to a file, you will see how handy it is to scroll down your computer screen and assess your research progress from time to time.

Information for the Working Bibliography.   When filling out a bibliography card or adding a source to your computer file, include the information you would need to find the source again or to include it in your paper's Works Cited section. Though you may eventually list many types of sources for your research, it is likely that a majority of them will be books and periodicals.

Book Sources.   In general, record the following information for any book you list in the working bibliography:

1. Library catalog call number
2. Author(s), editor(s), or translator(s)
3. Title (underlined), including the subtitle
4. Place of publication
5. Publisher
6. Publication date (or latest copyright date)
7. Brief note about the book's content or usefulness

Figure 4.1 shows how such information may appear on a bibliography card, using the style followed by the Modern Language Association (MLA). You should follow the form and punctuation you will use in your paper, if the form shown here is different. (MLA style is discussed further in Chapter 11. Other bibliographic styles are discussed in Chapter 12.)

PN1992.8
T3H43
1995

Heaton, Jeanne Albronda, and Nona Leigh Wilson
 Tuning in Trouble: Talk TV's Destructive Impact on Mental
 Health
 San Francisco: Jossey-Bass, 1995.

—— Has good discussions of experts and problems for guests

FIGURE 4.1   A bibliography card for a book (MLA style)

Periodical Sources.   Publications that are published at regular intervals are called *periodicals.* The information recorded on a bibliography card about an article from a periodical—such as a magazine, journal, or newspaper—will differ slightly from that for a book. It should include:

1. Author(s)
2. Title (in quotation marks), including the subtitle
3. Periodical name (underlined)
4. Volume number (for professional journals but not popular magazines)*
5. Date of publication
6. Page number(s) the article is found on
7. Brief note about the article's content or usefulness

If no author is given for a periodical article, begin the entry with the article title. Do not use *Anonymous* or *Anon.* in place of an author's name. If you have located the periodical through the *Reader's Guide* or another index, avoid using that source's forms and abbreviations. Either translate them into the bibliographic style of your paper as you write the data on your card, or make a new card when you later locate the periodical. Figure 4.2 shows a typical bibliography card (in MLA style) for a periodical article, but follow the style of your paper's bibliographical form if it is different.

Weinstein, Jack B.

"Considering Jury 'Nullification': When, May, and Should a Jury Reject the Law to Do Justice?"
American Criminal Law Review 30.2 (1993): 229-254.

— Says nullification may be appropriate and important to maintain

---

FIGURE 4.2   A bibliography card for a periodical (MLA style)

*See also Chapters 11 and 12 regarding issue and series numbers.

Gauging the Topic's Feasibility

At the start of your research, the working bibliography serves as an important check against beginning to work at length on an unfruitful topic. If your preliminary search for sources turns up too many—a dozen books and twenty magazine articles on your very topic, let's say—you will need to narrow the topic more or take a different approach to it (see Chapter 3). If you can find only one encyclopedia entry and a few magazine articles that discuss your research question, you will need to broaden your focus or select an alternate topic to research (see Chapter 3). In addition, check the working bibliography against the requirements of your assignment. For example, if your instructor wants you to use particular kinds of primary sources—original materials like diaries or unpublished papers—and none are available, you will need to select another topic.

Expect the working bibliography to change as you delete some works and add others throughout your research. Keep in mind, however, that the working bibliography's completeness is also essential to the success of your research. The more inclusive the working bibliography, the more thoroughly you will be able to study major ideas involved with the research topic. For these reasons, you will also need to understand how libraries organize and store information as well as how to use the resources available in them.

Using Bibliographies to Locate Sources

A list of related books or other written works is called a *bibliography* (hence, the name for the working bibliography). While all bibliographies provide information about each source's title, author, and publication data, they also vary in their emphasis and approach. A bibliography may be *selective* and include only a few works; it may *descriptive* and provide brief annotations or reviews; it may be *evaluative* and discuss the value of the sources it lists; or it may combine any of these approaches.

The most familiar kinds of bibliographies are those commonly found at the ends of scholarly books or their chapters, at the conclusions of encyclopedia or journal articles, or at the backs of a few popular periodicals like *Smithsonian* and *Scientific American*. These bibliographies are sometimes titled References, Works Cited, or Works Consulted, and they usually list the works that the article authors used to prepare their own discussions of their subjects. The Works Cited list that you will include at the end of your research paper will be such a bibliography.

Some complete reference works, however, are bibliographies only. That is, the entire purpose of a book published *as a bibliography* is to provide a list of sources on a topic. For example, you might go to a work titled *A Bibliography of Jazz,* by Alan P. Merriam, if you wanted a list of published works about jazz. The term *bibliography* is also sometimes referred to as a union catalog or list, a checklist, sourcebook, or index. Thus, G. Thomas Tanselle's *A Checklist of Editions of Moby Dick, 1851–1976* might be a useful bibliography to consult if you were studying that novel's publishing history. Regardless of what they are termed, you will need such whole-work bibliographies, as well as shorter ones listed within other works, to locate sources for your own working bibliography and to establish a larger base of materials to investigate for your research.

Becoming Familiar with General Bibliographies

Probably most helpful to researchers are *general bibliographies,* reference books that tell you about the bibliographies contained in other books.

Bibliographic Index.   One of the most useful general resources is the *Bibliographic Index: A Cumulative Bibliography of Bibliographies.* You can look up an author or subject in this comprehensive work to find other bibliographies that appear in books and periodicals.

As Figure 4.3 shows, an author entry in the *Bibliographic Index* may include bibliographies listed in works *by* an author, *about* an author, as well as *both by and about* an author. In addition to writing down all the usual information about a *Bibliographic Index* source, notice that you will also want to record where the bibliographies appear in the works cited. This information is given as the page numbers listed at the end of each entry. The bibliography card shown in Figure 4.4 records an entry from the *Bibliographic Index,* listing the work by Halford Ryan as well as the pages on which the bibliography of works about U.S. presidents appears.

Clinton, Bill, 1946–
  Metz, A. Reviews of President Bill Clinton's first two years and second year in office: an annotated bibliography. *Bull Bibliogr* v52 p211–27 S '95
  Metz, A. Reviews of President Bill Clinton's first year in office: an annotated bibliography. *Bull Bibliogr* v51 p355–97 D '94
  By and about
  U.S. presidents as orators; a bio-critical sourcebook; edited by Halford Ryan. Greenwood Press 1995 p374–5

FIGURE 4.3   An entry on "Bill Clinton" from the *Bibliographic Index*
Source: From *Bibliographic Index,* August 1995, p. 196. Copyright © 1995 by The H. W. Wilson Company. Reprinted by permission of the publisher.

Ryan, Halford, ed.
U.S. Presidents as Orators: A Bio-Critical Sourcebook
Westport, CT: Greenwood Press, 1995
Bibliography p. 374–375

FIGURE 4.4   A bibliography card for a book cited in the *Bibliographic Index*

Other General Bibliographies.   While the *Bibliographic Index* is probably the most available and practical general bibliography, others will also be useful to you. Theodore Besterman's *A World Bibliography of Bibliographies* (later updated by Alice Toomey) is international in scope and helpful for topics focusing on other countries or worldwide issues. It lists separately published bibliographies by subject, including those in books and periodicals.

The following list of general bibliographies includes those already discussed as well as others that can provide valuable assistance to your research:

Besterman, Theodore. *A World Bibliography of Bibliographies.* Lausanne, Switzerland: Societas Bibliographica, 1963. [See also the entry for Toomey, below]

The Bibliographic Index: A Cumulative Bibliography of Bibliographies. New York: Wilson, 1938–date.

Hilliard, James. *Where to Find What: A Handbook to Reference Service.* Rev. ed. Metuchen, NJ: Scarecrow, 1984.

McCormick, Mona. *The New York Times Guide to Reference Materials.* Rev. ed. New York: Times, 1986.

Sheehy, Eugene P., ed. *Guide to Reference Books.* 10th ed. Chicago: ALA, 1986.

Toomey, Alice F. *A World Bibliography of Bibliographies: 1964–1974.* 2 vols. Totowa, NJ: Rowan, 1977. [A supplement to Besterman's work of the same title, above]

Begin your research by consulting one or more of the general bibliographies described in this chapter. You can then go to the particular kind of bibliographic source, such as one of the following, to which they may refer you:

1. A bibliography of works used by an author to prepare his or her own discussion (those works listed at the end of an encyclopedia article, for example)
2. Bibliographies by or about one author (e.g., *Bibliography of the Works of Rudyard Kipling* or *Emily Dickinson: A Descriptive Bibliography*)
3. Bibliographies about one subject or subject field (e.g., *Checklist of Arizona Minerals* or *Bibliography of Mexican American History*)
4. Bibliographies describing materials relating to one country or region (e.g., *Bibliography of Africana*)

From these specific bibliographies, you will proceed to locate individual works by author and title (see Figure 4.5).

Searching Trade Bibliographies for Sources

People in the book trade, mainly librarians and booksellers, use trade bibliographies to buy, sell, and catalog books. You can use trade bibliographies to find out what books exist on your research topic; to get author, title, and publication data; and to find out if a book is still in print.

Subject Guide to Books in Print.   You will find the *Subject Guide to Books in Print* helpful in identifying current sources to include in your preliminary bibliography. Printed yearly, the *Subject Guide* can tell you which books on your research topic are in print. After writing down the information about any works listed, you can seek them out at your local library or ask about borrowing them through interlibrary loan.

Other Guides.   The *Subject Guide to Books in Print* is a version of another trade bibliography, *Books in Print*, which lists works in separate volumes by author, title, and subject. There is also *Paperbound Books in Print*, a good source to go to if you cannot find the hardbound edition of a

FIGURE 4.5   Moving from a general bibliography to an individual work

book in your library and are willing to try the local bookstore instead. *Books in Print* is often available online at college and university libraries, or you can access it from your home computer through some commercial services such as CompuServe. Figure 4.6 shows how the *Subject Guide to Books in Print* lists books under the subject *jury*.

For a listing and publication information about any book published in the English language, consult the *Cumulative Book Index (CBI)* for the year in question. If the *CBI* is not available at your library, the *Publisher's Trade List Annual* lists current and past books still in print from over 1,500 publishers.

The following trade bibliographies, including those already mentioned, are available at most libraries or bookstores:

American Book Publishing Record. New York: Bowker, 1960–date.
Books in Print. New York: Bowker, 1948–date.
Cumulative Book Index. New York: Wilson, 1898–date.
Paperbound Books in Print. New York: Bowker, 1955–date.
Publisher's Trade List Annual. New York: Bowker, 1873–date.
Subject Guide to Books in Print. New York: Bowker, 1957–date.

JURY
see also Grand Jury; Instructions to Juries
ABA, Committee on Jury Standards, et.al Standards
    Relating to Juror Use & Management: Tentative Draft.
    208p. 1982. 11.50 (*0-89656-603-5*, R-069) Natl Ctr St
    Courts.
Abbott, Walter F. Analytic Juror Rater. 142p. 1987. 31.00
    (*0-8318-0588-9*, B588) Am Law Inst.
—Surrogate Juries. LC 90-80485. 265p. 1990. 80.00
    (*0-8318-0607-9*, B607) Am Law Inst.
Abbott, Walter F., et. al. Jury Research: A Review &
    Bibliography. LC 90-75867. 346p. 1993. 31.00
    (*0-8318-0638-9*, B638) Am Law Inst.
The Anglo-American Jury: Keystone of Human Rights.
    1993. lib. bdg. 75.00 (*0-8490-8726-0*) Gordon Pr.
Antitrust Civil Jury Instructions (Supplement) LC 80-67740.
    88p. 1986. ring bd. 30.00 (*0-89707-215-4*, 503-0060-01)
    Amer Bar Assn.
Austin, Arthur D. Complex Litigation Confronts the Jury
    System: A Case Study. LC 84-19500. 120p. 1984. text
    ed. 55.00 (*0-313-27009-6*, U7099, Greenwood Pr)
    Greenwood.
Berger, Richie E. & Lane, Frederick S., 3rd. Vermont Jury
    Instructions. 400p. 1993. ring bd. 85.00 (*1-56257-293-8*)
    Michie Butterworth.

FIGURE 4.6 An entry on "jury" from the *Subject Guide to Books in Print*

Using Indexes to Locate Sources

Bibliographies can tell you what books are published, but they do not list the individual items that may be included within works. Indexes, however, can help you find single works—articles, stories, poems, essays, and other written pieces—located *within* books and periodicals. There are general indexes to periodicals and books as well as specialized indexes to particular kinds of works or subjects.

Periodical Indexes

Publications printed at regular intervals (or periods) are called *periodicals*. These include magazines, journals, and newspapers of every type and description. Because they are published more frequently than encyclopedias or books, periodicals are valuable sources of current information and opinion. Articles appearing in both popular and scholarly periodicals are indexed in a variety of sources. Use these indexes to identify possible areas to explore for research.

Popular Magazines.   In addition to journals and newspapers, periodicals also include popular magazines written for general audiences and usually available at newsstands or the local supermarket. *Newsweek, Ms., Psychology Today, Field and Stream, Penthouse, National Geographic,* and *Rolling Stone* are examples. Popular magazines like these can be useful for exploring a potential research focus and acquiring helpful background information. Because they are aimed at general audiences and vary greatly in their authority, however, articles in magazines may not be suitable for every kind of research. They are best used when you need current, non-technical information and opinion about a subject. When in doubt about using magazines, consult your instructor.

Magazine Indexes.   You are probably already familiar with the *Reader's Guide to Periodical Literature,* an index to more than 200 of the most popular magazines in the United States. (The *Reader's Guide* and its use are also discussed in Chapter 3.) The format for information in the *Reader's Guide* is representative of that used in most other periodical indexes. Articles are listed alphabetically by author and subject; each entry includes the author's name, article title, name of the periodical, the date and volume number of the periodical, and the page numbers of the article. Figure 4.7 shows a typical entry from the *Reader's Guide.*

While the *Reader's Guide* is no doubt the most comprehensive of the magazine indexes, you should not overlook others that include publications it does not index. For example, *Access,* issued three times a year, includes 150 or more magazines not included among those indexed in the *Reader's Guide.* Using *Access,* you can find articles printed in such maga-

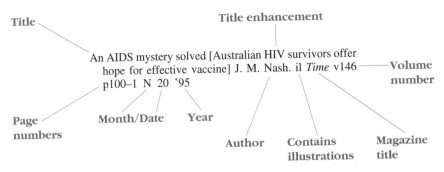

FIGURE 4.7 An excerpt from the *Reader's Guide to Periodical Literature*

Source: From the *Reader's Guide to Periodical Literature*, September 1989. Copyright © 1989 by The H. W. Wilson Company. Reprinted by permission.

zines as *Woman's Day, TV Guide, Penthouse,* and *Bicycling,* sources that can provide you with insight to popular taste or current information on well-known individuals.

To find very current articles with slightly different viewpoints than those often found in many mainstream publications, you might want to consult the *Popular Periodical Index* and the *Alternative Press Index.* The first of these indexes such magazines as *MacWorld, Playboy, English Journal,* and *Columbia Journalism Review;* the second includes over 200 so-called alternative publications such as *Green Peace, Feminist Studies,* and *Canadian Journal of Political and Social Theory.*

In addition to these print sources, you will find a number of magazine indexes available online or on CD–ROM. Many college and university libraries, for example, provide CD–ROM resources such as *Magazine Article Summaries* or *Magazine Index Plus,* each of which indexes over 400 magazines. In addition, many college and university library computer facilities offer InfoTrac, which includes several popular magazine and newspaper indexes as well as individual newspapers. Commercial services such as America Online, CompuServe, and Prodigy provide online search access to the archives of popular magazines such as *Newsweek, Time, U.S. News & World Report, McClean's,* and a host of others.

For her research paper on the American system of jury selection, Nancy Prado used her own computer at home to access CompuServe's *Magazine Database Plus.* She used the key words "jury selection" to get the list of possible sources shown in Figure 4.8. Note that abstracts of these articles were also available, if Nancy had wished to retrieve them. While such at-home research is appealing, remember that you must normally pay a fee for using a commercial service to conduct a search or retrieve information.

While you will obviously want to consider the *Reader's Guide* as your primary index to popular magazines, remember that you can locate useful

Magazine Database Plus   Article
Selection Menu

1   Unreasonable doubt. (O. J. Simpson acquittal) (Editorial)
    (Cover Story), the New Republic, Oct 23, 1995 v213 n17 p7(2).
    Reference #A17618819   Text: Yes (1639 words)   Abstract: Yes

2   Jury dismissed: the institution from the Dark Ages. (O. J.
    Simpson acquittal) (Unreasonable Doubt? Simpson, Race *
    America) (Cover Story),The New Republic, Oct 23, 1995 v213
    n17 p10(4).
    Reference # A17618821   Text: Yes (1488 words)   Abstract: Yes

3   My peers? Yeah, right. (item from 'Fat Girl' indicates that the
    California Supreme Court upheld the right to remove a juror
    who was 'overweight and poorly groomed') (Beat the Devil)
    (Brief Article) (Column), The Nation, July 31, 1995 v261 n4
    p121(1).
    Reference # A17361368   Text: Yes (181 words)   Abstract: No

FIGURE 4.8   Entries from *Magazine Database Plus,* an online database from
CompuServe
Source: Reprinted with permission of CompuServe, Inc.

sources in various other indexes, too. For easy reference later, the following list includes indexes already mentioned as well as others you may wish
to consult:

Access, 1975–date (includes only magazines not indexed in the
Reader's Guide).

Alternative Press Index, 1969–date (covers politically "left" publications).

California Periodicals Index, 1978–date (indexes magazines about California cities and lifestyles).

Catholic Periodical and Literature Index, 1930–date.

Children's Magazine Guide: Subject Index to Children's Literature,
1948–date.

Consumer's Index to Product Evaluations and Information Sources,
1973–date.

Index to Jewish Periodicals, 1963–date.
Index to Periodicals By and About Blacks, 1950–date.
Magazine Article Summaries, 1984–date (available on CD–ROM).
Magazine Database Plus, 1980–date (available online through CompuServe and at many college and university libraries).
The Magazine Index, 1977–date (appears on microfilm and duplicates the *Reader's Guide* and *Access*).
Magazine Index Plus, 1980–date (available on CD–ROM).
Periodicals Abstracts Ondisc, 1986–date (microfilm).
Physical Education Index, 1978–date (indexes magazines covering nutrition, fitness, and sports).
Physical Education/Sports Index, 1973–date (includes magazines devoted to particular sports).
Popular Periodical Index, 1978–date.
Reader's Guide to Periodical Literature, 1900–date (available in print and on CD–ROM).
Resource/One Ondisc, 1986–date (microfilm; available online through DIALOG [File 484] as *Newspapers & Periodicals Abstracts*).

Knowing Which Index to Consult.   If you are unsure about which index includes a particular popular magazine, refer to a copy of the magazine itself. The table of contents will often tell you where the magazine is indexed. If it does not, consult one of the following sources, but remember that these publications try not to duplicate each other. You may have to consult more than one before you find the particular magazine you want to know about:

Chicorel Index to Abstracting and Indexing Services. New York: Chicorel Library, 1978.
Magazines for Libraries. Ed. Bill Katz and Linda Katz. New York: Bowker, 1995.
Standard Periodical Directory. New York: Oxbridge, 1988.
Ulrich's International Periodicals Directory, 1993–94. New York: Bowker, 1995.

Journals.   Periodicals written for scholars or audiences with special expertise in a subject are called *journals.* These periodicals report on current issues, original research, and results of surveys and experiments. They also often include book reviews, which are themselves useful for your research. Journals are written by informed authorities for an audience of similarly informed or interested people. The level of knowledge or experience required to read them easily varies from very accessible ones, like the film journal *Movie Maker,* to more technical ones, like *Accounts of Chemical Research.*

Journal Indexes. Numerous indexes list journal articles covering subjects in nearly every field of study and interest. Four of the most widely used in the social sciences and literature and languages are discussed here:

1. *Social Sciences Index.* Since nearly every subject has implications for social consequences, check general social science indexes on almost any topic you research. A major source to consult in this field is the *Social Sciences Index,* which lists articles in over 250 scholarly journals covering such subjects as anthropology, economics, environmental studies, history, law, philosophy, political science, and sociology. As Figure 4.9 suggests, a check of the *Index* may not only yield sources for research but also suggest new relationships and emphases for you to consider.

2. *Social Sciences Citation Index.* A valuable resource in the behavioral and social sciences is the *Social Sciences Citation Index (SSCI).* This source indexes approximately 2,000 scholarly journals and is also available through online databases. Citation indexes are useful both for locating published journal articles and identifying authorities who have written on your research subject. Since it is composed of four separate indexes—Citation, Source, Permuterm Subject, and Corporate indexes—this work requires familiarity before it can be consulted efficiently.

   a. The Permuterm Subject Index of *SSCI* is useful at the start of your research, when you need to become acquainted with the key terms related to your subject or need to discover who has written about it. The Permuterm Subject Index lists articles by subject headings,

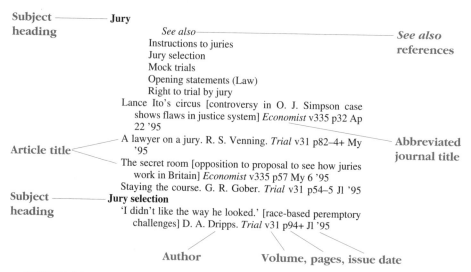

FIGURE 4.9   Entries from the *Social Science Index*

Source: From *Social Science Index,* September 1995, p. 333. Copyright © 1995 by The H. W. Wilson Company. Reprinted by permission.

followed by associated terms or subheadings. As Figure 4.10 shows, looking up the subject "television" in the Permuterm Index would yield a large number of more particular subheadings and authors whose journal articles treated them specifically. The entries under "television," for example, show an article on the topic of "adolescents" and television by L. Bernard. By using the Source Index, you could find the title of the source in which Bernard's article appears.

b. The Source Index provides publication information about each of the authors ("sources") listed in the Permuterm Subject Index and published in periodicals covered by *SSCI*. In addition, it also indicates the number of references made to each entry by other authors and lists those authors and where their works appeared. Thus, once you had found L. Bernard's name in the Subject Index under "television—adolescents," you could look him up in the Source Index for full information on what he had written. The entry would also list other authors who have cited his article. Figure 4.11 shows a complete Source entry for Bernard's article on adolescents and television.

c. Next, suppose you also wanted to find out more about L. Bernard's work. *SSCI*'s Citation Index will tell you (1) how many times and where a particular author has published during the time covered by the index and (2) what authors have made reference to the entries indicated for that author. Note that the Citation Index does not

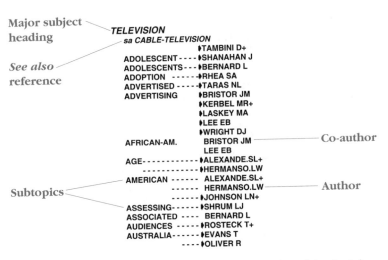

FIGURE 4.10 An excerpt from the Permuterm Subject Index of the *Social Sciences Citation Index*

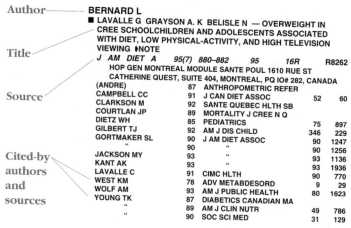

Author ——— **BERNARD L**
■ LAVALLE G GRAYSON A. K BELISLE N — OVERWEIGHT IN
CREE SCHOOLCHILDREN AND ADOLESCENTS ASSOCIATED
WITH DIET, LOW PHYSICAL-ACTIVITY, AND HIGH TELEVISION
VIEWING ♦NOTE

Title

J AM DIET A   95(7) 880–882   95   16R   R8262
HOP GEN MONTREAL MODULE SANTE POUL 1610 RUE ST
CATHERINE QUEST, SUITE 404, MONTREAL, PQ IO# 282, CANADA

Source

	(ANDRE)	87	ANTHROPOMETRIC REFER		
	CAMPBELL CC	91	J CAN DIET ASSOC	52	60
	CLARKSON M	92	SANTE QUEBEC HLTH SB		
	COURTLAN JP	89	MORTALITY J CREE N Q		
	DIETZ WH	85	PEDIATRICS	75	897
	GILBERT TJ	92	AM J DIS CHILD	346	229
	GORTMAKER SL	90	J AM DIET ASSOC	90	1247
	"	90	"	90	1256
Cited-by	JACKSON MY	93	"	93	1136
authors	KANT AK	93	"	93	1936
	LAVALLE C	91	CIMC HLTH	90	770
and	WEST KM	78	ADV METABDESORD	9	29
	WOLF AM	93	AM J PUBLIC HEALTH	80	1623
sources	YOUNG TK	87	DIABETICS CANADIAN MA		
	"	89	AM J CLIN NUTR	49	786
	"	90	SOC SCI MED	31	129

FIGURE 4.11   An author entry from the Source Index of the *Social Sciences Citation Index*

list titles of individual publications by an author. Instead, it lists the periodical and date when an article appeared (see Figure 4.12).

You should use the Citation Index to gauge an individual author's authority on the subject (indicated by the number of publications and the frequency of citations by other authors). Also use the

Column
heading ——— **BERNARD JP**   VOL PG YR

BERNARD JPA				
72 PARTI COMMUNISTE FRA				
MACEY O	ECON SOCIET	24	122	95 B
BERNARD JLR				
Authors
70 Z PHONETIK	23	113		
HARRINGT J	LANG SPEECH	37	357	94
BERNARD JT				
90 NEUROLOGY	40	154		
MEYERS CA	CNS DRUGS	3	56	95 R
BERNARD L				
45 AM J SOCIOL	50	534		
HELMESHA.RC	CAN J SOC	19	461	94
90 POLITICAL LANGUAGE I		P13		
BESWICK SF	J ASIAN AFR	29	172	94
BERNARD LC				
90 J CLIN EXPT NEUROPSY	5	715		
BEETAR JT	ARCH CLIN N	10	57	95
90 J CLIN EXPT NEUROPSY	12	715		
ARNETT PA	CLIN NEURPS	9	17	95
SIMON MJ	J CLIN PSYC	50	913	94
94 HLTH PSYCHOL BIOPSYC				
BELAR CD	PROF PSYCH	26	139	95

Volume,
page, and
year

FIGURE 4.12   An author entry from the Citation Index of the *Social Sciences Citation Index*

Citation Index to locate articles by other authors in the field, looking up the names listed there in the Source Index later.

d. The Corporate Author Index of *SSCI* has the same format as the Citation Index. Rather than citing persons, however, this index lists associations, leagues, corporations, and other groups who author publications.

Figure 4.13 summarizes the relationships among the separate indexes comprising the *Social Sciences Citation Index* and typical citation indexes in other fields of study. In addition to the *SSCI*, the following reference works include source, citation, and Permuterm indexes, as described here:

Arts and Humanities Index, 1977–date.
CompuMath Citation Index, 1968–date.
Science Citation Index, 1961–date.

3. *MLA Bibliography.* If you are researching a topic in languages or literature, consult the Modern Language Association's *MLA International Bibliography of Books and Articles on the Modern Languages and Literature.* This work's title is fully descriptive of its use and focus. Bound together as a single, inclusive volume and subtitled *Classified Listings with Author Index,* the *MLA Bibliography* divides articles on languages and literature into five distinct areas:

National literatures (subvolumes I and II)
Linguistics (III)
General literature (IV)
Folklore (V)

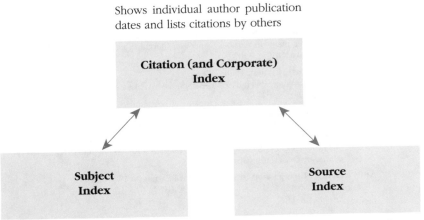

FIGURE 4.13   A summary of indexes included in the *Social Sciences Citation Index*

Locating an author or work in the *Classified Listings* is a step-by-step procedure:

a. Turn to the appropriate subvolume.

b. Find the section for the appropriate time period of your subject.

c. Find the alphabetical listing for the author or work you seek.

To locate items in the *MLA Bibliography* by subject, you will need to use a second, separate volume, the *Subject Index,* which is organized alphabetically.

Figure 4.14 shows entries from the *Subject Index* of the *MLA Bibliography* on author "Samuel Clemens" (who wrote using the pseudonym "Mark Twain"). Figure 4.15 is an entry from the *MLA Bibliography's Classified Listings with Author Index* on Twain's novel *The Adventures of Huckleberry Finn.*

4. *Humanities Index.* A good source for articles on religion, philosophy, literature, or any of the performing arts—such as dance, television, opera, drama, or film—is the *Humanities Index.* It includes entries from over 200 scholarly journals and follows *Reader's Guide* form in listing information. Figure 4.16 shows an article entry about "Mark Twain" taken from the *Humanities Index.*

CLEMENS, SAMUEL (1835–1910)
See also classified section: 1:7574 ff.
Used for: Twain, Mark.

    American literature. 1800–1899.
    Howells, William Dean. Relationship to CLEMENS, SAMUEL. Includes biographical information. I:7919.

    American literature. Criticism in *New York Tribune* (1870). 1800–1899.
    Hay, John. Treatment of Western American literature; especially Harte, Bret; CLEMENS, SAMUEL. I:7902.

    American literature. Fiction. 1800–1999.
    Treatment of utopia; especially CLEMENS, SAMUEL; London, John Griffith. Dissertation abstract. I:7369.

    American literature. Fiction. 1800–1899.
    Melville, Herman. Treatment of women; relationship to myth; the quest; compared to CLEMENS, SAMUEL; Hemingway, Ernest. Application of theories of Campbell, Joseph: *The Hero with a Thousand Faces;* Neumann, Erich: *Die grosse Mutter.* Dissertation abstract. I:8140.

    American literature. Fiction by Afro-American writers. 1900–1999.
    Point of view compared to CLEMENS, SAMUEL: *The Adventures of Huckleberry Finn .* I:8700.

FIGURE 4.14   An entry on "Samuel Clemens" from the *Subject Index* of the *MLA Bibliography*

Source: Reprinted by permission of the Modern Language Association of America from the *MLA International Bibliography* (Subject Index), 1984, p. G235. Copyright © 1985 by the MLA.

American literature / 1800–1899

CLEMENS, SAMUEL (1835–1910) / *Novel* / *The Adventures of Tom Sawyer (1876)*

Novel / *The Adventures of Huckleberry Finn (1884)*

[7039] Abderabou, Abdelrahman A. "The Human Dimensions in Multicultural Relations: A Critical Study of Twain's *Huckleberry Finn.*" *JEn* . 1986 Sept.; 14: 1–5. [†Treatment of black-white relations.]

[7040] Anderson, David D. "Mark Twain, Sherwood Anderson, Saul Bellow, and the Territories of the Spirit." *Midamerica* . 1986; 8: 116–124. [†Treatment of spiritual journey; relationship to American experience compared to Anderson, Sherwood: *Winesburg. Ohio;* Bellow, Saul: *The Adventures of Augie March* .]

[7041] Barrow, David. "The Ending of *Huckleberry Finn:* Mark Twain's Cryptic Lament." *CCTEP* . 1986 Sept.; 51: 78–84. [†Narrative ending.]

[7042] Berry, Wendell. "Writer and Region." *HudR* . 1987 Spring; 40(1): 15–30. [†Treatment of place; escape; relationship to community; the individual; society.]

[7043] Bird, John. " 'These Leather-Faced People': Huck and the Moral Art of Lying." *SAF* . 1987 Spring; 15(1): 71–80. [†Treatment of Finn, Huckleberry (character): relationship to falsehood.]

FIGURE 4.15 An entry from the *Classified Listings with Author Index* from the *MLA Bibliography*

Source: Reprinted by permission of the Modern Language Association of America from the *MLA International Bibliography* (Classified Listings with Author Index), 1987, p. 175. Copyright © 1987 by the MLA.

Subject heading ⟶ **Twain, Mark, 1835–1910**

about

A Connecticut Yankee in Jane Lampton's South: Mark Twain and the regicide. M. L. Sargent. *Miss Q* 40:21–31 Wint '86/'87

Article title ⟶ Huckleberry Finn and the minstrel show. A. J. Berret. *Am Stud* 27:37–49 Fall '86

Abbreviated journal title ⟶ Jim and Mark Twian: what do dey stan' for? S. Railton. *Va Q Rev* 63:393–408 Summ '87

Killing time with Mark Twain's autobiographies. L. A. Renza. *ELH* 54:157–82 Spr '87

Pudd'nhead Wilson: Mark Twain and the limits of detection. J. S. Whitley. *J Am Stud* 21:55–70 Ap '87

Repetition and recollection: the unconscious discourse of Mark Twain's Autobiography. M. C. Gwin. *Lit Psychol* 33 no3/4:120–31 '87

Satire deceit in the ending of Adventures of Huckleberry Finn. D. Kaufmann. *Stud Novel* 19:66–78 Spr '87

Volume ⟶ Twain's Huckleberry Finn. P. Wasserstein. *Explicator* 46:31–3 Fall '87

Page numbers ⟋   Publication date   Author

FIGURE 4.16 Entries on "Mark Twain" from the *Humanities Index*

Source: From the *Humanities Index,* April 1987–March 1988. Copyright © 1987, 1988 by The H. W. Wilson Company. Reprinted by permission.

Notice that most of the journals cited are published quarterly rather than monthly. Thus, for the article "Twain's Huckleberry Finn," published in the *Explicator,* a *Fall 1987* publication date is cited rather than the month and year.

Journal Article Abstracts.   Journals and the articles they contain are listed for nearly every field of study in a number of specialized indexes. You can often save time by reading an *abstract,* a condensed version of an article, in one of the many abstract references providing such article summaries. Most abstracts are identified by number and indexed according to subject in the abstract source itself. Figure 4.17 shows a summary of an article from *Psychological Abstracts* on *disclosure,* the therapeutic process of revealing private information about oneself. As the example shows, an abstract gives all the information you need—author, title, date, volume, page numbers—to cite the abstract in your Works Cited section or to locate the complete article. If you intend to read both the abstract and the complete article during your research, make a separate working bibliography card or computer file entry for each.

While abstracts are useful for general or background information, they should not serve as major sources for your research paper's discussion. Instead, use a journal abstract to determine whether the original article may be useful enough to seek out and read fully. If it is, use the publication information provided by the abstract to find the article and read it in complete form.

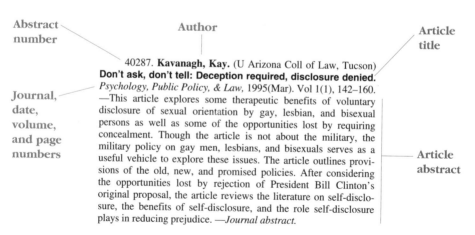

FIGURE 4.17   An article abstract from *Psychological Abstracts*

Many specialized journals titled as indexes also include abstracts. Familiarity with the common indexes of your research field will acquaint you with those that do. The following list provides a small sampling of the many indexes and abstracts available at most college and public libraries:

Applied Science & Technology Index, 1913–date (available online).
Art Index, 1929–date (available online).
Art Literature International, 1973–date (available online).
Biological & Agricultural Index, 1913–date.
Business Periodicals Index, 1958–date.
Child Development Abstracts and Bibliography, 1927–date.
Education Index, 1929–date (available online).
Film Literature Index, 1973–date.
General Science Index, 1978–date (available online).
Hispanic American Periodicals Index, 1974–date.
Historical Abstracts, 1914–date (available online).
Humanities Index, 1974–date (available online).
Index Medicus, 1960–date (available online).
Index to Legal Periodicals, 1908–date (available online).
Index to United States Government Periodicals, 1974–date.
Nutrition Abstracts and Reviews, 1931–date.
Pollution Abstracts, 1970–date (available online).
Psychological Abstracts, 1927–date (available online).
Public Affairs Information Index, 1915–date.
Social Sciences Index, 1974–date [previously part of *Social Sciences and Humanities Index,* 1965–74] (available online).
Women Studies Abstracts, 1972–date.

If you need to know if a particular journal is listed in an index or abstract, consult the comprehensive references given in Appendix B or one of these index sources:

Harzfeld, Lois. *Periodical Indexes in the Social Sciences and Humanities: A Subject Guide.* New York: Scarecrow, 1978.
Owen, Dolores B. *Abstracts and Indexes in the Sciences and Technology: A Descriptive Guide.* 2nd ed. New York: Scarecrow, 1984.

Newspaper Indexes

Newspapers report current facts and opinions. While they do not provide the studied or scholarly insights journal or magazine articles offer, newspapers contain valuable current information about such subjects as economics, social trends, politics, sporting events, crime, and fashion. Not all newspapers are indexed, but you can use those that are to find the date of an event. Once you have the date, you can locate information about the event in any nonindexed newspaper.

   New York Times Index.   You will find the *New York Times Index* (1851–date) available in book form, microfilm, or online at most libraries. As an index to the *New York Times,* it lists news stories by subject and provides summaries of them. Similar to the *Reader's Guide* in its entry format, the *Index* cross-references items with *see* and *see also;* indicates whether an article is short (*S*), medium (*M*), or long (*L*); and lists the date, section, and column number for each item.

   Figure 4.18 shows an abstract of a *New York Times* article about a new school program aimed at raising children's intelligence through increasing their self-esteem. Such abstracts are helpful when you are investigating a

DOCUMENT TYPE:	News;	Newspaper	
LANGUAGE: English		RECORD TYPE:	ABSTRACT
AVAILABILITY: UMIACH		CATALOG NO.:	600001.01
length: long	(18+ col inches)		

ABSTRACT: Efficacy, the favorite program of New York City Schools Chancellor Rudy Crew for fostering self-esteem in children and revitalizing the schools, is discussed. Efficacy training, which theorizes that intelligence is learned and is not innate, represents an attempt to motivate and instill a sense of esteem in children by setting high goals and providing examples of individual achievement. However, some critics claim that efficacy is just another grand prescription doomed to fail.

DESCRIPTORS: Curricula; Education reform; Public schools; Self image

NAMED PERSONS: Crew, Rudolph F

GEOGRAPHIC NAMES: New York City New York

FIGURE 4.18   An abstract of a newspaper article accessed online from the *New York Times Index* (via Newspaper Abstracts Daily via DIALOG)

Source: Copyright © by The New York Times Company. Reprinted by permission.

possible research topic or trying to determine whether it would be useful to locate the entire article. Remember that even if you are unable to find the original article, abstracts such as this can also become documented sources in your paper. (See pp. 272–273 for listing an online abstract in the Works Cited section of a paper).

Other Newspaper Indexes   Like the *New York Times,* other major newspapers—such as the *Chicago Tribune, Christian Science Monitor, Los Angeles Times, Wall Street Journal,* and *Washington Post*—are also individually indexed. You can find and compare articles in several of these and other newspapers at the same time by consulting the following comprehensive general indexes:

Index to Black Newspapers, 1977–date (on microfilm).

National Newspaper Index, 1979–date (carries last 4 years of the *New York Times* and, depending on the library's selection, the *Atlanta Constitution, Boston Globe, Chicago Tribune, Christian Science Monitor, Los Angeles Times, Wall Street Journal,* and *Washington Post;* available online through DIALOG [File 111] and Knowledge Index).

Newsbank, 1980–date (indexes articles from over 450 U.S. newspapers; available in print, CD–ROM, and online).

Newspaper Abstracts OnDisc (CD–ROM), 1985–date, monthly (libraries that subscribe get the *New York Times* and select among the *Atlanta Constitution, Boston Globe, Chicago Tribune, Christian Science Monitor, Los Angeles Times, Wall Street Journal,* and *Washington Post;* available online as *Newspaper and Periodical Abstracts*).

Newspaper and Periodical Abstracts, 1985–date, monthly (available online through DIALOG or an OCLC FirstSearch; same as *Newspaper and Periodical Abstracts* on CD–ROM, above).

NEXIS, 1977–date (indexes over 50 national newspapers, including the full text of the *New York Times;* available online).

Newspapers Online

Many newspapers are now online independently, making current and past issues available on the Internet or through commercial providers such as America Online, CompuServe, and Prodigy. The following is a brief list of some of the individual newspaper indexes now available online:

Boston Globe Online, last 7 days–date (archives available online through the World Wide Web: http://www.boston.com/globe/glohome.htm).

Chicago Tribune, 1985–date (current daily issue and archive searching available online through America Online).

New York Times Index, 1851–date (available in print, microfilm, and CD–ROM as well as online through *NEXIS* [see p. 79].

Philadelphia Enquirer, current daily only (available through the World Wide Web: http://www.phillynews.com.inq/front-page/).

San Francisco Chronicle, current daily only (daily online issues of the *San Francisco Chronicle* and *San Francisco Examiner* are available from The Gate, the newspaper's World Wide Web page: http://www.sfgate.com; archive searching is expected in the future).

San Jose Mercury News, no date provided (current daily issue and archive searching available online through America Online).

TimesLink, 1990–date (provides archive searching for the 1990–91 issues of the *Los Angeles Times;* available at libraries and through Prodigy).

USA Today, current daily only (available on the World Wide Web: http://www.usatoday.com/).

Wall Street Journal Interactive Edition, current daily only (available online through the World Wide Web: http://update2.wsj.com/welcome.html; also indexed in various other resources listed earlier).

Other newspapers also may be indexed locally. Use the *Gale Directory of Publications and Broadcast Media 1996 & Update* (Detroit: Gale, 1995) to locate, by state and then by city, publishers of small and large newspapers nationwide, or check with your library for newspapers you need information about. Almost any newspaper is available by writing to the local library or arranging for a microfilm copy through interlibrary loan.

Periodical Files or Serials Lists

Magazines, journals, and newspapers available in your library are listed in a periodicals file or serials list. The list may be in book form, on microfiche, or online at a computer terminal, with each periodical title listed alphabetically. Under the title of the periodical, such lists typically provide publication information, a description of the periodical, its location in the library, and the issues included in the library's collection. Entries without call numbers are shelved alphabetically in the library's periodical section. Figure 4.19 shows an entry from a library serials lists.

Indexes to Literature in Collections

Most indexes direct you to complete works addressing one major subject almost exclusively. Quite often, however, you need only a certain *part* of a work—say, a brief discussion of a minor subject, a single essay or

```
           Title:  American Health
     Other Title:  A.H.
   Dates Covered:  Vol.1, no.1 (Mar./Apr. 1982) -
       Published:  [New York, N.Y. : American Health
                   Partners, c1982-]
     Description:  v. : ill.; 28 cm.
      Subject(s):  Health—periodicals
                   Health—periodicals
           Notes:  Title from cover.
         Library:  BIOMED LIB Call number: W1 AM227
     Library has:  U3N1-3, 5-9 (1984) b4-7 (1985-88)
                   U8N1 (1989)
                   Library has current subscription
```

FIGURE 4.19   A periodical entry from a library serials file

chapter, or other selection. Fortunately, you do not have to hunt through the indexes of several different books to see if the material you want is included. Instead, you can consult subject indexes that locate material within complete works:

> *Biography Index.* New York: Wilson, 1946–date.
> *Essay and General Literature Index.* New York: Wilson, 1900–date.

The *Biography Index* lists information on people who have been written about in books or in the more than 2,000 popular and scholarly periodicals it cites. The *Biography Index* includes an alphabetized index, giving the date of birth, nationality, and occupation of each person listed in the volume. A second index cites individuals according to occupation. The *Biography Index* is available both in printed form and online as a database. Note that the printed version (see Figure 4.20) provides multiple examples of sources on a topic; however, the online database version (see Figure 4.21) gives only one entry at a time—a factor to consider if you must pay for searching for entries online.

The *Essay and General Literature Index* locates essays and parts of books for which there are no descriptive titles. Suppose, like student Mark Stevenson, you wanted to find some material about the influence that television talk shows have on children. By checking the *Essay and General Literature Index*, Mark was able to locate an essay titled "Television: Aesthetics and Audiences" in a work edited by P. Mellencamp, titled *Logics of Television* (see Figure 4.22).

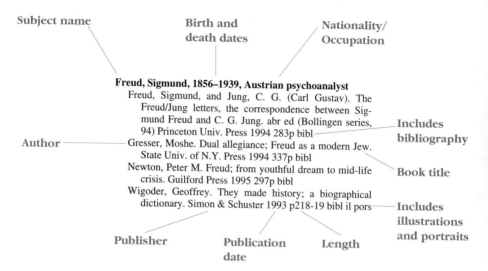

Subject name

Birth and
death dates

Nationality/
Occupation

Freud, Sigmund, 1856–1939, Austrian psychoanalyst
Freud, Sigmund, and Jung, C. G. (Carl Gustav). The
Freud/Jung letters, the correspondence between Sigmund Freud and C. G. Jung. abr ed (Bollingen series,
94) Princeton Univ. Press 1994 283p bibl

Author —————— Gresser, Moshe. Dual allegiance; Freud as a modern Jew.
State Univ. of N.Y. Press 1994 337p bibl
Newton, Peter M. Freud; from youthful dream to mid-life
crisis. Guilford Press 1995 297p bibl
Wigoder, Geoffrey. They made history; a biographical
dictionary. Simon & Schuster 1993 p218-19 bibl il pors

Includes
bibliography

Book title

Includes
illustrations
and portraits

Publisher

Publication
date

Length

FIGURE 4.20   An entry on "Sigmund Freud" from the *Biography Index*

Source: From the *Biography Index,* September 1986–August 1988, p. 765. Copyright © 1986, 1987, 1988 by The H. W. Wilson Company. Reprinted by permission.

Author

Subject
name

Book title

Number
of pages

Library call
numbers

Newton, Peter M
Freud, Sigmund: 1856–1939
Freud
from youthful dream to mid-life crisis
Personal Name Main Entry
Guilford Press:us
1995
United States
297 p.
bibliography
0-89862-293-X:$21.95: (acid-free paper)
Nonfiction
Biography
Government pub code: n
Dewey Decimal No. / Edition: 150\.19\092B:20:0
LC Class No: 94-27901
Freud, Sigmund: 1856–1931: Austrian psychoanalyst:
      Psychoanalyst
Full Encoding
AACR2
Monograph
950411

Subject birth
and death
dates

Publication
information

Category

Subject
occupation

FIGURE 4.21   An entry from the *Biography Index* Database

Source: From the *Biography Index* database, 1995. Copyright © 1995 by The H. W. Wilson Company. Reprinted by permission.

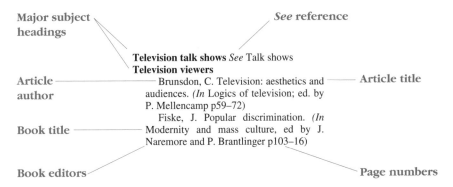

FIGURE 4.22 An excerpt from the *Essay and General Literature Index*

Source: From the *Essay and General Literature Index, 1990–1994*, p. 1633. Copyright © 1990, 1991, 1992, 1993, 1994 by The H. W. Wilson Company. Reprinted by permission.

Pamphlet Indexes

Libraries often maintain collections of pamphlets and other uncataloged printed material in *vertical files* (so named because items in them used to be filed standing upright rather than in file drawers). Pamphlets, flyers, newsletters, and other printed information distributed by local government agencies, clubs, businesses, and individuals are usually filed alphabetically by subject. Used appropriately, pamphlets can add fresh perspective to your research:

1. They can provide current information.
2. They usually discuss local issues or specific minor topics not addressed by other sources.
3. The presentation of technical material is generally written for the nonspecialist.
4. They often reflect opinions not available in other sources.

Remember that pamphlets and similar materials are sometimes written for other purposes than solely reporting information in an objective fashion. Weigh the content, authority, and objectivity of any pamphlet before relying on it too heavily in your research.

Besides investigating the vertical file of your own library, also consult the *Vertical File Index: A Subject Guide to Selected Pamphlet Material* (1935–date). Use this source to identify and order various pamphlets, brochures, and posters directly from their publishers. Figure 4.23 shows an entry from the *Vertical File Index* for a pamphlet on AIDS.

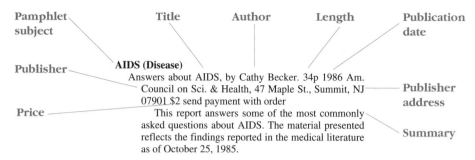

FIGURE 4.23   An entry from the *Vertical File Index*

Source: From the *Vertical File Index,* March 1986. Copyright © 1986 by The H. W. Wilson Company. Reprinted by permission.

In addition, the United States government also publishes thousands of pamphlets and other small information items every year. Check your library's holdings, or consult the *Monthly Catalog of United States Government Publications* (discussed later in this chapter).

Finally, the most direct means of acquiring pamphlets and other such material is to go directly to places related to your research topic (see Chapter 5). Along with getting a firsthand perspective on your research, you may also discover pamphlet material unavailable in any other way.

Indexes to U.S. Government Publications and Documents

The documents that the United States government prints include reports, bibliographies, dictionaries, guidebooks, maps, posters, pamphlets, directories, magazines, and other resources. All government publications are sent to designated depository libraries; there are two per congressional district and several others named in each state according to a range of criteria.

Many state, county, and college libraries serve as depositories for federal publications. Most of these, however, *select* the publications they receive because of the quantity available. Consequently, you may find that your own library either has no government documents available or has only a limited selection. If you know what document you want, ask your library to get it for you (usually in microform) through interlibrary loan. You can also write to this address to order a free copy of any government publication:

Superintendent of Documents
Government Printing Office
Washington, DC 20402

Locating Government Documents in Printed Forms. The printed forms of United States government documents are not always easy to locate. In most libraries, they are not cataloged with other related material nor are they always shelved in the same areas. Indeed, you will find that the call numbers given for government publications are not those of either the Dewey Decimal or Library of Congress systems. Instead, each documents is assigned what is known as a *Superintendent of Documents (SuDoc)* number and shelved according to the issuing agency, rather than the subject. The first letter in the SuDoc number indicates the government issuing agency (*J = Justice Department, L = Labor Department,* and so forth). The number following the letter is assigned by the Library of Congress for cataloging purposes. Thus, a publication with a SuDoc number such as *S 1.65/3:2734* is produced by the State Department and would be located with the other materials published by that agency.

The nature of this system prevents your browsing to find government material by subject and remains complicated, even for researchers with experience. Until you become familiar with government indexes and documents, you would be wise to work with a librarian to locate what you need.

Commercial as well as government-published guides to federal documents abound. The most comprehensive and generally up to date is:

> *Monthly Catalog of United States Government Publications.* Washington, DC: GPO, 1895–date (annual; also available online from DIALOG).

The *MC,* as the *Monthly Catalog* is known, lists the subject, author, title, and complete publishing data, including price, for all publications from United States government agencies. Published monthly, the *MC* supplies information from approximately 2,000 new government publications in each issue.

You can locate a publication by first consulting the Subject Index of the *MC* (see Figure 4.24). Then use the entry number given there to find the complete listing in another part of the *Catalog* (see Figure 4.25).

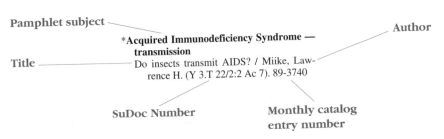

FIGURE 4.24   An entry from the Subject Index of the *Monthly Catalog*

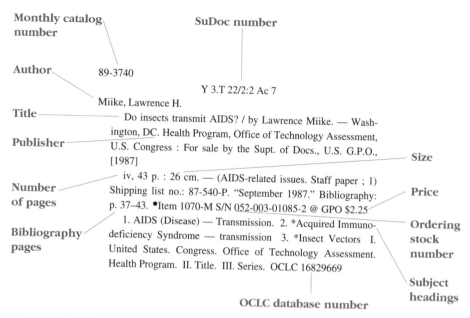

Monthly catalog number

SuDoc number

Author

Title

Publisher

Number of pages

Bibliography pages

89-3740

Y 3.T 22/2:2 Ac 7

Miike, Lawrence H.
Do insects transmit AIDS? / by Lawrence Miike. — Washington, DC. Health Program, Office of Technology Assessment, U.S. Congress : For sale by the Supt. of Docs., U.S. G.P.O., [1987]
 iv, 43 p. : 26 cm. — (AIDS-related issues. Staff paper ; 1)
Shipping list no.: 87-540-P. "September 1987." Bibliography: p. 37–43. •Item 1070-M S/N 052-003-01085-2 @ GPO $2.25
 1. AIDS (Disease) — Transmission. 2. *Acquired Immunodeficiency Syndrome — transmission 3. *Insect Vectors I. United States. Congress. Office of Technology Assessment. Health Program. II. Title. III. Series. OCLC 16829669

Size

Price

Ordering stock number

Subject headings

OCLC database number

FIGURE 4.25   A pamphlet entry from the *Monthly Catalog*

Keep in mind that the *MC* is a bibliography; it therefore lists complete works, not the articles they include. You can, however, refer to the subject headings (Figure 4.25) given in the *MC* entry to decide whether the publication contains information that would be useful to you.

For an index to government periodicals and serial publications that does include the articles, consult one of the following, published by Public Affairs Information Service (PAIS):

PAIS International, 1972–date (available on CD–ROM or online as "PAIS").

PAIS International in Print, 1991–date.

Public Affairs Information Service Bulletin, 1915–76.

Similar to the *Reader's Guide*, *PAIS* indexes about 1,500 periodicals, books, pamphlets, mimeographed materials, and state and city publications about government and legislation, economics, sociology, and political science.

If your research requires that you examine the reports of congressional committees, testimony of witnesses in congressional hearings, communications from the president to the Senate or House, or committee-prepared background on new legislation, consult the Congressional Information Service (CIS) annual *Index:*

Congressional Information Service. *Annual Index and Abstracts to Publications of the United States Congress.* Washington, DC: Congressional Information Service, 1970–date.

This useful source appears monthly, with quarterly cumulations and an annual cumulation titled *CIS/Annual.* The *Annual* itself comprises two volumes, *Subjects and Names* and *Abstracts.* Use the first volume to search out a listing for a subject or a person's name; then use the *Abstracts* volume to get full information, including a summary of any report or activities.

The guides to government documents listed here are only three of the hundred or more indexes and catalogs available. Every department of the government—from the Agriculture Department to the National Science Foundation to the Veterans Administration—publishes thousands of pages of information yearly. In addition to those sources discussed here, some 2,900 U.S. government publications in 83 subject areas are listed and annotated in:

Bailey, William G. *Guide to Popular U.S. Government Publications.* Littleton, CO: Libraries Unlimited, 1993.

Locating Government Sources Online

State and Local Government Online Resources. Most city, county, and state governments now provide public records and other important information online through a home page or another accessible form. In California, for example, you can use the California State Senate Gopher (gopher://gopher.sen.ca.gov) to access state government documents and connect with other related Gophers. If you were investigating a topic pertinent to New York City, you could check New York City Information (http://www.cs.columbia.edunyc/) to find statistical or historical information. Contacting the South Florida Environmental Reader (mail to: sfer-requesti@mthvax.cs.miami.edu) would be important for any research project relating to that area's local environment.

You should investigate any such online resources whenever you are researching issues related to local government or cities or nationwide topics that may have local impact. Contact a local bookstore for a directory of state or regional online services, or telephone relevant local agencies directly to ask about their online offerings. The Internet directories listed in the following section should also be helpful in finding online addresses for local information.

Federal Government Online Resources. To reduce paper consumption and to improve the accessibility of public information, more and more federal government information is being placed online each year.

Various types of information—ranging from government research data to congressional reports to the names and addresses of members of the House and Senate—are available today through the Internet. You can get information about the president's daily activities at the White House (http://sunsite.unc.edu/white-house/white-house.html) or access Prodigy or America Online to read presidential speeches or the latest White House press releases. You can also go online to read the national *1990 Census Report* (gopher://gopher.micro.umn.edu) or to review proposed bills or all congressional legislation since 1973 (telnet://locis.loc.gov).

Online government sources can be used free of charge when accessed directly over the Internet; others can be accessed through commercial providers, who charge fees for their services. The following are some of the most useful government resources to access online:

Bibliography of Senate Hearings (monthly bibliographies of Senate hearings and library publications: ftp://ftp.ncsu.edu).

Congressional Quarterly (CQ) (newsletter reporting congressional actions and including reports and other items relating to Congress: gopher://gopher.cqalert.com; *CQ* is included in NEXIS and abstracted weekly by DIALOG; fee based).

Congressional Record, 1985–date (official transcript of the activities of the U.S. House and Senate).

Executive Branch Resources (provides information about resources pertaining to the executive branch of the federal government and its various departments: http://lcweb.loc.gov/global/executive. html).

GENFED (General Federal Library) (comprehensive collection of federal legal materials, including case law, Supreme Court decisions, regulations, and publications; fee based: telnet://meaddata.com).

Historical Documents of the U.S. (collection of U.S. historical government documents, dating back to the Revolutionary War and extending to modern times: gopher://wiretap.spies.com11/Gov/US-History).

Internet *Federal Register* (provides the full text of the *Federal Register:* (gopher://gopher.internet.com).

Legislative Branch Resources (menu of resources pertaining to Congress and web pages of various congressional members).

MEGA (Combined Federal/Sate Case Law) (combined library that offers all federal and state case law provided on the LEXIS service; fee-based: telnet://nex.meaddata.com).

Supreme Court Decisions (full texts of Court decisions: ftp://marvel.loc.gov).

U.S. Federal Government Information (government data categorized according to each government source, such as the Justice Department: gopher://gopher.micro.umn.edu).

In addition to these online resources, a number of widely available guides and Internet directories are helpful, including the following:

Hahn, Harley, and Rick Stout. *The Internet Yellow Pages.* 2nd ed. Berkeley, CA: Osborne-McGraw, 1994.
Lent, Max. *Government Online.* New York: Harper Perennial, 1995.
Maxwell, Christine, and Jan Grycz Czeslaw, eds. *New Riders' Official Internet Yellow Pages.* Indianapolis, IN: New Riders, 1994.
Whitely, Sandy, ed. *The American Library Association Guide to Information Access.* New York: Random: 1994.

Reviewing Your Library Search

Before assuming that your search for available library sources is complete, take the time to review your working bibliography for balance and comprehensiveness. You will need sources reflecting a variety of viewpoints and depth of coverage. The number of books, magazines, journals, newspaper articles, or other sources you will need depends upon your topic and the research requirements of your instructor.

Thoroughly review your sources before proceeding too far with any of the activities described in the next chapter. That way, you can better decide how researching beyond campus and community libraries can next benefit your research most.

W O R K I N G   W I T H   O T H E R S

Establishing a working bibliography will be easier if you share insights and experiences with a classmate along the way. Use the following suggestions to review your understanding of library resources and the working bibliography discussed in this chapter.

- Share your knowledge of the campus library's general bibliographies, indexes, and abstracts with a classmate. Briefly explain the differences among each of these types of reference sources. Does each of you know where these resources are located and how to use them?

- Exchange working bibliographies with a classmate, preferably someone researching a topic related to your own. What differences do you see in the way you are both recording information? Has either of you overlooked a source that should be included in the bibliography?

- Explain citation indexes such as the *Social Sciences Citation Index* or another that you are familiar with. How might you use such indexes in your own research? If you do not understand how to use a citation index, team up with a classmate and ask a campus librarian to show you how to use these useful (but complex) resources.

- Locate the abstract for a published journal article, and compare it to the original. Does the abstract accurately summarize the article's major ideas? Would it make any difference if you read an abstract rather than an original article for your research?

- Located in major cities across the nation, Government Printing Office (GPO) bookstores provide hundreds of government publications, some for free and some for sale. Check the local telephone book to see if there is a GPO bookstore near you. If there is, you will find it rewarding to visit the bookstore with a friend to find current sources for research.

- Exchange working bibliographies from time to time with a classmate to review each other's list of sources. Are there an adequate number and variety of sources? Are the sources current enough? Are the sources varied enough in the points of view they represent?

CHAPTER **5**

Researching beyond the Campus Library

As you collect and study materials for the research topic, you will want to broaden your investigations by looking beyond campus and community libraries. Going out in the community to observe sites and activities related to your research topic, for example, is an exceptionally valuable way to understand it more thoroughly. Special library and museum collections can provide scarce primary and secondary sources especially relevant to local and regional subjects. You can also interview experts or people with uncommon opinions and experiences, use surveys and questionnaires to collect original data, listen to radio and television programs, or get first-hand opinions by attending lectures, addresses, and speeches on issues of community and world importance.

Getting more familiar with your research topic in any of these ways provides concrete experiences with which to illustrate and to verify your research. These approaches put you directly in touch with the people, places, events, and objects most closely relevant to your research and understanding of the topic.

Using Primary and Secondary Sources

Going beyond your campus and community libraries also provides opportunities to work with both primary and secondary materials in your research. The majority of books and magazine articles you consult in the library are *secondary* materials, information compiled and interpreted by someone else. Such research sources are valuable in providing information and expert insights that would be unattainable otherwise. For most undergraduate research, secondary materials provide the foundation as well as most of the materials for studying and writing about any subject.

Primary research, on the other hand, results in your discovering your own information and opinions. When you research onsite, interview an authority, conduct a survey, or attend a lecture, your own observations and the materials you examine firsthand are primary sources. You may also do primary research in a library by studying letters, diaries, manuscripts, or literary works or by examining unpublished reports and research collected by others.

For instance, in a marine science course, you might do primary research charting the migration of Atlantic salmon; in a physics lab, you could do primary research measuring air samples to determine local pollution levels. As you can tell from these examples, working with primary materials means getting information directly from original sources and interpreting it on your own. (See also Chapter 1 on primary and secondary sources.)

Compared to secondary sources, primary sources are often harder to come by and using them may require more independent judgment in assessing their credibility and value. In fact, *both* kinds of sources will need close critical reading and thinking on your part (see Chapter 7). As you examine such materials, be alert to discrepancies in content or disagreement with other sources and take care to distinguish between facts and opinions. Keep in mind that your goal in reading both primary and secondary sources is to synthesize their content and gather support for your own conclusions.

Observing Onsite

Reading as much as you can on a subject is essential to knowing it well and being able to make the most of related information. Researching onsite, however, to see and study something firsthand, engages your insight differently. By going to the places and events most directly connected with your topic, you will better understand that topic's importance in other people's lives. While books and articles can tell you about the plight of people who are homeless and living on the streets of America, you will understand their condition far better by visiting local state or federal agencies to talk directly with people trying to assist the homeless. If you are researching the problem the United States faces in disposing of its thousands of tons of trash every week, visit the local city or county dump. The experience may not be wholly pleasant, but you will understand the problem as never before.

Going onsite to explore your research topic more thoroughly will inspire other creative means to gather information for your research. Depending upon your purpose, you may need to make onsite observations to complete your research in several ways:

- *Record behavior:* For example, record social gestures of children at play; describe the actions of police officers making an arrest; test the responses of animals to human and nonhuman sounds.

■ *Describe conditions:* Characterize damage from a hurricane; investigate conditions at an animal research laboratory; report on the working environment of air traffic controllers.

■ *Examine primary material:* Compare organically and nonorganically grown fruits and vegetables; study a museum painting; examine a historical document; take notes at a lecture or interview.

While onsite observation may appear more interesting in some ways than library research, remember that it is not easy to do effectively. Accurate observation and reporting of data are difficult, even for a trained researcher. Thoughtful preparation before you get onsite can make the difference between conducting a research study and a tourist visit.

To ensure the effectiveness of your onsite studies, follow these steps for any observation research you do:

1. *Plan your onsite research as early as possible.* List it in your research schedule, along with any arrangements you will need to make for reservations, permissions, tickets, or transportation. For any onsite visit, ask ahead of time about limitations or required authorizations. If you plan to use a camera or tape recorder at the site, find out if such equipment is allowed. In addition, be sure to schedule enough time to complete the objectives of your research visit.

2. *Make a checklist of what you want to observe.* If you will be studying patients in a hospital ward, include the frequency, conditions, and extent of the behaviors to note. If you are making a study of playground equipment at city parks, make a checklist to record the types, conditions, and times of use and nonuse. If you are studying a historical document, list the features you want especially to note. Keep any checklist limited to what you can observe and record with accuracy. It is easy to get so caught up in observing as to forget the purpose of your visit. Once onsite, *use* the checklist to keep your activities focused on the research question you seek to answer. Also add to the checklist as needed.

3. *Take notes during and right after any onsite observation.* Use your research notebook to record factual descriptions of any artifacts or other objects you examine as part of your research study. In an appropriately labeled separate area of the notebook, write down any personal impressions and ideas for later use.

4. *Collect pamphlets, brochures, maps, and other explanatory materials about your topic or about any artifacts you observe at the site.* (Make certain that you never remove any artifacts themselves or other objects that are parts of an exhibit or observation site, however!) You need not bring home a whole library, but collecting available materials can prove valuable later. You might need to review the materials again or draw more exten-

sively upon them than you had originally planned. Make bibliography cards for all such materials if you think you might use them in your paper (see Chapter 4).

The onsite investigation you do now for a research paper will prepare you for the kind of advanced field or laboratory research you may do later for other college courses or a career. It requires training for such observational research to be carried out effectively and for its results to carry any authority. Check with your instructor about your plans before proceeding too far, and exercise careful judgment when you incorporate the results of your investigation in your paper. Done with care and used as a supplement to your other research, any one of the activities described here can enrich the content and individualized approach of your research paper.

Researching Society and Museum Libraries

You can spend an interesting afternoon exploring your city's museum and private society libraries. These facilities may help you discover research ideas and locate primary and secondary resources that might be unavailable at academic and public libraries.

Society Libraries

Local as well as national societies exist in every part of the United States, varying in size as well as purpose. Sometimes called *clubs, lodges, federations, associations,* or *leagues,* such societies are formed by people sharing interests in particular subjects. The libraries they sponsor for their own collecting and research purposes can often provide unusual or hard-to-find primary sources for your research.

Investigate the societal organizations in your local area. You will find groups interested in nearly every subject imaginable: the Civil War, gardening, people with disabilities, bird watching, genealogy, literary topics, the environment, and star gazing, to name just a few examples. Almost every region has at least one local historical society, a good place to start for any topic on a local issue.

The members of such groups range from beginning enthusiasts to informed amateurs and scholars. Any members can provide assistance with your topic or may be willing to serve as the subject for an interview.

A society library may be open only to experienced researchers or perhaps just members; nonmembers may pay a small fee for public use. To locate society libraries near you, consult the telephone book or one of the sources listed later in this chapter (see Finding Special Libraries and Museums).

Museum Libraries

Local museums are excellent sources of information and bibliographic materials on dozens of subjects, including art, history, literature, science, and popular culture. Not only can pamphlets and exhibit materials prove useful primary resources for your research, but the museum's own library may also be available for limited public use.

Check ahead of time with the museum staff about research privileges and the availability of materials for your topic. If you cannot use the materials in the museum library, take advantage of the museum exhibits. You can add available information about them to your list of bibliographic sources. It is also likely that someone on the museum library staff may be able to give you information or direct you to other libraries and resources.

Finding Special Libraries and Museums

The telephone book's Yellow Pages are the handiest reference to societies and museums in your area. In addition to the *American Library Directory* (mentioned in Chapter 2), a number of excellent guides to special libraries and museum collections found nationally are available. Entries from the *Directory of Special Libraries and Information Centers,* for example, indicate the size and type of collection a library has, if it is a government depository, and whether it offers computerized information services (see Figure 5.1). Use such sources as the *Directory of Special Libraries* to locate materials in your local area or to investigate the possibilities of acquiring them in microform or through interlibrary loan. Other guide sources to investigate include the following:

★ 15003 ★
Solano County Library - Special Collections (Rare Book)
1150 Kentucky St.
Fairfield, CA 94533   Phone: (707)421-6510
Founded: 1914.   **Special Collections:** Donovan J. McCune Collection (printing history, rare books; 1500 volumes); U.S. and state government documents depository (5000 volumes); local history (500 volumes). **Services:** Interlibrary loan; copying; collections open to the public; Donovan J. McCune Collection open to the public by appointment. **Automated Operations:**   Computerized cataloging, acquisitions, and circulation. **Computerized Information Services:**   DIALOG Information Services; OnTyme Electronic Message Network Service (electronic mail service). Performs searches free of charge. **Networks/Consortia:** Member of North Bay Cooperative Library System (NBCLS). **Remarks:** FAX: (707)421-7474.

FIGURE 5.1   Entry from the *Directory of Special Libraries and Information Centers*

Source: Taken from *Directory of Special Libraries and Information Centers,* 15th Edition (Vol. I, Part 2, O–Z, p. 1556). Edited by Janice DeMaggio and Debra M. Kirby. Copyright © 1992, Gale Research, Inc. Reproduced by permission. All rights reserved.

American Library Directory: 1994–95. New York: Bowker, 1994.

Ash, Lee, and William G. Miller, comps. *Subject Collections: A Guide to Special Book Collections and Subject Emphases as Reported by University, College, Public, and Special Libraries and Museums in the United States.* 2 vols. New York: Bowker, 1993.

Directory of Libraries. Washington, DC: World Bank, 1992.

Directory of Registered Environmental Organizations. Upland, PA: Diane, 1993.

Directory of Special Libraries. 2 vols. Detroit: Gale, 1994.

Hudson, Kenneth, and Ann Nicholls. *Directory of World Museums and Living Displays.* New York: Grove's Dictionary, 1986.

Piccirelli, Annette. *Research Center Directory.* 2 vols. Detroit: Gale, 1994.

Wheeler, Mary B. *Directory of Historical Organizations in the United States and Canada.* Nashville, TN: American Association for State and Local History, 1990.

Museums Online.   Thanks to the Internet, you can visit many museums from home. The Smithsonian Museum, in Washington, DC, for example, can be reached through Smithsonian Online, which is available on America Online and with partial access by ftp (ftp://photo1.si.edu). Smithsonian Online provides information about current displays and photographs as well as excerpts from museum exhibits. You can also visit the University of California's Museum of Paleontology and WWW Subway (http://ucmp1.berkeley.edu/subway.html) for a multimedia museum display, paleontology database information, and links to other museums and World Wide Web sites around the world. By traveling the Internet, you can also go to the Natural History Museum of London (http://www.nhm.ac.uk/) or other relevant museum sites around the world (http://www.comlab.ox.ac.uk/archive/other/museums.html), collecting valuable information for your research.

Finding Other Sources of Research

Not all useful collections of books, magazines, pamphlets, business reports, tax ledgers, production schedules, flowcharts, policy statements, consumer profiles, and case histories are stored in places called *libraries.* Your community and its surrounding area undoubtedly offer hundreds of places to investigate for research materials. Here are a few of the most common:

- Foreign consulates and embassies provide information covering the education, health care, politics, history, art, and economics of their respective countries.
- Large businesses and corporations maintain collections of data and reference materials pertinent to their operations.

- Hospitals and state and local health departments offer brochures on disease and health care and maintain small libraries for staff research.
- Radio and television stations maintain transcripts of news broadcasts, documentaries, and interviews as well as biography files and reference sources.
- Newspaper offices keep files of past issues that may not be available at libraries.
- Chambers of Commerce provide visitors and interested investors with financial reports, tax schedules, transportation studies, and related business information.

In addition, police departments, social service agencies, water and power departments, zoos, museums, churches, and forestry services all keep records and will provide printed information on a variety of subjects to anyone interested. Your family dentist probably has a small library for his or her own practice, and many of your friends or relatives no doubt have collections of resources about hobbies or special topics. Someone in your family undoubtedly has a scrapbook, a genealogy record, letters, mementos, a diary, or old news clippings that have been stored in a closet or garage for years.

In short, everyone collects information, and libraries are anywhere people store it. Think about and look into all the possible local resources for information as you begin to do your research. Remember to make out a preliminary citation card for any material you investigate in public agencies or business and private collections. Follow the appropriate form for each type, and give the necessary information (see Chapter 4).

Interviews

An *interview* can provide you with current information and personal insights that may not result from consulting other sources. In addition, information from an interview can add a dimension of human interest to a paper that might otherwise be mainly statistical or simply monotonous for other reasons. Taped interviews and those conducted on television or radio allow you to hear from experts and well-known personalities who might otherwise be unavailable to you. The most profitable interviews, however, can be the ones you conduct yourself, directing the questions to focus specifically on the primary information you need for your research paper.

Determining the Purpose

Because of the time required to prepare for and conduct an interview, assess its usefulness and purpose beforehand. Do not include an interview in your research only to add a primary source to your paper's bibliography or just to avoid learning about your topic through more ordinary materials.

Instead, use an interview when your critical assessment of the paper's sources indicate a need to strengthen certain areas of your thesis argument or to balance the paper's discussion with other points of view.

An interview will be useful to your research any time it fulfills one or more of the following purposes:

- Provides more current information than other sources
- Samples opinions or viewpoints not usually presented elsewhere
- Answers questions other sources have not sufficiently addressed
- Gives you examples to illustrate and support other research
- Records the responses of a recognized authority to questions specifically focused on your research topic or research question

Selecting the Right Person

The value of interview research depends significantly upon the choice of the *interviewee,* the person to be interviewed. Remember that not everyone interested in or connected with a research topic qualifies as a good subject to interview. Your neighborhood mechanic may be an expert on the difficulties of repairing or getting parts for certain models of cars, but the local Nissan dealer will know more about consumer trends in auto buying. Your chemistry professor may have some opinions about how his Ford Bronco behaves on mountain roads, but the ideas of a professional test driver will carry a lot more weight in a paper discussing automobile safety standards.

People with knowledge about your research subject are probably easier to locate than you might think. You may already know family members or friends who would be valuable subjects. Certainly, the professors on your own college campus are knowledgeable about or directly involved with many types of research topics. City, county, and government employees—from police officers to engineers to social workers—are also informed and usually willing sources to consult. Local societies, associations, hospitals, museums, private businesses, and political organizations are just a few of the many other places you will find people to discuss your research with you. Use your local telephone directory or the Chamber of Commerce to contact businesses in your community. You can also use the *Directory of Special Libraries* (described earlier) to locate individuals with special knowledge or experience in almost any subject.

Scheduling the Appointment

It is usually appropriate to schedule an interview a week or two ahead to allow you and the interviewee time to prepare. Contact the person by telephone or letter, identifying yourself and the purpose of the interview. Establish a few ground rules that you both agree upon concerning permissible subjects, tape recording, approval to quote, and so forth. Be sure to indicate the approximate amount of time you will need (1 to 1-1/2 hours is generally long enough). Make your introduction concise and polite, something like this:

> My name is Jeanette Carson, and I'm a student at Bluffs College. I am doing a research paper on air traffic control problems in our area, and I wondered if I could have an hour of your time for an interview. I'd like to find out about conditions at the local airport and what plans there may be for changes there in the future.

Ask the interviewee what day, time, and place would be convenient, and adjust your own activity schedule accordingly.

Preparing for the Interview

Avoid using valuable interview time to ask needless or unfocused questions. Do a sufficient amount of preliminary reading and thinking about the research topic beforehand. Then plan and write out a list of questions focusing on information needed for your research. Use these questions to direct the interview, but do not follow them so strictly that you inhibit the discussion. In order to evoke the interviewee's ideas on the topic, avoid questions that promote only "yes" or "no" responses. Twelve to fifteen questions should allow enough time for you and the interviewee to get acquainted, discuss your topic, and pursue any helpful digressions in detail.

Conducting the Interview

Be on time to the interview, and come equipped with pencils or pens and a notebook (and a tape recorder if the interviewee has agreed to its use). Avoid taking notes or taping the first few questions and answers until your subject gets used to the situation.

Start the interview with a general inquiry about the person's background and interest in the interview topic. Then move on to the questions you have prepared. Maintain a polite, attentive manner while you listen and ask questions. Allow time for the interviewee to complete his or her responses. When clarification or additional information would be helpful, ask follow-up questions, such as "Why do you feel the data are unreliable?" or "I don't know what a tokamak reactor is. Can you explain it to me, please?"

Interview Structures

Some researchers favor a *structured* interview, which restricts responses to interview questions and keeps the discussion closely focused. However, an *unstructured* approach, which allows the discussion to move with the interests of the interviewee, can often generate more useful material. Avoid getting bogged down in clearly irrelevant subjects, but do not worry too much if your interviewee brings up unexpected topics: Brief digressions about an exceptional incident or a personal triumph may yield rich new insights or information for your paper. If the discussion wanders too far afield, return to your prepared questions to bring things back into focus.

Quoting from the Interview

If you do not tape the interview, take careful notes throughout the session. Make a point of quoting authoritative, insightful, or fascinating comments word for word. Because they come from a live interview source, such remarks will add rich authority and interest to your final paper. At the completion of the interview, read aloud any direct quotations you have written down to check their accuracy with the interviewee.

Interview Length

Try to keep to the hour or so you had originally scheduled so the interviewee does not run out of time. That way, you will not have to schedule a second meeting in order to get all of your questions answered.

Before the interview ends, briefly read over or summarize all of your notes for the interviewee to hear and to suggest additions or changes, if necessary. Be sure to thank the person for the interview. Take the time later to send a follow-up note, again expressing your appreciation and indicating how helpful the interview was to your research paper.

Figure 5.2 contains an excerpt from Nancy Prado's interview with Professor Robert Jamieson, a practicing attorney who also teaches at the law school at her campus. To guide the interview, Nancy used questions she had prepared and typed ahead of time. Notice that she recorded her own summaries and Professor Jamieson's words while conducting the interview.

Using Telephone or Mail Interviews

A number of factors—including your and the interviewee's schedules and proximity to one another—may make a telephone or mail interview more practical than meeting personally. Because of the cost of telephoning and the limited discussion allowed by mail, however, both types of interviews require more planning than a personal conference might.

Telephone Interviews.   A telephone interview is convenient, but it can also can be expensive. Another drawback is that it forfeits your opportunity to meet directly with the authority you have chosen to interview. Use your best telephone personality to encourage your source to enjoy the discussion enough to talk freely and to volunteer information. To avoid

---

4. As an attorney yourself, do you think you should serve or be allowed to serve on juries?

Yes—sees it as a civic responsibility. Lawyer's presence may not make a big difference. "People will still see the evidence the way they want to." Attorneys could "bring a little extra insight" to their own part of the decision.

5. A lot of people hold a pretty low opinion of juries and the jury process right now. How do you feel about juries?

Trusts juries. They represent the community, or they are supposed to. Admits that juries can be manipulated, but most jury decisions are "the right ones."

FIGURE 5.2   Prepared questions and handwritten notes from a personal interview

catching the interview subject at an inconvenient time, use the first telephone call to set up a time for the actual interview. Then follow these suggestions while conducting the telephone interview:

1. After introducing yourself again and reminding your source why you called, state how much time you think the interview will take and whether the call is local or long distance. This will prompt each of you to keep the discussion focused and to use the time productively.

2. Let your telephone interviewee know that you will be recording or taking notes during your discussion.

3. If you have not already done so, tell a little about yourself and your interest in the topic.

4. Briefly summarize your research and findings up to now.

5. Ask the interviewee to describe his or her background in or experience with the topic.

6. At this point, you will probably find that your interview questions enter naturally into the conversation. If not, this is a good time to begin asking them.

7. Keep track of your time on the telephone to avoid running up a huge bill or taking up too much of the person's time.

8. Thank the interviewee for talking with you, and ask if you may call again if you have questions about anything that was said.

People who take the time for interviews like to know the results. Once you have completed your paper, write or call to thank your interviewee again. If you can, explain how the information from the interview helped your research or was used in the paper itself.

Mail Interviews.   Interviews done by mail allow the interviewee to answer your questions more carefully and on his or her own time. In addition, written responses provide accurate notes for your paper and usually give you more details to work with. You can also use mail interviews to correspond with several persons at once, thus getting multiple replies to the same questions.

Of course, a drawback to mail interviews is that, like those done over the telephone, you lose the opportunity of meeting and talking directly with your sources. In addition, people responding to mail interviews may not always do so quickly enough to meet researchers' deadlines. Rather than count on one particular source for an interview, contact more than a single person for mail interviews or be prepared to go forward with your research should a response not arrive soon enough.

If you decide to use a mail interview in your research, follow these suggestions:

1. Write or call ahead to find out if the person is willing to respond to your inquiry.

2. If your source agrees to respond, prepare a list of questions to be answered in writing.

3. Keep the questions specific and their number to a minimum. Asking "What can you tell me about the recent decline in Alaska's grizzly bear population?" is too broad: Your respondent will not know where to begin or end. Something like "How important has the recent increase in logging been to the decline of Alaska's grizzly bear population?" gives the question focus and shows you have done your research.

4. Avoid asking too many questions. You do not want to hand the interviewee a burdensome writing task, which may be refused or done poorly because of its size. Ten to twelve questions focused on the topic or research question itself will probably be enough.

5. In a cover letter sent with the questions, explain the purpose and scope of your research project, how extensive the answers should be, and when you need to have the responses returned. Include a stamped envelope with your address on it.

6. Once you have received the responses, promptly acknowledge their receipt with a thank-you letter to the interviewee. A brief follow-up note after the paper is finished can describe your use of the interview and, again, your appreciation of the correspondent's help.

One overall suggestion should be emphasized separately: The interview source will respond more willingly if he or she sees that you are serious enough about your research to write with care. Make necessary revisions to a draft before writing and sending out a final version of any correspondence. Check a dictionary for help with spelling. Consult your college writing handbook for questions about grammar, style, and letter formats.

Online Interviews.   Interviewing someone online offers the immediacy of a telephone interview but at a lesser cost, usually. Moreover, with an online interview, you have the added convenience of being able to print or download the interview for later review.

You can contact many kinds of experts through Internet newsgroups or special discussion groups, listed in resources such as *New Riders' Official Internet Yellow Pages* or other Internet guides (see Chapter 6). Online services such as CompuServe and America Online often provide opportunities for discussions and interviews with experts or celebrities in a number of fields. Recently, for example, Vice President Al Gore was interviewed online by CompuServe customers and Michael Jackson answered questions from his fans on America Online.

If you know the name of someone you would like to interview, you can find out if he or she has an Internet e-mail address through the IBM Whois server. To do so, send mail to the IBM Whois server (nic@vnet. ibm.com), and in the body of the text, include a message beginning with the word *whois* followed by the last name of the person you are attempting to contact, a comma, and then his or her first name. If you want to know whether President Clinton has an Internet e-mail address, for example, include the following message in the body of your e-mail: *whois clinton, bill.*

You can also locate people on the Internet by using *Finger,* a search tool that can provide names, home addresses, telephone numbers, and other personal information about individuals whose e-mail names and addresses you know. Many college and university systems have Finger capabilities. If you are not familiar with this tool, follow onscreen directions for using Finger.

Documenting the Interview

For any type of interview, make a preliminary citation card ahead of time. If you make use of the interview in your paper, include it in the Works Cited list, following one of the appropriate forms outlined in Chapters 10 and 11. Shown in Figure 5.3 is a sample bibliography card for a personal interview. Other than the identification of the type of interview conducted, information for a telephone or mail interview would be similar.

Robert Curry.
Personal interview. Nov. 24, 1995

FIGURE 5.3   A bibliography card for a personal interview

Surveys

If your research topic calls for characterizing the opinions, behaviors, or conditions of people in your local area, you may want to conduct a survey. A *survey* could provide statistical data for statements like "When asked if they would flirt with a friend's date, nearly two-thirds of the 350 students surveyed answered 'yes.'" You could also use a survey to learn the percentage of people in your city who are satisfied with their personal physicians or to find out how many hours a week students on your campus study. Surveys are also useful when you need to identify trends or make comparisons among groups or individuals (see Figure 5.4).

As with an interview, think ahead of time about the purpose of conducting a survey: What value will the evidence you collect bring to your paper, and how might these results relate to the information provided by other sources? Most importantly, consider how you will use the survey to support your paper's thesis.

Using Published Surveys

When should you use the results of published surveys versus those of surveys you have conducted yourself? Surveys of your own are best done to compare the characteristics of a local population with surveys done on a larger basis by others. For example, you may want to compare local attitudes about hunting with those identified by a national poll. Or you may want to compare the opinions of a certain group with the facts the rest of your research uncovers.

Whenever possible, however, it is generally best to use published surveys. So before you set up your own survey, check the statistical resources in your library. It is very likely that others have already compiled the kind

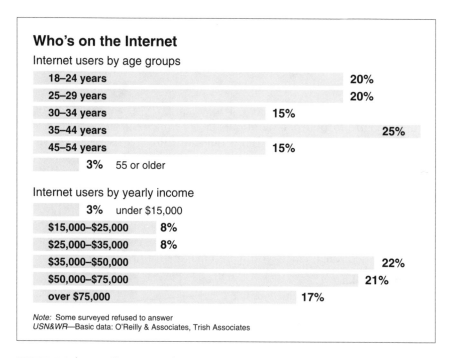

FIGURE 5.4 An illustration of survey results showing Internet users by age and yearly income groups

Source: From "Who's On the Internet?" (p. 24), *U.S News & World Report.* Copyright, Oct. 9, 1995, U.S. News & World Report.

of information you want or can use. The following sources are only a few that provide statistical data, rankings, comparisons, and public opinion polls for nearly every subject and locality:

American Statistics Index. Washington, DC: Congressional Information Service, 1973–date.

The Complete Book of American Surveys. New York: New American Library, 1980.

The Gallup Report. Princeton, NJ: Gallup Poll, 1965–date.

Statistical Reference Index. Washington, DC: Congressional Information Service, 1980–date.

Conducting Your Own Survey

Once you decide to conduct a survey of your own, remember that no survey is ever entirely accurate. A survey with even a fair degree of accuracy requires training to design and conduct. In addition, correctly interpreting a survey's results is usually a job for experts.

For the most part, expect to treat the results of any survey as *supplemental* to your other research. In most cases, it will be more descriptive than conclusive about, let's say, attitudes as to whether the United States should spend more money on fighting drugs through education.

Devising a Questionnaire.   To get started, you will need to devise a questionnaire to poll people about the information you want to know. You will get the best results from a questionnaire that is relatively short, easy to answer, and focused upon a single problem or related issues. The following suggestions will help you design a questionnaire that will be simple to administer and analyze for results:

1. *Define the questionnaire's purpose.* Begin by making a list of the specific information you want to gather. If you were researching the impact of the home video rental craze, you would make a list like this:

I want to know:
- Why people rent video movies
- How often people watch home videos
- What kinds of videos they watch
- How they feel about commercials in rental videos
- How they feel about X-rated videos
- How much they pay for video rentals

Having defined what you want to know, you are ready to write your questions.

2. *Decide upon a question-and-answer format.* Frame your questions and their answers to suit the information you seek. Several types of questions and responses are possible.

    a. Open-ended questions allow respondents to answer in whatever way they choose. The variety of responses such questions allow, however, can make answers difficult to interpret and summarize. At the same time, responses to open-ended questions can also provide more details than answers to other types of questions, and they often reveal unexpected, useful information.

    Examples of open-ended questions:

- Why do you think watching movies as videos at home has become such a popular form of entertainment in the United States?
- What do you think the government should do to prevent oil spill disasters from tanker ships in U.S. coastal waters?

Because open-ended questions require more time to answer orally or in writing, you will get better results using no more than five or six per survey.

b. Controlled-response or multiple-choice questions allow respondents to choose from a limited number of answers.
Example of a controlled-response question:

- The government should tighten controls on tanker ships transporting oil within 10 miles of any U.S. coastline.
  _____ Agree   _____ Disagree   _____ Undecided

Be careful that each controlled-response question includes an adequate representation of answers. Had the question above allowed only "Agree" and "Disagree" responses, people who were undecided would not be able to answer truthfully or might not answer at all. Yes-or-no questions—like "Do you rent video movies more than three times a month?"—may suit one purpose or reveal some of the information you seek. Giving more choices, however, always provides data for you to make more comparisons among respondents. For example:

- How many times a month do you rent movie videos?
  _____ 1–3 times   _____ 4–7   _____ 8–12
  _____ More than 12   _____ Never

Unlike open-ended questions, controlled-response questions are convenient for respondents to answer quickly, and their results are easy to describe quantitatively.

3. *Word your questions carefully.* The way you ask a question will significantly influence the response it prompts. To prevent biasing answers, keep your language objective. Asking "Do you favor passing stronger laws to protect our valued coastal environments from careless destruction by oil tankers?" unfairly loads the question. Anyone answering "no" may be made to feel he or she does not value the environment and approves of careless destruction. Rephrase the question to be more objective: "Do you favor stronger regulation of oil tanker ships operating in or near the U.S. coast?"

Also avoid asking questions that seem to implicate the respondent. People feel uneasy about admitting their shortcomings or being made to appear in a negative light just because of the way a question is worded. Asking "Do you ever cheat on examinations?" puts respondents immediately on the defensive. Making the question more hypothetical, asking "Would you ever cheat on an examination?" will probably fulfill your research needs and get more accurate responses.

Carefully review the wording of each question in your questionnaire. Consider whether each question is free of bias and offers the respondent a chance to answer accurately. Before administering the questionnaire for research purposes, try it out on yourself and a few friends. Also ask your instructor to look it over and make suggestions. Once you are satisfied that the questionnaire will meet your needs, you are ready to administer it to a representative survey population.

Sampling a Population.   In research, the word *population* refers to all the members of a group. A *sample* is a representative portion of the population (see Figure 5.5). When researchers study a group of any kind, they make generalizations about it based upon sampling the population. Sampling is important to research because examining every individual person or item in the group is usually impractical or impossible.

Good survey results are derived from an accurate sampling of the research population. You will get the best results from sampling by following these guidelines for a survey:

1. *Define the survey population.* Who gets surveyed and who does not will obviously affect the results of your questionnaire. Begin by carefully defining the population you intend to poll.

If you intend to study the characteristics of inner-city youth gang members, how will you define the population?

- What constitutes a *gang?*
- What kind of gangs will you study?
- Which participants in gang activities are actually members?
- What age range is meant by *youth?*

These and similar kinds of questions show the need for analyzing the population and describing it accurately throughout your research.

2. *Use random sampling.* The more diverse your sample, the more accurate the results. Narrowing your sampling to one kind of group lessens its representativeness. If you want to know how many people think watching television dulls creativity, do not ask only male college students or only those who refuse to watch television at all. A good sampling would include males and females of all ages and educational levels, of varied interests and occupations, and of a range of television-viewing habits.

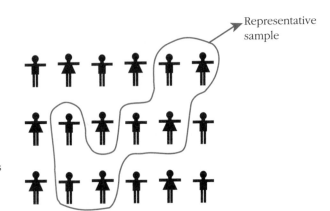

FIGURE 5.5   The population and representative survey sample

3. *Take an adequate sample.* Common sense may be your best guide to how large a sample you will need. Since it allows for more variety, a large sample is generally more accurate than a small one. The opinions of 15 people in a population of 1,000 has little practical value. On the other hand, a random sampling of 500 of those individuals represents a significant number for consideration. In general, large populations require proportionally larger samplings, and larger samplings carry more significance than smaller ones.

Polling the Population. Administer the questionnaire at varied times and places to the population you have identified. Choose a *polling* method that ensures getting a random sample and a good response rate. The results of a recent national telephone survey of married couples were widely challenged because people may have answered in ways to please their spouses (who may have been in the next room listening to the survey response). Another survey to find out what times people wanted college classes offered was criticized because it was done only during the day, while most people who might have preferred night classes were at work.

Almost every survey procedure has drawbacks, but you can safeguard results by consistently considering whether your method leaves out any particular group or overemphasizes the participation of another. If you survey customers at a video store to study their rental habits, include people of various ages and genders; who come in at all hours of the day on both weekdays and weekends; who are married and single; and so on.

Analyzing the Findings. Having administered the survey questionnaire, analyze your findings. Compare the results with other research data you have collected and try to account for any major differences. Review your questions and sampling procedures to check for bias. If you have used the survey to gather statistical data, include information about the various statistical tests (validity, margin of error, and so forth) you have used to verify your results. As you incorporate the survey results in your research paper, include a description of the survey population and the procedures used to administer the questionnaire. Include a copy of the questionnaire in your paper's appendix.

Documenting the Survey

Make a working bibliography card as soon as you decide to conduct a survey. Since in most cases you will not be citing the name of a particular respondent to your survey or questionnaire, list yourself as the author. Figure 5.6 shows the bibliography card for a survey such as you might administer as part of your own research. No separate card is made for the survey questionnaire, since it is part of the survey itself.

Randall, Steve.

Survey. Oct 11, 1995

FIGURE 5.6   A bibliography card for a self-administered survey

NOTE: The information given here on surveys can produce excellent results for the kind of research topics and assignments usually undertaken by college undergraduates. If your research depends heavily upon extensive survey information that you collect yourself, consult a more thorough resource, such as one of the following:

> Alreck, Pamela L., and Robert B. Settle. *Survey Research Handbook.* Burr Ridge, IL: Irwin, 1994.
>
> Fink, Arlene, and Jacqueline Kosecoff. *How to Conduct Surveys: A Step by Step Guide.* Newbury Park, CA: Sage, 1985.
>
> Foreman, E. K. *Survey Sampling Principles.* New York: Dekker, 1991.

Speeches and Lectures

Listening to Community Speakers

One good way to gain more familiarity with your research topic is to listen firsthand to what others have to say about it. Watch local newspapers and community announcements for upcoming events related to your research topic. It is likely that such occasions will feature presentations by recognized authorities or groups of informed spokespersons. If you know of a particular organization that may be sponsoring a conference or public meeting, get its number from the telephone directory and call about future scheduled meetings and speakers.

Use your imagination about where to hear public speakers on your research topic. Remember that public speeches and addresses include everything from your minister's sermon about marriage to a city council member's harangue on taxes.

Attending Campus Lectures

Take advantage of the opportunities presented on your own or neighboring campuses. Consult the campus newspaper and college organizations about visiting scholars, faculty addresses, and club debates. Consult a course syllabus or ask a particular professor when he or she will be lecturing on your research topic. Remember that you may need permission to sit in on lectures for courses you are not enrolled in.

Documenting Speeches and Lectures

Using your research question as a focus, make a checklist of important points to listen for, and take careful notes on any lecture or public address. You may be able to use a tape recorder, or the presentation may be available on video tape later from the sponsoring organization. Check ahead of time about both possibilities.

In addition, be sure to record necessary information for a bibliography card about the event. Include the speaker's name and position and the date, place, and occasion of the presentation (see Figure 5.7). Follow the form shown in Chapters 10 and 11 if you include the lecture or speech in the Works Cited list of your paper. If the information is not available when you hear a speaker, consult the sponsoring organization later for the documentation details you need.

NOTE: For historic speeches made by well-known individuals, consult the appropriate volume of the *Speech Index* in your library. Speeches made as recently as last week are available from the *Public Affairs Information Service (PAIS) Bulletin* or the online database PAIS (see Chapter 2). You

Rastall, Glen
"Is Clean Air Enough to Ask?"
Three Cities Conference
Denver, CO
6 Oct. 1996

FIGURE 5.7   A bibliography card for a speech

The following transcript of President Clinton's June 13 address to the nation was provided by the White House.

THE PRESIDENT: Good evening. Tonight I present to the American people a plan for a balanced federal budget. My plan cuts spending by $1.1 trillion. It does not raise taxes. It won't be easy, but elected leaders of both parties agree with me that we must do this, and we will.

We're at the cutting edge of a new century, living in a period of rapid and profound change. And we must do everything in our power to help our people build good and decent lives for themselves and their children. . . .

FIGURE 5.8   Excerpt from a speech by President Clinton (June 13, 1995), accessed from an online source

can also access the full texts of many famous speeches—such as President Kennedy's inaugural address or Martin Luther King, Jr.'s, "I Have a Dream" speech—online at Speeches and Addresses in the US (gopher://wiretap. spies.com/11/Gov/US-Speech). Recently made presidential speeches are available in CompuServe's Politics file or on America Online. Figure 5.8 shows an excerpt from one of President Clinton's recent addresses to the nation, which was accessed online through America Online.

Radio and Television

Investigating the Past

Use radio and television programs to put your research in touch with people and events from the past as well as the present. Many early radio and television productions—ranging from the nightly news to old radio dramas like *The Shadow* and popular television comedies like *I Love Lucy*—are commercially available today on tape or video.

One excellent source is the Vanderbilt Television News Archive, an outstanding video tape collection of major news broadcasts and documentaries since 1968. To find out what the archive and other such sources hold, consult your library's copy of the *Television News Index and Abstracts*

(Nashville, TN: Vanderbilt Television News Archives, Vanderbilt University, 1972–date [monthly]). You can use taped material to study historical events at the times they were first reported to the world over radio or television.

Researching Current News

Using current radio or television broadcasts as a basis for research requires both alertness and planning. Check the newspapers regularly or scan *TV Guide* to keep informed about weekly programs related to your research topic. In addition, a brief telephone inquiry to the local radio or television station may yield information about future programs to watch for. Even if you are unsure about a program's content ahead of time, make a checklist of the things you especially want to note for your research. Using a checklist will help you take notes and keep your attention focused.

Taping a Broadcast. A good deal of the time, you will have little or no advance notice of a program airing. In such a case, listen or watch carefully, taking notes throughout the broadcast and checking them during commercial breaks. If you have the equipment, use a tape recorder to record a radio broadcast or a VCR (video cassette recorder) to record a television program while you are tuned in and taking notes. You can review the recordings later, filling out your notes and taking down the bibliographic information for a preliminary citation card. If you cannot get all the information you need during a single broadcast of the program, find out when it may be presented again; check listings for it in the newspaper or, for television broadcasts, consult recent weekly issues of *TV Guide* or *Facts on File* at the library.

Using Transcripts. Anytime you miss a radio or television show completely or need to study its contents more closely, you may be able to send for a *transcript,* a printed copy of the broadcast. Transcripts of news broadcasts, documentaries, interviews, talk shows, and even some entertainment programs are often available upon request from major radio and television stations. Issue-oriented television programs—like *60 Minutes, Dateline,* and those produced by the Public Broadcasting Service (PBS)— offer program transcripts on a regular basis. Transcript availability is usually announced during a radio and television broadcast, but you can always call the station to make sure. For transcripts of past radio programs, consult your library's set of *Summary of World Broadcasts by the British Broadcasting Corp.* (microform, 1973–date) or for television, a source like *CBS News Television Broadcasts* (microform, 1963–date).

For information about publications and broadcasts for radio and television, as well as for a complete listing of radio stations and their addresses in the United States, the *Gale Directory of Publications and Broadcast*

Media 94 is a useful source. The full title and other bibliographic information is given here to show the range of material it provides:

> *Gale Directory of Publications and Broadcast Media 94: An Annual
> Guide to Publications and Broadcasting Stations, Including News-
> papers, Magazines, Journals, Radio Stations, Television Stations,
> and Cable Systems.* 3 vols. Detroit: Gale, 1994.

Documenting Radio and Television Programs

Make out a preliminary citation card for any radio or television program you intend to include in your research. Figures 5.9 and 5.10 show the
information to include for both kinds of sources. If you include a radio or
television program in your paper's list of Works Cited, follow the forms
suggested in Chapters 10 and 11.

> "California and the State of U.S. Education."
> With John Jameson.
> NBC Radio. KNBC, Los Angeles
> 7 May 1994

FIGURE 5.9   A bibliography card for a radio program

> "Where Is the Rest of the Universe?"
> Prod. Peter R. Baker
> Narr. Richard Chamberlain
> PBS. KCET Los Angeles
> 15 April 1993

FIGURE 5.10   A bibliography card for a television program

Public Print Sources

Printed information is everywhere in American society. Pamphlets, circulars, government documents, newsletters, posters, and advertisements tell us almost more than we want to know about our world. Though you will need to weigh the authority and objectivity of any such printed sources, you should not overlook the current information about people, events, or products they can provide for research.

Finding Materials

The Vertical File.   The vertical file collection of your campus or community library is a good place to start finding such materials as pamphlets (see Chapter 2), or you may collect a variety of public print items by visiting offices, laboratories, factories, zoos, museums, or other locations related to your research topic (see Observing Onsite, earlier in this chapter).

Public print items not found in a library or by directly visiting a source may be available by mail. Your library's copy of the *Vertical File Index: A Subject Guide to Selected Pamphlet Material* (1935–date) will provide information about what products exist and how to order them directly from their publishers. If you decide to order something, do so promptly. Pamphlets and similar materials are not permanently stocked. Also, your order may take several weeks to arrive.

U.S. Government Publications.   As the nation's largest publisher, the United States government yearly produces thousands of publications: documents, brochures, pamphlets, posters, guidebooks, directories, photographs, and newsletters. The various branches of government annually publish current information on thousands of subjects, including cities, people, roads, lakes, diseases, housing, agriculture, education, technology, employment, and wildlife.

Some 1,400 academic, law, and public libraries across the nation are depositories for most documents printed by the United States government. In addition, nearly every state also has at least one such library designated as a Regional Depository Library to receive and store *all* publications distributed by the Government Printing Office (GPO). Any librarian can tell you which libraries near you receive government documents and which may be regional depositories, or you can consult a helpful guide to information sources, such as the following:

Lent, Max. *Government Online.* New York: Harper-Perennial, 1995.
Lesko, Matthew. *Information U.S.A.* New York: Viking-Penguin, 1986.

Berman, Claire

  Raising an Adopted Child
  Public Affairs Committee,
  New York, 1993

FIGURE 5.11   A bibliography card for a pamphlet

To find out about published government pamphlets and related materials, consult the *Monthly Catalog of United States Publications* (1895–date) or the *Public Affairs Information Service (PAIS) Bulletin* (1915–date) at a library or online through a computer database like DIALOG (see Chapter 4). If the material you want is not at your library, you can usually get it through interlibrary loan.

Documenting Public Print Sources

Make out a bibliography card for any public print sources you intend to use in your research (see Figure 5.11). If you include an item in your paper, list it in the Works Cited section.

WORKING WITH OTHERS

Educational research shows that some of the most effective learning takes place among communities of learners. Take advantage of that fact: Let your friends and classmates know when you intend to investigate sources beyond the campus library. More than likely, you will find that they can share in your efforts or at least increase your enthusiasm with their own fresh insights and enjoyment of the topic. If you do team up with a classmate to do research beyond the campus or community library, consider the following suggestions ahead of time.

- Before visiting a research location with someone else, decide about sharing transportation, how long you will stay, and roughly what each of you hopes to accomplish.

- Share the responsibility of finding out about local private libraries, businesses, hospitals, or other sites that may be of value to you and others. Make a list of such places, and divide the work of telephoning or visiting them in person to get information needed before deciding to visit a site together.

- Make checklists of the specific activities each of you expects to accomplish during an onsite visit. Discuss these lists together, checking for any omissions and ensuring that your plans do not conflict.

- If your topics overlap in any way, you may be able to work together on an interview or in conducting a survey. (If your topics do not overlap, it may still be possible to poll people about more than one issue with a single survey instrument.) Work together on setting up and conducting the interview or survey. Formulate questions and analyze results together to make sure that each of you gets the information you need.

- Attend public presentations together or agree ahead of time that one of you will go and take careful notes for both. (Be sure your instructor allows you to use another's notes as part of your own research, however.) You can do the same with radio and television programs by deciding ahead of time who can most conveniently listen to or record a particular broadcast. Prepare a checklist and take good notes for any of these kinds of activities, especially if the notes will be used by someone else.

- You and your collaborator may find it convenient to collect pamphlets or other material for each other onsite or to order certain material together from the *Vertical File Index*. Talk about your individual needs to see what kinds of material you can work toward acquiring together.

6

Researching Online and through the Internet

Computers have created entirely new and exciting ways to access information and conduct research. If you have used a computer at your local or university library to locate sources there or elsewhere, you may already be familiar with some of the many information-searching programs connected to databases, the Internet, or other telecommunications sources. And if you have a computer and a modem (a device that allows your computer to connect with other computers) at home, you may have already "surfed" the Internet or used one of the many types of services offered by commercial online providers such as CompuServe, Prodigy, America Online, and the Microsoft Network. Because these and other sources provide access to computers throughout the world, the researcher with a modem has access to the entire world's library of computer-stored information—and literally, at his or her fingertips. The keys are knowing what there is to access and how to access it.

Using a Database for Research

Although not all the information you might access by computer will be the kind stored in a database, the majority of what you need for research purposes will be. A *database* is a collection of information stored in a computer and available to other computers through a modem (plus computer) hookup. Libraries and commercial providers subscribe to commercial vendors, whose systems provide access to hundreds of separate databases on a fee-for-use basis. Databases incorporate hundreds of general indexes and journal abstract sources, even the complete texts of a variety of sources:

Books	Journals	Government reports
Newspapers	Reviews	Conference proceedings
Magazines	Dissertations	Financial reports

Databases exist for hundreds of subjects, ranging from agriculture and chemical compounds to the stock exchange and Japanese technology. A large database like AGRICOLA, which covers agriculture and related subjects, contains over 2.5 million records. A national database vendor such as DIALOG, to which many libraries subscribe, can search over 300 such separate databases, offering access to more than 175 million records.

You will find it fairly simple to conduct a database search through a college or university library or from your own computer at home. For instance, when student Nancy Prado, the author of the research paper on jury selection (see Chapter 10), was seeking journal articles, she went to the Legal Resource Index, a database listing articles on law and government. When Nancy used the descriptors "jury" and "selection" for her search, she received a list of several articles whose abstracts she could then choose to read online, to print immediately, or to download (i.e., copy) to a disk. One of the articles she chose to print for later reference is shown in Figure 6.1.

JOURNAL NAME: ABA JOURNAL   80 40(1) Oct, 1995
SOURCE FILE: LRI FILE 150
ISSN: 0747-0088
GEOGRAPHIC CODE: NNUS
ABSTRACT: Lawyers should be allowed to serve as jurors for their own benefit, to improve public perceptions of the profession, and to help improve the conditions jurors face. Lawyers who have served as jurors nearly always say the experience will help them perform better in court. Exempting the profession from jury duty stirs resentment by others and is too drastic a solution to limited problems. Lawyers are not more likely to make bad jurors than are people with any other training or background.
DESCRIPTORS: Jury selection—Laws, regulations, etc.; Attorneys—Laws, regulations, etc.
    REVISION DATE: 951021

FIGURE 6.1   An example of a database search report

Source: From "At Issue: A Jury of Your Peers—Is it in the best interest of justice to have lawyers serve on juries? Yes: It's everyone's duty—including lawyers," by Colleen McMahon, "No: The temptation to take over is too great," by Larry D. Sharp, *ABA Journal,* Copyright © 1995 American Bar Association. Reprinted by permission of the *ABA Journal.*

If you use campus library facilities, you probably have access to a number of databases for free or for a minimal cost. Accessing databases at home is possible by making direct billing arrangements with a commercial server or a provider such as CompuServe or America Online. Keep in mind that while they are handy, database searches done from home can be very expensive (unless they are part of the services supplied by the provider). Plan to use at-home searches to supplement your research or to access sources you could not otherwise reach through your campus library or another library accessible via the Internet.

Researching through the Internet

Possibly the most significant resource for worldwide communication and research is the *Internet,* a network composed of thousands of other networks and computers around the world. These individual networks and computers share the information and even the capabilities they have with each other, with the result that anyone accessing the network can obtain all of the information and even some of the capabilities of every computer on the Internet.

While it is not the purpose of this chapter to tell you everything you need to know about accessing the Internet, familiarity with a few basic concepts will aid your understanding of discussions that follow.

Internet Addresses

Each individual computer linked to the Internet is accessible through an Internet address called a *URL (uniform resource locator).* The URL for the online history resources located at the University of Virginia, for example, is *gopher://gopher.lib.virginia.edu.* While addresses such as this may look formidable, you need not be an expert about URLs or the Internet to use them.

Simply put, an Internet address is divided into domains and subdomains; periods, slashes, and colons are used to separate these various parts of the address. As with any address, these parts are essential in identifying what or whom to connect with and where. Of course, in this case, the address is given to a computer in order to locate something or someone at a site on the Internet. Any error or omission in the address will make the transmission undeliverable. For this reason, you must enter the URL exactly to connect successfully with a remote address.

One of the important things to understand about an Internet URL is that the actual address follows the slash and the information that precedes it.

The first part of the URL (i.e., before the slash) identifies the kind of system or *search tool* that is needed to access a particular source. For example:

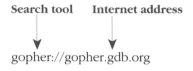

gopher://gopher.gdb.org

Note that this particular URL uses a search tool called *Gopher* (described later in this chapter) to locate the address and information represented by *gopher.gdb.org*.

Depending upon the kind of search tool you use and what capabilities your computer has, you may need to enter only the address portion of the URL (i.e., after the slash). Clearly, for research purposes, it is important for you to know what kind of search tool is required to access a resource and whether your computer has that capability.

Using Online/Internet Search Tools

If you have used a computer in the library to locate sources there or somewhere else, you may already be familiar with some of the information-searching programs connected to databases, the Internet, and other telecommunications sources. Of course, it is not always necessary to know which kind of search system you are accessing when you seek sources and information via computer. Even so, being familiar with certain terms and what search processes they make available will help you take advantage of the benefits such "search engines," as they are called, offer to anyone doing research (see also Figure 6.3, pp. 127–29).

The World Wide Web

Often written as *WWW* and spoken of as "the Web," the *World Wide Web* is the gateway to all of the resources available on the Internet and one of the most popular means of accessing those resources in textual, graphic, or sound format. Much of the information on the Internet is available in text form only; however, resources including *www* as part of their address are usually rich in text and artwork.

Connecting with a web address (i.e., a URL) takes you to what is known as a *home page,* or main document, which in turn can link you to additional data or other websites. Web pages have *hypertext* capabilities, which allow you to access additional information on related subjects. By selecting certain highlighted words, or hypertext, you can jump automatically to whole new documents. Figure 3.6 (p. 40) shows an example of a web document with hypertext words. Selecting one of these words would transport you to more information about that subject.

In addition, you can use the web's search capabilities to find and connect with websites offering information you need for research. For example, you can connect with *Yahoo,* a comprehensive directory that indexes thousands of World Wide Web pages by main and subcategories. You can access many valuable, searchable indexes to websites all over the world, including Yahoo, through the following web addresses, or URLs:

Web "Search Engine"	*URL*
Info Seek	http://www.infoseek.com
Lycos	http://fuzine.mt.cs.cmu.edu/mlm/lycos-home.html
OpenText	http://www.opentext.com
Web Crawler	http://webcrawler.com.html

World Wide
  Web Worm
	http://www.cs.colorado.edu/home/mcbryan
	  /WWWW.html

Yahoo	http://www.yahoo.com

Telnet

Telnet connects your computer to another computer at a different site and allows you to read files stored on that computer and run some of its programs. The files accessed through Telnet are textual resources, programs with files and databases such as directories, indexes, abstracts, lists of public documents, stock quotations, and libraries' listings of their catalogs and collections. If you were researching privacy issues such as wiretapping and credit reporting, for example, you could use the Telnet address *telnet://teetot.acusd.edu* to access factsheets, position papers, copies of legislation, and press releases provided by the Privacy Rights Clearinghouse. Addressing *telnet://locator@locator.nim.nih.gov* would access the National Library of Medicine Online Catalog System, which has listings of nearly 5 million information items relating to medicine, biomedicine, the health sciences, and the history of medicine.

FTP

FTP (file transfer protocol) allows you to retrieve files from or send files to another computer at a remote distance. Using FTP, you can download (i.e., retrieve) software from another computer or copy text files, graphics, or audio and video programs right to your own computer and store them for later use. For instance, you could strengthen your research on trends in radio programming by using FTP to retrieve sound files of actual radio shows from *ftp://ni.funet.fi* (path = */pub/sounds/**). To access a copy of President Clinton's speech on the twentieth anniversary of the *Apollo* moon landing, you could use FTP to address *explorer.arc.nasa.gov* and retrieve a file (*apollo.ann*) with the complete text.

Gopher

Gopher is a search program that allows you to choose among successively narrower menus of resources or related resources at its own or another site. Suppose, for example, that you were interested in getting information about nutrition from a worldwide perspective. You could begin by accessing the Gopher server menu for the United Nations World Health Organization (*Gopher.who.ch*). The menu would present you with successively more focused menus to select from, such as these:

First menu choice	WHO's Major Programmes
Second menu choice	Food & Nutrition
Third menu choice	Int'l Conference on Nutrition, Rome, 1993

Working from the last menu, you would be able to access information about topics presented at the 1993 Rome conference and find other resources with an international perspective.

Archie and Veronica

Both Telnet and FTP require you to know the addresses of the computers and the names of the files you want to access. Two other search programs—named *Archie* and *Veronica* (apparently playfully named after the popular comic book friends)—are also useful and frequently referenced on the menus you will encounter online. (Another more locally focused search tool, known as *Jughead,* also searches titles but is rarely referred to by name in a system.)

Archie is useful when you know the names of the FTP files you want to access (or even parts of the names) but do not know the address (server and path) by which to get to those files. Suppose, for example, that you wanted to find the *Apollo* anniversary speech by President Clinton but did not know the address of the FTP site that held the file. You could ask an Archie server to locate the site for the file *apollo.ann* or, if you did not know the file's name, to locate files with the word *apollo* in their titles. The

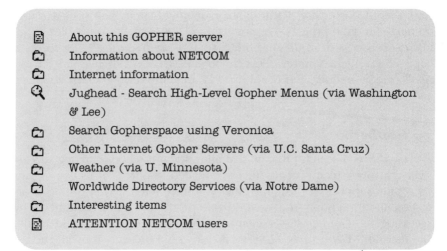

FIGURE 6.2   The NETCOM Gopher server menu
Source: Reprinted with permission from NETCOM On-Line Communication Services, Inc.

Archie system would return a list of FTP site addresses storing files that matched your request. Using Archie for such searches can save a great amount of time and effort, sparing you from searching large numbers, perhaps hundreds, of FTP sites to find the files you want.

Veronica is an efficient means of accessing a particular Gopher server with the specific information you are seeking or a directory of Gopher servers from which you can select one that meets your needs. You connect with Veronica by first arriving at a Gopher menu that offers a selection specifically referencing it by name, such as *Search titles in Gopherspace using Veronica* (see Figure 6.2). Once you select such an option and enter a keyword or keywords, the Veronica search system bypasses all other Gopher servers until it locates and connects you to a server, another directory, or menus with the information you seek. Using Boolean operators such as *AND* or *OR* with your keyword requests (*juries AND selection,* for example) allows you to narrow the search criteria in ways that save time.

WAIS

WAIS (wide area information service) performs keyword or subject searches through the indexes of other servers to find relevant sources. It then ranks those sources according to the frequency with which the keyword or words appear in them. You can successively narrow a search by modifying the keyword or keyword string until you find a source significantly focused on your topic.

Once you have accessed WAIS through a local public server, you can select a source and ask WAIS to search its index for any files containing a keyword or words. WAIS returns a list of sources, ranked on a scale of 1 to 1,000, for you to select from. For example, if you entered the key phrase "ozone," WAIS might return a list such as this:

marsys-int	1,000
USDOS	783
osea-news	528

You could select any of these database sources to find files on your topic. Keep in mind, however, that WAIS searches all terms as the same, regardless of the meanings you intend. If you enter the term "salmon," for example, WAIS will return a list of sources that includes discussions of salmon fishing, salmon biology, salmon cooking, and so forth. For this reason, you should be careful about the keywords you enter and expect to get unwanted sources among your choices.

WAIS searches databases with a variety of sources, including text, sound, and images. You will need to work from a computer system adequately equipped for such media to take advantage of the full potential of WAIS.

Other Resources

Most campus libraries have information and designated staff to assist individuals who have questions about using computers to search available databases or access the Internet. As with other library resources, use them when you need help.

You can also use the Internet's own resources for information about using the search programs described in this chapter. The SURAnet Network Information Center and a number of universities provide brief guides to using these powerful research tools at the following Internet addresses:

Telnet	ftp://ftp.sura.net
FTP	ftp://ftp.sura.net
Gopher	gopher://gopher.micro.umn.edu
Archie	ftp://archie.ans.net
Veronica	ftp//ftp.cso.uiuc.edu
World Wide Web	telnet://info.cern.ch

In addition, bookstores today abound with Internet directories and "how to" books about getting the most out of the Web, using search tools, and simply accessing the entire potential of the Internet. The following titles are representative of the books available, but also check your local campus bookstore and others for current resources that may match your needs:

Campbell, Dave, and Mary Campbell. *The Student's Guide to Doing Research on the Internet.* Reading, MA: Addison-Wesley, 1995.

Nelson, Stephen L. *Field Guide to the Internet.* Redmond, WA: Microsoft, 1995.

Maxwell, Christine, and Czeslaw Jan Grycz, eds. *New Riders' Official Internet Yellow Pages.* Indianapolis, IN: New Riders, 1994.

Also consult the following online resources, depending on what topic you are researching:

Academic Index, 1976–date.

AGRICOLA (U.S. National Agricultural Library), 1970–date.

Arts & Humanities Search (Arts & Humanities Citation Index), 1980–date.

Biography Index, 1984–date.

CancerLit, 1963–present.

ERIC (Educational Resources Information Center), 1966–date.

Historical Abstracts, 1973–date.

Legal Resource Index, 1980–date.

Magazine Index, 1959–1970 and 1973–date.

MEDLARS/MEDLINE (Medical Literature Analysis and Retrieval System), 1965–date.

Mental Health Abstracts, 1969–date.

National Newspaper Index, 1979–date.

PAIS International (Public Affairs Information Service), 1972–date.

Philosophers' Index, 1940–date.

PsychINFO (Psychological Abstracts), 1967–date.

Public Opinion Online (POLL), 1940–date.

SOCIAL SCISEARCH and/or SCISEARCH (Social Science Citation Index and Science Citation Index online), 1972–date.

See Figure 6.3 for an overview of the Internet search tools discussed in this chapter.

PROGRAM	FUNCTION	RESEARCH USE	EXAMPLE
Telnet	Connects you to another computer and lets you access its files and run its programs.	Log in as "Guest Telnet" to read information files stored at one site, such as directories, indexes, abstracts, lists of public government documents, and university libraries' databases of catalogs and collections.	Addressing *telnet: //locator@locator. nlm.nih.gov* gets you the National Library of Medicine Online Catalog System, with listings of nearly 5 million items relating to medicine, biomedicine, the health sciences, and the history of medicine.
FTP (File Transfer Protocol)	Allows you to retrieve (download) files from or send (upload) files to a remote computer. You must know the address of the site and know (or learn once there) the names of any files you want to access.	Log in as an "anonymous" user and use your e-mail address as a password to download or copy government documents, books, software, multimedia, text files and images, bibliographies, and live audio and video programs to your own computer.	Get a list of names, addresses, e-mail addresses, and telephone and fax numbers for the President, First Lady, Vice President, and members of the Cabinet at *ftp://nifty. andrew.cmu.edu/pub /QRD/info/govt /cabinet.*
Gopher	Allows a choice among a series of hierarchical, successively narrower menus of resources or related sources at that particular Gopher site or at another site to which it will connect you.	Search a topic to narrow it, find related headings, or discover a new subject as you search for sources in databases, indexes, bibliographies, and government documents. Gopher can also connect you to WAIS databases, WWW sites, FTP sites, and more.	*Gopher://Chicano /LatinoNet* leads to these successive menus: 1. Library to Databases 2. Description of Chicano Databases 3. Chicanos: A Checklist to Biographies 4. Bibliographies of works on Caesar Chavez and Joan Baez

FIGURE 6.3　Internet search tools for research

PROGRAM	FUNCTION	RESEARCH USE	EXAMPLE
World Wide Web (WWW)	Provides hypertext links to text, graphic, and sound files as well as links to additional WWW sites, Gopher servers, or search programs.	Use the *http://* protocol to access web pages from which you can follow hypertext to find and retrieve (download) text information and images such as graphics, maps, and charts and sound files with musical recordings and speeches.	Accessing *http://www.fbi.gov* takes you to the home page of the Federal Bureau of Investigation (FBI). You can use hypertext selections to jump to information on the Oklahoma City bombing case or get updates on the FBI's investigation of the Unabomber.
Archie	Searches among FTP sites in its database and presents a list and addresses of those with file names that include your "string," or search terms. You can restrict the number of results returned.	Save time by searching individual FTP sites to find file names or programs and their addresses. Access by Telnetting to an Archie server, or go through a Gopher menu.	Use e-mail or Telnet to instruct an Archie server to "find genius." You would receive a response listing the names and FTP site addresses of files that contained "genius" or other phrases you included in the request.
Veronica	Similar to Archie; scans Gopher directory titles and resources (documents, graphics, movies, and sound) worldwide. Checks Gopher site titles for matches with user's keywords, and then lists those as a menu for the user's selection and connection.	Save time searching by keywords instead of menu by menu at various Gopher sites. Access through the address of a Veronica server, or go through a Gopher menu. "Jughead," which sometimes accompanies Veronica, searches directory titles.	Entering the keyword "homeless" as the search string results in a list of accessible Gopher menu titles such as "Amendments to McKinney Homeless Assistance Act," "Homeless Services," and "Homeless Youth and Teens Report, 1994."

FIGURE 6.3   Continued

PROGRAM	FUNCTION	RESEARCH USE	EXAMPLE
WAIS (Wide Area Information Service)	Performs keyword searches in databases of full-text, sound, and image files. Some WAIS "engines" rank files according to the frequency of keyword appearances in them. A drawback is that WAIS returns file names with *any* occurrence of a keyword.	Access by Telnetting to a public WAIS server or through a Gopher, WWW menu, or other tool. Use WAIS-related menus to get to a directory of servers or list of *sources*. Then use keywords to go from sources to full-text files.	Entering the keyword "refugees" takes you to a list of sources, including "Refugee Resettlement Program: Proposed Allocations to States FY 1995." Choosing this source takes you to the March 8, 1995, *Federal Register,* with the full text of this report.

FIGURE 6.3 Continued

WORKING WITH OTHERS

Begin immediately with your classmates to share information about using the library's resources on campus or exploring the Internet or other online resources from your own home-based computer. Although researching via computer may seem a little scary at first, your confidence and expertise will grow with each new effort. Explore the web, search databases through CompuServe or America Online, chat with experts from across the United States, e-mail classmates about research questions, or download files from other universities. You will find that researching online and sharing your experiences with others will make your efforts not only more effective but more enjoyable, as well.

- With a friend or classmate, find out what computer facilities and services are available at your campus library and which databases can be accessed using them. Discuss each other's knowledge of or experience in accessing such databases.

- If you are not familiar with the types of online or Internet search tools described in this chapter, ask your campus librarian about participating in introductory sessions that explain these resources. You may also be able to share some of your research time working alongside a classmate who has experience in using the library's online programs.

■ Find out if any of your classmates subscribe to commercial services such as Prodigy, CompuServe, and America Online. Compare your experiences with such services, and discuss how they may be of use to your research projects. Consider how you might utilize chat groups, e-mail, database searches, Internet access, or other services to aid your research. If you do not subscribe to a commercial service and have a modem on your home computer, ask your classmates to recommend one to get started with. You may want to investigate the free trial periods offered by many of the leading commercial providers.

■ Use e-mail or another form of online communication to share your daily or weekly research results with a classmate. Use such communication as an opportunity to ask questions, try out ideas, or share resources with one another. You will find that sharing in these ways will keep your enthusiasm going and help you finish your research paper on time.

■ Join one or more of your classmates to browse campus or local bookstores for online or Internet guides that may contain information helpful to your research. Look through Internet directories, for example, to see what resources may be available on your research topic. Or if you are unsure about how to access or use the Internet, browse through some sources that provide this information. Discuss these sources with your classmates to see if they have recommendations or can perhaps lend you resources of their own. Remember, too, that you may be able to check out such materials from your campus or city library, rather than purchase them.

Most colleges offer introductory, short-term classes about using computers or the Internet. If you are not experienced in such matters or want to strengthen your knowledge, investigate these courses and enroll in one or more as soon as you can. Doing so will prove useful for more than one semester's research assignment. For added enjoyment, ask a friend or classmate to take a class with you so you can share experiences.

CHAPTER 7

Reading and Recording Information

An accurate understanding and interpretation of sources is integral to the value of your research paper's content. Conduct your research to make the most efficient use of your own time and the resources available. Careful reading, accurate notetaking, and thoughtful evaluation as you examine a source will ensure good results.

Planning Your Reading

Avoid putting the time and thinking about your topic at the mercy of haphazard reading. Once you have established a working bibliography, use the source's title, publication information, author's name, and length to estimate its place in your research needs. Naturally, you cannot always know in advance what a source contains, but planning your reading will make the best use of sources and time.

The following suggestions will help you plan an efficient use of reading time:

1. Review the working bibliography to consult general sources first: magazine articles, histories, and other broad discussions. This will allow you to organize your research of available materials.

2. When selecting sources to read, consider their intended audience as well as your own purposes. Popular magazines will be your best resources when you need general ideas, current opinions, or recent developments; turn to more scholarly journals and books for detailed studies and recognized authorities on the topic.

3. Once familiar with a topic through reading general sources, move next to those sources that treat the topic specifically or in detail. It is best to

work in such sources as soon as you can do so comfortably. This way, you avoid having to read through general ideas that are repeated throughout several different sources.

4. Plan your reading to examine no more than one or two related aspects at a time. This will organize notetaking and focus your thinking on the material. For example, Nancy Prado made a point to read first a journal article and then a book that specifically addressed how the American jury selection system works. Take care to keep your bibliography and your reading balanced. Consulting different viewpoints will enhance your understanding of the topic and allow for comparing opinions as you read.

5. Finally, you can waste a lot of valuable time and energy running back and forth from the periodicals room to the book stacks or from one campus library to another. When possible, organize your reading activities around types of sources and their locations. This will prevent your omitting a potentially valuable source because you do not have time to go back for it.

Types of Reading

Skimming

Skimming is a way of reading quickly to find out what is said. Rather than read everything in a selection, look for key words, main ideas, subheadings, illustrations, and other features related to your research question. The goal in skimming a source is not to read it thoroughly. Rather, find out if it has the kind of information you seek, and if it does, determine what to read more closely.

Skimming Books.   Before spending time on a close reading, first skim a book to evaluate its possible usefulness. Use the book's major components to determine its contents and scope:

1. *Start with the title.* A main title alone may be too general to indicate a book's subject, or it may not accurately reflect the book's focus. Main titles such as *Lucy's Child* or *Verdict for Justice,* for example, give no hint of the books' respective contents. The full titles of these works, however, more completely suggest their subjects:

> *Lucy's Child: The Discovery of a Human Ancestor*
> *Verdict for Justice: The American Jury System on Trial*

Attention to a complete title can tell you if a particular book is something you want to examine more closely, put off reading until later, or ignore altogether.

2. *Consult the table of contents.* Here, you will find a list of the chapters included in the book and the pages on which they begin. A quick exami-

nation of the table of the contents and of any promising chapters will tell you whether to return to the book later for more detailed study.

Let's say, for example, that you were interested in researching the topic *animal intelligence*. A general bibliographic source, such as the *Essay and General Literature Index,* might refer you to a work titled *Through a Window,* anthropologist Jane Goodall's account of her studies of chimpanzees in the Gombe region of East Africa. The table of contents (see Figure 7.1) for Goodall's book lists at least one especially relevant chapter, The Mind of the Chimpanzee. You would skim this chapter first to assess its usefulness and then examine others whose titles also suggest they might address your topic or research question. If your skimming indicated any chapters that merited further study, you would make out a bibliography card for the book so you could return to it later.

3. *Search the index.* In case small segments of information on your topic also appear in other places than the chapters you consult, turn next to the index located at the back of the book. A nonfiction book usually includes

Contents

1.	GOMBE	1
2.	THE MIND OF THE CHIPMANZEE	12
3.	THE RESEARCH CENTRE	24
4.	MOTHERS AND DAUGHTERS	32
5.	FIGAN'S RISE	43
6.	POWER	53
7.	CHANGE	65
8.	GILKA	75
9.	SEX	85
10.	WAR	98
11.	SONS AND MOTHERS	112
12.	BABOONS	124
13.	GOBLIN	138
14.	JOMEO	151
15.	MELISSA	161
16.	GIGI	178
17.	LOVE	191
18.	BRIDGING THE GAP	206
19.	OUR SHAME	217
20.	CONCLUSION	235
	Appendix I. Some thoughts on the Exploitation of Non-Human Animals	245
	Appendix II. Chimpanzee Conservation and Sanctuaries	251
	Acknowledgments	257
	Index	263

FIGURE 7.1 A table of contents listing the chapters in a book

an index, an alphabetical list of the topics, subtopics, ideas, places, and names mentioned in it. The page numbers after each entry tell where to find it in the book. In addition to looking for a topic by name in the index, also search for it under a major term. In Jane Goodall's book on chimpanzees, for example, the index lists *mind, brain, intelligence, 12–23, 206–9* under the term *chimpanzees.*

Sometimes you need to look for a topic under a synonym or closely related term. If you found no entries in a book's index under *alcoholism,* for instance, you should next look under related terms, such as *substance abuse, addiction, drinking,* or *encounter group.*

In addition to skimming a book's table of contents and index, also look for other useful features:

- The *preface* or *introduction* to a book may give an overview of the subject or suggest that particular book's approach to it.
- An *appendix* (plural *appendices* or *appendixes*) provides additional information on topics discussed in the book and may include maps, graphs, charts, or other helpful material.
- A *glossary* lists special terms and their definitions, as they relate to the book's subject.
- A *bibliography* may guide you to other books or resources.

If you do not read closely and take notes from a book when you first skim it, use the working bibliography card to record the author and title as well as a brief note on what you found and the relevant page numbers. Return to the book later when you know more about what you need from it.

Skimming Periodical Articles.   You can usually skim articles in magazines, journals, and newspapers more quickly than those in books. Titles of periodical articles are usually more specific than book titles, and they often include subheadings to label and organize content for readers. Articles in most scholarly science journals, such as *Journal of Marine Research* and *Journal of Applied Psychology,* are organized according to guidelines recommended by the American Psychological Association (APA). Articles in APA form are often divided into major sections boldly labeled as Abstract, Introduction, Method, Results, Discussion, and References. Use these headings to skim such journal articles for the information you seek as well as to organize and label any notes.

To skim a periodical article, scan it quickly, paying attention to features such as boldfaced headings, subsections, and illustrations. Skim the first sentence of each paragraph or subsection to identify its main idea. You may want to read the last paragraph or two closely to understand the author's conclusions. If you think the article is worth reading more thoroughly later, make a note on the back of the bibliography card to review it.

Close Reading

Close reading requires careful attention to all the words and sentences in a selection to understand its full meaning. After you have skimmed a source and decided to read all or part of it closely, you read carefully to comprehend ideas and record information. While these two purposes can undoubtedly overlap, awareness of them as separate activities will help focus your notetaking and organize your thinking as you read.

Reading for Meaning. Reading to comprehend meaning involves recognizing main ideas as well as making inferences about what you read. As you read any material, pay attention to key ideas and statements that support an overall point.

The Thesis or Summary Statement. In most articles or chapters in books, you will recognize a thesis or summary statement that explains the author's major point. (Review the discussion of thesis statements in Chapter 3.) The main point usually appears near the beginning of a discussion but not necessarily. Wherever it occurs, the main point dominates the text. All the other ideas, sentences, paragraphs, and examples relate to it. Make a habit of identifying the main point of any material you read. As you read and take notes, consciously relate the main point to the other ideas in the text.

Topic Sentences. The topic sentence contains the paragraph's major idea, the concept that all other elements in the paragraph support or explain. Supporting ideas for a thesis may occur as the topic sentence stated at the beginning, middle, or end of a paragraph. In the following paragraph, the topic sentence occurs in the first sentence. Notice how all other sentences help to build upon the idea stated in the topic sentence:

Topic sentence	Regular cocaine users put up with many unpleasant drug effects. Restlessness, irritability and apprehension are common.
Examples support the topic sentence	Users tend to become suspicious and even display paranoid symptoms—frequently changing locks and phone numbers, doubting friends and showing inappropriate anger or jealousy. All this derives from cocaine's impact on the sympathetic nervous system—the network that controls "flight or
Transition word signals *additional* details	fight" responses to fright. In addition, even at fairly low doses cocaine may cause tremors, cold sweats, and grinding of teeth. At higher doses, vomiting and nausea may result, along with muscle pains, a disoriented feeling and dizziness—followed, in some cases, by life-threatening seizures.

—Ira Mothner and Alan Weitz, *How to Get Off Drugs: Everything You Should Know to Help Someone You Love Get Off—and Stay Off—Drugs, Including When to Seek Help and Where to Find It* (New York: Simon and Shuster, 1984) 75.

When reading this paragraph for ideas, note particularly the main idea stated as the topic sentence. Use the main idea to focus your attention on the examples and details that develop the topic sentence further.

Implied Topic Sentences.   Sometimes the main idea in a paragraph is implied, rather than stated directly. In these cases, the author feels that the point of the paragraph is obvious, and it is up to the reader to understand the central meaning. This paragraph by Annie Dillard, for example, avoids stating in an outright topic sentence that a jungle is crowded with unusual and somewhat threatening varieties of life:

> Unseen in the jungle, but present, are tapirs, jaguars, many species of snake and lizard, ocelots, armadillos, marmosets, howler monkeys, toucans and macaws and a hundred other birds, deer, bats, peccaries, capybaras, agoutis, and sloths. Also present in this jungle, but variously distant, are Texaco derricks and pipelines, and some of the wildest Indians in the world, blowgun-using Indians, who killed missionaries in 1956 and ate them.
>
> —Annie Dillard, "In the Jungle," *Teaching a Stone to Talk: Expeditions and Encounters* (New York: Perennial-Harper, 1988) 57.

You should read such a paragraph as you would any other, paying attention to how the ideas and information fit together to present an overall picture or main idea. When reading paragraphs with implied main ideas, always sum up the main point in your own words, and make it a part of your notes.

Taking Effective Notes

You will need to take good written notes on all the information collected during your research. The notes will help organize your thinking about what you investigate as well as provide general ideas, quotations from authorities, and specific data when you write the paper. Since you cannot remember everything you discover about a topic, develop and follow a consistent system of notetaking that will help you select, organize, and record information.

What to Take Notes About

Your research notes will be more useful if you recognize in advance what to record from your reading. Certain information needs to be written down each time you take any kind of notes about a source:

1. The title and author of the source (You will also need to include the publisher's name, as well as the place and date of publication, if you

have not made a working bibliography card for each source consulted during your research.)

2. The page number(s) from which the material is taken
3. The content you want to record

In general, the content of your notes should reflect your close, critical evaluation and analysis of the source. Summarizing the source is a valuable way to ensure your own understanding. Doing so also provides a reference that will be useful later, whether as a reminder as to what the source is about or to provide the documentation needed in your Works Cited list. As you evaluate a source, make notes about the author's authority on the subject, the use and kinds of evidence presented, and your overall impression of the author's effectiveness. Consider these questions:

- What facts or opinions seemed to contradict those you found in other sources?
- What ideas agree with those of other writers and with your own conclusions about the topic?

As with the answers to these and similar questions, focus your notes upon content that will assist you in thinking critically about the source and its use in your research paper.

Note Format

Arrange note information any way that is convenient and makes for easy reference. Consistency in the way you record page numbers, identify direct quotations, and add your own commentary is essential for accurate interpretation of the notes later.

Figure 7.2 shows a typical arrangement of essential note material on one of Nancy Prado's notecards. Nancy labeled the card with the heading Problems with Jury Duty and used it for notes on an article titled Jury Duty on Trial. Notice that only the source's author, identified by a first initial and last name, is needed on the notecard. Nancy had previously recorded the author's complete name, the full title of the source, and all relevant publishing information on a separate bibliography card. In order to make her notes clearly understandable later, Nancy punctuated each section of quoted material clearly and added the notation *quote* next to it in the margin. She also indicated her own analysis with the notation *mine* and used parentheses to separate and identify page numbers.

Note Content

Using your research question as a guide, you will find that a good deal of your notetaking will be based on evolving intuition: As a preliminary thesis or response to the research question begins to form from your read-

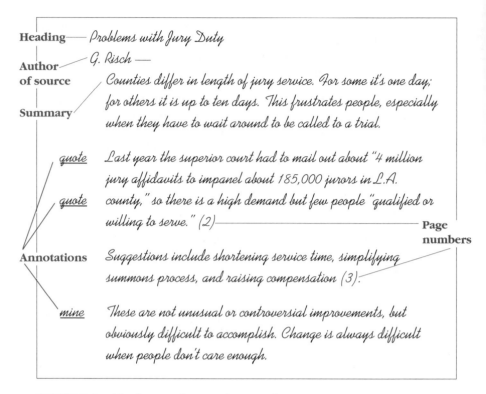

Heading — *Problems with Jury Duty*

Author of source — *G. Risch* —

Summary — *Counties differ in length of jury service. For some it's one day; for others it is up to ten days. This frustrates people, especially when they have to wait around to be called to a trial.*

quote   *Last year the superior court had to mail out about "4 million jury affidavits to impanel about 185,000 jurors in L.A.*

quote   *county," so there is a high demand but few people "qualified or willing to serve." (2)* — **Page numbers**

Annotations   *Suggestions include shortening service time, simplifying summons process, and raising compensation (3).*

mine   *These are not unusual or controversial improvements, but obviously difficult to accomplish. Change is always difficult when people don't care enough.*

FIGURE 7.2   The format of a typical notecard

ing, you will start to recognize what things to record in your notes. Taking more notes, you will also begin to recognize how the pieces of collected information fit together to support one or more major ideas that may form an answer to the research question or seve as the basis of a preliminary thesis for the paper. The further you progress in your research, the more you will recognize with increasing certainty what material to record.

Before starting research, review the sample papers in Chapter 10 and Appendix A. Examine them to acquaint yourself with the kinds of ideas and information that make up a research paper. Naturally, you will not know all the information needed from your research sources until you begin writing the paper; however, your increasing sense of what you will eventually say about the topic should help identify material for notes. Depending upon your topic and your own knowledge of the subject, the contents of the notes will include a wide variety of information:

1. Take notes to record background information that you need to understand the research topic better. If you are investigating welfare fraud, you may first need to learn about the extent of the problem, existing laws, facts

about the history of state assistance programs, or the legal definitions of terms. Eventually, your reading and notes on such material will supply the broad understanding necessary to research and write effectively on the topic. Expect the background notes on any subject to decrease as you learn more about it and begin focusing on supporting a preliminary thesis.

2. Take notes to summarize general ideas supporting your preliminary thesis statement. Your preliminary thesis will probably shift in focus or change completely as you pursue your research. Groups of major ideas will emerge from your reading, changing your thinking or the emphasis of the preliminary thesis.

You will find it easier to organize your notes on such ideas by listing them under subtopic headings. As Nancy Prado did her reading research on jury selection, for example, she recorded her notes under headings such as Problems with Jury Duty, Peremptory Challenges, Nullification, and Juror Qualifications. As Nancy gathered additional ideas about her topic, she added more headings, discontinued a few, and eventually merged others under new headings. In doing so, Nancy found a way to organize her notes and to begin identifying categories of ideas to include in her paper (see Figure 7.3, p. 141).

3. Take notes on explanatory information such as histories, definitions of terms, plot summaries, biographical data, and other material that you may need to provide for your readers. For a paper about former Soviet President Mikhail Gorbachev, you may need notes about the form of the Soviet government, background on the 1991 coup attempt, or information about the highlights of his political career. A paper on cocaine use would need notes for defining terms such as *crack* and *freebasing,* for example.

4. Take notes to record quotations, examples, and anecdotes that will illustrate or support your ideas in the paper. Quoting an eloquently stated opinion or the words of a recognized expert lends interest as well as authority to your own discussion (see Using Quotation, Chapter 9). For instance, in a paper on computer viruses, you could use specific examples from an interview with an expert on the subject. A paper on problems faced by new U.S. immigrants might include an anecdote about someone's first attempt to register for school or to apply for a job.

5. Take notes on little known facts or questionable and controversial ideas about your topic. Even if accurate, facts and opinions that are not commonly known or may seem questionable to your paper's reader need to be carefully recorded and supported by documentation. For instance, selected research may suggest people can actually lose weight by *thinking* themselves thin, but your readers may not accept this assertion or may believe you have misunderstood the facts. To prevent losing credibility, take good notes to describe the research fully and indicate an authoritative source for it in your paper. (See Chapters 10–12 on citing such sources.)

6. Take notes to record statistical figures, such as percentages, weights, amounts of money, ratios, and dates that are not commonly known, as well as the sources in which you found them. Your readers may need to know that Americans throw away 160 million tons of trash each year or that 55% of American women in 1993 worked outside the home. Figures like these can add precision to your paper's discussion and also convincingly support and illustrate your ideas. Take notes on all such figures related to your research question. The frequency with which you come across such statistics in your research will determine whether they are commonly known or need to be documented. (See Chapter 10 about documenting figures.)

The notes from material such as that mentioned here will shape your thinking during the research stage. Expect to take more notes than you will actually need, and do not hesitate to write down anything you think may be of importance later. Eventually, you will combine the material from your notes with your own ideas, as well as those of others you cite in the research paper.

Figure 7.3 shows one of Nancy Prado's notecards for a discussion of the results of so-called scientific jury selection procedures. Notice how Nancy used her notes on the original source material to illustrate and support the main idea of a paragraph in her paper:

Original from source

Media accounts of jury selection bear involuntary witness to our widespread belief that jury selection determines all. Race especially gains privileged status in popular accounts of why verdicts turn out as they do, as if it were obvious not only that justice does not cross racial lines but also that a juror's race always outweighs the competing or overlapping influences of class, gender, or education. . . .

My conclusions about this science of jury selection will be straight forward. Empirically, there is no evidence that it works.

—Jeffrey Abramson, *We, the Jury: The Jury System and the Ideal of Democracy* (New York: Basic-Harper, 1994) 143–45.

Notes as used in the paper

While the significance of such indicators remains unclear, attorneys use peremptory challenge rights to create juries whose members have the attitudes or education levels believed to be most promising in getting the desired verdicts. Some consultants suggest that clergy, teachers, and lawyers do not make desirable jurors because they are too often sought out for advice and tend to be too opinionated. Attorneys are also usually advised to avoid selecting bank and management

---

Jury Selection — Results

J. Abramson —

quote *The public still believes that jury selection "determines all" (143), especially in cases where race is important, as if it*
quote *outweighed "class, gender, or education" (144).*

He doesn't subscribe to trying to pick a certain type of jury by
quote *any "scientific" method. "Empirically, there is no evidence that it works" (145).*

mine *People are too complex and the dynamics of being on a jury have an important role in how jurors make a decision. Group identity is not always a necessarily important factor.*

FIGURE 7.3   Notes used in writing the paper (see paragraph on pp. 140–41)

employees as jurors because they "are trained to give or take orders [and] they expect others to conform as well" (Simon 262). Although there is little empirical evidence that such quasi-scientific methods of selecting juries work (Abramson 145), attorneys and the public continue to believe that these methods are important in shaping verdicts. Moreover, people's faith in such methods is renewed each time the outcome of a trial seems explainable in terms of jury demographics, such as gender, education, and other factors (Abramson 144).

Where to Record Notes

While everyone has his or her own method for taking notes, some are more useful for preparing a research paper than others. Again, *consistency* is the key to any successful notetaking. Decide early on a system that you will follow. A regular routine for storing notes and registering information will keep them from getting lost and prevent omissions that may cause extra work later.

Record your notes in a legible and accurate fashion. It is easy to become confused later about note contents. Be consistent about listing or marking bibliographic data, source summaries, quotations, page numbers, and your own comments. (See Chapter 9 on how to punctuate quotations and quote accurately.) Mark your notes in a way that clearly separates and identifies each. As mentioned earlier, notations such as *mine, quote, summary,* and the like can keep note content clearly identified (see Figure 7.2).

Decide how or on what you want to store your notes. There are plenty of options. Notecards, a notebook, photocopies, or a computer are common preferences. You will probably vary your method from time to time to suit certain kinds of information, but using one medium throughout your research is most efficient. In general, the best method is one that consistently fits your work habits and meets the needs of your research materials.

Notecards.   Keeping your notes on cards offers the greatest flexibility and convenience. Notecards can be arranged or shuffled to suit any order you need, and you can easily add or take out cards as your research progresses. Use cards big enough to record plenty of information. Large 5″ × 8″ cards provide ample space for recording notes, commentary, and bibliographic information. Use a separate card for each source. Include subtopic headings to categorize your notes (see Figures 7.2 and 7.3) and to group cards in the same categories later. Keep the cards bound with a rubber band, and carry them with you when doing research.

A Research Notebook.   For some topics, especially those requiring extensive notes or columns of figures, recording all your research ideas in a single notebook is also a good idea. Notebook pages allow plenty of room for adding your own extensive commentary or other remarks to your notes, and a bound notebook keeps all your work together for easy use. If you have been keeping a research notebook, use a major part of it to record reading notes. This will make other research material (research schedule, observations, survey questions, etc.) more accessible for review when working with your notes or their sources. You can cut and paste various sections of the notebook pages together for easy reference when you start to write your paper.

Photocopies.   Photocopied materials are not notes but the basis for notes. Nonetheless, considerations of length, complexity, availability, or your need for precise data may make it necessary to photocopy portions of printed research sources. Photocopying is a valuable aid to any researcher, though overreliance on it can become expensive and doubly time consuming: You will still have to reread the contents of photocopied material and make notes on it before writing your paper.

Figure 7.4 shows the kind of notes Nancy Prado made on a photocopy of material about jury duty in Los Angeles County. She decided to photo-

Before 1968

During the last 25 years, juries across the nation have undergone major changes. Before the passage of a 1968 federal law, <u>most jurors were chosen by a jury commissioner from a select group of upstanding citizens in the community.</u> They were mostly white, middle-class men. Today's juries contain more women and more minorities.

How many serve

Only (17%) of the adult American public has served on a trial, according to the 1990 study, and only (45%) have been called to serve.

Juror qualifications

Los Angeles county selects jurors from voter registration and Department of Motor Vehicles lists. The county mails more than 3 million questionnaires a year to determine who is eligible to serve. Jurors must be citizens, 18 or older, and have no felony record.

Gloria Gomez, manager of juror services for the county, said only 15% to 18% of the residents mail back the questionnaires.

Jury pool #

The office of the jury commissioner then mails out about 400,000 to 500,000 summons a year. About half of those who are summoned perform jury duty, according to Gomez.

FIGURE 7.4 A photocopy on which notes have been added in the margin

Source: From Maura Dolan, "Demographics Favor Racial Parity for O. J. Simpson Jury," *Los Angeles Times* 25 Sept. 1994: A22. Copyright, 1994, Los Angeles Times. Reprinted by permission.

copy the page, rather than record notes from it, because of the many statistics it included and her uncertainty about which ones she might want later for her paper. In this way, Nancy used the photocopied material to supplement her notetaking, not replace it.

On Computer. Computers can make storing and using research notes both easier and more difficult. On the positive side, storing research notes on a computer allows you to revise them with follow-up commentary, to reorganize them according to developing subtopics, and to merge them once you get to the writing stage. A separate file for sources listed in the working bibliography is also a good idea: You can update and alphabetize the list as you need, adding it to the paper when you have finished writing the text. If your computer software program has outlining features, you can use the topic headings from notecards to create a working outline.

There are also some drawbacks to keeping your notes on computer. Unless you have regular access to a computer and are in the habit of working consistently with one for your academic needs, you may need to use an additional method of notetaking, as well. Remember that you will not always have a computer available wherever you do research, and you will regularly have to transcribe handwritten notes and other collected data into the computer almost daily. Unless your computer program does it for you, you will also need to make back-up copies of all your material on a regular basis to prevent loss due to a machine or program malfunction.

Too many methods of storing information result in misplacing notes and wasting time trying to consolidate results. For all your notetaking, avoid using loose sheets of paper, more than one notebook, or too great a mixture of ways to store your research notes. Choose a means of storing notes that prevents loss while still allowing flexibility, organization, and ease of use.

Types of Notes

Your notes are a literal record of what you learn about the research topic. In addition to recording your findings, taking notes prompts you to read sources critically. In the act of reading and taking notes, you organize and reinterpret information for yourself, thereby understanding it better. (A drawback to photocopying materials is that it postpones this important critical process.)

Different research sources and your individual responses to them will require varying kinds of notes. Though books and periodicals will supply the majority of your note content, notetaking will also be important for recording what you learn from other kinds of sources: Onsite observations; pamphlets and other literature; responses to interview questions; films, radio, and television broadcasts; and public speeches or lectures will also require good written notes. While your way of recording information will vary with each kind of source, the following methods are basic to all notetaking:

- Summary
- Paraphrase
- Direct quotation
- Combination notes

As this lists suggests, the majority of your notes will represent a condensation of information. You should know the differences among these major kinds of notes and how to use them effectively in your research, including giving proper acknowledgment to your sources.

Summary.   In writing a summary, you reduce what was originally said in a source by restating it more briefly in your own words. You summarize original material by eliminating unimportant ideas and condensing essential ones to a single statement or two. Since your goal is to reduce without distorting meaning, you must understand the original well before attempting to summarize it.

How much you summarize from a source depends upon your purpose. You may summarize large portions of a work, such as the action of a novel, the development of a scientific theory, or the content of a journal article. To summarize large amounts of content, read the whole piece closely, at least twice. Take notes as you read, looking for main ideas or subdivisions of the content (see Close Reading, earlier in this chapter). Then combine your notes by reducing their content into a few sentences that summarize the whole. Read your summary carefully several times. Add or delete content until you have condensed the original without distorting or leaving out important parts.

In summarizing any entire work or large portions of it, your aim is to reduce the whole piece by including only the main ideas. Smaller portions of a work are summarized in much the same way, though you can be more selective about what you summarize. In most research notetaking, you need to condense and record only the information most relevant to your topic, research question, or thesis. This could mean summarizing only a few sentences or a single paragraph, if that is all the information relevant to your research.

Mark Stevenson used such selective notetaking to summarize information from one of the sources he read for his paper on television talk shows. The following paragraph from that source provided him with statistical data about the number of children watching talk shows:

> Given their popularity with adult viewers, it is not surprising that children are exposed to Talk TV, but the actual number of child viewers is alarming. In 1990, there were 448,000 children and 742,000 teenagers watching Oprah, 400,000 viewing Geraldo, and another 500,000 apiece tuning into Sally and Phil. Even with overlap, these numbers make it clear that millions of our country's children are soaking up the same doses of pathology, perversity, and interpersonal aggravation that their adult counterparts tune in to every day. And for every problem the shows create for adult viewers, there are other and more serious troubles for children.
>
> —Jeanne Albronda Heaton and Nona Leigh Wilson, *Tuning in Trouble: Talk TV's Destructive Impact on Mental Health* (San Francisco: Jossey-Bass, 1995) 169.

Mark recorded his summary of this paragraph on a notecard with the heading Children Viewers. Notice that in writing the following summary, he omitted irrelevant information from the paragraph but did record a quotation, which he later incorporated into his research paper:

Children's audience probably as large as adult. In 1990, 448,000 to 742,000 children were watching Oprah. Between 400,000 and 500,000 were watching Geraldo, Sally, and Phil Donahue. Children are "soaking up the same doses of pathology, perversity, and interpersonal aggravation" (169) as adults.

While the purpose of a summary is to condense an original, it should not be so abbreviated as to lose its usefulness later. Mark's summary included several specific facts as well as the author and page number from the original source. He recorded the other source information needed for preparing the Works Cited list on a separate bibliography card (see Chapter 4). Like Mark, you may occasionally want to summarize information using fragmentary phrases—such as *Children's audience probably as large as adult*—or your own shorthand for reducing language. It is best, however, to write summaries in complete sentences. Doing so will help you better grasp the content as you record it and ensure that you will be able to understand it later.

Paraphrase.   A good paraphrase clarifies a source's content by recasting it into your own words. Whereas a summary seeks to condense or eliminate length, a paraphrase restates the original almost line by line. The result is that a paraphrase is usually about the same length as the original, but the words are your own. Remember that proper citation of the source must always accompany any paraphrase.

You should paraphrase whenever the language or content of the original cannot be adequately summarized. This often happens with technical and scientific material, in which the detailed content or language may be unsuitable for condensing to notes or for use in your paper. At other times, you may paraphrase by combining original details and language with your own wording in order to shorten the content. In general, paraphrase whenever doing so will make your notes more useful and the information clearer to your paper's readers.

The following excerpt demonstrates material suitable for paraphrase. The example is from an article published in *TESOL Quarterly*, a journal written for linguists and (as the title acronym indicates) Teachers of English to Speakers of Other Languages (TESOL). The paragraph summarizes research on the relationship between notetaking and learning by students who are native and nonnative speakers of English:

> There appears, in other words, to be a need to rehearse information noted down rather than just to take notes on information imparted via lecture format. Incorporating a review-of-notes condition into the present design might have yielded quite different results and might have tested the delayed effect, not just

the immediate effect, of the encoding hypothesis. In sum, results of the present study suggest that note taking without opportunity for review of notes is of questionable utility for either American or international lecture attendees.

—Patricia Dunkel, Shitala Mishra, and David Berliner, "Effects of Note Taking, Memory, and Language Proficiency on Lecture Learning for Native and Nonnative Speakers of English," *TESOL Quarterly* 23 (1989): 547.

The language and content in this excerpt may be appropriate for the author's intentions and the journal's audience. For the purposes of notetaking, however, and for better understanding by your paper's readers, the passage should be paraphrased.

A good paraphrase effectively recasts original language for better clarity and readability. A poor paraphrase simply changes the words of the original or mixes the original with rephrased material. Compare the following paraphrase with the original paragraph above:

A poor paraphrase

There seems, then, to be a necessity for rehearsing note content instead of just taking notes on lecture information. Including a note review in the current plan may have given different results and tested not only the immediate effect but also the delayed effect of the encoding hypothesis. In summary, the findings of this study suggest that taking notes without the chance to review them has questionable usefulness for American or foreign lecture students ("Effects of Note Taking" 547).

This is a poor paraphrase because it merely substitutes new words for the language of the original. A good paraphrase, on the other hand, translates the *meaning* of the original by effectively recasting its language into clearer form:

A good paraphrase

Students need to review lecture notes rather than simply write down information presented in lecture. If this research study had included the practice of reviewing notes, the delayed as well as the immediate effect of notetaking on learning might have been tested. Overall, however, it seems that notetaking alone, without the practice of reviewing notes, may have little value for any lecture student, whether native or nonnative speaking ("Effects of Note Taking" 547).

Because you are adding your own wording and using your own sentence structures, a good paraphrase should sound like your own writing. This does not mean that you should take credit for the paraphrased material, however. Notice that the preceding paraphrase correctly cites the title (shortened for convenience) and page number of the original source. Be sure to record the page number of any paraphrased original on your notecard, and cite the source for any paraphrase when it appears in your paper.

Direct Quotation. Use a quotation when you need to record a source's precise language, whether spoken or written. The emphasis here is on *need:* You should quote because the original language is necessary or the sense cannot be conveyed by other words. You may need to use quotations for the following purposes:

1. *To capture individual authority or interest:* An authority, a well-known person, or another individual should be quoted when his or her own words would be more important or more interesting to your reader. For example:

> Hillary Rodham Clinton probably spoke for all working mothers when she asked, "What power wouldn't I trade for a little more time with my family?" (Carlson 36).
> —Margaret Carlson, "At the Center of Power," *Time* 10 May 1993: 28–36.

> Dr. Robert Webber, head of research for the New York Cancer Institute, says a person's attitude "can influence susceptibility to disease more than most of us realize" (102).

> "I got my father to let me ride the mule to school one day. As I came over the hill toward the schoolhouse, a cub black bear came out of the bushes behind us. The mule turned and saw the bear, gave a sort of loud snort, and took off! I could hardly hold on, but I did. The next thing I knew, the mule and me had raced through the front door of the schoolhouse and landed smack in the middle of a geography lesson" (Satler 129).

Used in appropriate amounts to illustrate points or demonstrate character, direct quotations from individuals add liveliness and credibility to your paper's discussion.

2. *To ensure accuracy:* Exact language is often needed to define special terms, describe conditions, or report results. The precise language that scientific, medical, and technical sources rely upon for accuracy cannot always be preserved in a summary or paraphrase. In these cases, it is usually best to use direct quotations:

A complex number in trigonometry can be represented on a two-dimensional diagram: "The horizontal axis is the real axis and the vertical axis is the imaginary axis. The number $\underline{a} + \underline{b}i$ is represented by a point drawn $\underline{a}$ units to the right of the origin and $\underline{b}$ units up" (Glenn 82).

"Ibuprofen is one of several nonsteroid anti-inflammatory drugs used to reduce inflammation, relieve pain, or reduce fever. All nonsteroid anti-inflammatory drugs share the same side effects and may be used by patients who cannot tolerate Aspirin" (Simon and Silverman 317).

Legal discussions may require quotations to ensure strict interpretation or adherence to given laws:

Our Constitution states that "No person shall be convicted of treason unless on the testimony of two witnesses to the same overt act, or on confession in open court" (III, 3).
—U.S. Constitution, Art. III, Sect. 3.

The court decreed that, in cases of divorce, an indignity is any "affront to the personality of another or a lack of reverence for the personality of one's spouse" (Gifis 284).
—Steven H. Gifis, *Law Dictionary* (New York: Barton's, 1984) 284.

In instances such as these, you may need quotations to ensure precise meaning or to emphasize the accuracy of your own understanding of the material.

3. *To illustrate unique language:* Sometimes language is more important for its uniqueness or emotional power than its ability to convey meaning. In discussing a literary work, for instance, a quotation demonstrates the author's use of language to create meaning and tone. You might quote an example like the following from John Steinbeck's *Grapes of Wrath* to illustrate how he describes the onset of the great drought that created the "dust bowl" conditions of his novel's setting:

"The dawn came, but no day. In the gray sky a red sun appeared, a dim circle that gave a little light, like dusk; and as that day advanced, the dusk slipped back toward darkness, and the wind cried and whimpered over the fallen corn" (Steinbeck 2–3).
—John Steinbeck, *The Grapes of Wrath* (New York: Viking, 1939) 2–3.

In other instances, a memorable phrase or a particularly telling remark can often reveal more than any paraphrase could capture:

Those of us who are well fed may find it difficult to understand that people who are homeless are grateful for whatever is available. As Benjamin Franklin once said, "Hunger never saw bad bread" (40).
—Benjamin Franklin, *Poor Richard's Almanac, 1773* (Philadelphia: Rosenbach, 1977) 40.

As government cutbacks in social and educational programs increase, the need for volunteers becomes even greater. We should remember the words of John F. Kennedy, who said, "Ask not what your country can do for you—ask what you can do for your country."
—John F. Kennedy, Inaugural Address, Washington, DC, 21 Jan. 1961.

Who had the right to sign memos for the president in his absence? "Everybody and nobody," according to one White House source (Miller 91).

These examples demonstrate situations in which the use of direct quotations is appropriate and effective. Remember, however, that too many quotations will dilute the quality of your discussion. By depending on quotation instead of paraphrase, you will decrease your analysis of the material during notetaking. Furthermore, by including too many quotations in your paper, you may bury your own ideas and make your readers do all the thinking. Avoid excessive quotation by summarizing and paraphrasing whenever possible. If a quotation adds something that a paraphrase or summary cannot, be sure it fits one of the situations described here.

Whenever you use a quotation, be sure to quote all words and punctuation *exactly as they appear in the original.* Mark your notecard clearly to indicate that the material is a direct quotation and to show all necessary punctuation and page numbers. Notice that each of the examples given earlier cites the source for the quoted material. Such citation is an absolute requirement any time you use a quotation in your paper.

Combination Notes.   Combining summary, paraphrase, and quotation in your notes or the paper itself allows for adapting source material to your own style and fitting it into a discussion. When combining notetaking methods, take care to identify for yourself which notes are summary, paraphrase, or quotation so as not to misrepresent the material later in your paper.

Plagiarism

Unfortunately, beginning writers of research papers sometimes fall into committing *plagiarism,* using another person's language or ideas without acknowledgment. Some plagiarism results from borrowing from a source and consequently forgetting to acknowledge its author in the paper. At other times, plagiarism occurs because the student writer purposely wishes to take credit for the words or ideas of another. Intentional or not, however, all plagiarism is theft: It is taking what belongs to someone else and using it dishonestly.

To avoid commiting plagiarism in your research paper, make sure any notes you take are complete and accurate and that you will be able to acknowledge their sources later. As you write the paper, remember that any time you use someone else's words, expressions, or ways of thinking about something, you must give credit to the source. You will be committing plagiarism if you do not.

Acknowledging a Source. To acknowledge a source, name it at the same time you present its words or ideas in your paper. Whether the language presented is your own or the source's makes no difference. The idea is as important as the words used to express it. Notice how sources are named directly within the text in each of these examples:

MLA (Modern Language Association) Style

The first life forms probably began appearing about 3,000 million years ago in a kind of "prebiotic soup of organic molecules" (Gregory 233).

People who argue for legalizing drugs believe that they are not really as dangerous as we think or that truly unsafe drugs would never be widely used (Nadelmann 56).

APA (American Psychological Association) Style

While classification of children's drawings shows some similarity among individuals (Kellog, 1970), Golomb (1981) emphasizes the difficulty of interpreting development by comparisons with models.

Number-Reference Style

If we assume that phobic neuroses can be effectively treated by desensitization,[1] there still remains the problem of treating multiple afflictions. Roth's work in this area suggests several useful approaches.[2]

(See Chapters 10–12 for instruction on documentation following these various styles.)

In addition, each source you cite in the text of the paper must be listed on the Works Cited or References page. If you fail to acknowledge your sources in these ways, you are guilty of plagiarism, which can have such serious consequences as a failing grade on the research paper, failing the course, or even being expelled from college.

Avoiding Plagiarism.   Because of the ethical and practical seriousness of plagiarism, give scrupulous attention to avoiding it throughout your
research. Following these guidelines will keep you from making mistakes
that might result in unintentional plagiarism:

1. *Understand and use correct notetaking methods.* Know the differences
among summary, paraphrase, and quotation as well as when and how to
use them correctly. (See the preceding discussion for the proper uses of
these methods.)

2. *Take accurate and legible notes.* Record page numbers clearly for any
material you summarize, paraphrase, or quote as well as for any figures or
uncommonly known facts you borrow. Annotate your notes by adding
comments such as *my words, quoted, summary, her idea,* and so forth
(see Figure 7.2). Remember that faint periods and ambiguous quotation
marks will later be easily overlooked or misread. Use heavy, bold punctuation, especially for quotation marks and any punctuation included within
quotations.

3. *Know what to document.* You must cite in your paper's text and document in the Works Cited or References page(s) the source for any words,
expressions, ideas, organization of ideas, facts, or lines of thinking you borrow or adapt. This means that your notes will always need to include the
title, author's name, and publication facts about the source as well as specific page number(s) for any information you record. (See Chapter 4 on
what to record on bibliography cards for books and magazines.)

Whenever you quote directly, for example, or even paraphrase what
another writer has said, you must cite the source for that material. Similarly,
if you state in your paper that "three-fourths of the American public favor
raising the tax on cigarettes," tell where you got such information. If you
rely particularly upon one source for your extended description, let's say,
of how a typical nuclear power plant operates, give credit to that source. In
each of these cases, make sure that your notes include specific page numbers and other documentation information you will need in the paper.
(Chapters 10–12 describe necessary documentation information and forms
for various kinds of sources.)

Your paper will not need to document information that is *common
knowledge*—ideas or facts that are generally well known or basic to a field
of study. Understandably, you may not be able to judge what information
is considered common until you have done a fair amount of research on
your topic. Thus, when beginning research on *dinosaurs,* for example,
you may not know that they lived during what is called the Mesozoic Era.
Similarly, when first investigating the topic *heroin,* you may not know that
the main effects of this narcotic occur in both the nervous and digestive
systems. After you have consulted three or four sources on your topic,

however, you will be able to recognize what information is common knowledge.

It is always a good idea, of course, to record complete documentation for any information you find. Do so during initial reading and notetaking until you have a sense of what is common knowledge for your subject. As you later write the paper, however, remember that you should not cite sources for commonly known facts and ideas.

4. *Make a bibliographic card for every note source.* You cannot give credit to a source if you lack the information to do so. Fill out a bibliography card for each source you take notes from, and *consistently* record the title, author's name, publishing date, and other data necessary to acknowledge the work in your paper. (See Chapter 4 on what to record for various sources.)

5. *Acknowledge sources in your paper.* Follow the correct form for citing sources in the body of your paper as well as for listing them on the Works Cited or References pages (see Chapters 10–12).

A final word: Do not underestimate the potential problem of plagiarism, but do not let it distort your perception of the research paper, either. You are encouraged to use and build upon the work of others—though naturally, your paper should not simply become a patchwork quilt of other people's words and ideas. Borrow and always acknowledge when you must, but remember that your own ideas are the most important ingredient of the paper.

Critically Evaluating Sources

The critical evaluation of source materials will continue throughout your research. As your understanding of your topic changes, so, too, will your estimation of your sources. In turn, your opinion of each source's value or authority will shape the way you think about the topic and read or take notes.

Consequently, evaluation of sources should not come only after your research has been completed but before and during your reading, as well. This is because in thinking judgmentally about a source, you also think critically about its content. You may decide not to bother reading a source at all or to take entirely different kinds of notes because of what you decide about its value. By consulting the opinions of others about sources, you can learn which ideas are considered important or what others have found controversial. You can study sources more efficiently because you know what to look for as you read and take notes.

Developing Critical Judgment

In part, your judgment of a source's authority and value to your research will develop out of your own reading in the field. The more you learn about your subject, the more perceptive you will become about sources. Some that were impressive at the start of your research may eventually seem inadequate; the importance of others will emerge only as your research becomes more complete.

To gauge the reliability of an individual author's work, critically assess it in terms of its overall effectiveness in areas such as these:

- *Fairness:* Does the author demonstrate knowledge and consideration of other viewpoints and research in the field? Is there discussion of opposing viewpoints as well as application and citation of other works or authorities?
- *Logic:* Has the author supported his or her ideas with valid evidence? Is the presentation logical, and has the author avoided bias and common fallacies of logic?
- *Evidence:* Do the examples and other evidence presented fairly reflect current data? Is there a clear separation of fact and opinion?
- *Authority:* Does the author refer to qualified experts or establish his or her own credentials to speak with authority on the subject?

You should apply these and other similar criteria as you begin to take notes from research sources and also when you begin writing your paper and integrating source material into the text. Give extra consideration to how you use information from a source that appears unreliable in any of the areas described above.

Consulting Other Opinions

Because you cannot read everything written on your research topic, you will want to consult those sources who have the greatest authority or whose ideas are most valuable to your discussion. While your own broad reading on a topic will help judge the expertise and usefulness of some sources, you may also need opinions from others more familiar with the field. After locating a particular source, such as a book or a scholarly journal article, use your library's general reference sources to find out how others reacted to it.

Using Book Reviews.   Critical discussions like those published in the *New York Times Book Review,* the *Times Literary Supplement,* and scholarly journals give you the opinions of experts about a work's strengths and weaknesses. Book reviews can help you learn more about a topic as well as about the book and its author's standing in the field.

PRESTON, RICHARD. The hot zone. 300p il $23/Can$31
1994 Random House
   614.5   1. Ebola virus 2. Epidemiology 3. Animal ex-
perimentation
   ISBN 0-679-43094-6   LC 94-13415

SUMMARY: This volume focuses on the viruses Ebola and
Marburg, named "for the places where they were first de-
tected, [and] classified as 'Biosafety Level 4' because they
are more lethal than HIV but also highly contagious. This
is the story of their recent escape from the . . . African rain-
forest to big centres of human population via modern roads
and planes. . . . Ebola and Marburg are filoviruses or thread
viruses. . . . [Preston argues] that these viruses have
'jumped species' from monkeys to humans at precisely the
time when human activity is threatening the habitat and
survival of other primates." (New Sci) Glossary.

FIGURE 7.5 A sample entry from *Book Review Digest*

Source: From *Book Review Digest,* Vol. 91, No. 5, August 1995, p. 438. Copyright © 1995 by
The H. W. Wilson Company. Reprinted with permission.

The most useful resource for general book reviews is *Book Review Digest (BRD)* (New York: H. W. Wilson, 1905–date). Drawing upon reviews
published in nearly one hundred general periodicals and scholarly journals, *BRD* summarizes a book and any reviews written about it (see Figure
7.5). Because *BRD* usually includes several reviews for each work listed,
use it to avoid having to consult multiple sources to learn about a book or
its author. If you need more information than summarized versions provide, use *BRD* to locate the complete reviews in their original publications.
Note that *BRD* is also available online (1983–date) through DIALOG or
CompuServe's IQuest.

In addition to *Book Review Digest,* reviews of scholarly books and articles are available in most of the specialized indexes discussed in Chapter 3.
The following indexes are also useful for general and scholarly works:

Book Review Index. New York: H. W. Wilson, 1905–date.
Current Book Review Citations. New York: H. W. Wilson, 1976–date.
Index to Book Reviews in the Humanities. Williamston, MI: Thomson,
   1960–date.
Technical Book Review Index. New York: Willis, 1961–date.

Using Citation Indexes. The number of times an author has published in a field, which journals have carried his or her work, and how others have valued it are all important considerations in evaluating a source.
Computer-produced periodical indexes such as *Arts & Humanities Citation
Index, Science Citation Index,* and *Social Science Citation Index* provide
information such as the following:

- What other current and past work an individual has authored
- What other authors have cited the work, as well as where and when
- Where a work has been reviewed
- Where follow-up studies, corrections, or applications have been described
- Where the article is summarized as an abstract in the major journals for the field

Available in print or online, citation indexes can supply information to help judge a work's originality, authority, and application. Citation indexes list mainly journal articles, but some books are included, as well. Remember that citation indexes are usually organized as three different volumes: *permuterm index, source index,* and *citation index.* Using key words from a work's title or the name of an author, you can use any one of the indexes to locate information. (See Chapter 4 on citation indexes and how to use them.)

Evaluation Criteria

While it is essential to consult the work of recognized authorities in order to integrate their ideas with your own thinking, not all your research information will come with identifiable credentials. In general, a source will be useful to your research if it meets one or more of the following criteria:

1. It was written by a reliable authority whose methods and reasoning appear valid. Not everything you use in your research has to (or should) be written by someone with a PhD, but the author's education, experience with the topic, and reputation should play a major part in your evaluation and use of a work.

2. It offers facts and ideas other sources do not.

3. It sets forth facts and ideas that do not contradict known concepts or other works without good evidence.

4. It demonstrates knowledge and consideration of other viewpoints and research in the field. Look for discussion of opposing ideas and also the application and citation of others' works.

5. It is current in terms of both publication date and information. Remember that knowledge changes more rapidly in some fields than others. Ideas in the humanities, for example, tend to remain consistent longer than those in the sciences, where constant research and new technology change existing knowledge daily.

Apply these criteria both when you begin to take notes from your research sources and when you begin writing your paper and integrating source material into the text.

W O R K I N G   W I T H   O T H E R S

The diligence required for reading and taking notes can seem less demanding when you share your progress and results with others. As often as possible during this period, take time to discuss your work with a friend, or compare your reading and notetaking with those of a classmate. Telling others about what you have read will give you a better perspective on what you have done so far. Consider these suggestions as you share your research reading and notetaking with another.

- Compare your techniques for skimming and close reading with those used by a classmate. What differences can you identify that may suggest ways to improve your own approaches? Can you provide the other person with any tips?

- Discuss the notes you take and compare your method of notetaking with that of your classmate. Does a comparison reveal you are taking the right kinds of notes? Are you taking too few? Too many?

- Find out how someone else stores his or her research notes. Can you suggest any ways to improve upon your friend's method or your own? What problems have you each had with notetaking? Were you able to solve them?

- Show the person you are working with a sample of how you record a quotation or paraphrase in your notes. Does your method seem adequate? Discuss the concept of plagiarism. Do you both understand what it means? What has your instructor said about it?

- Compare your evaluations of the sources from which you have both read and taken notes. Have you used the same criteria to evaluate such sources? Are there others that would also be useful?

- Using *Book Review Digest* or library citation indexes can be difficult. Discuss these sources with your collaborator to make sure you both understand their benefits and how to use them.

Sharing your thoughts about your reading will help you to understand and to evaluate your sources more thoroughly than thinking about them alone. Continue discussing these and any other aspects of your research with a classmate or friend.

CHAPTER **8**

Planning
Your Paper

You should no sooner write a research paper without having a plan than you should build a house without having a blueprint. Depending upon your writing skills and the way you prefer to work, a plan can range from a rough sketch of your major ideas to a detailed outline. Planning the paper will get you started writing and help direct your efforts any time you are unsure of how next to proceed. Rather than simply plunge into the act of writing your research paper, take the time beforehand to organize your ideas and plan the best use of your research. Once you have a plan, you will be prepared to adapt your writing methods to carrying it out.

Using Your Research Notes

Plan your paper by first reviewing notes you recorded from library materials and other research sources. Your goal at this point is to get an overall view of your topic, as represented in the notes. Reviewing the notes will also show what you have to work with in terms of ideas and information for the paper.

Arranging and Studying Your Notes

Read carefully through the notes several times, studying their contents and observing subheadings and other clusters of information. Relate the contents of each set of notes to the information in other sets as you proceed. The goal here is to see how your notes—all the pieces of information you have collected—fit together. What picture do they make in terms of answering the research question?

You may find it useful to merge separate groups of notes with previously different subheadings or to arrange the notes in a particular order, such as a chronological or cause-effect sequence. (Having notes on cards makes such rearranging easy, as does having them on computer. If you use a notebook to record notes, cut out each section so you can rearrange the notes as needed.) In your review of the notes, look for examples, anecdotes, quotations, and statistics that appear particularly useful or striking. Consider how these and other content relate to your research question or a preliminary thesis statement.

Reviewing the Research Question

Although the planning stage is not the place to begin a new research topic, you may need to modify the focus of your research question and its answer before proceeding further (see Chapter 3). After reviewing your research notes, take time to consider what research question and answer they best support. If you began your research by asking What effect does early fame have upon the adult lives of child stars? a review of your notes may suggest a different approach: What factors contribute to successful adult lives for child stars? A slight change such as this may promote fuller use of your research material and help you frame a more precise final thesis statement.

Reviewing the Preliminary Thesis Statement

The preliminary thesis statement you devised earlier to guide your research may still be sufficient, or it may need to be revised to reflect your note material and any modification in the original research question (see Chapter 3). Write the research question and thesis statement at the top of a notebook page or other sheet of paper. Underneath, list the topic headings from your notecards. As you do so, include under the various headings the major ideas or examples that should be part of the paper. Do not worry too much whether you list information in some final order or if it will indeed be part of your paper. At this stage, you simply want to see how major ideas relate and how accurately the thesis statement describes the note material. As you compare the research question, note material, and preliminary thesis, consider the extent to which they relate. Modify the preliminary thesis as needed to match the research question as well as the ideas and information on the notecards.

Devising a Final Thesis Statement

The thesis statement asserts the main idea controlling your paper's content and organization. In turn, every part of the paper's content supports the thesis statement by explaining it further or offering evidence and examples that show it is accurate. Your thesis will grow out of the thinking you do about the research topic and from deciding on a focus for the information collected from your sources.

A good thesis statement is not devised quickly. It will probably be revised several times before and during the writing of the paper so that it conforms to the evolving content. You may also need to add or delete content during the writing stage in order to support the thesis statement more closely. Good planning of the thesis before you write can help you avoid making too many alterations later.

Writing an Effective Thesis Statement

State the thesis statement as a single sentence, perhaps as two, if necessary. Your goal is to convey your main point concisely but fully. That will help the reader recognize the relationship among ideas and the emphasis of your paper.

Most thesis statements are expressed as *claims,* argumentative assertions about which people will disagree. There are three types of claims:

1. Claims about *facts* argue that something exists, causes something else, or is defined in a particular way:

Alien beings are making routine flights over the United States.

TV talk shows are corrupting Americans' morals.

Freedom of the press means complete freedom to print any information of interest to the public.

2. Claims about *value* make subjective statements about the worth of something:

The Internet will have a profound impact on education.

Billy Budd remains the finest example of Melville's sense of justice.

Current research about the causes of Alzheimer's disease will benefit future generations.

3. Claims about *policy* state what action should be taken:

Limits should be imposed on congressional terms of office.

Americans should be encouraged to carpool.

Additional funding needs to be provided for early childhood education programs.

Like any effective argument, a claim needs to be supported by evidence and a clear pattern of reasoning that logically connects the evidence to the claim. If your claim has developed with your research and notetaking, you will have this support.

Remember, too, that a good thesis (or claim) invites readers' interest. Rather than state the obvious, the thesis should promise a discussion worthy of the time needed to read the paper. Avoid weak thesis statements that only summarize known facts and conditions, that are too general to state clear arguments about topics, or that state intentions:

Weak (summarizes known facts)	AIDS is a usually fatal disease in which the body's immune system fails to resist infection.
Better	People with AIDS should have legal access to promising new drugs without having to wait for their approval by the U.S. Food and Drug Administration.
Weak (too general)	The drug problem is something we need to solve.
Better	Antidrug campaigns are most effective when designed and targeted for specific local populations.
Weak (intention only)	This paper will show that the moral content of children's cartoons is too ambiguous to present acceptable behavior models.
Better	The moral content of children's cartoons is too ambiguous to present acceptable behavior models.

As the "Better" examples above demonstrate, a good thesis statement focuses the paper's discussion on a central idea. In most cases, you will need to experiment several times to find the exact wording for the thesis, and you may need to reword it again during or after writing the paper. The more focused you can make the thesis when planning the paper, the easier writing the body of the paper will be.

Reviewing Your Paper's Purpose

The overall purpose of your paper is determined by what you plan to tell your audience and your strategy for presenting information on the topic. A research paper that primarily intends to persuade the reader of the author's viewpoint about a topic has an *argumentative* purpose; one that minimizes expression of the author's ideas and seeks mainly to present information for the reader's benefit is *informative*. In order to organize your discussion material effectively, you should plan your paper with one of these two major purposes in mind.

An Argumentative Purpose.   In an argumentative paper, remember to keep your position on the topic consistent and clearly related to the thesis throughout. Your thesis *statement,* or a form of it, should appear more than once in the introduction and perhaps only once again in the conclusion of the paper. The thesis *idea,* expressed in varying ways to match the context, should be a continuous concept that runs more or less explicitly through each section of the argumentative paper. An argumentative paper about the challenges of raising an adopted child, for example, would emphasize the thesis throughout the discussion:

Introduction leads into thesis

. . . Raising an adopted child can pose unexpected problems for even the most loving of parents.

Topic sentence restates thesis idea

One difficulty adoptive parents have to overcome is an often unrecognized desire that the adopted child is actually theirs. "I feel like she is one of my own" is a warm expression of closeness, but it may also reflect the wish that the adopted child had been born into the family. . . .

Successive paragraphs develop thesis further

Raising a child of another race presents adoptive parents with additional and sometimes overwhelming challenges. Experts, in fact, are divided over the wisdom of interracial adoptions. . . .

Becoming the parent of an adopted child can get even more difficult when there are other biologically parented children in the family. . . .

Thesis statement idea is continued

The difficulties of raising an adopted child are certainly real, but they are not insurmountable. When parents learn ahead of time . . .

An Informative Purpose. In an informative paper, the thesis will receive less emphasis than the information you provide the reader. Keep the content focused on information rather than issues, and maintain a reasonable balance in the material you provide about each subject discussed. To avoid stuffing an informative paper with unneeded material, create topic sentences that control the content and focus of all paragraphs.

Notice how the following discussion blurs its informative purpose by introducing facts and issues (here, shown boldfaced) not related to the topic sentence or the writer's purpose:

Informative topic sentence	Several studies document sustained changes in sexual behavior within the gay male population resid-
Irrelevant facts and issues	ing in various U.S. cities. **Researchers had difficulty gathering certain kinds of data because some gay men are hesitant to share information or identify themselves as gay, evidence that social disapproval is still a concern for many gay males in American society.** Anti-AIDS programs seem to be working, as shown by contrasting the results of a 1984 study of San Francisco men with those found more recently in a New York study showing an even greater decline in risk-related activity.

Which Purpose Is Appropriate? Deciding whether your paper's purpose is argumentative or informative depends upon your research assignment, your research material, and how important your own interpretation, viewpoint, or evaluation is to the discussion. Your research material will determine, for example, whether you are prepared to argue for or against allowing females to serve in U.S. combat forces (argumentative paper) or should instead report on the growth of opportunities for women in the armed services today (informative paper).

Comparing the Purposes of Sample Papers

Because Nancy Prado's paper on the need to reform the American system of jury selection seeks to persuade readers of her research conclusions, it has an argumentative purpose (see her paper in Chapter 10). Similarly, Mark Stevenson's paper on television talk shows is argumentative in that he demonstrates how these programs have likely gone too far to survive the backlash by the great numbers of people who find them offensive (see Appendix A). Both of these writers recognized that their topics provided enough unsettled questions or controversy to call for further discussion and reasoned conclusions.

Daniel Nguyen's research paper reviewing the current literature on AIDS research, on the other hand, is an informative paper. Daniel seeks to inform his readers more than convince them of any particular viewpoint (see Appendix A).

Using Your Paper's Purpose for Planning

Unless your assignment requires a particular purpose for your paper, decide whether it will be more effective as an argumentative or as an informative paper. Keep your purpose in mind as you construct an outline for the paper.

Working with an Outline

An *outline* is a tool to assist you in organizing and writing the paper. You will understand and appreciate the use of an outline best by keeping certain principles in mind:

■ An outline assists you by organizing material and providing a pattern to follow as you write. It gives your reader an overview of the paper's discussion and major ideas.

■ There are two general types of outlines: informal and formal. You may wish to use the informal type for your own writing needs, perhaps using it later to create a formal outline of the paper. A formal outline is more effective for planning a paper, especially a longer one, but it also takes more preparation.

■ Some writers work best by drafting a working plan or outline before they write and making changes as needed. Others prefer to complete the outline after the paper is finished, using it as a means to check the paper's organization and emphases. You should follow the practice that works best for you.

■ Since writing is a creative and recursive process, the outline and the paper's content will necessarily change at times to consistently reflect each other.

Both informal and formal outlines are discussed in the following pages. Which type you work with depends upon your writing preferences and the requirements of your research assignment.

An Informal Outline

If you are not required to make a formal outline for your research paper, you may want to work from an informal one. Though such an outline is informal and intended for your use only, it still requires careful planning to be useful.

Begin by writing your paper's title at the top of a work page, with the final thesis right below it for easy reference. After reviewing your notecards, list the major categories of ideas for the paper in a logical sequence, perhaps under headings such as Introduction, Body, and Conclusion to get started or until more specific major headings occur to you. It will probably help if you number the categories and leave enough space between them to add supporting material from notes later.

Since the informal outline is solely for your own use, make notations, additions, or deletions as you need to while organizing and writing the paper. Under the proper subheadings, include important facts, dates, and examples that you want to include in the paper. Feel free to write full sentences: At some point, you may want to add them directly to the paper.

Figure 8.1 shows the informal outline for Nancy Prado's paper on the need to reform the American system of jury selection. Though Nancy was required to submit a formal outline with her paper, she felt more comfortable beginning with her own loosely structured plan. She followed her informal outline to write most of the paper and then used it later to construct a formal topic outline (see later in this chapter). Nancy found her informal outline helpful to her writing, but she also recognized that the form and structure required by a formal topic outline demonstrated the organization of ideas in the paper better. In fact, she used the formal topic outline as a guide when she revised her paper's first draft. A comparison of the informal outline in Figure 8.1 with the final topic outline (see the Appendix to Chapter 10) shows the changes, additions, and deletions Nancy made when she wrote the paper.

A Formal Outline

A formal outline differs from an informal one by following a standard format and organization. The formal outline subdivides categories of information, designating each category by different letters and numbers and by separate headings. The degree of importance or inclusiveness of each head-

---

Flawed Justice: Why and How the American Jury System Must Be Reformed

Thesis: If we are to restore the public's confidence in jury decisions and in the justice system as a whole, this nation must begin by reforming the processes by which jurors are selected to render justice in the courtroom.

Introduction
- - Highly publicized trials like the O. J. Simpson case and others have undermined this nation's confidence in the jury system.
- - Surveys show that people have very little confidence in juries.

Body
1. Too few people are actually involved in serving on juries- -too homogenous
   - - most people avoid jury duty, especially educated professionals
   - - a "dumbing down" process takes place
2. Jury selection practices
   - - peremptory challenges allow attorneys to dismiss anyone, with no cause given
   - - jury consultants and the idea of "scientifically" selecting a jury (Abramson 145)
   - - some evidence that jury shaping works- -Marion Barry case, William Kennedy Smith trial
   - - Simpson trial "was over with the jury pick" (Greenburg 39)
3. Jury decisions
   - - nullification- -juries can ignore law if it leads to "unjust verdict" (Kerwin and Shaffer 140)
   - - if nullification is increasing, all the more reason to examine jury selection process
4. Juror qualifications
   - - "twelve prejudiced, gullible dolts" (Wishman ii)
   - - jurors cannot always understand instructions or the case evidence
   - - ignorance has led to bad decisions- -Brown & Willamson suit
5. Ways to remedy the problem
   - - must have all citizens take part, "no excuses" (Kaplan 59)
   - - some states are reforming jury selection and other rules- -Florida and Colorado examples
   - - legal organizations are also recommending reforms- -more technology and opposed to peremptory challenge
   - - British example

Conclusion
- - need to institute changes
- - if the jury system loses credibility, could lose the jury system

---

FIGURE 8.1   Nancy Prado's informal research paper outline

ing is shown in the outline by successive indentation; that is, the less important a category, the more it is indented under more significant categories:

I. Major heading
   A. Minor heading
      1. Detail heading
         a. Example heading
         b. Example heading
            (1) Minor example heading
            (2) Minor example heading
      2. Detail heading
   B. Minor heading
      1. Detail heading
      2. Detail heading
   C. Minor heading, etc.

Subdivisions within headings can continue even further than shown here, though most rarely need to go beyond the level of example headings (*a, b,* etc.).

As the above example demonstrates, the headings within a formal outline are each part of a whole. If you subdivide a topic heading, it must have at least two parts. Thus, every *I* will have at least a *II*, every *A* a *B*, every *1* a *2*, and so on:

I. National parks
   A. Size
      1. Public-use areas
      2. Primitive areas
   B. Types
      1. Recreation
      2. Preservation

Outlines for papers and articles written for the sciences or business may use a decimal outline, in which decimal divisions indicate successive headings:

1. Major heading
   1.1 Minor heading
      1.1.1 Detail heading
      1.1.2 Detail heading

1.1.2.1 Example heading

1.1.2.2 Example heading

1.2 Minor heading

1.2.1 Detail heading

1.2.2 Detail heading

2. Major heading, etc.

Types of Outlines

A Topic Outline.   Each heading in a topic outline is worded as a noun (College) or nounlike phrase (Applying for Admission, To Enroll in Classes). Keep all headings brief and clearly related to the major heading.

A topic outline can appear easy to compose, but be aware that its level of generality can cover up weaknesses in organization or content. The advantage to a topic outline is that it is brief and identifies the main points of discussion quickly:

I. Reduction of the rain forests

  A. Questionable benefits

    1. Increased farm land

      a. Cleared forest

      b. New farmers

    2. Timber for export

    3. Intracontinent trade

    4. Modernization

      a. New roads

      b. Hydroelectric dams

  B. Environmental effects

    1. Failure of land to support farming

    2. Loss of plant and animal species

      a. Numbers

      b. Potential uses

    3. Extermination of primitive cultures

      a. Relocation

      b. Modernization

      c. Disease

    4. Disruption of major rivers

    5. Increase in the greenhouse effect

II. International response

A Sentence Outline.   A sentence outline requires more planning and writing than a topic outline, but its completeness will prove more useful when you begin to write the paper. You can incorporate complete sentences from the outline into the paper as topic sentences for successive paragraphs:

I. Despite progress in utilizing the Amazon more productively, development is producing disastrous results with worldwide consequences.

  A. The eight nations through which the Amazon runs have had high expectations that its development would prove beneficial.

    1. The Amazon forest has been cleared to provide increased farm land.

      a. Some 20% of the state of Rondonia is under development.

      b. Farmers receive free land.

    2. The exportation of rare hardwoods has increased since restrictions have been removed.

    3. The building of roads and clearing of the Amazon River have increased the possibility for intracontinent travel and trade throughout Amazonia.

    4. The changes have helped modernize many primitive areas of the Amazon.

      a. Dams and roads are making it possible for Amazon people to reach new areas to live.

      b. Electricity has improved living conditions.

  B. Attempts to utilize the Amazon's rich forest and land, however, are having devastating effects on the region.

    1. The nutrient-poor soil will not support farm crops.

    2. Hundreds, perhaps thousands, of valuable plant and animal species have already been lost because of development.

      a. A four-mile area of forest may support over 1,500 different species of life.

      b. Many of these have valuable uses in medicine or industry.

A Paragraph Outline.   A paragraph outline provides a summary of the main parts of the outline. You should be careful to develop each paragraph fully as a unit. Remember, however, that since each paragraph in such an outline represents an entire section, it is not developed enough to fit directly into the paper:

I. Reduction of the rain forest

    A. The elimination of millions of acres of Amazon rain forest has provided many Amazonians with the opportunity of clearing and owning their own farms. In the western state of Rondonia, some 20% of the land has been cleared to provide new farm land for those who will settle there. Exports of hardwood have increased significantly from the massive reduction of the forest, and modern roads have allowed increased travel and trade. New hydroelectric dams provide electricity for hospitals and other modern advantages.

    B. Attempts to utilize the Amazon's rich forest and land, however, are having devastating effects upon the region. Since the nutrient-poor soil will not sustain crops, clearing millions of acres of forest to provide new farm land has proven dismally unsuccessful. Worse yet, hundreds, perhaps thousands, of valuable plant and animal species have already been lost because of development. A four-mile area of forest may support over 1,500 different species of life, many of which have valuable uses in medicine or industry.

Creating Your Own Outline

To begin the outline for your paper, start by arranging your notecards or other materials into main categories, assigning each a major heading designation indicated by a roman numeral. For example, an outline from notecards for a paper on current research findings about drug addiction might begin this way:

I. Definition   **Major headings**

II. Causes

III. Effects

IV. Treatment

Next, review the note material included in each major heading category. If you have enough material for at least two minor categories, add them as subdivisions. The number or letter identifier of each new level of subdivision should align with the text portion of the preceding level. Note that the *A* below aligns on the preceding entry, *Definition*. Follow this style:

   I. Definition
      A. Problem of defining   **Minor headings**
      B. Use and abuse
      C. Prevalent types
  II. Causes
      A. Social factors   **Minor headings**
      B. Psychological needs
      C. Genetic origins
 III. Effects
      A. Physiological   **Minor headings**
      B. Psychological
      C. Societal
 IV. Treatment
      A. Chemical substitutes   **Minor headings**
      B. Clinical therapy
      C. Support groups

Now examine the note material included within each of the minor categories to determine whether you have enough material to subdivide into at least two detail headings. If so, include them in the outline, using arabic numerals (*1, 2, 3,* etc.) and aligning them on the appropriate indent (as explained earlier):

   I. Definition
      A. Problem of defining
          1. APA definition   **Detail headings**
          2. WHO definition
      B. Use and abuse
          1. Stable addiction   **Detail headings**
          2. Unstable addiction
      C. Prevalent types
          1. Physiological   **Detail headings**
          2. Psychological

II. Causes

    A. Social factors

        1. Alienation   **Detail headings**

        2. Drug availability

    B. Psychological needs

        1. Personality disorders   **Detail headings**

        2. Stress and trauma

    C. Genetic origins

        1. Neurologic vulnerability   **Detail headings**

        2. Alcoholism

Most outlines do not require extensive enough development to need example headings. If you wish to include them, however, repeat the processes described above, using small letters (*a, b, c*):

II. Causes

    A. Social factors

        1. Alienation

            a. Familial   **Example headings**

           b. Economic

        2. Drug availability

            a. Cocaine   **Example headings**

           b. Alcohol

    B. Psychological needs

        1. Personality disorders

            a. Antisocial behavior   **Example headings**

           b. Low self-esteem

        2. Stress and trauma

            a. Overachievers   **Example headings**

           b. War veterans, etc.

Guidelines for the Formal Outline

■ Although not always necessary, it is a good idea to include the thesis statement at the top of the outline for a research paper (see the outline for the sample research paper in Chapter 10).

■ Align each new level of subentry below the previous-level entry (see last section and examples).

■ Align headings of the same level on the same indent. Do so by aligning the periods following the number or letter identifiers:

I. _____
   A. _____
      1. _____
      2. _____
   B. _____
II. _____
   A. _____ , etc.

■ Word headings to maintain the same parallel forms, generally as noun phrases (Addiction) or nounlike phrases such as gerund phrases (Treating addiction) or infinitive phrases (To treat addiction). Which form you use will depend upon the grammatical parallelism of your outline:

Unparallel headings
  I. Defining addiction
    A. Difficult to define
    B. Some uses and abuses
    C. Prevailing types
  II. Causes of addiction
    A. Societal
    B. Your own personality
    C. Genes also contribute

Parallel headings
  I. Definition
    A. Problem of defining
    B. Use and abuse
    C. Prevalent types
  II. Causes
    A. Social factors
    B. Psychological needs
    C. Genetic origins

Once you have completed a satisfactory outline for the paper, write your final thesis statement at the beginning of the outline, as well. The thesis statement and outline will direct your writing and help to keep the content and main idea consistent.

A Review of Basic Patterns of Development

Planning the organization and exposition of your paper's content should include considering the standard patterns that underlie most people's thinking about a subject. Writers employ these patterns to provide a structure for their ideas and for developing a discussion. Narration, description, definition, and analogy are minor patterns that can sustain brief discussions or whole paragraphs in long works. The major patterns—argumentation, comparison-and-contrast, classification, and cause-and-effect—are useful structures for longer compositions like the research paper. These four major patterns can support a paper's purpose by providing logical methods for organization, development, and expression.

The patterns of development described in the following sections may be used as outline structures for your research paper or combined with other outline models. They may also serve as development patterns for smaller sections of the outline and the paper.

Argumentation

Arguing a position requires presenting opposing viewpoints and refuting or qualifying each reason for opposition to your argument. The structure for arguing a position is often determined by the nature of the pro and con arguments discussed. The following outline demonstrates a typical argument pattern:

   I. Thesis

     A. Background

     B. Thesis position

  II. Ideas opposing thesis

     A. First reason

     B. Second reason

 III. Support for thesis (refutation)

     A. First reason

     B. Second reason

 IV. Conclusion

Another argumentation pattern might take this form:

   I. Introduction

     A. Background to the problem

     B. Thesis statement

II. Body

    A. Opposing viewpoint

        1. Reason

        2. Reason

    B. Thesis position (refutation)

        1. Reason

        2. Reason

    C. Solution proposal

III. Conclusion

Comparison-and-Contrast

Although it is possible to write an entire paper that either compares or contrasts two or more things, a more common practice is to combine the two approaches into a comparison-and-contrast pattern.

One method of comparison-and-contrast examines each subject separately in terms of selected features:

   I. Japanese education   **Subject 1**

     A. Levels   **Feature 1**

     B. Access   **Feature 2**

     C. Standards   **Feature 3**

  II. U.S. education   **Subject 2**

     A. Levels   **Feature 1**

     B. Access   **Feature 2**

     C. Standards   **Feature 3**

 III. Conclusion

A second method compares and contrasts subjects directly by examining the same features:

   I. Education levels   **Feature 1**

     A. Japan   **Subject 1**

     B. U.S.   **Subject 2**

  II. Access   **Feature 2**

     A. Japan   **Subject 1**

     B. U.S.   **Subject 2**

III. Standards   **Feature 3**
   A. Japan   **Subject 1**
   B. U.S.   **Subject 2**
IV. Conclusion

Classification

The process of classification is similar to that of comparing and contrasting: identifying the qualities that put things into the same category or distinguish one category from another (e.g., drug therapy programs: behavior versus encounter). Begin by identifying the principle by which items will be classified (e.g., types of children's toys, kinds of legal statutes, ways to purchase a car). Next, designate the categories to which the items belong. Your discussion of the topic would then describe the items in such a way as to differentiate them from other items and categories:

   I. Principle of classification: Types of therapy
  II. Categories of classification
     A. Behavior therapy
       1. History
       2. Examples
     B. Encounter therapy
       1. History
       2. Examples
     C. Gestalt therapy
       1. History
       2. Examples
     D. Interactional approach
       1. History
       2. Examples
  III. Conclusion

Cause-and-Effect

Cause-and-effect patterns are useful for showing how one event or circumstance causes another event or circumstance. Direct and indirect causes may be discussed as well as recommendations for any problem or condition they have created. For example, a paper discussing the problem of decreasing numbers of insect pollinators (such as bees, moths, and butterflies) might develop from a cause-effect outline such as the following:

I. Problem or condition: Severe reductions in insect pollinators
II. Causes
    A. Direct: Loss of habitat
    B. Direct: Use of pesticides
    C. Indirect: Increased human population
III. Effects
    A. Direct: Loss of natural vegetation
    B. Direct: Declines in commercial crop production
    C. Indirect: Loss of species diversity
    D. Indirect: Threats to human health
IV. Solution (recommendation)

APA and Scientific Patterns

A paper following the guidelines of the American Psychological Association (APA) or one discussing research, methodology, and conclusions for a scientific study may be organized as follows:

I. Introduction
II. Methodology
III. Results
IV. Discussion
V. References

Creating a Title

Many writers prefer to create a title after the paper is finished so that it accurately reflects the content and focus. Others create the title along with the thesis statement and outline as an additional reminder to themselves during the writing stage of the paper's focus. Whichever you prefer, take the time to devise a title that indicates (1) what the paper is about and (2) what approach you have taken toward the subject. The following titles meet these criteria:

A Critical View of Tax Shelters

Why New York Is America's Best-Loved City

Families: Do They Really Exist Anymore?

Use a subtitle (added following a colon) when it provides additional focus:

Teen Music: Can Mean Lyrics Hurt You?

Sleaze T.V.: Viewers Are Saying No

Avoid vague, high-sounding, or cute titles that hide the paper's content and approach:

Vague	Youths at Risk
Overblown	A Brief Examination of the Cause-and-Effect Relationship of Lower-Than-Average Grades among College Transfer Students
Cute	The "Purrrfect" Pet: Cats as Support Animals

Remember: Do not underline or use quotation marks around the title of your own paper, unless it is named in your text. (See Chapter 13 for guidelines on placement and spacing when typing the title.)

W O R K I N G   W I T H   O T H E R S

The more completely you plan the research paper at this point, the more smoothly you will proceed with writing it. Planning the paper with the help of a friend or classmate will ensure that you are actually ready to write and that the logic of the paper's organization is apparent to others. Take the time to share your research material and to discuss the following major points from this chapter with someone else.

■ Review the research question and your notes with another person to be sure you have enough material to support a thesis statement. Point out the examples you intend to include in the paper.

■ Does your friend or classmate feel there are enough examples in the notes to support your thesis? Discuss any quotations you plan to include in the paper as well as your reasons for doing so.

- Ask the person you are working with to state the final thesis statement in his or her own words. How could the thesis be stated more effectively?

- Ask whether the paper seems to be informative or argumentative in its purpose. Can the other person offer any advice on which one of these approaches might work best for your paper? If you are working with a classmate, what purpose will his or her paper support?

- Look over the outline for the paper together. Does it meet the requirements of the assignment? Does the proposed content support the thesis? Is the organization of material logical and effective? Should any headings be changed, moved, or deleted? Is the form for the outline correct?

- What pattern of development is best for this paper? Briefly summarize the approach the paper will take. Decide together whether that approach seems appropriate for your thesis and purpose.

- Evaluate the proposed title for the paper. Does it clearly indicate the paper's subject and the author's position? Can the two of you think up any other appropriate titles together?

If possible, share your writing preparation with more than just one person, especially if you have lingering questions about any particular aspects of the paper. Be sure to ask others to review their plans with you, also. You will find that discussing another's plans for writing the research paper will provide valuable insights about your own readiness.

CHAPTER **9**

Writing
Your Paper

Once you have completed a carefully planned outline, writing your paper should proceed fairly smoothly. Plan to write the paper over several days, expecting to make changes, to run up against writer's block for short periods, or even to make another visit to the library. But do not despair: Such hurdles are always overcome. They rarely prevent a paper from getting written if the author has been working diligently up to this point.

Reviewing Your Preparation for Writing

Before actually starting to write, take time to review what you have prepared so far to support the composing process:

- A final thesis statement
- A clear purpose (argumentative or informative)
- Notecard material
- An outline of the projected paper

You will need to draw upon all of these as you write the paper. Keeping your purpose, thesis, outline, and notecards nearby as you work will help generate ideas and keep the paper organized.

Preparing to Write

Progressing in Stages

Your paper will undoubtedly go through several versions before it is completed. It is usually helpful to work from successive drafts, though writers vary in the way they like to proceed with any paper.

Revising as You Write.   Some writers prefer to write, revise, and fi-
nalize each part of the paper fairly thoroughly before moving on to the
next part. This system works well when you have a strong outline and
need to have a sense of completing one part of the paper before moving
on to the next. A drawback is that you can get bogged down finetuning a
single section: You may spend so much time trying to get one part just
right that you lose momentum for writing.

Revising a Whole Draft.   A more practical method of writing is to
create the paper in three draft stages, usually in rough, revised, and final
forms:

1. In the *rough draft,* aim to get as much of the paper's content written
   down as you can. Do not worry much about spelling, copying whole
   quotations, or even fully documenting sources.
2. In the *revised draft,* review the writing style, make improvements in
   the order of ideas, add supporting details, and check to see that you
   have fully developed and supported the thesis statement.
3. For the *final draft,* check spelling and punctuation closely, make sure
   all documentation is accurate in form and content, and generally
   check the paper to see that it conforms to the standards of the research paper assignment.

Whether you revise as you write, prefer to work with whole drafts, or
use a combination of approaches is really up to you. The important thing is
to write consistently, following the outline you prepared or changing it
when necessary to maintain organization and focus in the paper.

Determining an Appropriate Style

Before you begin to write, decide how you want to sound to your
paper's audience. The semiformal style and language you use for most college papers is also appropriate for the research paper; however, because
the research paper is not a personal essay, pay particular attention to matters of voice and tone, qualities that influence how your writing affects the
reader.

Voice.   Avoid using the personal pronoun *I,* since in most cases, the
paper is not about you but about your research findings and conclusions.
Avoid saying *I think . . .* or *I found that . . .* unless you are reporting
your own efforts and they are relevant to the immediate subject under discussion. For instance:

Though Cranston and others have argued for changing the law, **I
found** most police personnel in favor of the current statute.

In most cases, express your ideas in a third-person voice that remains objective and allows focus on the subject:

> Though Cranston and others have argued for changing the law, **most police** personnel favor the current statute.

Tone.   Throughout the paper, write in a tone that is consistent with the paper's purpose, subject, and audience. *Tone* is the writer's attitude toward the subject and the audience. It can be formal, serious, humorous, sarcastic, ironic, or any other quality evoked by the language and style of expression. Which tone you adopt for your paper will depend upon the subject and your attitude toward it. Obviously, some subjects require a certain tone just because of their nature. The subject *AIDS* would undoubtedly require a serious tone, for example. A sarcastic or humorous tone would be unusual for a research paper, though some subjects might be effectively handled in one of these ways (a paper about *designer clothing for pets,* for example).

Considering the Audience

Since most readers will not share your familiarity with the paper's topic, anticipate what they will need to understand to follow the paper's discussion most easily. Be alert as you write to include necessary information and definitions that will assure the clarity and effectiveness of your discussion.

Defining Unfamiliar Terms.   Review your topic to identify unfamiliar names, terms, and concepts that you should define for the reader. Make sure you understand such items yourself, and be prepared to define them for your audience. Unless it is the subject of your discussion, you normally will not define a common term (e.g., *nuclear reactor, Pentagon, dolphin*). Brief mentions of well-known individuals seldom require further identification, but explain any persons, terms, or concepts that may be unfamiliar to your reader:

Individual identified	At this point, Madison turned to his friend Elbridge Gerry for support. Gerry was also a member of the Democratic-Republican Party, and he later became Madison's vice-president. Madison had hoped . . .
Major term defined	The <u>Electra complex</u>, which Sigmund Freud first identified, is today defined as a normal emotional crisis in females resulting, at an early stage of psychosexual development, from sexual impulses toward the father

and jealousy of the mother (Heber 112). This is the Electra complex that Sylvia Plath once stated the speaker of her poem "Daddy" was attempting to resolve . . .

Note that in the second example, *Sigmund Freud* is not identified, since readers would likely be familiar enough with his name to understand this brief mention. The same is not true for *Elbridge Gerry,* mentioned in the first example.

Using Appositives.   When possible, keep definitions and explanations from interrupting the text by using *appositives,* which are descriptive words or phrases that qualify or rename the terms that precede them. Notice that an appositive is usually connected by a comma to the term it identifies (shown in bold in the following examples):

At this point, Madison turned for support to his friend Elbridge Gerry, **also a Democratic-Republican and later Madison's vice-president.**

The poem can be understood in the context of Freud's theory of an Electra complex, **a normal emotional crisis in females resulting, at an early stage of psychosexual development, from sexual impulses toward the father and jealousy of the mother** (Heber 112).

Simplifying Difficult Terms.   Avoid overdefining terms or defining those that may be simply sophisticated or unfamiliar to you. Use a simple term when possible, especially if a more complex term is going to show up only once in the paper. Thus, rather than burden the reader with a term like *microcom networking protocol* when discussing computer functions, use instead *a method for detecting and correcting errors in data transmissions.* Your reader will also probably follow a discussion about the human immune system more easily if you refer to *erythrocytes,* for example, simply as *red blood cells.*

Explaining Special Uses of Common Terms.   Familiar terms that you use with special meanings in the paper or that are used synonymously with other familiar terms may require clarification. For instance, one student writing about the responses of black readers to Mark Twain's *The Adventures of Huckleberry Finn* realized that the term *black* had several popular definitions and could carry special implications for many readers. Since the student decided to use *black* to denote what several of her sources called by various other names—*African American, Black,* and *Negro*—she included the following note near the end of her paper to define what she meant by the term and why she preferred to use it:

¹For consistency and to reflect the most common usage today, I have throughout this paper used the term <u>black</u> to refer to the people several of my sources have called <u>African American, Black</u>, and <u>Negro</u>. As Jane Carson has observed in her essay "Words and Culture," <u>black</u> remains the most recognized and consistently used term among different races in U.S. society (67).

In general, sensitive consideration of your audience will help you decide which terms need defining and which do not. As you prepare to write the paper, be sure to have on hand the information you may need to provide any necessary definitions or explanations.

Writing the Paper

The Introduction

The introduction announces the paper's topic, presents the thesis statement, and engages the reader's interest in what the paper will say. There are no rules as to how long an introductory section should be. An overly lengthy introduction, however, can lose the paper's focus and eventually cause the reader to wonder what you are getting at. How you go about introducing the paper's topic and thesis will depend upon your own writing preferences and the material you need to include before moving to the body of the paper.

Starting with an Anecdote.   Introduce the paper with an anecdote (a brief account of an incident) when it helps to illustrate or lead into the topic. For instance, a paper on Japanese ownership of U.S. properties could open with a humorous anecdote that is directly relevant to the paper's topic and leads into the statement of the paper's thesis (which is boldfaced in all examples):

When President George Bush attended the funeral of the late Japanese Emperor Hirohito in January 1989, comedian Jay Leno quipped that "as President of the United States, [Bush] figured he should meet the owners" (Holger 39). Leno's remark demonstrates the extent to which the American public is both aware of and nervous about the amount of Japanese ownership in the United States. . . . While the concerns expressed are justified, however, **Americans should view the expansive Japanese presence in the United States as a positive stage in this country's global development.**

Introducing the Topic's Significance. Point out the importance of a topic by demonstrating its widespread effect or important consequences:

The crack and cocaine epidemic in the United States has gone beyond killing the users to addicting children even before they are born. All across the United States today, doctors are delivering babies whose symptoms range from all-out dependency on crack or heroin to major brain and organ damage due to the mother's use of drugs. The problem is so great that next year, more babies born in the United States will die from drug addiction than in any other country in the world (Keeler 23). **Though federal and state programs to educate the young have reduced their numbers, drug-dependent pregnancies seem destined to continue in this country for some time.**

Offering Statistics. Statistics provide a quick and concrete way to interest a reader in the topic:

Americans today throw away 160 million tons of garbage and trash a year, roughly 3.5 pounds a day apiece. That is enough to spread 30 stories high over 1,000 football fields. The average family of three sends 29 bags of trash to the dump every month, but in five years, one-third of our present landfills will be full ("Buried" 57). The question facing the United States today is: Where will we bury all the mountains of garbage and trash in the future? Right now, no one has an answer, but **states are scrambling to resolve a problem that, if not settled soon, literally threatens to bury us in trash.**

Quoting an Authority. Quoting an authority allows you to agree or disagree with the opinion expressed, or the quotation can emphasize the importance of the paper's topic. A paper on Mark Twain could open with this quotation by another author, Nobel Prize winner Ernest Hemingway:

"All modern literature comes from one book by Mark Twain called <u>Huckleberry Finn</u>," wrote Ernest Hemingway in 1935. "It's the best book we've had" (22). Although most literary critics and scholars, as well as the general reading public, would agree with Hemingway's assessment, Mark Twain's <u>The Adventures of Huckleberry Finn</u> is also one of the most controversial classics on American bookshelves. Indeed, <u>Huckleberry Finn</u> has borne a long history of staunch criticism and debate, first over what white audiences viewed as its common vulgarity and, increasingly in this century, over what many perceive as its racist and demeaning portrayal of black characters. **The result has been a concerned, often outraged black response to** <u>**Huckleberry Finn**</u> **that centers not only upon the work's language and characterization but upon its consequent value as literature, as well.**

Reviewing a Controversy.   If your paper is taking a position on or examining a controversy, you may want to review general issues before discussing the major arguments in depth:

The American public's long-standing debate over gun control has taken on new urgency of late because of the widespread availability and use of assault-style weapons. Gun-control advocates fear that awesome, rapid-fire weapons like the Uzi and AK-47 are giving drug lords and other criminals the ability to outgun the police. They want these kinds of weapons banned, but gun enthusiasts say that would mean the end of their right to own such guns, too. Pro-gun advocates argue that the Constitution guarantees them the right to bear arms, including Uzis and AK-47s. **The recent debate has set off a flurry of political reactions that seem to have upset everyone but the criminals it originally centered upon.**

Summarizing the Literature.   A summary of the recent literature presents an overview of issues related to the paper's topic. The introductory summary below focuses on the positions of black critics on the issue of the literary value of *The Adventures of Huckleberry Finn* and the question of banning the novel:

Black critics of Mark Twain's <u>The Adventures of Huckleberry Finn</u> continue to define the novel's strengths and weaknesses along both literary and racial lines. Kenny J. Williams, for example, recognizes several flaws in characterization and plot but ends by calling the novel a "classic." Richard K. Barksdale sees the novel as great because of its ironic rather than simply positive view of black and white friendships. **The one point on which both of these critics agree, however, is that Twain's** <u>**The Adventures of Huckleberry Finn**</u> **is too important a book to go unread by any generation of Americans.**

Providing Background Information. Set the stage for a discussion by providing the reader with background information on the topic:

> Though the first airplane flight by the Wright brothers in 1903, as well as the early rocket experiments of Dr. Robert Goddard, certainly laid the foundations for space flight today, the real leap in progress came in 1957 when the Soviet Union launched the first orbiting satellite. That success was followed by several more Soviet firsts: the first long space flight, the first man in space, the first woman in space, and the first walk in space. The United States began catching up to the Soviets in the early 1960s with President John F. Kennedy's promise to land a man on the moon before the end of the decade. **When the first moon landing did take place in 1969, it changed the United States's commitment to space exploration in ways no one had expected.**

Defining a Key Term. Define a central term, and explain its relationship to the discussion:

> The Electra complex, which Sigmund Freud first identified, is today defined as a normal emotional crisis in females resulting, at an early stage of psychosexual development, from sexual impulses toward the father and jealousy of the mother (Heber 112). This is the Electra complex that Sylvia Plath once stated the speaker of her poem "Daddy" was attempting to resolve. **An examination of the Electra complex theory, in fact, reveals the psychosexual sources for the basic structure and major images of Plath's remarkable poem.**

The Body

The body of the paper develops the thesis statement according to the sequence of ideas planned in the outline. You should write the body of the paper as if it were an unfolding discussion, advancing one major idea at a time. Each paragraph should state a main idea, which is developed by supporting discussion and examples and followed by the next logical point for development. Your goal is to examine the topic fully while integrating your research material to support and develop the thesis statement.

Writing Effective Paragraphs. As you compose the body of the paper, avoid writing paragraphs that amount to little more than a collection of other writers' ideas and examples. Each paragraph in the paper should contain at least one idea of your own, usually expressed as the topic sentence. The paragraph should gain development from further discussion and supporting examples, with your own analyses and commentary weaving the various parts together.

Transitions show the relationship between words, sentences, and paragraphs. Use transitions (boldfaced in the following example) to give your writing *coherence,* which is the logical flow and connection of ideas:

> We cannot blame the activities of humans entirely for acid rain, **however.** Volcanic eruptions and forest fires, **for example,** release substantial amounts of sulfur and nitrogen compounds into the air. **In addition,** microbial processes in oceans and coastal mud flats the world over generate constant amounts of gaseous sulfur compounds. **Finally,** nitrogen oxides in the air result not only from the action of soil bacteria but also from the heat produced by lightning. Studies indicate, **in fact,** that natural emissions of sulfur and nitrogen are roughly equal to those produced by humans (Cordova 258).

The above paragraph also demonstrates *unity* because the content relates to the single idea expressed in the topic sentence: We cannot blame the activities of humans entirely for acid rain. Everything in the paragraph's examples and discussion directly relates to the topic sentence.

Writing in the Appropriate Tense.   In discussing a work of literature, use the present tense to write about what is said or to describe actions or events occurring within the context of the work:

> As the hero of the book <u>The Great Gatsby</u>, Jay Gatsby projects an ambiguous greatness that is as much owed to his idealism as his past. When Nick reminds Gatsby that he cannot repeat the past, Gatsby responds, "Why of course you can!" (115). Following this comment, Nick describes Gatsby as looking intently around him, as if the past itself were just out of reach.

In discussing other kinds of subjects, use the tense appropriate to the event described. Note how the tense shifts in this paragraph as the discussion moves from the past to the present:

> Three years ago, the small, economically depressed town of Blytheville wanted a Japanese steel firm to build its new 500-acre steel mill there instead of elsewhere. To convince the Japanese of the town's potential, citizens invited corporate officials to visit, even hosting dinners and community sports events in their honor ("Blytheville"). In a similar

manner, American-owned microchip manufacturers are today busily courting Sony, Hitachi, NEC, and Mitsubishi in hopes of gaining much-needed Japanese assistance in technology and production costs.

Integrating Sources.   The paper's content is a discussion of what your research has led you to understand about the topic. You will need to draw upon your research sources for examples, authority, certain kinds of facts, and effective expressions. Rather than simply add these to the paper, however, you should blend your research into the discussion as part of your own way of understanding the topic. The research material should fit logically and linguistically into the paper's discussion. Irrelevant material, no matter how interesting or otherwise important, should be omitted.

The following discussion uses source material without integration, preventing the voice of the paper's author from coming through:

Though such analyses may amount to little more than posttrial hindsight, the advice of jury consultants in the O. J. Simpson case appears to have been credible. Decision Quest, Inc., a consulting firm for the defense, guaranteed seating a jury with a low educational level by advising Simpson's attorneys to reject anyone who

Use of colon isolates quotation from the writer's discussion

read a newspaper regularly:

Only two of the jurors graduated from college, and most said they derived their information from tabloid TV, a factor Decision Quest found correlated directly with the belief that Simpson was not guilty.

Overquoting obscures writer's point

One declared that she read nothing at all "except the horse sheet." The jurors eventually tuned out during the weeklong interrogation of the state's hapless LAPD criminalist Dennis Fung. (Miller 39)

In the opinion of some lawyers, "Simpson's defense team took a giant step toward his acquittal the day the

Overuse of sources

jury was seated" (Greenburg). "The defense built the kind of jury they wanted and the state had to sit and let them do it," said one trial analyst (Lord 24). "They got

Sources not integrated

what they paid the consultants for," said another (Jordan). According to Paul Lisneck, a Chicago-based trial consultant, the O. J. Simpson case "was over with the jury pick" (Greenburg).

The following version shows a better integration of sources and clearer expression of the writer's own ideas:

Use of selected quotations and paraphrase condenses material and keeps writer's ideas prominent	Though such analyses may amount to little more than posttrial hindsight, the advice of jury consultants in the O. J. Simpson case appears to have been credible. Decision Quest, Inc., a consulting firm for the defense, guaranteed seating a jury with a low educational level by advising Simpson's attorneys to reject anyone who read a newspaper regularly. While one juror said that she read nothing at all "except the horse sheet" (Miller 30), the majority of jurors selected said they derived their information about national and world events from tabloid TV, "a factor Decision Quest found correlated
Source material condensed	directly with the belief that Simpson was not guilty" (Miller 39). So effective was the defense strategy in using peremptory challenges to eliminate better-educated jurors that, according to Paul Lisneck, a Chicago-based trial consultant, the O. J. Simpson case "was over with the jury pick" (Greenburg).

As this second example demonstrates, you should weave source material into your own commentary and explanation, pruning quotations to highlight important ideas.

Using Quotations.   Use direct quotations to give examples and lend authority or whenever a summary would forfeit precision or lose the effectiveness of the original. Except as explained below, maintain the exact wording, spelling, and punctuation of the original any time you quote.

Quotation Marks.   Quotation marks separate your own words from those of another. In general, include all quoted words, phrases, and sentences of less than four lines between quotation marks. The following example demonstrates the integration and clear indication of quoted material with the writer's own sentences:

The speaker in Plath's "Daddy," for example, expresses her seething bitterness over the men in her life who have failed to return her love. Thus, she claims her father is "a devil" and her husband "a vampire" who "drank my blood." Though the speaker says at the end of the poem that she is "through" with anguishing over her father's death and lost affection, her words seem more insistent than certain. As Carol Langer points out, "The poem's intensity of tone and imagery suggest there is yet more grief than has found words" (45).

Note that titles of short poems such as "Daddy" are also included between quotation marks.

Selection.   Since few statements from your sources will require full presentation, omit unnecessary words when you quote. Rather than quote a whole sentence, integrate fragments of the original into your own sentence:

Original

"A book so clearly great, yet with such evident defects, poses a difficult critical problem."

—Henry Nash Smith, Introduction, *Adventures of Huckleberry Finn* by Mark Twain (Boston: Houghton-Riverside, 1958) v.

Integrated quotation

Almost since its first appearance, readers have been divided over the work literary historian Henry Nash Smith describes as "a book so clearly great, yet with such evident defects" (v).

Original

"The genesis of speech is not to be found in the prosaic, but in the poetic side of life: the source of speech is not gloomy seriousness, but merry play and youthful harmony."

—Otto Jespersen, *Language: Its Nature, Development and Origin* (London: Allen and Unwin, 1922) 154.

Integrated quotation

Though Jespersen holds that the origins of speech are "not to be found in the prosaic" or in "gloomy seriousness" (154), language is nonetheless a practical medium before it is anything else.

Exceptions to Quoting Exactly.   In most cases, a quotation must reproduce words, phrases, and sentences exactly as they appear in the original. Occasionally, however, a quotation may be made clearer or used more effectively with slight alteration of grammar or wording. While some changes are permissible, remember that they must be made in accordance with accepted practices as well as with care not to distort the original meaning of the quotation. Follow these guidelines:

■ *Initial capital letters:* If you incorporate a quotation that is a complete sentence into a sentence of your own, you must maintain the capitalization of the original or show any changes in brackets:

Original	"War is the father of all." (Heraclitus)
Original sentence and capitalization	It was Heraclitus who said, "War is the father of all."
Quotation integrated, capitalization changed	Heraclitus believed that "[w]ar is the father of all."

Clearly, the use of brackets in the above sentence is awkward. To avoid the need for brackets, quote only part of the original sentence, when possible:

Heraclitus believed that war is "the father of all."

■ *Ending punctuation:* You may change or omit the ending punctuation of the original when you add the quoted material to your own sentence:

Heraclitus said, "War is the father of all," but I disagree.

or

Although Heraclitus believed that war is "the father of all," we cannot let that point of view lead us into war.

Though the original sentence ended with a period after *all,* it is understood that the punctuation in these examples may have been changed to fit grammatically with the second writer's own sentence structure.

Other than the two cases discussed here and following, you must indicate all other changes in the original material with the use of brackets or ellipses.

■ *Brackets:* Square brackets may be used to change or add to the original wording of a quotation. If your typewriter or computer does not have square brackets, leave spaces for them as you type the paper and add them later in ink. Do not confuse brackets [ ] with parentheses ( ).

As with ellipses (discussed in the following section), alter original wording sparingly to avoid interrupting your text with cumbersome punctuation or explanatory material. Use brackets only as needed for the following purposes:

1. To alter a quotation for grammatical accuracy:

    Original   "Herst finally realized he was not familiar with those types of locks" (Gross 21).

    Quotation altered   According to Gross, it was only then that "Herst finally realized he [Houdini] was not familiar with those types of locks" (21).

2. To enclose the term *sic* (meaning "thus" or "so") to reassure the reader that you have quoted accurately despite an error in the source:

    Bruner claims that Elizabethan drama "went idle and then died with Shakespeare's death in 1621 [sic] and the advance of the Great Plague in 1665" (117).

    William Shakespeare died in 1616, not 1621. The addition of *sic* in square brackets following the erroneous date acknowledges the error in the original without altering it.

3. To clarify a quotation's meaning:

    As Alan Shears argues in <u>The Dollar Abroad</u>, "These fluctuations [in the value of the dollar] are not just economically important. They can make or break world peace efforts" (34).

4. To add material between parentheses:

    Yates manages to tell us a number of intriguing details about the members of Sylvia Plath's family (e.g., "Otto [Sylvia's father] grew up speaking German and Polish" [126]).

5. To explain added emphasis:

    Williams argues that the greatness of Hemingway's style lies in its "<u>integrity of form and level of detail</u>" [emphasis added], not in its romanticism" (74).

    An alternate method that avoids interrupting the text is to follow the quotation with an explanation of the change, placed in parentheses (following the page number):

    Williams argues that the greatness of Hemingway's style lies in its "<u>integrity of form and level of detail</u>," not in its romanticism" (74; emphasis added).

■ *Ellipses:* Omit unnecessary material from a quotation or show that it is part of another sentence in the original with the use of three spaced periods (. . .), called *ellipsis points.* Ellipses can indicate the omission of words, phrases, or sentences, but their use should never misrepresent the meaning or context of the original material.

The guidelines below demonstrate uses of ellipses to quote from the following sample passage:

> "When commercial computer users upgrade to newer versions, they soon discover that even the trash bin is no longer an option for the old models. The heavy metal content of computers qualifies them as hazardous waste. The cost of disposing of old computers can grow to be a problem even for the big companies" (Langley 60).

1. To omit material from within a sentence:

    > As Langley points out, "When commercial computer users upgrade to newer versions . . . even the trash bin is no longer an option for the old models" (60).

    Note that this use of ellipses calls for a space before and after each period.

2. To omit beginning material:

    > Although the recycling of such technology is on the increase, the sheer expense involved in ". . . disposing of old computers can grow to be a problem even for the big companies" (Langley 60).

    Though the above method is acceptable, avoid cluttering your sentences with unnecessary ellipses. Instead, introduce the quoted material using the word *that,* with no punctuation between it and the quotation:

    > Although the recycling of such technology is on the increase, the sheer expense involved is so great that "disposing of old computers can grow to be a problem even for the big companies" (Langley 60).

3. To place omitted material at the end of a sentence:

    > Langley (60) points out that even for companies such as IBM, the "cost of disposing of old computers can grow to a be a problem. . . ."

Note that in this situation, with the source page citation included *before* the quotation, three spaced periods are required for the ellipsis and a fourth period (after the last word) is needed to end the sentence. Another method is to give the source page citation *after* the quotation. The final period is then separate from the three spaced ellipsis points (i.e., after the final parenthesis):

> Langley points out that even for companies such as IBM, the "cost of disposing of old computers can grow to a be a problem . . ." (60).

4. To omit sentences in the middle of a quotation:

> Langley has shown that when "commercial computer users upgrade to newer versions, they soon discover that even the trash bin is no longer an option for the old models. . . . The cost of disposing of old computers can grow to a be a problem even for the big companies" (60).

Note that there is no space before the period ending the first sentence, but there are spaces before and after the ellipsis points that follow it.

5. To omit paragraphs from a long quotation, using a continuous line of spaced periods to indicate the ellipsis:

> When commercial computer users upgrade to newer versions, they soon discover that even the trash bin is no longer an option for the old models. The heavy metal content of computers qualifies them as hazardous waste. The cost of disposing of old computers can grow to be a problem even for the big companies.
>
> . . . .
>
> Many of the recycling efforts were led by computer companies who saw in doing so the opportunity to solve their own and their customers' problems. The winners in this situation appear to be third world countries anxious to get their hands on anything even close to an old 386 model. A side business has consequently sprung up of parts and repair middlemen who see to it that the machines are ready to sell and operate. (Langley 60)

Do not indent the first line of a single paragraph when you quote it, even though it may have been indented in the original. But note that when quoting *two or more* paragraphs that were indented in the original, you must indent the first line of each paragraph three spaces, as shown in the previous example.

6. To omit lines of poetry from a quotation:

You stand at the blackboard, daddy,

In the picture I have of you,

. . . .

I was ten when they buried you.

At twenty I tried to get back, back to you.

I thought even the bones would do. (Plath 53)

—Excerpt as submitted from "Daddy" from *Ariel* by Sylvia Plath from *The Collected Poems of Sylvia Plath,* edited by Ted Hughes. Copyright © 1963 by Ted Hughes. Copyright Renewed. Reprinted by permission of HarperCollins Publishers, Inc.

Long Quotations.   Any quotation that is longer than four typed lines should be set off as a block and indented ten spaces from the left margin. Introduce the quotation with a complete sentence and a colon (unless the context calls for some other kind of structure and punctuation):

Colon introduces quotation after complete sentence

It is difficult, however, to enforce these rules, and they say nothing about eliminating those individuals whose education or experience might make it difficult for attorneys to control a jury. One experienced trial attorney expresses the matter this way:

All potential jurors . . . inevitably bring with them the views and biases built into their race, religion, age, and gender. These preconceptions supposedly influence the eventual verdict as much, if not more than, the evidence presented at trial. The task of the lawyer, therefore, is to outsmart the system—to figure out the demographics of justice and manipulate it during jury selection by eliminating jurors with the so-called wrong personal characteristics. (Abramson 143)

The Conclusion

The conclusion to your research paper is as important as every other part, possibly even more so. Here is where you will summarize, evaluate, restate for emphasis, place in perspective, and finally drive home the major ideas and lasting impressions you want a reader to take away from the paper. Do not disappoint your audience with an ending that does no more than restate what has already been said. Make the conclusion of your paper as interesting and insightful as possible, something worth the reader's further consideration.

Devising an Effective Conclusion. While there is no single way to conclude any research paper effectively, two guidelines should be observed:

1. Reemphasize the thesis statement without repeating it word for word.
2. Be sure the last paragraph clearly signals a conclusion about what has been said.

Avoid the temptation to introduce new issues or list unanswered questions in the conclusion. Instead, offer your reader content that brings the discussion to a logical close.

The following examples demonstrate common approaches to concluding a research paper discussion. You will notice that some closings combine more than one approach.

Reemphasizing the Thesis Statement. Make certain your reader grasps the main point of your paper by emphasizing the thesis again in the conclusion. Rather than simply repeating the thesis statement word for word, emphasize key words and concepts that represent the thesis in the context of the conclusion itself. The final paragraph of Mark Stevenson's paper on television talk shows, for example, echoes the paper's thesis that such programs have offended or alienated too many people to survive in their present form:

> In providing such opportunity, the talk shows have indeed gone too far, for they have moved into realities which, once examined, cannot remain entertaining. As we watch the lives held up for examination and exposed on our screens, our better judgment tells us they deserve another kind of forum than Geraldo or Ricki Lake can provide. It is for this reason that as talk shows change, as they surely must to survive at all, their alteration will result less from mere matters of taste than from an overruling, collective conscience as to what is fair and decent.

Presenting a Quotation. An eloquent or particularly striking comment by a voice other than your own can effectively sum up your position or significantly affect your reader's awareness. The writer of a paper on *The Adventures of Huckleberry Finn,* for example, felt she wanted her readers to recognize that the conflicting concerns surrounding the novel were rooted in its power as a great literary work. For this reason, her conclusion returned to the quotation from Ernest Hemingway that appeared at the beginning of the paper:

> Huckleberry Finn has come a long way from what made it the "veriest of trash" for white audiences in the nineteenth century. Today, the book acts for black as well as white readers as what another black writer, David L. Smith, calls "a trigger to outrage" (5), a classic work of art that stirs reflection and humanity in all of us. In this sense, The Adventures of Huckleberry Finn is perhaps, after all, just what Ernest Hemingway insisted, "The best book we've had" (Hemingway 22).

Providing Direction or Offering Solutions.   If your paper has explored a problem or traced its effects, provide your audience with a direction for action or point out realistic solutions. For instance, an informative paper dealing with new developments in the treatment of AIDS might conclude with the following suggestions for further action:

> As actress Whoopi Goldberg said, we can all learn to do something about AIDS: "If you're a carpenter, you could build a ramp that would allow more mobility for someone in a wheelchair. A good cook could provide hot meals for someone living nearby" (43). What can you and I do to help? Start by finding out about state-sponsored AIDS projects or other concerned groups in your community. Join them. Take part. You'll find you have more to offer in the war against AIDS than you ever thought possible.

Evaluating Results.   Use the conclusion of your paper to evaluate significant effects or to describe and analyze results. A research report on experiments to identify color preferences among different ethnic groups, for example, might conclude with an analysis of major problems encountered and their influences on the project results. The following paragraph concludes a research paper discussing attempts by world governments to preserve threatened species and environments through international agreements:

> As these cases demonstrate, international treaties alone cannot overcome worldwide threats to fragile ecosystems and endangered species. The Third World countries in which threatened entities are

found are often too debt ridden to enforce agreements, preserving instead what are referred to as "paper parks" that exist only in writing (Golob and Brus 349). Written global agreements to save wetlands or threatened plants and animals will never be enough, however, without the recognition of people everywhere that nature is neither ours to control nor to destroy. Without such recognition, human beings themselves may become the most endangered species on the planet.

Providing a Broader Perspective.   Just as the paper's introduction has led your reader to a closer examination of the topic, so, too, should the conclusion lead away from it to a broader perspective. An examination of a historical event, for example, would conclude by discussing its relationship to later events or its relative significance today. In a literary study, move from discussing the work itself to seeing it in the context of the author's life or other works:

Sylvia Plath was nearing her thirtieth birthday in the month that she composed "Daddy" and several other of her strongest poems. As her marriage to poet Ted Hughes began falling apart during this time, Plath used her anger and pain as catalysts to transform her earlier dependency on male authority figures into spiteful, creative independence. It is no surprise that "The Jailer," "Fever 103°," "Ariel," and "Lady Lazarus" all echo "Daddy" in their vivid images of rebirth and purification mixed with angry renunciation of males. The speaker of "Lady Lazarus" rises "out of the ash" the way the poet's genius itself seemed to rise out of her own suffering and spiritual rebirth. Plath's suicide four months after writing "Daddy" and these other late poems only adds a further, harsh validity to the psychological and spiritual complexity of all her work.

Other Backmatter

The concluding section of your research paper will be followed by a separate page(s) of content notes (see Chapter 10) and a separate Works Cited page(s) (see Chapter 11), in that order. Documentation of sources cited in the paper (see Chapter 10) will appear both in the body of the text and in the Works Cited page(s).

Preparing a Final Draft

By now, your research paper should have a well-developed introduction, body, and conclusion, followed by any necessary content notes or foot-notes and the Works Cited page(s). What you have written at this point will most likely represent 95% or more of the paper's final content. Any remaining material will come through performing three important last steps: revising, editing, and proofreading. These steps understandably often overlap during the process of revision. Conscientiously following through on each of them, however, will ensure that nothing is left out of your paper and that everything you have done so far is in its most effective and final form.

Revising

Few papers can be written thoroughly with only a first draft. You will undoubtedly need to make some revisions in the arrangement of the paper's major parts to ensure its general readability, to be certain that it forms a whole, and to know that everything is in the right order. Since up to now, you have no doubt been deeply engrossed in the act of writing the paper, set it aside for another day or two. When you return to it, you will read it through with a fresh eye.

Begin your revision by looking at the overall paper as an investigation and discussion of the research subject. Does the content develop a smoothly connected *discussion* rather than an assemblage of quotation and paraphrase? Does the paper exhibit unity and coherence as a whole and in the development of its paragraphs? Look for transitions that make the writing clear and flowing.

Review each part of the paper as follows:

1. Reread the *introduction*. A good introduction will arouse a reader's interest in the subject and the discussion that follows. The thesis statement should be clearly stated and follow logically from the introductory material itself.

2. Is the *body* of the paper developed sufficiently? Is there a logical progression of ideas among individual paragraphs? Remember that the thesis statement idea should be prominent throughout the paper. Check each paragraph for its relationship to the thesis.

3. The *conclusion* should be worth reading. Make sure it offers sufficient content without beginning or alluding to a new subject of discussion. The paper's thesis statement should be emphasized again in the conclusion, but avoid just repeating it word for word.

Revise the paper by rearranging large parts of the content as needed. You can accomplish this by drawing arrows or making notes on the draft itself, or you can cut and paste various parts in the desired order. If you are writing on a computer, use the "copy" and "move" functions of your software to rearrange text. How much you need to revise will depend upon what you recognize is needed, but do not fall into the trap of starting the paper all over again. If you have followed your outline and provided logical connections between major parts of the paper, rearranging some parts or editing others should be sufficient to prepare for the final typing.

Editing

Editing involves making changes to the text in order to strengthen the content and writing style. This is when you will need to improve the paper's language or edit sentences and paragraphs for weak style or development. Edit for these purposes:

1. Reread each paragraph to see that it has a topic sentence related to the paper's thesis. Be alert to noticeably long paragraphs that may need trimming or division. Paragraphs that are surprisingly short may need to be combined with others or developed more with examples. At the same time, check for paragraphs that may be "stuffed" with research information irrelevant to the thesis. Edit such paragraphs out of the paper, or revise them as needed. Be sure that each paragraph offers examples and that they support or explain the topic sentence.

2. Edit the paper's language to sharpen vocabulary. Be sure that all central terms are defined for the reader and that any complex terms are used only when necessary. Avoid the passive voice where possible, and use strong, active verbs in place of weaker constructions. Vary your paper's style and vocabulary to avoid repetition and to add precision; weave paraphrase and quotation into your own sentence structures:

> As Brewer **points out,** "Though certainly admirable, Twain's stylistic versatility could sometimes become a major weakness" (66).

> Brewer (66) **says** that Twain's versatility was at times also a great weakness.

> Brewer **has argued** that Twain's versatility was at times also a great weakness (66).

> Other critics **agree** with Brewer (66) that Twain's versatility was at times also a great weakness.

A dictionary or thesaurus can provide alternatives for any words that may be frequently repeated in the paper. If you are editing on computer, these references are likely available with your software. Also use the "find" function to locate words or phrases you tend to overuse.

3. Edit to avoid sexist language, wording that discriminates against males or females by inaccurately portraying them in stereotypical ways. The following sentence, for example, demonstrates erroneous sexual stereotyping of male and female roles:

> A nurse's salary can improve a great deal once she has two or three
> years of experience. A doctor, however, has to complete his residency
> requirement in a hospital before he sees much increase in income.

Language such as this is sexually biased because it implies that all nurses are female and all doctors are male. Using *he or she* in place of the single pronouns may eliminate some of the bias, but such use can sound awkward if repeated. A better way is to construct sentences using plural nouns and pronouns:

> Salaries for **nurses** can improve a great deal once **they** have two or
> three years of experience. **Doctors,** however, have to complete **their**
> residency requirements in a hospital before **they** see much increase in
> income.

Another way to avoid bias is to omit the use of pronouns altogether:

> Salaries for nurses with two or three years' experience can improve a
> great deal. Doctors, however, have to complete residency requirements
> in a hospital before seeing much increase in income.

Also edit to remove language that discriminates against groups of various ages, ethnicities, sexual preferences, exceptionalities, and so on.

Proofreading

Proofread your paper several times to make minor corrections in spelling, punctuation, and typing. Do not make the mistake of relying upon others to proofread for you. Even if someone else has typed the final version, you will find that your own acquaintance with the research material is an essential safeguard against misspellings or omissions of content.

If you have written your paper on a computer, make use of its "spellcheck" function. Depending on what software you use, you will be able to check for misspelled words and perhaps repeated words, as well.

Do not rely on the computer, however, as your only means of proofreading. Keep in mind that a "spellcheck" will identify only words that are misspelled, not those that are used incorrectly (e.g., *form* vs. *from* and *county* vs. *country*). You will still need to read the paper.

Correct small typing mistakes and other errors neatly by hand, using correcting fluid and ink. If there are very many such corrections, however, preserve the paper's neatness by retyping and reprinting some pages. After you have carefully read the final version several times and made necessary corrections, share the paper with others who can proofread it again for you with a fresh view of the language and content.

WORKING WITH OTHERS

Rather than wait until the entire paper is completed, discuss your efforts with others throughout the planning and writing stages. If it helps, set up a regular meeting time at two- or three-day intervals to discuss your progress. Such a pattern will help to keep your writing on schedule.

You will find that talking over your progress with others during the writing stage of the research paper can help you get over writer's block and test the paper's effectiveness as you work. Having someone else review the final draft of the paper for revision and editing purposes is always a good idea.

After you have proofread the paper yourself, ask a friend or classmate to look it over, too. Listen carefully as he or she responds to these or any additional concerns about which you have questions or would value responses.

- Often another person's immediate reaction or interest in a paper can be a measure of how well it is written. Ask your friend or classmate how he or she responds to the paper. Is it readable? Is the discussion interesting?

- How effective does your reader feel the paper's introduction, body, and conclusion are? What areas are particularly strong? Do any weak parts need more development or revision?

- Does the paper have a clear, logical organization? Is the thesis supported throughout?

- Proofread the paper together. If you are working with a classmate, take turns reading each other's papers. Indicate any mistakes with small checks in pencil in the paper's margin. Discuss the checked places together to be sure about any changes needed in the paper.

■ Next to your instructor, a classmate is probably the best judge of the paper's use of sources and their proper citations. Ask his or her opinion on these matters, and be prepared to follow through with any you feel are important to the paper's total effectiveness.

As you discuss your paper with others during the writing and revision stages, listen carefully and take notes whenever you can. Try not to hurry this important sharing session. The more time you spend reviewing each other's papers, the more confident you can be of your own paper's strengths. While working with other classmates during this time, remember to offer the same serious attention to their papers as you have asked them to give yours.

CHAPTER **10**

Acknowledging Sources

Intext Citation and Content Notes (MLA Style)

In addition to the discussion of the research topic, your completed paper will also include documentation of the sources you have cited and, in some cases, content notes that provide further information about your research. You must always give credit in the paper for any ideas and language you borrow directly or adapt from other sources, although you should not cite sources for information that is common knowledge. (See the discussion of plagiarism and common knowledge in Chapter 7.)

Following a Standard Documentation Fomat

Generally speaking, entries in the Works Cited section at the end of the paper tell the reader what sources you have borrowed from in writing the paper's content. Such general acknowledgments, however, do not tell the reader precisely what was taken from a source and where or show how it was used in the paper's discussion. Consequently, documentation formats used in writing for various disciplines also include either intext citation of sources or endnotes or footnotes to convey this kind of precise acknowledgment of sources.

This chapter describes the methods of documentation recommended by the Modern Language Association (MLA), a nationwide association of

teachers and scholars that sets standards for publishing papers about literature and modern and classical languages. Documentation formats used by
writers in other disciplines are discussed in Chapter 12.

MLA Documentation

MLA documentation style requires up to three methods of acknowledging
sources in a research paper: (1) parenthetic intext citation of sources, (2)
full documentation in the Works Cited page(s), and when appropriate to
the paper, (3) content notes. All sources cited in text or mentioned in the
content notes must also appear in the Works Cited page(s). These methods
of documentation are preferred by the MLA, though some schools and
journals still use footnotes or endnotes. Which documentation method you
use may depend upon your subject and the format your instructor wants
you to follow.

Using Intext Citation

Intext citation means identifying the source of any borrowed material
immediately as it appears, right in the text of the paper. (An intext citation
is only the first such acknowledgment you will give each of your sources;
the Works Cited section of your paper will list each source again, giving
complete publication information.) Intext citation requires the minimum information a reader would need to find the item in the Works Cited page(s)
of your paper or in the cited material itself. In most cases, this means giving the author and page number(s) for the source you are crediting:

Author	According to Berman, adopted children "want to be con-
	nected with a past heritage or a genealogical history"
Page number	(119).

This example demonstrates intext citation form for a single author.
Note, however, that no citation is needed when you refer to an author's entire work, rather than a part of it:

Alice Walker's The Color Purple examines people's hopes and dreams
with great sensitivity.

For citing authors, titles, and other kinds of information, follow the
guidelines given in the following sections:

1. PLACEMENT OF ITEMS

When the identity of an author is important for purposes of clarity, emphasis, or authority, include the name in your text as you introduce a quotation or paraphrase. Place the page number(s) of the source in parentheses at the end of the borrowed material:

Author cited with quotation	Donald R. Griffin, author of <u>Animal Minds</u>, points out that "Darwin and many others have been impressed with the fact that sleeping dogs sometimes move and vocalize in ways that suggest they are dreaming" (258).
Author cited in paraphrase	Donald R. Griffin, author of <u>Animal Minds</u>, points out that many scientists have interpreted the movements and sounds of sleeping dogs as evidence that they dream (258).

When your major emphasis is on the content of the borrowed material, however, include the author's name in parentheses with the page number(s):

Many scientists, including Charles Darwin, have "been impressed with the fact that sleeping dogs sometimes move and vocalize in ways that suggest they are dreaming" (Griffin 258).

Many scientists, including Charles Darwin, have interpreted the movements and sounds of sleeping dogs as evidence that they dream (Griffin 258).

NOTE: Be certain that you do *not* place a comma between the author's name and the page number(s). MLA citation form calls for listing the author's name and the page numbers *without punctuation,* as in the preceding examples. In addition, never use *p.* or *pg.* before the page number(s).

An author's name should appear only once in any intext acknowledgment. Include the author's name in the text or in the parentheses following, but not in both:

Incorrect: Author named in both text and parenthetic citation	Ex-ambassador to Japan Mike Mansfield believes that the relationship between Japan and the United States "holds the promise of well-being for nations and peoples around the world" (Mansfield A12).

2. CITING AN AUTHOR, EDITOR, OR CORPORATION

In general, treat individuals, editors, corporate authors, and others who would normally be considered responsible for producing a work as its author. Note that the intext citation form for an author and editor does not distinguish between their roles. In the Works Cited section of the paper, however, the designation *ed.* (for "editor") differentiates between them for your reader. The following examples demonstrate alternative techniques for placement of author names:

Single author

Despite the current international squeeze on U.S. markets, the Clinton administration has at least managed to lower the huge trade imbalance by a significant fraction and strengthen export growth at the same time (Kennedy 528).

Single editor

As Robert J. Slater insists, "If we can't learn from the younger generation, it's because we don't really want to" (77).

Corporate author

A report by Western Trends, Inc., showed that more than fifty percent of those surveyed distrusted the current jury system ("Survey").

The U.S. Department of Health and Safety reports that death from ATVs (all-terrain vehicles) has increased by over 15% a year since 1987 (76).

In a case such as the last one, in which the name of the source is long or perhaps similar to that of another source, the MLA suggests citing the name in the text discussion, rather than within a parenthetical citation. Long intext citations, as well as other parenthetical material, break up the content and impair the reader's concentration.

3. CITING MORE THAN ONE AUTHOR

Cite both authors by their last names if there are two, but cite only the first author's last name followed by *et al.* ("and others") if there are three or more authors:

For Two Authors:

Authors
introduced
in text

Naisbitt and Aburdene claim we are approaching the day when "virtually all women will work except for a few months or years when they are raising children full-time" (7).

Parenthetic citation of authors   We are approaching the day when "virtually all women will work except for a few months or years when they are raising children full-time" (Naisbitt and Aburdene 7).

For Three or More Authors:

Authors introduced in text   According to studies by Mathers et al., AIDS is decreasing only in specifically targeted areas of the United States (72).

Parenthetic citation of authors   We know that AIDS is decreasing only in very narrow, specially targeted areas of the United States (Mathers et al. 72).

4. CITING MULTIPLE WORKS BY THE SAME AUTHOR

When listing more than one source by the same author in the Works Cited page(s), give the author's name in the citation, followed by a comma, followed by the name of the source and the page number(s):

Plath's poetry has long been recognized as exhibiting a "good deal of disturbance with proportionately little fuss" (Alvarez, "Poetry" 26).

Entries for Alvarez's work would appear in alphabetical order by title in the Works Cited page(s). After the first entry, additional works listed would show three unspaced hyphens for the author's name:

Alvarez, A. "Poetry in Extremism." The Observer 14
    March 1963: 26-33.
- - -."Sylvia Plath." Tri-Quarterly 7 (1966): 65-74.

5. CITING TITLES

Cite titles of sources only when (a) there is no author's name provided or (b) you need to distinguish between one source and another by the same author—for example, *The Sun Also Rises* and *The Old Man and the Sea,* by Ernest Hemingway. In both cases, use recognizable, shortened versions of the titles when they are cited: *Sun* for *The Sun Also Rises; Huck Finn* for *The Adventures of Huckleberry Finn;* and so on. (See Chapter 13 for common abbreviations for literary titles.)

Examples within this text follow current MLA and APA preferences for using underlining, rather than italics, for titles of published works. The text also explains, however, that either option is acceptable for research papers and that students should check with their instructors if they wish to use italics.

Also follow these guidelines in citing titles:

- If there is no author to cite, describe the issuing magazine, newspaper, agency, or other authority when you introduce the borrowed material:

  A recent article in <u>Science News</u> reports that researchers have genetically engineered mice with "powerhouse" hearts. The transgenic mice have up to one hundred times more of the protein receptors that contribute to the heart pumping blood ("Gene Therapy" 303).

  A weekly science newsmagazine has reported that researchers have genetically engineered mice with "powerhouse" hearts. The transgenic mice have up to one hundred times more of the protein receptors that contribute to the heart pumping blood ("Gene Therapy" 303).

  The Works Cited entry for either form would look like this:

  "Gene Therapy Fashions Supermouse Hearts." <u>Science News</u> 7 May 1994: 303.

- To distinguish between material taken from different sources by the same author, cite page number(s) and shortened titles in parentheses, as follows:

  The strongest of Hemingway's male characters embrace rituals of disciplined courage as a part of their roles in life. We see this in the fine, respectful precision of the great Belmonte when he enters the "territory of the bull" (<u>Sun</u> 135) and again when the old fisherman vows to "be worthy of the great [Joe] DiMaggio who does all things perfectly even with the pain of the bone spur in his heel" (<u>Old Man</u> 68).

6. CITING INDIRECT SOURCES

Though it is always best to consult a source directly for any material you adapt from it, you may not always be able to do so. In a case in which you cannot locate the original source of a quotation, cite the source you have, preceding it with *qtd. in* ("quoted in"):

As two ex-Secretaries of State, Henry Kissinger and Cyrus Vance, warned in a recent <u>Foreign Affairs</u> article, "America's ability to influence events abroad . . . will be determined in a large part by how rapidly we get our economic house in order" (qtd. in "Fitting" 80).

The inclusion of *qtd. in* with the source citation indicates that the writer did not take the quotation from the actual *Foreign Affairs* article by Kissinger and Vance but instead got it from an article with the shortened title, "Fitting." The Works Cited entry for this citation would include only the indirect source, not the *Foreign Affairs* article by Kissinger and Vance:

"Fitting into a Global Economy." U.S. News & World Report 26 Dec.
1994: 80-82.

7. CITING MULTIPLE SOURCES

If you borrow an idea mentioned in more than one source, give credit in the paper to all sources. Always cite multiple sources parenthetically. Separate the sources with semicolons:

Social researchers and defenders of television talk shows say that, in
providing such opportunities for otherwise silent or misunderstood
individuals to be heard, the programs perform a valuable outlet and a
needed service to society (Priest 73-91; Cabot 19).

Each source would then appear in the paper's Works Cited section in the normal manner.

NOTE: Citing multiple sources parenthetically in text is cumbersome and may interfere with your reader's concentration. Given this, you should cite multiple sources in text sparingly and only when necessary. If you need to list more than three sources, cite them in a note, rather than parenthetically in text (see Using Content Notes, later in this chapter).

8. CITING VOLUME AND PAGE NUMBERS

For a work in more than one volume, cite the volume number, followed by a colon, followed by a space and the page number(s):

Freud believed in a process he called free association to uncover the
hidden meanings of dreams (V: 221).

9. CITING PAGE NUMBERS OF CLASSICAL WORKS

A classical work remains in demand long after its author's death. Once its copyright has expired, such a work may be published in several editions by different publishing houses. Classical works such as *The Adventures of Huckleberry Finn* and *The Scarlet Letter,* for example, appear in several editions, each published by a different publisher and each bearing the same material but on differently numbered pages. Since your reader may have an edition with a different pagination than yours, give the page number for your source, followed by a semicolon and the chapter, book, section, or other parts abbreviated and numbered, as well:

> Twain satirizes monarchies by having Huck give Jim a brief lesson about kings and dukes (130; ch. 22).

> The main character in Dostoyevsky's <u>Crime and Punishment</u> tries to convince himself that he has "killed a principle" rather than another human being (271; pt. 3; sec. 6).

When discussing a classic poem such as *Paradise Lost* or *Canterbury Tales,* line numbers will also be more useful to your reader than page numbers of an edition he or she may not have. Omit page numbers, and cite the work by divisions such as canto, book, part, line(s), scene, or act. Use abbreviated or shortened titles (see Chapter 13), followed by numbers separated with periods to represent the work's divisions. Thus, "*PL* 2.428–29" would indicate "part 2, lines 428–29," of John Milton's *Paradise Lost:*

Reference to a poem	Milton's Satan exhibits "monarchal pride/Conscious of highest worth" (<u>PL</u> 2.428-29) when speaking early in the poem. Later, however, he is described as "Squat like a toad, close at the ear of Eve" (4.799-800).

Similarly, discuss a drama (such as Shakespeare's *Macbeth*) by providing line, scene, and act numbers: "*Mac.* 3.2.25–38." Roman numerals, instead of arabic (as shown here and above), are acceptable if they appear in the source or if your instructor prefers them. (See Chapter 13 on numbers.)

10. CITING NONPRINT SOURCES

Nonprint sources such as an interviews, recordings, and television and radio speeches have no page numbers. Cite each of these kinds of sources by giving the author's name in the text or parenthetically. The author's name in the Works Cited list will key your reader to the type of work referred to:

Text entry	Governor Barrington said he would be sorry to see opponents of the bill "use the law to fight against justice."
Works Cited entry	Barrington, Alan. Personal interview. 18 Oct. 1995.
Text entry	As one critic complained, "It's not certain that Shakespeare knew what he was doing at the end of <u>Hamlet</u>, so why should we?" (Carter).

Works Cited entry Carter, Andrew R. "What <u>Hamlet</u> Cannot Tell Us—And What It Can." National American Literature Conference. Boston, 20 May 1995.

11. CITING MULTIPLE PAGE REFERENCES TO THE SAME WORK

When discussing a short story, novel, long poem, or play throughout the paper, do not repeat the author's name for each reference. In general, name the author and title once, and cite only page numbers after that:

> In <u>The Old Man and the Sea</u>, Hemingway's fisherman believes firmly in his own courage, of being "worthy of the great DiMaggio" (68). He recalls days when, much younger, he felt he could "beat anyone if he had to" (70). Though he eventually loses his great fish, the old man insists that "man is not made for defeat" (103), and the novel ends with his "dreaming about the lions" (127).

When discussing any written work, omit the author's name after the first page citation:

> The old fisherman believes firmly in his own courage, of being "worthy of the great DiMaggio" (Hemingway 68). He recalls days when, much younger, he felt he could "beat anyone if he had to" (70).

To allow a reader to find quoted material in any edition of a prose work, include the chapter number after the page number, separated by a semicolon:

> The old fisherman believes firmly in his own courage, of being "worthy of the great DiMaggio" (Hemingway 68; ch. 4).

Using Content Notes

Content notes differ from the documentation appearing in footnotes or the Works Cited page(s) of your paper. You may find such notes helpful in providing additional commentary or explanations that are not immediately relevant to your paper's discussion. Be aware, however, that you should use such notes sparingly. Make a point to include important material in the main text of your paper. Reserve content notes for adding *necessary* qualifications or explanations when including them in the main text would otherwise interrupt your discussion.

To include content notes in your paper, follow these guidelines:

1. Refer your paper's reader to a content note by means of a superscript numeral, a raised arabic number immediately following the material to which the note refers:

Superscript numeral in text refers to numbered content note
According to a 1986 U.S. Supreme Court decision, lawyers are not supposed to eliminate potential jurors because of race or gender. It is difficult, however, to enforce this rule, and it says nothing about eliminating those whose education or experience might be the cause of their dismissal.[2] One experienced trial attorney . . .

The following content note refers to the correspondingly numbered material in the preceding paragraph:

Content note
[2]Judges can also dismiss jurors for a variety of reasons, ranging from health matters to violations of court restrictions. In the O. J. Simpson case, Judge Ito removed a juror because he believed she was meeting with a literary agent and intending to write a book about the trial (Gleick, "Disorder"). As Rubank has noted, jurors in high-profile trials often see this experience as "their 15 minutes of fame" (24).

2. Type superscript numerals—such as the numeral [2] shown here—by turning the typewriter roller up so that the typed number appears about a half space above the text, usually at the end of the sentence to which it refers, as here[2]. If you are writing on a computer, type the superscript numeral by using the appropriate function keys or commands in your word-processing program.

3. Do not space between the superscript number and any word or punctuation that precedes it.

4. Remember that superscript numbers for content notes should appear in numerical sequence throughout the text, regardless of what pages they appear on.

5. Place all content notes on a separate page(s) following the text of your paper; type the centered title Notes at the top of the page. (See the Notes

page of the sample research paper at the end of this chapter.) Content note entries should appear immediately below the title, each preceded by a raised number indicating the text material to which it corresponds (see the preceding example).

6. Any source you mention in a content note must also appear with complete documentation in the Works Cited page(s) of the paper. For instance, you would need to include the authors mentioned in the preceding example (*Gleick* and *Rubank*) in the Work Cited page(s), even if you did not also cite them in the paper's text.

Content notes can be used for a variety of purposes:

1. **TO ELABORATE ON MATTERS NOT STRICTLY RELEVANT TO THE TEXT DISCUSSION**

   [1]Oprah Winfrey made talk show history in 1985 when she disclosed on her own program that she had experienced repeated acquaintance rapes throughout her life (Priest 3). The disclosure was hailed by thousands of women who needed Oprah's example to confront their own victimization and to begin to heal their pain from it.

   [2]Sacks (149) points out that there has also been a parallel shift in the public's attitude toward people who are deaf. He claims the change from perceiving these individuals as pathetic victims to viewing them as uniquely empowered is demonstrated in two popular films: The Heart Is a Lonely Hunter (1975) and Children of a Lesser God (1986).

2. **TO ADD CLARIFICATION**

   [3]Not all biologists agree with Wilson's estimates. Lugo (81-90) argues that a slight shift in assumptions would predict a loss of only 9% of threatened species by the year 2000. If Lugo is correct, however, even a 9% loss from 5 million species would result in 450,000 extinct species.

   [4]This is not to say that Asians and Europeans consider all U.S. exports inferior. American-made clothing—especially denim jeans— and Hollywood films are still top-rated exports everywhere (Dorn 33).

3. TO EVALUATE OR COMPARE SOURCES

[5]Completed in 1993 and based on over 3,000 personal interviews, Hoag's study of reported marital disharmony among city-employed firefighters remains the most current and comprehensive work on this subject.

[6]Keeler's study of underachieving college students is based on interviews with college students and professors. A more persuasive viewpoint is expressed in Mike Rose's Lives on the Boundary (New York: Macmillan, 1989). Rose tells of his own underprivileged education and its relevance to his teaching and working with struggling minority students at UCLA.

4. TO PROVIDE STATISTICS

[7]A recent survey by U.S. News & World Report of 696 college seniors found that 95% could name Mark Twain as the author of The Adventures of Huckleberry Finn, while only 62% could name Geoffrey Chaucer as the author of the next best-known work, Canterbury Tales ("Reader's Block" 89).

[8]Laboratory results over a six-week period showed a loss of 3.05 mg of potassium, with a corresponding 9% decrease in fluid volume. Density measurements were not recorded during the first cycle of testing but were found during the second cycle to be 0.07% higher.

5. TO EXPLAIN METHODS OR PROCEDURES

[9]I interviewed Robert Nelson with the assistance of an interpreter, who conveyed my questions to him in American Sign Language (ASL), translating his responses orally to me. Nelson's words, as quoted in this paper, are the verbatim answers provided to me and recorded on tape by the interpreter, Louise Ibarra.

[10]Researchers induced three types of naturally occurring fungi—penicillium, acremonium, and uloclabium—into selenium-contaminated soil through addition of humus, regular aeration, and irrigation between 1983 and 1985. The fungi converted selenium to the less toxic gases dimethylselenide and dimethyldiselenide. See Golub and Brus (369).

6. TO CITE ADDITIONAL SOURCES

[11]For more information on Einstein's religious thinking, see Calder (143); Hoff (326-27); and Gamow (187). Einstein's argument with Niels Bohr on the origin of matter is recounted in Jason M. Collier's "Discussions of Genius," <u>New Mexico Journal of the Physical Sciences</u> 21 (1994): 4-11.

[12]See also Sacks (42), Luria and Yudovich (121), and Church (63).

7. TO SHORTEN MAJOR SOURCE CITATIONS

[13]All references and citations for this discussion of Darwin's early life are to <u>Charles Darwin: A Biography</u> (New York: Knopf, 1995), by Janet Browne.

[14]Ernest Hemingway, <u>The Old Man and the Sea</u>. Future citations in the text will be to page numbers only.

8. TO DEFINE IMPORTANT TERMS

[15]The term <u>phantasmal voices</u> refers to the sense of actually hearing speech, which people who are postlingually deaf may experience when they read lips. They do not, of course, actually hear speech. They instead translate the visual experience into an auditory correlate based on their memory of sound, as they knew it before becoming deaf. See Sacks (6).

The sample research papers in the appendix to this chapter and in Appendix A demonstrate the use of content notes to clarify and add information pertinent to the author's discussion. As you examine these papers, note how sources are used and given proper intext citation throughout.

WORKING WITH OTHERS

Check the accuracy of your paper's documentation by sharing the final draft with others. Seek advice about the effectiveness of any content notes, and encourage readers to make suggestions. The following suggestions may also be helpful.

- Ask your reader to note the placement and accompanying punctuation for each intext citation, as it appears in the paper. Check for complete parentheses and the use of a period following the closed parenthesis whenever a citation appears at the end of a sentence. Be sure that no comma separates the author's name and the page number citation, as in this correct example: *(Smith 65)*.

- Point out any unusual intext citations that you want your reader's opinions about. For example, look especially at multiple-author entries, works cited only by title, and citations of different authors with the same last name. Are these cited correctly in the paper?

- Discuss your rationale for each of the paper's content notes. Does your reader feel each note serves a useful purpose? Should any be reduced or rewritten?

- Use the sample paper that follows to compare your own and your reader's final drafts. Discuss major differences as well as any intext citations or content notes you have questions about.

A P P E N D I X

A sample student research paper follows on pages 219–37. Review the annotations throughout for guidelines on a variety of subjects. Consult the cross-references given for more information.

Center paper's title, your name, and course information on title page

Flawed Justice:

Why and How the American Jury System

Must Be Reformed

by

Nancy Prado

English 101

Professor T. Benfey

November 28, 1995

Prado ii

Outline

Thesis: The United States must reform the process by which jurors are selected to render justice in the court-room.

    I. Introduction: The lack of confidence in the American jury system

   II. Problems with the jury selection process

      A. Intention of cross-sectional juries

      B. Homogeneity of jury pools and juries

         1. Resistance to serving

         2. Exemption practices

      C. Peremptory challenges

         1. Jury consultants

         2. Jury-shaping practices and results

      D. Effects of limited jury composition

         1. Nullification

         2. Misunderstanding by the jury

  III. Corrective measures

      A. Elimination of exemptions

      B. Addressing needs of jurors

      C. Limitations on peremptory challenges

Annotations (margin notes):

Write thesis at beginning of outline

Use standard outline form

This outline is organized by topics

Last name and page number in running head; use lowercase roman numerals for preliminary pages and arabic numerals for text pages

Prado 1

Flawed Justice:

Why and How the American Jury System

Must Be Reformed

Repeat title on first page

Because of recent acquittals of defendants in several high-profile cases by juries who seemed to ignore
abundant evidence, many people believe the American
jury system is seriously flawed and in desperate need of
reform. Indeed, recent "not guilty" verdicts in such
complex cases as the first trial of the Menendez brothers and later that of O. J. Simpson[1] have raised national
concern about whether the courts and jury selection
system in the United States can work effectively for justice (Kaplan 58). According to respected writer and jour-
nalist Ellen Goodman, "The last trusted institution is
being doubted. . . . In the public mind, there is an
emerging suspicion that a verdict represents nothing
more than the idiosyncratic views of 12 individuals."
Mirroring an attitude shared across the nation, a recent
California poll reported that some 55 percent of those
surveyed had "only some or very little" confidence in
the ability of juries to decide criminal cases (Dolan A1).
Americans' belief in justice and their trust in the very
jury system intended to ensure it have clearly been
eroded by recent courtroom decisions across the land. If
we are to restore the public's confidence in jury decisions and in the justice system as a whole, this nation
must begin by reforming the processes by which jurors
are selected to render justice in the courtroom.

As one legal expert has stated in praise of the
United States's democratic jury system, "No other insti-

Use superscript number to refer reader to endnotes

Use ellipsis to indicate omitted content in quotation

Cite sources parenthetically in text

Thesis concludes introductory section

Prado 2

tution of government rivals the jury in placing power so directly in the hands of citizens" (Abramson 1). But it is precisely the questions of who comes forward and who gets selected to serve on juries that may lie at the heart of the current judicial process and its problems ("Jury"). Advocates of jury reform point to a nearly standardized process that seems, in too many instances, to promote overly homogeneous juries who lack diversity in education and experience and who increasingly ignore or grossly misunderstand evidence (Abramson 99-143; DiPerna 227-37).

One process that contributes to the homogeneity among juries is the way members are recruited for selection. Until just thirty years ago, juries were generally composed of people with higher education or recognized expertise; in many communities, civic leaders selected jurors from among their social, economic, and educational equals (Simon 87). Then, in 1968, civil rights legislation required jury pools to represent a cross-section of the population in order to eliminate previously existing elitist, exclusionary jury selection processes. Under present law, the goal in selecting a jury is to achieve a group of jurors who represent the diverse perspectives of race/ethnicity, religion, gender, and educational background found in the community (Abramson 180-81). Although legislation aimed at ensuring representative juries was sorely needed in the United States, current jury selection practices considerably undermine the law's intended effect.

Depending upon the location, for example, today's jury notices reach only about 50 to 70 percent of the

Cite work with no author by title

Separate citations of multiple sources with semicolons

Give only last 2 digits for 3-digit page numbers

Prado 3

adult population, and in some jurisdictions, up to two-
thirds of the people who receive jury notices simply ignore them (Adler 219). Nationally, only 20 to 30 percent
of those who even respond to jury summonses ever end
up serving on juries, while in some areas, such as Los
Angeles, that figure can be as low as 10 to 15 percent
(Adler 243). With the average juror pay nationwide at
roughly $5.00 per day, it is no wonder that the jury pool
often becomes limited to government workers, retired
persons, and low-paid workers. While it may be argued
that there is nothing inherently wrong with such individuals serving on juries, the consistent homogeneity
represented in their availability, education, and socio-
economic status defeats the need for greater diversity
and the presence of more educated professionals
among members of the jury pool.

    That such professionals are usually missing on ju-
ries results partly from a general resistance among all
potential jurists to the possibility of being sequestered
for long periods of time. Most jurors, including professionals, simply want to avoid the stress of confinement
and isolation. Thus, one survey found that up to 59 percent of potential jurors said they "would resist serving
on a jury if they had to be isolated from family and
friends. A majority also said they would try to get out of
a trial that lasted more than two weeks" (Dolan A18).

    Other potential jurors, especially educated profes-
sionals, avoid jury duty and the possibility of lengthy,
isolated sequestration out of concern for their private
beliefs, economic and professional interests, and need
to be available to serve their communities. In most

Margin annotations:
- **Consistently spell out or use numerals for percentages**
- **Quotation incorporated within text**

Prado 4

cases, selection processes tend to accommodate them.
In New York, for example, nearly anyone with a professional title- -including physicians, clergy, optometrists,
podiatrists, registered and practical nurses, embalmers,
Christian Science practitioners, sole business propri-
etors, police and fire personnel, licensed physical thera-
pists, and others- -is automatically exempt from service
on a jury. As a result of practices like these, "the jury
system has lost access to [such] people's special perspectives, their education and expertise, [and] their
contribution to the community profile" (Adler 219).

In most court cases, jurors who do show up and
who are eligible to serve are often less likely to be educated, involved citizens with varieties of expertise and
insight. This is why, in the opinion of well-known
Chicago Tribune columnist Mike Royko, "jury selection
is often a demonstration in the dumbing down of the
legal system. Anyone with an impressive education, a
high IQ or a professional job is usually given the boot."

A factor that further limits and distorts the pool of
jurors, and consequently skews the resulting jury, is the
practice of peremptory challenges. Such challenges "require no justification, no spoken word of explanation, no
reason at all beyond a hunch, an intuition" (Abramson
170). They allow attorneys on either side to dismiss
prospective jurors whom they believe might be hostile
to their case or are simply too independent minded to
be swayed by the presentation of evidence (Greenburg). About 30 percent of the 80 million Americans
who have been called for jury duty have been sent

Use double-dash to show abrupt interruption or addition of content

Brackets enclose material not included in original

Author named in text instead of parenthetically

Cite single-page source without page numbers

Prado 5

home because of an attorney's judgment, although in
the opinion of some, "many of those who are removed
appear to be more alert and unbiased than many who
are seated" (Adler 221).

According to a 1986 US Supreme Court decision, attorneys are not supposed to eliminate jurors because of
race or gender. It is difficult, however, to enforce these
rules, and they say nothing about eliminating people
whose education or experience might make it difficult
for attorneys to control a jury.[2] One experienced trial attorney expressed the matter this way:

Indent long quotations 10 spaces from left margin

> All potential jurors . . . inevitably bring with them
> the views and biases built into their race, religion,
> age, and gender. These preconceptions supposedly
> influence the eventual verdict as much, if not more
> than, the evidence presented at trial. The task of
> the lawyer, therefore, is to outsmart the system- -to
> figure out the demographics of justice and manipu-
> late it during jury selection by eliminating jurors
> with the so-called wrong personal characteristics.
> (Abramson 143)

source indented tation at , following d period

To determine during jury selection precisely
whom they want and do not want on a jury, attorneys
frequently hire high-priced jury consultants, professional analysts who offer "charts, focus groups, surveys
and psychological profiles that try to predict how potential jurors will vote," with the chief indicators being
"everything from race, income, and gender to personal
history and what kind of car they drive" (Gleick, "Rich"
42). While the significance of such factors remains

For author of multiple works, include relevant title in each citation

Prado 6

unclear, attorneys use their peremptory challenge rights to create a jury whose members have the attitudes or education levels they want. Some consultants suggest that clergy, teachers, and lawyers do not make desirable jurors because they are too often sought out for advice and tend to be too opinionated. Attorneys are also usually advised to avoid bank employees and management employees because they "are trained to give or take orders [and] they expect others to conform as well" (Simon 262). Although there is little empirical evidence that such quasi-scientific methods of selecting juries work (Abramson 145), attorneys and the public continue to believe in their importance in shaping verdicts. Their faith in such methods is renewed each time the outcome of a trial seems to be explainable in terms of jury demographics such as gender, education, and other factors (Abramson 144).

The extent to which jury shaping matters perhaps not to the outcome but to the handling of a case can be extremely significant. For example, research shows that "a woman juror is more likely to be intolerant of the complaints of her own sex and thus return a verdict unfavorable" to another female (Simon 262). In the William Kennedy Smith rape trial, jury research showed that conservative women over 40 were the type of juror most likely to acquit Smith. According to defense attorney Roy Black, "'They were most skeptical of claims made by younger women who would go out all night in bars,'" and the defense counted on this bias in making its case to the jury (Lacayo).[3]

Use single quotation marks within double for material enclosed in double marks in original

Prado 7

Not surprisingly, race and education are also major
factors for attorneys to consider in molding acceptable
juries. Take, for example, the Washington, DC, trial of
Mayor Marion Barry, who was charged with fourteen
felony counts after the FBI and police videotaped him
using cocaine. After Barry was acquitted of the charges,
jury consultants attributed the votes of older, poorer,
black jurors to their racial identification with him as
someone like themselves, an underdog or victim of the
establishment (Adler 265).

Though such analyses may amount to little more
than posttrial hindsight, the advice of jury consultants
in the O. J. Simpson case appears to have been more
credible. Decision Quest, Inc., a consulting firm for the
defense, guaranteed a jury with a low educational level
by advising Simpson's attorneys to reject anyone who
read a newspaper regularly. One juror said that she
read nothing at all "except the horse sheet" (Miller 39);
the majority of jurors selected said they derived their information about national and world events from tabloid
TV, "a factor Decision Quest found correlated directly
with the belief that Simpson was not guilty" (Miller 39).
So effective was the defense strategy in using peremptory challenges to eliminate better-educated jurors that,
according to Paul Lisneck, a Chicago-based trial consultant, the O. J. Simpson case "was over with the jury
pick" (Greenburg).

In the Simpson case and others in which peremptory challenges have been used to create juries easily
influenced and perhaps simply outsmarted by defense

Prado 8

attorneys, it has seemed to observers that some juries'
verdicts have clearly ignored the evidence because of
racial bias or some other cause. In many cases (and especially those with juries made up mostly of individuals
from minority groups), critics have charged that jurors
exercised <u>nullification</u>, a practice in which juries "disre-
gard a law if they feel that its strict application would
result in an unjust verdict" (Kerwin and Shaffer 140).

Separate two authors' names with *and*

    The Simpson case was one in which many per-
ceived nullification. It was, however, only one of a
growing number of cases in which juries composed
mainly of blacks and other minorities apparently disre-
garded significant amounts of evidence in order to, as
Martin Luther King, Jr., described such practices,
"arouse the conscience of the community" over larger
and more widespread social injustice existing beyond
the courtroom (qtd. in Hall 768).[4] Indeed, statistics
show that conviction rates in areas of the United States
with large minority populations are unusually low- -up
to three times lower for African American defendants in
some places, for example (Leo). If the nullification
movement continues to find expression in American
courtrooms, then it is all the more important that juries
be selected on the basis of their ability to understand
and their willingness to apply existing laws.

Use *qtd. in* to indicate indirect source

    Such a safeguard is not always so easily accom-
plished under current procedures, however. Refusal to
apply the law can often take the form of simply not understanding it or the evidence brought forward in a
case. Unfortunately, many jurors are simply not able to

Prado 9

comprehend or keep track of the confusing amounts of
evidence or complicated jury instructions presented to
them in complex trials, a fact that often leads to their
voting almost in ignorance about the facts of the case
they have heard. After studying several juries in action,
one legal expert described them as "lots of sincere, serious people who- -for a variety of reasons- -were missing
key points, focusing on irrelevant issues, succumbing to
barely recognized prejudices, failing to see through the
cheapest appeals to sympathy or hate, and generally
botching the job" (Adler 220).

No one would argue that jurors need to be experts
themselves to hear cases or that they must hold PhD degrees to serve effectively on juries. For jurors to make
informed decisions, however, they need to be able to
understand the testimony of witnesses, many of whom
are experts testifying about complex and sophisticated
subjects. At the same time, jurors must also be able to
interpret facts and follow the instructions of a judge
when he or she explains the law. Such is not always the
case, however. It is probably unfair and extreme to perceive juries as being made up of "twelve prejudiced,
gullible dolts incapable of understanding the evidence
or the law" (Wishman vii), as some critics do; however,
it is safe to say that the majority of those who actually
end up serving on juries find it more than challenging.
Studies show that most jurors cannot interact effectively with other jurors or judges and attorneys, nor can
they usually understand the huge amounts of complex
information and evidence presented to them in trials

Use roman
numerals
for page
numbers of
preface or
introduction

(Meyer A2). Although many judges discourage jurors
from taking notes while they listen to evidence being
presented in a trial, over one-third of judges nationally
explicitly forbid notetaking (Adler 239). Thus, it should,
be no surprise that juries "sometimes come down on
the wrong side of the law" (Meyer A2).

Lack of understanding and the failure of jurors to
clarify information can lead to unjust and even over-
turned verdicts. Thus, a 1992 death sentence case in
Chicago was thrown out on the basis of a court study
that showed that "75 percent of jurors in the local
courts didn't understand parts of the instructions"
(Adler 231). In another case involving an unfair competi-
tion lawsuit, filed by Brown & Williamson against a
rival tobacco company, jurors were given eighty-one
pages of instructions by the judge and had to rely on
memory alone to recall testimony that filled 108 volumes. Although the jury ultimately awarded $49.6 mil-
lion in damages to Brown & Williamson, the U.S.
Supreme Court later ruled that no "reasonable jury"
with adequate understanding of the evidence could
have concluded that the other company's actions were
illegal or that Brown & Williamson was entitled to any
damages whatsoever (Lacayo).

What is required to avoid these kinds of mistakes
and other weaknesses inherent in the current jury selection processes in the United States are major reforms
in the ways citizens are recruited and eventually selected to serve on juries. An underlying factor in all of
the weaknesses described so far has been the lack of

Prado 11

genuinely diverse pools of potential jurors, especially
those including educated professionals. To remedy this
problem, we must find ways to increase the sizes of jury
pools and broaden their community representation. Although jurisdictions in some states continue to excuse
individuals who have traditionally been seen as too in-
dispensable to serve as jurors, many other states have
begun to eliminate laws granting automatic exemptions
for certain classes of individuals, including doctors,
lawyers, teachers, and even judges (Abramson 249).
Every citizen needs to understand that his or her participation in jury service is essential to its very existence
and that "no one can have the right to be tried before a
jury unless we all feel an obligation to accept jury duty
in turn" (Abramson 248). In California, Los Angeles District Attorney Gil Garcetti has called for "mandatory
jury service- -no excuses allowed" (Kaplan 59) as a
means of increasing broader participation in juries.
Praiseworthy as such a goal may be, however, it misses
the reason people try to avoid jury duty in the first
place. States must simply do more to ensure people's
willingness to serve on juries and also take steps to
make doing so less burdensome.

Some states have already made progress in this direction. Florida and Colorado, for example, and many
counties in California require jurors to serve only one
day or for the length of one trial. This option has at-
tracted more professionals and others who have traditionally found ways to avoid taking part in jury duty.
Massachusetts, Colorado, and Connecticut require

employers to cover their employees' wages for the first
few days of jury service, after which the court pays $50
a day. The court rate is also paid to unemployed individuals who serve. In Minnesota, state and local courts
provide day care in order to allow parents with children
to be available for jury duty. Finally, some states have
considered holding court during evening hours to encourage more professionals to sit on juries (Meyer A2).

Other progress is being made through recommendations coming from national special focus groups, such
as the Fully Informed Jury Association, which promotes
juror rights (Adler 241), and the National Center for
State Courts' Center for Jury Studies, near Washington,
DC, which has recently unveiled a fifty-six-point reform
plan for strengthening jury selection and jury procedures within the courtroom. This plan calls for child
care and other supportive measures for jurors, including
time limits on trials, more use of technology such as
computers and video recordings of trials, and a bill of
rights guaranteeing jurors respect from attorneys and
judges and defining each citizen's right to serve on a
jury, rather than be dismissed without cause (Meyer
A18). Such efforts to review the jury system and pro-
pose reforms, controversial as they sometimes are, need
to be encouraged nationwide if we are to address the
roots of the problems afflicting current jury selection
processes.

In addition, states must also take steps to eliminate
attorneys' rights to peremptory challenges. The results
of the efforts put forth by the O. J. Simpson defense

Prado 13

team illustrate the extent to which such challenges can
alter and direct the composition of a jury. Such challenges restrict and homogenize juries in ways that undermine the full participation of the citizenry and that
deprive juries of their necessary diversity in perspective, experience, and education. As Jeffrey Abramson,
Professor of Politics at Brandeis University and author
of <u>We, the Jury</u> has pointed out, jury deliberations are
considered to be impartial only "when group differences are not eliminated, but rather invited, embraced,
and fairly represented" as parts of "the diversity of
views held in a heterogeneous society" (187). Although
attorney groups in several states are currently considering proposals that would limit the number of peremptory challenges that could be made in a case, it may ultimately prove more effective to eliminate the procedure
altogether from the American courtroom. Peremptory
challenging was eliminated in British courtrooms in
1988 and a process instituted wherein jurors are selected randomly from voter lists and not addressed by
attorneys until they have been sworn in and the trial
has actually begun. Such a process greatly reduces the
amount of time and frustration now required for jury selection in many American trials and also validates the
democratic and representative nature of the jury selection process (Adler 223-24). The United States would do
well to institute a similar system.

    Loss of faith in the effectiveness of juries has re-
sulted in a worldwide decline in their use in this century (Nolan). If the practice of trial by jury is to continue

Conclusion
summarizes
thesis and
general
content

Prado 14

in the United States, steps must be taken to improve the
jury selection process and to ensure that citizens of all
backgrounds and abilities have the opportunity to serve
on a jury. The problem of jury homogeneity and its vul-
nerability to undemocratic and erroneous decision making, even to the very extreme of nullifying existing
laws, needs to be addressed by immediate reform efforts. The lessons of the O. J. Simpson trial and other in-
cidents of national alarm cannot be ignored if we are to
ensure the future process of justice in this country.
Broadening the jury pool, eliminating most juror exclu-
sions, and abolishing peremptory challenges would
greatly improve many of the serious problems now undermining Americans' confidence in the U.S. jury system. The public and its leaders must become actively
concerned about the erosions already underway in the
jury system itself. If not, we assume the great and serious risk that juries and the duties they perform will become mere fruitless and pathetic imitations of justice.

Prado 15

Notes

Begin section on new page; center title

[1]Although both Lyle and Eric Menendez admitted to having murdered their parents, a jury found them not guilty when they were first tried together in 1991. The brothers claimed they had acted out of fear of being further abused by their parents. Their case was retried in 1996, and the second jury found both brothers guilty of murder. They were sentenced to life imprisonment without parole. In the O. J. Simpson case, despite what many felt was overwhelming evidence of guilt, a jury acquitted Simpson after a highly publicized, one-year trial, in which he was charged with the double murders of his wife, Nicole Brown Simpson, and her friend Ron Goldman in June 1994.

Clarifies or adds information that would interrupt text

[2]Judges can also dismiss jurors for a variety of reasons, ranging from health matters to violations of court restrictions. In the O. J. Simpson case, the judge removed a juror because he believed she was meeting with a literary agent and intending to write a book about the trial (Gleick, "Disorder"). As Rubank has noted, jurors in high-profile trials often see this experience as "their 15 minutes of fame" (24).

[3]This is not to imply, however, that attorneys in the case used peremptory challenges to exclude jurors on the basis of gender alone or to systematically shape the jury along gender lines. The Supreme Court forbid such uses of peremptory challenges in 1994. See Abramson 137.

Refers reader to sources listed in Works Cited

[4]Although highly controversial, nullification is explicitly legal in three states but only an implied or assumed jury right in the other forty-seven. For discussions of nullification, see Kerwin and Shaffer 140-46; Weinstein 239; and Holden.

Use semicolons to separate multiple sources

Prado 16

Works Cited

Abramson, Jeffrey. <u>We, the Jury: The Jury System and the Ideal of Democracy</u>. New York: Basic-Harper, 1994.

Adler, Stephen J. <u>The Jury: Trial and Error in the American Courtroom</u>. New York: Times Books, 1994.

DiPerna, Paula. <u>Juries on Trial: Faces of American Justice</u>. New York: Dember, 1984.

Dolan, Maura. "Jury System Is Held in Low Regard by Most." <u>Los Angeles Times</u> 27 Sept. 1994: A1+.

Gleick, Elizabeth. "Rich Justice, Poor Justice." <u>Time</u> 19 June 1995: 40-47.

- - -. "Disorder in the Court." <u>Time</u> 12 June 1995: 65.

Goodman, Ellen. "Today's Juror Must Carry the Baggage of Evolving Values." <u>Boston Globe</u> 21 Mar. 1994: 13. Online. Nexis. 5 Oct. 1995.

Greenburg, Jan Crawford. "Jury System Goes under the Microscope after Simpson Verdict, Some Specialists Argue for Big Overhaul." <u>Chicago Tribune</u> 8 Oct. 1995, chicagoland final ed.:1. Online. Dialog. 13 Oct. 1995.

Hall, Robert T. <u>Morality and Disobedience</u>. New York: Athens, 1971.

Holden, Benjamin A. "Color Blinded? Race Seems to Play an Increasing Role in Many Jury Verdicts." <u>Wall Street Journal</u> 4 Oct. 1995: A1.

"Jury." <u>The Encyclopedia Americana</u>. 1993 ed.

Kaplan, David A. "Disorder in the Court." <u>Newsweek</u> 16 Oct. 1995: 58-61.

Kerwin, Jeffrey, and David R. Shaffer. "The Effects of Jury Dogmatism on Reactions to Jury Nullification Instructions." <u>Personality and Social Psychology Bulletin</u> 17.2 (1991): 140-46.

Begin section on new page; center title

Book

Use + to indicate discontinuous pages

Alphabetize entries by authors' names

Use 3 unspaced hyphens for author's name when multiple works by same author

Include cross-referenced sources in Works Cited (see entry "King")

Online source without page numbers given

Encyclopedia article

Work with 2 authors

Prado 17

Work printed in another work

King, Martin Luther, Jr. "Letter from a Birmingham Jail." Morality and Disobedience. Ed. Robert T. Hall. New York: Athens, 1971. 767-73.   **Author with *Jr.* in name**

Lacayo, Richard. "Jury System in Trouble: Questionable Judgment." Time 13 Oct. 1994: 45.

Leo, John. "The Color of the Law." U.S. News and World Report 16 Oct. 1995: 24.

Meyer, Josh. "Small Vanguard Presses Its Case for Jury Reforms." Los Angeles Times 28 Sept. 1994: A1+.

Miller, Mark. "How the Jury Saw It." Newsweek 16 Oct. 1995: 37-39.   **Article in weekly magazine**

Nolan, Kenneth P. "Jury." Academic American Encyclopedia. Online. CompuServe. 27 Nov. 1995.

Royko, Mike. "Jury System Often Blind about Justice." Chicago Tribune 2 Mar. 1995, north sports final ed.: 3. Online. Dialog. 13 Oct. 1995.

Rubank, Larry. "Jurors Seeking Fame and Fortune." Psychology World 18 June 1995: 68-72.

Simon, Rita J. "Jury Nullification, or Prejudice and Ignorance in the Marion Barry Trial." Journal of Criminal Justice 20.3 (1992): 261-66.   **Article in journal**

Weinstein, Jack B. "Considering Jury 'Nullification': When, May, and Should a Jury Reject the Law to Do Justice?" American Criminal Law Review 30.2 (1993): 239-54.

Wishman, Seymour. Anatomy of a Jury: The System on Trial. New York: Times, 1986.

CHAPTER 11

Documenting Sources

The Works Cited List
(MLA Style)

The Works Cited list follows your paper's Notes section (or the paper's text if there are no notes), its pages numbered consecutively with those preceding it. Although often informally referred to as a *bibliography* (which is a broad list of *available works* on a subject), the Works Cited section is actually more precise: It is a summary listing each of the *sources named in the text*. For this reason, the Works Cited section of the paper reflects the focus and breadth of your discussion, and it serves as an aid to the research others may do on the subject.

What to Include

When compiling the list of sources for the Works Cited page(s), be certain to include every source you have mentioned in the paper but no others. List each source from which you (1) borrowed ideas or (2) quoted material or that you (3) named in a note. Sources included in the first two categories will also have previously been cited parenthetically in the text. Works mentioned in your paper's Notes will have received previous citation there, as well. Only works included in the text or Notes should appear under the heading Works Cited.

This undoubtedly means some, perhaps several, works that contributed background information or common knowledge to your research will not be listed on the Works Cited page. You may have consulted 50 sources during your research and ended up paraphrasing, quoting, or naming only 10 of them in your research paper. Only those 10 sources will be listed under Works Cited.

Works Cited Entries

The Works Cited section should provide the paper's reader with enough information to locate any of the works listed. The three basic units of information included for any kind of source are *author, title,* and *publication facts,* in that order. Some sources require additional information or may be cited with a special focus. In order to save the reader time and to ensure accuracy, follow the standard forms and abbreviations recommended for the discipline in which you are writing. (See Chapter 12 on documentation forms for other disciplines.) The discussion and examples that follow in this chapter conform to the documentation guidelines of the Modern Language Association, or MLA, and its publication *MLA Handbook for Writers of Research Papers,* 4th edition, by Joseph Gibaldi (New York: MLA, 1995).

Listing Works Cited Entries

In keeping with the MLA format, sources named on the Works Cited page should be listed alphabetically by the author's surname or, if no author is given, by the first word of the work's title. (If the title begins with the word *A, An,* or *The,* alphabetize by the second word in the title.) When listing more than one work by the same author, cite each work alphabetically by title, using three hyphens in place of the author's name after the first entry. (See the example for *Claiborne* in Figure 11.1.)

To prepare the list of entries, it is easiest to sort your bibliography cards into the desired order and then work directly from them. If you have entered the bibliography sources into a computer file, you may be able to utilize a "sort" function to alphabetize the list for you.

Formatting the Works Cited Page

To type the initial Works Cited page, center the title *Works Cited* one inch down from the top of the paper. Begin the first line for each entry flush with the left margin. Indent the second and all other lines for each entry five spaces from the left margin. Double-space throughout, including between entries (see Figure 11.1).

General Guidelines

The Works Cited entries for most sources will follow the standard order of author, title, and publication information. Note that the second and following lines of information for an entry are indented five additional spaces:

Martin 16

Works Cited

Joint
authors

Altman, Kenneth, and Shannon Moore. <u>Cycles of</u>
<u>Language Development: Three Studies</u>. Chicago:
Angar, 1994.

Calvin, William H. "The Emergence of Intelligence."
<u>Scientific American</u> Oct. 1994: 100-107.

Article in
magazine

Multiple
works by
same
author

Claiborne, Robert. <u>Our Marvelous English Tongue: The</u>
<u>Life and Times of the English Language</u>. New
York: Times, 1983.

- - -. <u>The Roots of English: A Reader's Handbook of</u>
<u>Word Origins</u>. New York: Times-Random, 1989.

Lighter, J. E. <u>Random House Historical Dictionary of</u>
<u>American Slang</u>. Vol. 1. New York: Random, 1995.

Source in
multivolume
work

Joint
editors

Marshall, Jeremy, and Fred McDonald, eds. <u>Questions</u>
<u>of English</u>. Oxford, Eng.: Oxford UP, 1994.

Malone, J. L. "Language." <u>Academic American Encyc-</u>
<u>lopedia</u>. Danbury, CT: Grolier Electronic, 1993.
Online. CompuServe. 18 Oct. 1995.

Encyclopedia
article/online
source

Source
included
in another
work

Mencken, H. L. "The American Language." <u>The</u>
<u>Treasury of the Encyclopedia Britannica</u>. Ed.
Clifton Fadiman. New York: Viking, 1992. 545-49.

Otter, Jane. "The First Noun and the Second Verb."
<u>New Language Journal</u> 11 (1995): 177-83.

Article in
journal

Unsigned
newspaper
article

"Spelling Was Never Easy." <u>New York Times</u> 17 Mar.
1995: B3+.

Turner, Kenneth. "Sign Language on the Net." <u>E-Lines</u>
(1995). 6 pars. Online. Internet. 6 Sept. 1995.

Article
from online
journal

Source
with more
than 3
authors/
editors

Washington, Patrick D., et al., eds. <u>Language for</u>
<u>Our Times: Essays on Communication and</u>
<u>Expression</u>. New York: Appletree, 1992.

FIGURE 11.1   Sample Works Cited Page: MLA Style

Book entry form Hawking, Stephen. <u>Black Holes and Baby Universes and Other Essays</u>. New York: Bantam, 1993.

Periodical entry form Lenat, Douglas B. "Artificial Intelligence." <u>Scientific American</u> Sept. 1995: 80-82.

When the entry for a source requires additional kinds of information, follow these sequences, as applicable:

For a Book
1. Author(s)
2. Title of section of the book (in quotation marks)
3. Title of the book (underlined or italicized—see p. 244)
4. Editor, translator, or compiler
5. Edition
6. Volume number of this book
7. Series title or number
8. Place, publisher, and date published
9. Page numbers for the part cited from this book (#2 above)
10. Number of volumes

These elements would appear as follows in the Works Cited entry for a book:

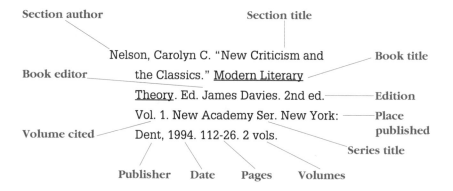

Section author **Section title**

Nelson, Carolyn C. "New Criticism and **Book title**
Book editor the Classics." <u>Modern Literary</u>
<u>Theory</u>. Ed. James Davies. 2nd ed. **Edition**
Vol. 1. New Academy Ser. New York: **Place published**
Volume cited Dent, 1994. 112-26. 2 vols.
Series title

Publisher **Date** **Pages** **Volumes**

For a Periodical
1. Author(s)
2. Title of the article (in quotation marks)
3. Title of the periodical (underlined or italicized—see p. 244)
4. Series title or number
5. Volume number (and issue number, if there is one)
6. Date of publication
7. Page numbers of the article cited

These elements would appear as follows in the Works Cited entry for a periodical article:

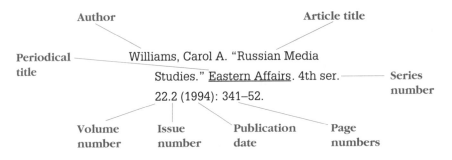

Authors' Names. A book, periodical, or other type of source may be written by one or several authors or an organization or group of some kind, or it may be the product of an editor, translator, or other type of compiler. Any one of these individuals or groups may be listed in the Works Cited section as the "author" of the work.

To list a source in the paper's Works Cited section, follow these general practices:

1. Cite the work alphabetically by the author's last name. If no author is given for a source, list it under the first word of its title (see the entry for *"Pyramids Repaired,"* below, and the section on Titles, p. 244):

Aldred, Cyril. Egypt to the End of the Old Kingdom. London: Thames & Hudson, 1982.

Bauval, Robert, and Adrian Gilbert. The Orion Mystery: Unlocking the Secrets of the Pyramids. New York: Crown, 1995.

Cairo Historical Foundation. Policies for Exploration and Excavation, 1991-93. Cairo, Egypt: 1994.

Hamblin, Dora Jane. "A Unique Approach to Unraveling the Secrets of the Great Pyramids." Smithsonian Apr. 1986: 39-42.

"Pyramids Repaired." Archaeology Feb. 1993: 23.

The Works Cited example in Figure 11.1 (see p. 240) also shows entries listed in alphabetical order by their authors' last names or by the first words of their titles.

2. Provide the author's name exactly as it is stated on the book's title page. Do not substitute initials for names when names are given (not *R. L. Atwood* instead of *Robert L. Atwood*). Do not omit initials when they are given (not *Carolyn Maitland* instead of *Carolyn M. Maitland*). Omit titles,

positions, and degrees, such as *PhD* and *MD*, but include suffixes that are essential parts of names, such as *Jr.:*

> Gates, Henry Louis, Jr. <u>Colored People: A Memoir</u>. New York: Vintage-Random, 1995.
>
> Kaye, Steven K. "Profits Across the Board." <u>U.S. News & World Report</u> 24 Apr. 1995: 68.
>
> Sabel, R. T. O., and S. Pallister. <u>Micro-Managing Profit and Loss: A Practical Guide for Small Businesses</u>. New York: Thresher, 1994.

Editors, Compilers, and Translators of Books. A work that is an anthology or collection is usually the product of an editor or compiler. List such persons alphabetically by their last names, followed by the abbreviation *ed.* (plural *eds.*) or *comp.:*

> Carrigan, Robert C., comp. <u>Astronomy Abstracts, 1994-95</u>. Creeley, MA: American, 1995.
>
> Jones, Steve, Robert Martin, and David Philbeam, eds. <u>The Cambridge Encyclopedia of Human Evolution</u>. New York: Cambridge UP, 1992.
>
> Michels, Greg, ed. <u>Governments of the West, 1991</u>. Austin, TX: Municipal Analysis, 1991.
>
> Nicholson, Colin, and John Orr, eds. <u>Cinema and Fiction: New Modes of Adapting</u>. New York: Columbia UP, 1992.

For the editor or translator of another writer's work, cite the person first whose work you are focusing upon in your paper:

Emphasis upon editor or translator	Bruccoli, Matthew J., ed. <u>The Short Stories of F. Scott Fitzgerald</u>. New York: Scribner-Simon, 1989. MacAdam, Alfred, trans. <u>The Campaign</u>. By Carlos Fuentes. New York: Harper Perennial, 1990.
Emphasis upon original author	Fitzgerald, F. Scott. <u>The Short Stories of F. Scott Fitzgerald</u>. Ed. Matthew J. Bruccoli. New York: Scribner-Simon, 1989. Fuentes, Carlos. <u>The Campaign</u>. Trans. Alfred MacAdam. New York: Harper Perennial, 1990.

(For citing the writer of an introduction, foreword, preface, or afterword, see section 29 later in this chapter.)

Titles.   List the title of a work exactly as it appears on the work itself. For a book, consult the title page, and include a subtitle if one is given. For the title of a periodical article, locate the first page of the article itself or check the periodical's table of contents for the exact title. Since punctuation between the main title and subtitle of a work is not usually shown, you may need to supply it. Always use a full colon followed by a single space to separate the main title and subtitle.

Underline the full title of a book, periodical, or other work published as an independent whole (e.g., a film, play, cassette recording, or other such work, as discussed later in this chapter). Note that these types of titles are underlined in the examples in this text. If your instructor agrees, you may use italics instead of underlining. Always place the title of a periodical article between quotation marks:

Book with subtitle	Valle, Galen Harris. <u>Teaching English in Asia: Finding a Job and Doing It Well</u>. Berkeley, CA: Pacific View, 1995.
Magazine article with subtitle	Silberman, Steve. "Home Sweet Home Page: The Missing Link Is You." <u>NetGuide</u> July 1995: 52-59.

(For the title of a work included in another work's title, see section 18 later in this chapter.)

Place of Publication, Publisher, and Date.   Since publishers for periodicals, unlike those for books, remain standard and are not essential to locating periodical material, do not include the names of publishers and places of publication for periodical entries on the Works Cited page.

For a book, consult the title page or the copyright page for publication facts. Give the place of publication first, followed by a colon, the name of the publisher, and the publication date:

Griffin, Donald R. <u>Animal Minds</u>. Chicago: U of Chicago P, 1992.

Place of Publication.   Give the name of the city in which the book was published. If the city may be unfamiliar to your reader, add the postal abbreviation of the state or country (*Upper Saddle River, NJ; Darwin, Austral.*):

Palmer, Eve. <u>The Plains of Camdeboo: The Classic Book of the Karoo</u>. Rev. ed. Johannesburg, S. Afr.: 1986.

Priest, Patricia Joyner. <u>Public Intimacies: Talk Show Participants and Tell-All TV</u>. Cresskill, NJ: Hampton, 1995.

When more than one city of publication is listed, give only the name of the first city mentioned.

Publisher's Name. Give the publisher's name in shortened form, omitting articles, business abbreviations (*Inc., Co., Ltd.*), and descriptions (*Publishers, Library, & Sons*):

Full publisher's name	*Shortened form*
E. P. Dutton	Dutton
Harcourt Brace Jovanovich, Inc.	Harcourt
Harper & Row Publishers, Inc.	Harper
Houghton Mifflin Co.	Houghton
McGraw-Hill	McGraw
W. W. Norton and Co., Inc.	Norton
Prentice-Hall	Prentice
Simon & Schuster, Inc.	Simon

For university presses, abbreviate *University* as *U* and *Press* with *P*. Do not use periods after either letter:

Full publisher's name	*Shortened form*
Cambridge University Press	Cambridge UP
Oxford University Press	Oxford UP
University of Chicago Press	U of Chicago P
University Press of Florida	UP of Florida

(See Chapter 13 for other examples and further guidelines for shortening publishers' names.)

Page Numbers. When citing part of a complete work (such as a chapter in a book or an article in a periodical), give the continuous page numbers on which the cited material is located. Do not use any abbreviation such as *p., pp.,* or *pg.* with page numbers.

For entries included in a book, give the page number(s) after the period following the work's publication date:

Aguilar, Luis Miguel. "The Huapango." New Writing from Mexico. Ed. Reginald Gibbons. New York: Tri Quarterly, 1992. 90-91.

Hardy, Thomas. "Channel Firing." Selected Poems. Ed. Andrew Morton. London: Dent, 1994. 75-76.

When listing a periodical article, give the inclusive page numbers for the entire article cited, listing the first page reference exactly as it is given in the source: *221–32; B2–4; Nov/6*. When the full article does not appear on consecutive pages (e.g., appears first on page 2 and then skips to page 8), give only the first page number followed by a plus sign:

Bower, Bruce. "Criminal Intellect." Science News 15 Apr. 1995: 232+.

Otis, John. "Cigars Are Back, Made in Honduras." San Francisco Chronicle 4 May 1995: A1+.

For a periodical issued on a daily, weekly, or monthly basis, include the day and month published, when they are given. Abbreviate all months except *May, June,* and *July:*

> Marshack, Alexander. "Images of the Ice." <u>Archaeology</u> July/Aug. 1995: 28-39.
>
> Robinson, J. "Geraldo's Showboating Makes Waves in Buzzard's Bay." <u>Boston Globe</u> 2 Aug. 1994: 58.

Index to Works Cited Forms

The rest of this chapter outlines standard MLA forms for sources listed in the Works Cited section of a research paper. Use the list below as a quick index to these forms when compiling and editing your own paper.

Books

1. A Book by One Author
2. More Than One Book by the Same Author
3. A Book by an Author Whose Name Includes Initials
4. A Book by an Anonymous Author
5. A Book by a Pseudonymous Author
6. A Work by a Classical Author
7. A Book by Two or Three Authors
8. A Book by More Than Three Authors
9. More Than One Book by the Same Multiple Authors
10. A Book with an Editor
11. A Book with Two or Three Editors
12. A Book with More Than Three Editors
13. A Book by a Corporation, Committee, Institution, or Other Group
14. The Proceedings of a Conference or Meeting
15. A Book in Multiple Volumes
16. A Single Volume Included in a Multivolume Work
17. A Part of a Volume Included in a Multivolume Work
18. A Book That Is Included in Another Book
19. A Book That Is Part of a Series
20. A Book That Is an Anthology or Collection
21. A Work That Is Included in an Anthology or Collection
22. A Work That Is Cross-Referenced to an Anthology or Collection
23. A Book That Is a Later Edition, Revision, or Reprint
24. A Book That Has Been Republished
25. A Book That Has Been Printed by a Division of a Publisher
26. A Book That Was Printed before 1900
27. A Book That Has Been Published in a Foreign Language

28. A Book That Has Been Translated
29. A Book with an Introduction, Preface, Foreword, or Afterword
30. The Bible
31. A Published Dissertation
32. An Unpublished Dissertation
33. A Government Publication
34. A Legal Citation

Magazines and Journals

35. An Article in a Journal with Continuous Yearly Pagination
36. An Article in a Journal with Discontinuous Pagination by Issue
37. An Article with No Author Named
38. An Article in a Weekly Magazine
39. An Article in a Monthly Magazine
40. An Article in a Series
41. A Published Interview
42. A Review in a Magazine or Journal
43. An Article Title That Includes Another Title
44. Letters, Comments, or Notes in a Journal or Magazine
45. A Dissertation or Article Abstract in an Abstract Journal

Newspapers

46. Standard Form for a Newspaper Article
47. An Unsigned Article in a Newspaper
48. Citing the Edition of a Newspaper
49. Citing the Pagination of a Newspaper

Other Sources

50. An Interview
51. A Public Address, Speech, or Lecture
52. A Letter
53. A Pamphlet
54. A Bulletin
55. An Article in a Microfilm Collection of Articles
56. An Advertisement
57. A Manuscript or Typescript
58. An Unpublished Paper
59. Material on a CD–ROM
60. Material on Diskette or Magnetic Tape
61. Material in Multiple Electronic Publication Forms
62. Material Accessed through an Online Database
63. Sources from Electronic Journals, Newsletters, and Conferences
64. Published Material Received as Electronic Text

65. A Work of Art or a Photograph
66. An Illustration, Table, Chart, or Map
67. A Cartoon
68. A Film, Video Tape, Video Disc, or Slide Program
69. A Television or Radio Program
70. A Recording

Works Cited Forms

Books

1. A BOOK BY ONE AUTHOR

Sheehy, Gail. New Passages: Mapping Your Life across Time. New
    York: Random, 1995.

Parenthetic citation form: (Sheehy 62).

2. MORE THAN ONE BOOK BY THE SAME AUTHOR

List multiple works by the same author (or editor) alphabetically by
title after the author's name. Substitute three unspaced hyphens and a period in place of the author's name after citing the first work. But if that author is an editor or writes a work with another person, list such works as
different entries:

Daiches, David. The Novel and the Modern World. Chicago: U of
    Chicago P, 1984.
- - -. The Scottish Enlightenment. New York: State Mutual Bank, 1986.
- - -. Two Worlds: An Edinburgh Jewish Childhood. Tuscaloosa: U of
    Alabama P, 1989.
Daiches, David, ed. A Companion to Scottish Culture. New York:
    Holmes and Meier, 1982.
Daiches, David, and John Flower. Literary Landscape of the British
    Isles: A Narrative Atlas. New York: Penguin, 1981.

Parenthetic citation forms: (Daiches, Novel 11); (Daiches, Scottish
334); (Daiches, Two Worlds 114); (Daiches, Companion 130);
(Daiches and Flower 64).

3. A BOOK BY AN AUTHOR WHOSE NAME INCLUDES INITIALS

Always use the same form for an author's name as given on the title
page of the work:

Auden, W. H. <u>Collected Shorter Poems: 1927-1957</u>. New York: Random, 1964.

Fitzgerald, F. Scott. <u>Tender Is the Night</u>. New York: Scribner's, 1951.

Parenthetic citation forms: (Auden 21); (Fitzgerald 91).

While it is not necessary to provide the full names of well-known authors, you may supply the full names in brackets, if you wish:

Auden, W[ystan] H[ugh]. <u>Collected Shorter Poems: 1927-1957</u>. New York: Random, 1964.

4. A BOOK BY AN ANONYMOUS AUTHOR

<u>Beowulf</u>. Trans. E. Talbot Donaldson. Ed. Joseph F. Tuso. New York: Norton, 1975.

Parenthetic citation form: (<u>Beowulf</u> 6).

5. A BOOK BY A PSEUDONYMOUS AUTHOR

Molière. <u>Le Misanthrope and Other Plays</u>. Trans. Donald M. Frame. New York: NAL, 1968.

To indicate the real name of an author published under a pseudonym, use square brackets followed by a period:

Molière [Jean Baptiste Poquelin]. <u>Le Misanthrope and Other Plays</u>. Trans. Donald M. Frame. New York: NAL, 1968.

Parenthetic citation form: (Molière 51).

6. A WORK BY A CLASSICAL AUTHOR

Sophocles. <u>Oedipus the King</u>. Trans. Stephen Berg and Clay Diskin. London: Oxford UP, 1989.

Virgil. <u>The Aeneid</u>. Trans. Robert Fitzgerald. New York: Random, 1983.

Parenthetic citation forms: (Sophocles 3.115–18); (Virgil 1.61).

7. A BOOK BY TWO OR THREE AUTHORS

Cite the first and last names of the first author in reverse order, separated by commas, and follow his or her name with the other authors' names in normal order. Use *and* before the last author's name:

Heaton, Jeanne Albronda, and Nona Leigh Wilson. <u>Tuning in Trouble: Talk TV's Destructive Impact on Mental Health</u>. San Francisco: Jossey-Bass, 1995.

Roueche, John E., Susanne D. Roueche, and Mark D. Milliron. <u>Strangers in Their Own Land: Part-Time Faculty in American Community Colleges</u>. Washington, DC: American Association of Community Colleges, 1995.

Parenthetic citation forms: (Heaton and Wilson 175); (Roueche, Roueche, and Milliron 140).

8. A BOOK BY MORE THAN THREE AUTHORS

For books with more than three authors, you have several options. You may cite all authors in the order in which they are listed on the source's title page:

Merit, Linda A., Carl H. Danz, Robert Ulrich, Janice Pohl, and Daniel M. Vance. <u>Families and Family Violence: A Report on the Effects of Intervention Counseling</u>. New York: Altran, 1994.

As you can see, however, citing all of the names could result in a lengthy parenthetic citation, which will interfere with your paper's text. To avoid such citations, you may also give only the first author's name (in reverse order), followed by a comma and the abbreviation *et al.* (meaning "and others"):

Merit, Linda A., et al. <u>Families and Family Violence: A Report on the Effects of Intervention Counseling</u>. New York: Altran, 1994.

Parenthetic citation form: (Merit et al. 132).

9. MORE THAN ONE BOOK BY THE SAME MULTIPLE AUTHORS

Cite all the authors in the first citation only; use three unspaced hyphens, followed by a period, in place of the authors' names in succeeding entries. List all works in alphabetical order by title (ignoring the words *A, An,* and *The* at the beginnings of titles).

Note that three hyphens can be used for successive entries only when the authors are *exactly* the same. Thus, the example below shows one work by *Richard Leakey,* followed by three he co-authored with *Roger Lewin* (listed by title in alphabetical order); the last entry shows a work by *Lewin* only:

Leakey, Richard. <u>The Origin of Humankind</u>. New York: Basic-Harper, 1994.

Leakey, Richard, and Roger Lewin. <u>Origins: The Emergence and Evolution of Our Species and Its Possible Future</u>. New York: Dutton, 1977.

- - -. Origins Reconsidered: In Search of What Makes Us Human. New York: Anchor-Doubleday, 1992.
- - -. People of the Lake: Mankind and Its Beginnings. New York: Avon, 1979.

Lewin, Roger. The Origin of Modern Humans. New York: Freeman, 1993.

Parenthetic citation forms: (Leakey 150); (Leakey and Lewin, Origins 102); (Leakey and Lewin, Origins Reconsidered 14); (Leakey and Lewin, People 20); (Lewin 82).

10. A BOOK WITH AN EDITOR

a. To Focus on the Work of the Editor

Karlin, Wayne, Le Minh Khue, and Truong Vu, eds. The Other Side of Heaven: Post-War Fiction by Vietnamese and American Writers. Willimantic, CT: Curbstone, 1995.

Morton, Andrew, ed. Selected Poems of Thomas Hardy. London: Dent, 1994.

Parenthetic citation forms: (Karlin, Khue, and Vu 170); (Morton 81).

b. To Focus on the Work of the Author

Bao, Vu. "The Man Who Stained His Soul." The Other Side of Heaven: Post-War Fiction by Vietnamese and American Writers. Eds. Wayne Karlin, Le Minh Khue, and Truong Vu. Willimantic, CT: Curbstone, 1995. 166–71.

Hardy, Thomas. "Channel Firing." Selected Poems. Ed. Andrew Morton. London: Dent, 1994. 75–76.

Parenthetic citation forms: (Bao 167); (Hardy, "Channel" 76).

11. A BOOK WITH TWO OR THREE EDITORS

Rees, A. L., and Frances Bozello, eds. The New History of Art. Atlantic Highlands, NJ: Humanities, 1992.

Danziger, Sheldon H., Gary D. Sandefur, and Daniel W. Weinberg, eds. Confronting Poverty: Prescriptions for Change. Cambridge, MA: Harvard UP, 1994.

Parenthetic citation forms: (Rees and Bozello 111); (Danziger, Sandefur, and Weinberg 33).

12. A BOOK WITH MORE THAN THREE EDITORS

Again, you have several options here. You may cite a book with more than three editors by naming each editor in the order given on the source's title page:

Humm, S. Randall, Beate Anna Ort, Martin Mazen Anbari, Wendy S. Lader, and William Scott Biel, eds. <u>Child, Parent, and State: Law and Policy Reader</u>. Philadelphia: Temple UP, 1994.

Parenthetic citation form: (Humm, Ort, Anbari, Lader, and Biel 40).

As this example demonstrates, however, including numerous names in the parenthetic citation makes it cumbersome to read and distracts from the paper's content. Unless there is a reason for including all the editors' names in the parenthetic citation and in the Works Cited section, it is generally better to give only the first editor's name, followed by a comma, *et al.* (meaning "and others"), and *eds.:*

Humm, S. Randall, et al., eds. <u>Child, Parent, and State: Law and Policy Reader</u>. Philadelphia: Temple UP, 1994.

Parenthetic citation form: (Humm et al. 16).

13. A BOOK BY A CORPORATION, COMMITTEE, INSTITUTION, OR OTHER GROUP

Act Up/NY Women and AIDS Book Group. <u>Women, AIDS, and Activism</u>. Boston: South End, 1992.

American Medical Association. <u>Guide to Prescription and Over-the-Counter Drugs</u>. New York: American Medical Association, 1988.

Sumner County Historical Society. <u>A Brief History of Sumner County 1871-1921</u>. Groveland, CO: Mineral, 1993.

Parenthetic citation forms: (ActUp/NY 61); (American 288); (Sumner 113).

These corporate authors' names have been shortened to avoid lengthy parenthetic citations that might interrupt the reader's attention to the text. (See additional guidelines for avoiding extended parenthetic citations for government authors in section 33.)

14. THE PROCEEDINGS OF A CONFERENCE OR MEETING

Include the place, date, and nature of the conference or meeting if they are not provided in the title:

Federal Bar Association Staff. <u>Conference on Advertising Law:</u>
<u>Proceedings of the Federal Bar Association</u>. September, 1994.
Washington, DC: Federal Bar Assoc., 1995.

<u>Preparing for Tomorrow: Communications in the Twenty-First Century</u>.
35th International Communications Conference, Detroit, MI:
Society for International Communications, 1995.

Parenthetic citation forms: (Federal 16); (<u>Preparing</u> 88).

15. A BOOK IN MULTIPLE VOLUMES

Mokhtar, G., ed. <u>General History of Africa: Ancient Civilization in</u>
<u>Africa</u>. Abr. ed. 8 vols. London: James Currey, 1990.

Shakespeare, William. <u>The Complete Works of William Shakespeare</u>.
Ed. David Bevington. 6 vols. New York: Bantam, 1990.

Parenthetic citation forms: (Mokhtar, vol. 2); (Shakespeare 3:445-46).

Give the inclusive publication dates if the volumes were published
over a period of years (*1989–93*). If some volumes have been printed but
others have not, include the phrase *to date* after the number of volumes (*4
vols. to date*) and leave a space after the hyphen following the beginning
date (*1993–*):

Boyd, Julian P., et al., eds. <u>The Papers of Thomas Jefferson</u>. 25 vols. to
date. Princeton, NJ: Princeton UP, 1950– .

Parenthetic citation form: (Boyd 3:221).

16. A SINGLE VOLUME INCLUDED IN A MULTIVOLUME WORK

If you are using one volume of a multivolume work, cite only the
number of the volume you are using (*Vol. 2*) and give the publication information for that particular volume, as well:

Norris, Robert S., Andrew S. Burrows, and Richard W. Fieldhouse.
<u>Nuclear Weapons Databook: British, French, and Chinese Nuclear</u>
<u>Weapons</u>. Vol. 5. Boulder, CO: Westview, 1994. 8 vols.

Parenthetic citation form: (Norris, Burrows, and Fieldhouse 121-22).

17. A PART OF A VOLUME INCLUDED IN A MULTIVOLUME WORK

To cite a part of a volume in a multivolume work, give the volume
number of the part you are citing before the place of publication (as shown
in the preceding example). Cite the inclusive page numbers of the material
after the publication date, followed by the total number of volumes:

Blair, Hugh. Lectures on Rhetoric and Belles Lettres. Ed. Harold F.
    Harding. Vol. 2. Carbondale: Southern Illinois UP, 1965. 116. 2
    vols.
Zayed, A. H. "Egypt's Relations with the Rest of Africa." General History of Africa: Ancient Civilizations of Africa. Ed. G. Mokhtar. Vol.
    2. Abr. ed. London: James Currey, 1990. 145-47. 8 vols.

Parenthetic citation forms: (Blair); (Zayed 145).

18. A BOOK THAT IS INCLUDED IN ANOTHER BOOK
Do not underline or italicize the title of a book when it is included
within the title of another work. Make sure, however, that you underline or
italicize the rest of the title:

Bloom, Harold, ed. William Faulkner's The Sound and the Fury. New
    York: Chelsea House, 1988.
Jaffe, Mare, ed. Three Great Novels of the Civil War: The Killer Angels
    by Michael Shaara; Andersonville by MacKinlay Kantor; The Red
    Badge of Courage by Stephen Crane. New York: Wings, 1994.

Parenthetic citation forms: (Bloom 120); (Jaffe 222).

19. A BOOK THAT IS PART OF A SERIES
Include the series name and number (when given) before the place of
publication. Use the standard abbreviation *Ser.* when the word *series* is part
of the series name:

Barrow, John D. The Origin of the Universe. Science Masters Ser. New
    York: Basic-Harper, 1994.
Dappon, Henry. Vanishing Species of the Americas. Wildlife Ser. 3.
    New York: Glenn-Golder, 1995.

Parenthetic citation forms: (Barrow 34); (Dappon 4).

20. A BOOK THAT IS AN ANTHOLOGY OR COLLECTION

Stevens, Wallace. Collected Poems. New York: Random, 1982.
Wagner-Martin, Linda, and Cathy N. Davidson, eds. The Oxford Book
    of Women's Writing in the United States. Oxford, Eng.: Oxford UP,
    1995.

Parenthetic citation forms: (Stevens 47);
(Wagner-Martin and Davidson 117).

21. A WORK THAT IS INCLUDED IN AN ANTHOLOGY OR COLLECTION

Give the name of the author of the work you are citing, followed by the work's title in quotation marks or underlined/italicized, depending upon how it is regularly indicated. Next give the title of the anthology or collection, followed, if appropriate, by the editor's or translator's name in normal order, which is preceded by *Ed.* or *Trans.* After the publication information, give the page numbers on which the work appears in the anthology or collection:

Chopin, Kate. "A Pair of Silk Stockings." The Oxford Book of Women's Writing in the United States. Eds. Linda Wagner-Martin and Cathy N. Davidson. Oxford, Eng.: Oxford UP, 1995. 63-67.

Stevens, Wallace. "The Palm at the End of the Mind." Collected Poems. New York: Random, 1982. 237.

Parenthetic citation forms: (Chopin 65); (Stevens).

22. A WORK THAT IS CROSS-REFERENCED TO AN ANTHOLOGY OR COLLECTION

When you cite two or more works from the same anthology or collection, cross-reference them to the editor of the larger work, which you must also cite separately. Give only the editor's surname after the name of the author and title of the work you are citing. Use no punctuation between the editor's name and the page numbers for the cited work. Omit *ed.* or other descriptive words in the cross-reference:

Baym, Nina, et al. eds. The Norton Anthology of American Literature. 3rd shorter ed. New York: Norton, 1989.

Faulkner, William. "That Evening Sun." Baym 2005-16.

Wright, Richard. "The Man Who Was Almost a Man." Baym 2118-26.

Parenthetic citation forms: (Baym 142-44); (Faulkner 2007); (Wright 2125).

23. A BOOK THAT IS A LATER EDITION, REVISION, OR REPRINT

Following the information on the title page or copyright page, indicate that a book is a later, revised, or reprinted edition by giving the edition number (*2nd ed.* or *3rd ed.*), a description (*Rev. ed.* for "Revised edition," *Abr. ed.* for "Abridged edition, or "*rpt.* for "reprinted"), or a year (*1972 ed*). For a work that has been revised by someone other than the original author, give the name of the reviser after the title (see the *Fowler* entry on the next page):

Christians, Clifford G., Mark Fackler, and Kevin B. Rotzall. Media
Ethics: Cases and Moral Reasoning. 4th ed. White Plains, NY:
Longman, 1995.

Fowler, H. W. Modern English Usage. Rev. Ernest Gowers. 2nd ed.
New York: Oxford UP, 1965.

Hirsch, E. D., Joseph F. Kett, and James Trefil. The Dictionary of
Cultural Literacy. 2nd rev. ed. Boston: Houghton, 1993.

Mokhtar, G., ed. General History of Africa: Ancient Civilizations of
Africa. Vol. 2. Abr. ed. London: James Currey, 1990. 8 vols.

Taylor, Michael J. H., ed. Jayne's Encyclopedia of Aviation. Rev. ed.
New York: Crescent, 1995.

Parenthetic citation forms: (Christians, Fackler, and Rotzall 221);
(Fowler 28); (Hirsch, Kett, and Trefil 72); (Mokhtar 160); (Taylor 8).

24. A BOOK THAT HAS BEEN REPUBLISHED

Cite a republished book by giving the original publication date after
the title and the recent date of publication at the end of the entry:

Cushing, Frank Hamilton. Zuni Folktales. 1901. Tucson, AZ: U of
Arizona P, 1992.

Parenthetic citation form: (Cushing 118).

You may also include supplementary information about the original or
later publication, as relevant to your purpose:

Cushing, Frank Hamilton. Zuni Folktales. Fwd. by John Wesley Powell.
1901. Tucson, AZ: U of Arizona P, 1992.

Parenthetic citation form: (Cushing 86).

25. A BOOK THAT HAS BEEN PRINTED BY A DIVISION
OF A PUBLISHER

Paperback versions of cloth-bound editions are often reprinted by divisions of the main publisher. If the title or copyright page carries a publisher's special imprint, list the division first, joined by a hyphen to the
name of the main publisher:

Abramson, Jeffrey. We, the Jury: The Jury System and the Ideal of
Democracy. New York: Basic-Harper, 1994.

Parenthetic citation form: (Abramson 116).

26. A BOOK THAT WAS PRINTED BEFORE 1900

Cite an early book as you would any other, but omit the publisher's name:

Melville, Herman. Redburn. London, 1849.

Parenthetic citation form: (Melville 200).

Note that the lengthy and descriptive subtitle common to many older books is usually shortened. The full title of Melville's *Redburn*, for example, is *Redburn: His First Voyage, Being the Sailor-boy Confessions and Reminiscences of the Son-of-a-Gentleman, in the Merchant Service.*

27. A BOOK THAT HAS BEEN PUBLISHED IN A FOREIGN LANGUAGE

Maintain capitalization, spelling, and punctuation of names and titles exactly as in the original. Include any special symbols (e.g., accent marks, umlauts) required by the respective foreign language:

Jaramillo, Maria Mercedes, Angelo Robledo, and Flor Maria Rodriquez-Arenas, eds. ¿Y las mujeres?. Medellin, Colombia: U de Antioque, 1991.

Parenthetic citation form: (Jaramillo, Robledo, and Rodriquez-Arenas 43).

28. A BOOK THAT HAS BEEN TRANSLATED

a. To Focus on the Translator

Reck, Michael, trans. The Iliad. By Homer. New York: Icon, 1994.

Parenthetic citation form: (Reck 90).

b. To Focus on the Original Author

Homer. The Iliad. Trans. Michael Reck. New York: Icon, 1994.

Parenthetic citation form: (Homer 202).

29. A BOOK WITH AN INTRODUCTION, PREFACE, FOREWORD, OR AFTERWORD

a. To Focus on the Author of the Supplementary Material

If the author of the introduction, preface, foreword, or afterword is also the author of the book you are citing, give only his or her last name after the word *By* (see the entry for *Dickey,* below). List the page numbers on which the supplementary material appears in the book:

Clinton, Hillary Rodham. Foreword. Health Care Choices for Today's
Consumer. By Marc S. Miller, ed. Washington, DC: Living Planet,
1995. iv-xii.

Dickey, James. Preface. Babel to Byzantium: Poets and Poetry Now. By
Dickey. New York: Farrar, 1968. ix-x.

Ice-T. Introduction. Uprising: Crips and Bloods Tell the Story of America's Youth in the Crossfire. By Yusuf Jah and Sister Shah'Keyah.
New York: Scribner, 1995. 9-23.

Parenthetic citation forms: (Clinton vi); (Dickey x); (Ice-T 14).

b. To Focus on the Author of the Work Cited

If you have referred in your paper to both the author of the work cited
and the author of the supplementary material, you will need to include
them each separately in the Works Cited list. For example, if you had cited
both *Hillary Rodham Clinton* and *Marc S. Miller* in your paper's text (see
the example for *Clinton,* above), your Works Cited list would include entries for both: the *Clinton* entry shown above and the following entry for
Miller:

Miller, Marc. S., ed. Health Care Choices for Today's Consumer.
Fwd. Hillary Rodham Clinton. Washington, DC: Living Planet,
1995.

Parenthetic citation form: (Miller 65).

As this example shows, when listing a work by its author, rather than
by the author of the supplementary material, you should use the abbreviation *Introd.* ("Introduction"), *Fwd.* ("Foreword"), *Pref.* ("Preface"), or
Aftwd. ("Afterword"), as appropriate, after the title of the work.

30. THE BIBLE

Do not list the Bible on your Works Cited page if you are using the
King James version. In the text of your paper, cite a book, chapter, or verse
of the Bible parenthetically, using standard abbreviations (see the example
below and on p. 326). Cite other versions of the Bible as you would a
book with an anonymous author:

New American Bible: Revised New Testament. Grand Rapids: Christian UP, 1988.

The Revised English Bible with Apocrypha. London: Oxford UP, 1990.

Parenthetic citation forms: (Gen. 2:11); (Matt. 1:2).

31. A PUBLISHED DISSERTATION

Underline or italicize the title of a published dissertation. Use the abbreviation *Diss.* for "Dissertation" after the title of the work and before the name of the degree institution. Include the year in which the degree was granted after the institution's name, followed by standard publication information (place, publisher, date). For works published by University Microfilms International (UMI), you may include the order number as supplementary material, if you wish:

Harris, Rachel. Picasso and the Evolution of Cubist Literature. Diss. U
   of Kansas, 1993. Austin, TX: Prairie, 1994.

Ramsey, Arnold G. On the Significance of Success Attitudes Among
   Elite College Athletes. Diss. U of Virginia, 1994. Ann Arbor: UMI,
   1993. 6239772

Parenthetic citation forms: (Harris 23); (Ramsey 182).

32. AN UNPUBLISHED DISSERTATION

For an unpublished dissertation, give the title in quotation marks, followed by the name of the institution granting the degree, a comma, and the date:

Allen, Annette Marie. "AIDS and the Aging: Are the Elderly Becoming
   the New At-Risk Population?" Diss. U of North Texas, 1994.

Parenthetic citation form: (Allen 126).

33. A GOVERNMENT PUBLICATION

Government agencies generate a multitude of documents in varying forms. The citation examples shown here are representative of the most common types. Observe these guidelines:

a. In most cases, treat the major agency as the author, followed successively by the subagency or -agencies. For United States government documents, it helps to remember that *departments* (e.g., Department of Health and Human Services, Department of Justice) oversee *bureaus, administrations, offices,* and the like (e.g., National Bureau of Standards, Maritime Administration, Office of Justice Programs).

b. Note the standard abbreviations for certain items when citing U.S. government publications. For instance, the *Congressional Record* is abbreviated *Cong. Rec.*; its page numbers begin with *H* or *S* to stand for the *House* or the *Senate* sections of the publication. Most United States government materials are printed by the *Government Printing Office,* abbreviated *GPO.*

c. If you list more than one entry by the same agency, do not repeat the agency name. Use three hyphens followed by a period for each successive entry by the same agency/author. The example below uses hyphens to stand for *United States* and *Dept. of Commerce,* as given in the previous entry:

Cong. Rec. 17 Mar. 1989. S2966. Florida State. Joint Committee on

Language Education. Standards for Elementary Grades Language

Instruction. Tampa: Greydon, 1988.

United Nations. General Assembly. Resolutions and Decisions. 42nd

sess. 15–21 Dec. 1987. New York: United Nations, 1988.

United States. Dept. of Commerce. Bureau of the Census. 1990 Census

of Retail Trade: Pennsylvania. Geographic Area Ser. Washington,

DC: GPO, 1990.

- - -. - - -. Bureau of Economic Analysis. Selected Foreign Investment

Fluctuation: Analysis. Washington, DC: GPO, 1993.

- - -. President. Public Papers of the Presidents of the United States. Bk.

2. 4 July-31 Dec. 1987. Washington, DC: GPO, 1989.

Parenthetic citation forms: Although you may cite the author of a government publication parenthetically—for example, *(United Nations, General Assembly 65–81)*—it is best to avoid interrupting the reader with a lengthy parenthetic citation. Whenever possible, name the author in the text and cite the page numbers in parentheses:

The report from the United Nations General Assembly shows worldwide crop yields have changed dramatically in the last seven years (225).

34. A LEGAL CITATION

Citations for sections of the United States Constitution, federal and state codes, as well as court cases are usually heavily abbreviated. If your paper requires several such citations, you may want to consult *The Blue Book: A Uniform System of Citation,* published by the Harvard Law Review Association (1991).

The following examples demonstrate common practice. Use these for comparison with your own legal source and as a guide for citation:

US Const. Art. 6, sec. 3.

12 US Code. Sec 2283. 1973.

Federal Financing Bank Act of 1973. 96 Stat. 879. Pub. L. 97-255. 1993.

New Jersey. Const. Art. IV, Sec 6.

To cite a court case, give the name of the case, using the abbreviation *v.* (for "versus") between the names of the litigants and ending with a period. Next list the volume and page numbers in the work cited, the kind of court that decided the case, and the year in which the case was decided:

People v. Keith. 741 F 2d 220 DC CA 3d 1993.

This entry shows that the case of *People v. Keith* was decided in the Third District Court of Appeals in 1993. The case is described in volume 741 of the *Federal Reporter,* second series, page 220.

Note that the name of a court case should be underlined or italicized in the text of your paper or in a parenthetic note but not in the Works Cited list.

Parenthetic citation forms: See the guidelines above for citing government authors and their works.

Magazines and Journals

Magazines and journals differ in their contents and intended audiences as well as in the information you need to locate and document for use in your paper. While magazines are generally published monthly or weekly, journals are published less frequently and often irregularly. For this reason, the publication information needed for a magazine and a journal differ significantly. For example, a magazine will likely have a weekly or monthly publication date (e.g., *May 24, 1994* or *August 1995*), whereas a journal will have a publication date indicating a more general time period (e.g., *Winter 1994* or *Vol. 4, no. 3, 1995*).

Volume and Issue Numbers. Volume and issue numbers are important for documenting journal articles. Each *issue* of a journal is usually numbered, and all the issues published in a single year make up one *volume* of that particular journal. Thus, the cover or title page of a particular journal may indicate that its contents comprise *Volume 2, number 2.* This information may be all that you have to locate the journal in the library or to document its contents in your paper. Although magazines also have volume and issue numbers, their more specific dates of publication make that information unnecessary for documentation purposes and for listing them in the Works Cited list.

Page Numbers. Another difference in documentation information between magazines and journals is in how issues are paginated. Magazines use *discontinuous* pagination, whereby each issue starts with page 1 and ends with any given page number. Although some journals also use discontinuous pagination, most use *continuous* pagination, in which each issue continues the numbering of pages from wherever the previous issue stopped. For instance, the first issue in a given year of a continuously paginated journal might begin on page 1 and end on page 260; the next issue would begin with page 261; and so forth. Each successive issue would continue pagination from where the previous issue stopped.

The distinctions between information needed to document sources from magazines and journals will become increasingly clearer to you once you begin working with such periodicals and following these guidelines:

**35. AN ARTICLE IN A JOURNAL WITH
CONTINUOUS YEARLY PAGINATION**

For an article in a journal with continuous pagination, give the author's name first, followed by the article title in quotation marks. Next give the journal title (underlined or italicized), the volume number, the publication year in parentheses, followed by a colon, and then the page numbers of the article, ending with a period. Do not include the issue number for a continuously paginated journal, since the volume number and sequential pagination are all that will be needed to locate the source:

> Bracher, Mark. "Doctor-Assisted Suicide: Psychoanalysis of Mass
> Anxiety." Psychoanalytic Review 82 (1995): 657-58.
> Ramsey, Norman F. "Science Teaching and Research in Universities."
> New Literary History 26 (1995): 591-600.

Parenthetic citation forms: (Bracher 657); (Ramsey 598).

**36. AN ARTICLE IN A JOURNAL WITH DISCONTINUOUS
PAGINATION BY ISSUE**

For an article in a journal with discontinuous pagination, begin with the author's name, the article title, and the journal title (formatted as just described for continuously paginated journals). Then give the volume number and issue number, separated with a period (*9.3*). Use a hyphen to show combined issues (*44.2-3*). Do not include the word *volume* or any abbreviations for it, such as *vol.* or *vols.* Following the volume and issue numbers, add the date in parentheses, followed by a colon and the page numbers:

> Moore, Kevin Z. "Eclipsing the Commonplace: The Logic of Alienation
> in Antonioni." Film Quarterly 48.4 (1995): 22-34.
> Raston, Elizabeth. "Potentials in Teen Suicide Patterns." Social Issues
> 10.3-4 (1995): 76-82.

Parenthetic citation forms: (Moore 31–33); (Raston 80).

37. AN ARTICLE WITH NO AUTHOR NAMED

Begin the entry with the article title, and follow the format for a magazine or journal, as appropriate. List the article alphabetically by its title, but ignore the word *A, An,* or *The* when it appears as the first word in the title:

"Can We Save Antarctica?" <u>Hemisphere Quarterly</u> 16.4 (1995): 34-40.

"A Most Perfect Fit." <u>Time</u> 14 Apr. 1993: 22-23.

Parenthetic citation forms: ("Can" 36); ("Most" 22).

38. AN ARTICLE IN A WEEKLY MAGAZINE

Gleick, Elizabeth. "Sex, Betrayal and Murder." <u>Time</u> 17 July 1995: 32+.

Parenthetic citation form: (Gleick 36).

Use a plus sign (+) after the first page number to indicate that the entire article does not appear on consecutive pages. Thus, the pagination for an article beginning on page 12 and continuing again on pages 17–19 would be indicated by *12+,* followed by a period to end the entry.

39. AN ARTICLE IN A MONTHLY MAGAZINE

Trefil, James. "Dark Matter." <u>Smithsonian</u> July 1993: 27-35.

Parenthetic citation form: (Trefil 31).

40. AN ARTICLE IN A SERIES

If the article in the series has the same title and author in each issue of a publication, list all bibliographic information, including serial publication dates, in one entry:

Dendam, Karl H. "The Artist's Only Muse." <u>Fine Arts Journal</u> 14 (1990): 112-19; 15 (1990): 253-61, 293-96.

Parenthetic citation form: (Dendam 14: 118).

If the series articles have different titles in various issues, list each separately. You may include a brief explanation at the end of the entry to indicate that the article is part of a series:

Varry, Joan. "Prisons." <u>Stateside</u> Dec. 1994: 55–67. Pt. 2 of a series.

Parenthetic citation form: (Varry 56).

41. A PUBLISHED INTERVIEW

Begin the entry with the name of the person interviewed, followed by a period; then add the term *Interview,* followed by the interviewer's name, if pertinent; end with a period. For the rest of the entry, include the information and follow the format used for a magazine or journal article, as appropriate:

Clinton, Hillary Rodham. Interview with Margaret Carlson. "'We've Had Some Good Times.'" <u>Time</u> 10 May 1993: 37.

Parenthetic citation form: (Clinton).

Note that the title of this sample entry has both double and single quotation marks around it, rather than just double (the usual style). Both are used here because double quotes were used around the title in the original publication. Single quotes always go *within* double quotes, as shown. (For listing other sources of interviews, see section 50.)

42. A REVIEW IN A MAGAZINE OR JOURNAL

Follow the reviewer's name and the title of the review with *Rev. of,* followed by the title of the work reviewed, a comma, the word *by,* and the name of the work's author. Use appropriate abbreviations, such as *ed.,* ("editor"), *trans.* ("translator"), and *dir.* ("directed"), instead of *by,* as needed. List a review for which no author's name is given by its title. Include the name of the magazine or journal, along with the remaining publication information, as appropriate:

> Lind, Michael. "American by Invitation." Rev. of <u>Alien Nation: Common Sense About America's Immigration Disaster</u>, by
> Peter Brimelow. <u>New Yorker</u> 24 Apr. 1995: 107-10.
> "The Theater." Rev. of Samuel Beckett's <u>Waiting for Godot</u>, dir.
> Eve Adamson. <u>New Yorker</u> 4 Sept. 1995: 12.
> *Parenthetic citation forms:*   (Lind 109); ("Theater").

43. AN ARTICLE TITLE THAT INCLUDES ANOTHER TITLE

Put the title of the periodical article you are citing in quotation marks and underline or italicize any titles of whole works within it. Included titles that are usually written in double quotation marks should be cited with single quotation marks inside double, as in the second example:

> Cosgrove, Peter. "Snapshots of the Absolute: Mediamachia in <u>Let Us Now Praise Famous Men</u>." <u>American Literature</u> 67 (1995): 329-58.
> Rody, Caroline. "Toni Morrison's <u>Beloved</u>: History, 'Rememory,' and a
> Clamor for a Kiss." <u>American Literary History</u> 7.1 (1995): 92-119.
> *Parenthetic citation forms:*   (Cosgrove 330); (Rody 104).

44. LETTERS, COMMENTS, OR NOTES IN A JOURNAL OR MAGAZINE

> Harris, Angela. Letter. <u>Harper's</u> May 1994: 9.
> Rossman, Gary. "Frost's 'Desert Places,'" <u>The Explicator</u> 27.3 (1987): 21-22.
> Walsh, Thomas, and Natasha Walsh. "Patterns of <u>Who/Whom</u> Usage."
> <u>American Speech</u> 64 (1989): 284-86.
> *Parenthetic citation forms:*   (Harris); (Rossman 22);
> (Walsh and Walsh 284-85).

45. A DISSERTATION OR ARTICLE ABSTRACT
IN AN ABSTRACT JOURNAL

Abstract journals publish condensed versions of scholarly and professional works, such as articles and dissertations. When you list an abstract in the Works Cited portion of your paper, give the original publication information about the abstracted work first; follow this information with the underlined or italicized title of the abstract journal; then give the volume number, year (in parentheses), and item or page number of the abstract. Whether you list an item number or page number will depend upon the journal source. Some journals, such as *Psychological Abstracts* and *Current Index to Journals in Education,* use an item number with each abstract entry; others, such as *Dissertation Abstracts* and *Dissertation Abstracts International,* use a page number.

If the title of the journal does not indicate that the item you are citing is an abstract, include the word *Abstract* (capitalized but not underlined, italicized, or in quotation marks) immediately after the original publication information (see the entry for *Keely* below).

Use the abbreviation *DA* for *Dissertation Abstracts* and *DAI* for *Dissertation Abstracts International,* followed by the volume number and then the date in parentheses. Give the page number on which the abstract appears, including the series letter (*A* denotes "humanities and social sciences"; *B,* "the sciences"; *C,* "European dissertations"):

Haldeman, Melissa Anne. "The Effects of Motivation, Anxiety, and
  Visualization on Creative Behavior." Diss. U of California, Los
  Angeles, 1992. <u>DAI</u> 52 (1992): 1846A.

Keely, Robert A. "Economic Reward as Educational Motivation: Factors
  in College Students' Perseverance and Success." <u>Research in
  Higher Education</u> 36 (1995): 432-39. Abstract. <u>Current Index to
  Journals in Education</u> 37 (1996): item LR275964.

Robbins, Michael T. "Hiding in Cyberspace: Inhibition and Online
  Addiction." <u>Journal of Psychology and Technology</u> 20 (1995):
  17-26. <u>Psychological Abstracts</u> (43): item 10B5854.

Parenthetic citation forms: (Haldeman); (Keely 435);
(Robbins).

Newspapers

46. STANDARD FORM FOR A NEWSPAPER ARTICLE

For each newspaper article, provide the name of the author, the article title (in quotation marks), and the newspaper title (underlined or italicized), as well as the publication date, section (if appropriate), and page number(s). If the place of publication is not part of the title, supply it in square brackets after the newspaper name (but not underlined or italicized). When the pages on which an article appears are not continuous, give only the first page number and a plus (+) sign, with no intervening space:

> Rollins, Fred. "Teachers Say Yes to Parents in the Classroom."
> Newsday [Garden City, NY] 9 July 1994: 2+.
>
> Schmitt, Eric. "Admiral's Remark Puts Navy on Hot Seat Again." San
> Diego Union Tribune. county final. 19 Nov. 1995: A1.
>
> Wildermuth, John. "Elections Bad Bets for Card Parlors." San Francisco
> Chronicle 10 Nov. 1995: A1+.
>
> *Parenthetic citation forms:*   (Rollins 4); (Schmitt); (Wildermuth A20).

Note that when a newspaper article is only one page, just the author's name is included in the parenthetic citation (see *Schmitt,* above). For an article without an author, just the shortened title is included in the parenthetic citation (see following example in section 47).

47. AN UNSIGNED ARTICLE IN A NEWSPAPER

When no author's name is given, list the article alphabetically in the Works Cited list by its title:

> "X-Generation Tells It Like It Is." Boston Globe 17 Sept. 1993: A2.
>
> *Parenthetic citation form:*   ("X-Generation").

48. CITING THE EDITION OF A NEWSPAPER

The front page, or *masthead,* of a newspaper indicates if the issue is a particular edition, such as a *national, final,* or *county* edition. Because different issues of newspapers contain different information, it is important to list the specific edition used, when one is given. When it is, designate the edition after the date:

> Lee, Jessica. "Senate Says No to Limits on Lawsuits." USA Today 5
> May 1995, weekend ed.: 1A.
>
> Rohter, Larry. "A Witness Says He Lied, But the Execution Is On." New
> York Times 25 Oct. 1995, natl. ed.: sec. 1:9.
>
> *Parenthetic citation forms:*   (Lee); (Rohter).

49. CITING THE PAGINATION OF A NEWSPAPER

Newspapers vary in pagination practices, and some even change paginating formats for different editions of their own publications. A few have continuous paginations (see the entry for *Washington,* below), while many others have paginations that combine section letters or numbers with page numbers (*B3* or *4-2,* see *Bannon,* below). If no section letter or number is included in the pagination, you must add the abbreviation *sec.* to show the "section" of the indicated page (see *Franklin,* below). As explained elsewhere, cite the first page number followed by a plus sign (+) for an article that does not appear in full on consecutive pages:

> Bannon, Lisa. "Is the Debonair 007 Too Old to Charm Grunge Generation?" Wall Street Journal 7 Nov. 1995: B1+.
>
> Franklin, Stephen. "Colorblind Hiring Brightens Up Small Firms." Chicago Tribune 18 Sept. 1995, sports final ed.: sec. 4:1.
>
> Washington, David. "Courts Assailed As Ineffective." New York Times 4 Mar. 1995: 32.

Parenthetic citation forms: (Bannon B1); (Franklin); (Washington).

Other Sources

50. AN INTERVIEW

For an interview you have conducted yourself, list the name of the interviewee first. Indicate the type of interview, and give the date on which it was conducted:

> Nguyen, Phan. Personal interview. 10 Nov. 1993.
>
> Tomlinson, David. Telephone interview. 7 Jan. 1995.

To list a published or recorded interview, start with the name of the interviewee, followed by *Interview* (unless a title makes it obvious; see section 41). If there is a title for the interview, include it in quotation marks:

> Clinton, Hillary Rodham. Interview with Margaret Carlson. "'We've Had Some Good Times.'" Time 10 May 1993: 37.
>
> Edwards, Robbie. "An Interview with Robbie Edwards." Profile 12 July 1995: 34-35.
>
> Gore, Al. Interview. "Gore CompuServe Conference." On the Info Highway 11 Jan. 1994: Online. CompuServe. 10 April 1994.

Parenthetic citation forms: (Clinton); (Edwards 34); (Gore).

51. A PUBLIC ADDRESS, SPEECH, OR LECTURE

If the presentation has a title, place it in quotation marks and provide information about the occasion, place, and date of the presentation. For any presentation without a title, provide a descriptive phrase after the speaker's name:

Adams, Hazard. "The Dizziness of Freedom; or, Why I Read William
Blake." Ninth Annual Faculty Lecture. U of Washington, 5 Nov.
1984.

Whitson, Carol. Address. City Council Meeting. Branning, MI, 24 Feb.
1994.

Yamada, Mitsuye. "The Current Trend to Silence Artists: A Call to
Action." English Council of California Two-Year Colleges Annual
Statewide Conference. Newport Beach, CA, 21 Oct. 1995.

Parenthetic citations forms: (Adams); (Whitson); (Mitsuye).

52. A LETTER

a. For a Letter Published in Another Work

Cite the letter's author first, followed by the descriptive title of the letter in quotation marks. Next, add the date of the letter and, if the editor has
assigned one, its number. After including standard information about the
source in which the letter is reprinted, include the page numbers for the
letter:

Eliot, T. S. "To John Quinn." 13 Nov. 1918. In <u>The Letters of T. S. Eliot</u>.
Ed. Valerie Eliot. Vol. I. San Diego, CA: Harcourt, 1990. 177-79.

Parenthetic citation form: (Eliot 178).

b. For an Unpublished Letter

Describe the material, including the date on which it was written, the
collection in which it was found (if any), and the place in which it is now
located:

Eliot, T. S. Letter to Bertrand Russell. [4] Jan. 1916. Mills Memorial
Library. McMaster University, Hamilton, OH.

Parenthetic citation form: (Eliot).

c. For a Letter Written to You

Cite as follows:

Cheney, Sharon. Letter to the author. 4 Feb. 1995.

Parenthetic citation form: (Cheney).

53. A PAMPHLET

Pamphlets are listed the same as books:

<u>Cats and More Cats . . .</u> Millpark, MI: Newsway, 1994.

Nolan, Kenneth C. Gangs in Your Neighborhood. Sante Fe, NM: Trend, 1995.

US Public Health Service. Have You Seen This Virus? Washington, DC: GPO, 1994.

Parenthetic citation forms: (Cats 24); (Nolan 2); (US Public Health 1).

54. A BULLETIN

Energy Resource Commission. Intra-State Waste Management Ordinances. Department of Energy, Bulletin JRB-5. 3 Sept. 1986. Washington, DC: GPO, 1991.

Harding, Frederick. Marital Status and Employee Benefits. Bulletin 43. Sacramento, CA: State Dept. of Employment, 1994.

Parenthetic citation forms: (Energy Resource Commission 36); (Harding 102).

55. AN ARTICLE IN A MICROFORM COLLECTION OF ARTICLES

Periodical articles available in microform versions may be available through reference sources such as *Newsbank* or other services available at the library. List such an article as you would any periodical entry (see sections 35–45), and then add relevant information about the microform source, including its title (underlined or italicized), volume number, year (in parentheses), and identifying numbers and descriptions (*fiche 16, grids 2–3*):

Ruiz, Maria R. "B. F. Skinner's Radical Behaviorism." Psychology of Women Quarterly 19.2 (1995): 161-79. Newsbank: Welfare and Social Problems 10 (1995): fiche 1, grids B1-7.

Parenthetic citation form: (Ruiz 170).

56. AN ADVERTISEMENT

Begin with the name of the company or product that is the subject of the advertisement or, if it is in print form, the title, heading, or first words of the advertisement (without underlining/italics or quotation marks), followed by a period. Then add the word *Advertisement* and another period. Add remaining information about where and when the ad appeared, as shown here:

Ford Aerostar. Advertisement. NBC. 6 June 1994.

Get a Hard Copy of Cyberspace. Advertisement. Wired July 1995: 179.

Parenthetic citation forms: (Ford); (Get).

57. A MANUSCRIPT OR TYPESCRIPT

Bradley, Frederick. "Art and Science in the Nuclear Age." Unpublished
essay, 1994.

Hadley, Joyce. Notebook 7, ts. Hadley Collection. Trinity Coll., Hartford.

Joyce, James. "Penelope." Ts. Huntington Library, Pasadena, CA.

Parenthetic citation forms: (Bradley 4); (Hadley 23); (Joyce).

58. AN UNPUBLISHED PAPER

Brenner, William G. "The Good, the Wise, and the Ugly in Faulkner's
World." Unpublished paper, 1995.

Parenthetic citation form: (Brenner 2).

59. MATERIAL ON A CD–ROM

a. For a Source from a Periodically Published Database

Many of the sources available on CD–ROM are simultaneously included in databases for periodicals (newspapers, magazines, and journals)
because they are also available in print or microfilm versions. When this is
the case for a CD–ROM source you need to list in your Works Cited section
(such as a journal article), provide all of the information you would normally include for such a work, along with information about the CD–ROM
source.

To list CD–ROM material that also appears in another version, give the
author's name (if provided), followed by the publication information for
the other form of the material. Then provide the title (underlined or italicized) of the database in which the other form of the source is listed followed by the publication medium, vendor, and publication date of the
CD–ROM, in that order and separated by periods:

Hastie, Reid. "Is Attorney-Conducted Voire Dire an Effective Procedure
for the Selection of Impartial Juries?" The American University
Law Review 40 (1991): 703-26. InfoTrac: Magazine Index Plus.
CD-ROM. Information Access. Nov. 1995.

"Number of Hospitals in Decline." New York Times 8 Mar. 1994: B2+.
New York Times Ondisc. CD-ROM. UMI-Proquest. Sept. 1994.

Silby, Caroline Jane. "Differences in Sport Confidence among Elite
Athletes with Different Perceived Parenting Styles." DAI 54
(1995): 3145A. U of Virginia, 1994. Dissertation Abstracts Ondisc.
CD-ROM. UMI-Proquest. Dec. 1995.

Parenthetic citation forms: (Hastie 720); ("Number" B4); (Silby).

If the CD–ROM gives no page numbers for a source, avoid parenthetic citation by using the author's name in the text ("Carter has shown . . ."). If all of the information needed for entries like those just listed (such as vendor name) is not given, cite what is available:

Crane, Graham T., ed. The Complete Works of William Shakespeare. New York: Cleo, 1990. CD-ROM. 1994.

Parenthetic citation form: (Crane).

b. For Material Not Indicated as Appearing in a Periodically Published Database

If the CD–ROM bears no information stating that its contents are available in another form and so listed in a periodically published database, provide only the necessary information about the CD–ROM itself. Give the author's name (if provided), followed by the title of the material accessed (in quotation marks), the date of the material, the title of the database (underlined or italicized), the publication medium, the vendor name, and the CD–ROM's publication date, in that order (separated by periods):

Michelucci, James L. "Market Trend Analysis: Bookstar Inc." 18 Feb. 1993. Business Database Plus. CD-ROM. Information Access. Oct. 1993.

United States. Dept. of State. "Immigrant Population Centers." 1993. National Trade Data Bank. CD-ROM. US Dept. of Commerce. July 1994. U.S. Population by Age: Urban and Urbanized Areas." 1990 U.S. Census of Population and Housing. CD-ROM. US Bureau of the Census. 1990.

Parenthetic citation forms: (Michelucci); (United States, Dept. of State).

c. For Material That Is Not Periodically Updated after Publication

Some information on CD–ROM is not intended to appear periodically or to be regularly updated. Cite such a source as you would a book, but include the publication medium after the title:

The Best of the Mayans. CD-ROM. Research International, 1995.

The Oxford English Dictionary. 2nd ed. CD-ROM. Oxford, Eng.: Oxford UP, 1992.

Parenthetic citation forms: (Best); (Oxford).

If you are citing only part of a work, give the name of that part first:

"Leopards." Animals of the World. CD-ROM. New York: Chestnut,
1994.

Parenthetic citation form: ("Leopards").

60. **MATERIAL ON DISKETTE OR MAGNETIC TAPE**
Cite a source located on diskette or magnetic tape as you would a book
or part of a book, with a description of the medium following the title:

"John Keats." English Romantic Poets. Diskette. Atlanta, GA: Craft,
1994.

"Manchester College." Peterson's College Database. Magnetic tape.
Princeton: Peterson's, 1992.

Westerman, Kenneth. The Simple Universe. Diskette. New York:
Science, 1993.

Parenthetic citation forms: ("John Keats"); ("Manchester");
(Westerman).

If the source on diskette or magnetic tape has a printed version, give
information about that version first:

Harmon, Philip M. From Platonism to Stoicism: The Story of Greek
Philosophy. Chicago: U of Chicago P, 1987. Magnetic tape.
Boston: Eastend, 1992.

Parenthetic citation form: (Harmon).

61. **MATERIAL IN MULTIPLE ELECTRONIC PUBLICATION FORMS**
When electronic publications are issued and packaged together as a
single product, include each medium in the Works Cited listing:

Smolan, Rick, and Jennifer Erwitt. Passage to Vietnam: Seven Days
Through the Eyes of Seventy Photographers. Sausalito, CA: Eight
Days, 1994. CD-ROM, video disc. International Research. 1995.

Parenthetic citation form: (Smolan and Erwitt).

62. **MATERIAL ACCESSED THROUGH AN ONLINE DATABASE**
a. **For a Source Also Available in a Printed Version**
When the source you retrieve through a database also appears in another form (such as a journal article), provide all the information normally
included for such a work as well as information about the database source.

Begin by giving the author's name (if available), followed by the title and full publication data about the work as it appears in the other form. Next list the title of the database (underlined or italicized), followed by the publication medium (*Online*), the name of the computer service, and the date of your access to the material, in that order:

> "Number of Hospitals in Decline." New York Times 8 Mar. 1994: B2+.
> New York Times Online. Online. Nexis. Sept. 1994.
>
> Priest, Patricia Joyner. "Self-Disclosure on Television: The Counter-
> Hegemonic Struggle of Marginalized Groups on Donahue." DAI 53
> (1993): 2147A. U of Georgia, 1992. Dissertation Abstracts Online.
> Online. Information Access. 10 Sept. 1995.
>
> Van Ness, Daniel. "Preserving a Community Voice: The Case for Half-
> and-Half Juries in Racially-Charged Criminal Cases." John
> Marshall Law Review 28.1 (1994): 1-56. Legal Resource Index.
> Online. Dialog. 16 Nov. 1995.

Parenthetic citation forms: ("Number" B4); (Priest); (Van Ness 32).

If you are unable to find all of the information about the source (such as the computer service name), provide as much information as you can:

> "Number of Hospitals in Decline." New York Times 8 Mar. 1994: B2+.
> New York Times Online. Online. Sept. 1994.

Parenthetic citation form: ("Number" B4).

b. For a Source Not Indicated as Appearing in a Printed Version

If the material you retrieve from a database does not indicate that it is also available in a printed version, give only the information required for the database source. First, give the author's name (if provided), followed by the title of the material accessed (in quotation marks), the date of the material (if given), the title of the database (underlined or italicized), the publication medium, the vendor name, and the date of your access to the material, in that order:

> College Board. "1995-96 Test Dates." College Board Online. Online.
> CompuServe. Nov. 1995.
>
> "Jury." Academic American Encyclopedia. Online. Prodigy. 20 Sept.
> 1995.
>
> "Microsoft Corporation: Patent Applications Summary." Disclosure.
> Online. Dialog. 25 Jan. 1993.

Parenthetic citation forms: (College); ("Jury"); ("Microsoft").

63. SOURCES FROM ELECTRONIC JOURNALS, NEWSLETTERS, AND CONFERENCES

Treat material from an electronic source, such as an electronic journal, newsletter, serial, or conference, as you would its printed counterpart. The only difference is that you must also include information about the electronic format of the material and where you accessed it.

Begin by giving the author's name (if provided), followed by the document title (in quotation marks) and then the title of the journal, newsletter, or other source in which the document appeared (underlined or italicized). Next, state the volume and issue numbers, followed by the publication date in parentheses. Following the date, state the publication medium (*Online*), the name of the computer network, and your date of access, in that order:

Childs, Margo T. "Battered Wives Deserve Attention." ReaLines 2
    (Apr. 1994): 3 pp. Online. Internet. 3 Oct. 1995.

"Lone Star Equity: State Asks Court to Give Law a Chance." Daily
    Report Card 3.19 (1993): n. pag. Online. Internet. 27 Mar.
    1995.

Sapontzis, S. F. "The Nature of the Value of Nature." Electronic Journal
    of Applied Philosophy 3 (1995): 39 pars. Online. BITNET. 17 July
    1995.

Parenthetic citation forms: (Childs 2); ("Lone Star");
(Sapontzis par 24).

Note that electronic sources sometimes appear without dates, volume and issue numbers, and the usual pagination of printed articles. You may need to indicate "no pagination" with the abbreviation *n. pag.* (see the entry for *"Lone Star Equity"* above) or show the number of paragraphs using *par.* or *pars.* (see the entry for *Sapontzis*). In the parenthetic citation, add a comma after the author's name: (*Sapontzis, par. 24*).

You may also give the electronic address you used to access the material you cite, either because your instructor requires it or you want to provide more information for the reader. If you give an address, include the word *Available* at the end of the entry and before the address:

"True Lies from Hollywood." Academe This Week (19 Dec. 1995-1 Jan.
    1996). n. pag. Online. Internet. 27 Dec. 1995. Available
    gopher://chronicle.merit.edu:70/11/.

Parenthetic citation form: ("True Lies").

64. PUBLISHED MATERIAL RECEIVED AS ELECTRONIC TEXT

A great number of complete works, especially literary and historical texts, are now available from the Internet or through commercial computer networks. The full texts of Shakespeare's plays, for example, are available free over the Internet, as are Aesop's tales and copies of the Declaration of Independence and the Constitution of the United States. Since such electronic texts may vary in reliability, assess each for its sufficiency for your research and study purposes. At the very least, check to see that an electronic text bears a title, editor's name, and edition information.

To cite electronic texts in the Works Cited section of your paper, begin by giving the author's name (if provided), followed by the title of the text (underlined or italicized), followed by the publication information. Next, state the publication medium (*Online*) and then the name of the repository (such as a library or archive) from which the text was accessed. Complete the entry with the name of the computer network and your date of access, in that order:

> Dante. <u>La Divina Commedia</u>. Ed. Riccardo Scateni. Online. Centre for
> Advanced Studies, Research and Development, Sardinia, Italy.
> Internet. 24 June 1995. Available http://www.crs4.it/~riccardo
> /DivinaCommedia/DivinaCommedia.html.

> Hawthorne, Nathaniel. <u>The Scarlet Letter</u>. Ed. Thomas Rowley. New
> York: Harper, 1970. Online. University of Minnesota Lib. Internet.
> 10 Aug. 1995.

> United States. National Institute on Alcohol. <u>Research Summary, 1993-
> 94: A Report to the Chairman, Health and Welfare Committee, U.S.
> Senate</u>. 28 Jan. 1994. Online. U of California San Diego. Internet.
> 12 Sept. 1995. Available gopher://infopath.ucsd.edu.

Parenthetic citation forms: (Dante, Purg. V); (Hawthorne 65); (United States, National Institute 24).

65. A WORK OF ART OR A PHOTOGRAPH

Give the name of the artist when known, followed by a period and the title; underline or italicize the title if the work is a painting or sculpture. For any art you view personally, list the proprietary institution and, if not indicated in the institution's title, the city in which the work is found:

> Rodin, Auguste. <u>The Thinker</u>. Metropolitan Museum of Art, New York.

Refer to such a work of art in text, rather than in a parenthetical citation: *Rodin's* The Thinker *shows . . .*

Cite a photograph or another reproduction of a work of art the same as above, but also add publication information about the source of the reproduction:

Moore, Henry. Recumbent Figure. Illus. 842 in History of Art. By Charles Minot. New York: Harper, 1992.

Van Gogh, Vincent. Self-Portrait. The Louvre, Paris. Illus. in Vincent by Himself. Ed. Bruce Bernard. Boston: Little, Brown, 1985. 279.

Parenthetic citation forms: (Moore); (Van Gogh).

(These forms are acceptable, but you should normally name the artist and the work in the text.)

66. AN ILLUSTRATION, TABLE, CHART, OR MAP

Birds of California. Chart. San Diego, CA: Walson, 1995.

Mexico. Map. Chicago: Rand, 1995.

"Two Views of Modern Human Origins." Illus. in Richard Leakey, The Origin of Humankind. New York: Basic, 1994. 87.

Parenthetic citation forms: (Birds); (Mexico); ("Two").

67. A CARTOON

Trudeau, Gary. "The Far Side." Cartoon. Washington Post 29 Jan. 1990. D8.

Maslin, Michael. Cartoon. New Yorker. 21 and 28 Aug. 1995: 87.

Parenthetic citation forms: (Trudeau); (Maslin).

68. A FILM, VIDEO TAPE, VIDEO DISC, OR SLIDE PROGRAM

For a film, list the title (underlined or italicized), followed by the name of the director, the distributor, and the year of release, in that order. Add other information you feel is relevant. To focus on one person's involvement, cite him or her first, followed by a description of his or her role:

Reiner, Rob, dir. and prod. The American President. Perf. Michael Douglas and Annette Bening. Columbia/Castle Rock, 1995.

Forrest Gump. Dir. Robert Zemeckis. Perf. Tom Hanks. Paramount, 1995.

Parenthetic citation forms: (Reiner); (Forrest).

For a video cassette, video disc, slide program, or filmstrip, begin with the title (underlined or italicized), followed by the medium, the distributor (including location, if available), and the release date (if available). Specify individual performances or roles as for a film entries (see above):

Building a Successful Medical Transcription Business. Video cassette.

Health Profession Institute, 1993.

Climbing the Rockies. Sound filmstrip. Colorado Environments, 1995.

Hanks, Tom, perf. Forrest Gump. Dir. Robert Zemeckis. Video disc.

Paramount, 1995.

Shakespeare, William. All's Well That Ends Well. Prod. Johnathan

Miller. Video cassette. New York: Time-Life, 1981.

Parenthetic citation forms: (Building); (Climbing); (Hanks);

(Shakespeare).

69. A TELEVISION OR RADIO PROGRAM

List the name of the episode or segment (in quotation marks), followed by the title of the program (underlined or italicized). Next give the title of the series (if any), the name of the network on which the program appeared, the call letters and city of the local station (if any), and the broadcast date, in that order. Cite the names of individuals and their roles after the program title, or list them first if your focus is primarily on their work:

Springer, Jerry, host. "Wild Teens." Jerry Springer. KCAL, Los

Angeles. 28 Oct. 1995.

"Superabled." Dateline NBC. Rpt. John Larson. NBC. KNBC, Los

Angeles. 27 Dec. 1995.

Parenthetic citation forms: (Springer); ("Superabled").

70. A RECORDING

London, Jack. The Call of the Wild and Other Stories. Audio tape. Read

by Arnold Moss and Jack Dahlby. Listening Library, CXL 517.

1987.

Tchaikovsky, [Peter Ilyich]. The Nutcracker. Cond. Leonard Slatkin.

Saint Louis Symphony Orchestra. RCA, D216 A3. 1985.

Parenthetic citation forms: (London); (Tchaikovsky).

W O R K I N G   W I T H   O T H E R S

As with intext citations and the content notes for the paper, you will appreciate another reader's assurance that the Works Cited section is done correctly. Share the final draft of your paper with a friend or classmate in these ways.

- Ask your reader to assist in checking to see that every source cited intext or in the Notes section of the paper is also included on the Works Cited page(s). An easy way to do this is to list each author or work as you read the draft and then compare the list with the entries on the Works Cited page(s).

- Draw your reader's attention to any unusual entries, such as multiple works by the same author, single artist performances, or video discs. Check these entries together to see if they appear in correct form.

- It is not always easy to cite online or other electronic sources accurately in your paper's text or Works Cited section. Review all such citations with your classmate, and discuss any you are unsure about. Check these entries against the guidelines and examples presented in this chapter.

- If you are working with a classmate, compare his or her Works Cited entries with your own. Note any differences in the way you have each listed similar kinds of sources, and discuss them. Make changes as necessary.

- Finally, encourage your reader to look for omissions of underlining or italics, quotation marks, colons, or periods in the Works Cited entries. Make corrections before you type or print out the final version of the paper.

CHAPTER 12

Alternative Documentation Styles

Author-Date (APA and *Chicago*), Number-System, and CBE

Research papers written for most college English courses follow the Modern Language Association (MLA) author-page documentation style discussed in Chapters 10 and 11. Papers for other subjects, however, often require different documentation formats. Writers in the social, biological, medical, and applied sciences; education; fine arts; and humanities (excluding literature) follow formats recommended by their own professional associations or leading journals. Documentation in these disciplines differs from MLA style in the way sources are cited in the text and the References section.

In general, papers that do not use the author-page, MLA style of documentation follow one of three other basic formats:

1. *Author-date style:* This style is generally associated with the American Psychological Association (APA); in fact, it is often called *APA style.* However, author-date format is also recommended by *The Chicago Manual of Style,* a leading reference work for writers and editors, for papers in most of the sciences and humanities (see pp. 312–14).

In APA author-date style, sources are cited parenthetically in the text by the author's last name and the work's publication date:

> The changes that Kilner (1983) traced demonstrate further patterns of
> simplification and reduction (Shore, 1995).

All sources cited in the text are fully documented in a References section at the end of the paper.

2. *Number-system style:* This documentation format is often called *CBE style,* as it is used primarily by the Council of Biology Editors; it is appropriate for most papers in the applied sciences (see pp. 306–12).

In this style, raised superscript numerals in the text—like this[5]—refer to numbered sources listed at the end of the paper in a References, Literature Cited, or References Cited section.

3. *Footnote or endnote style: The Chicago Manual of Style,* 14th ed. (Chicago: University of Chicago Press, 1993), considers author-date style the most practical means of documentation for all papers in the natural sciences and most of those in the social sciences. For some papers in the humanities, however, the use of footnotes or endnotes is recommended. In sum, notes are appropriate for papers about subjects that may require numerous or extended explanations or definitions apart from the regular text; such papers are usually written for very specific and knowledgeable audiences.

In this style, raised superscript numerals in the text refer to explanatory notes and documented sources appearing either at the bottoms of pages as footnotes or at the end of the paper as endnotes in a Notes section. The advantage of using notes is that explanatory-type information can be presented along with source citations in the same place.

NOTE: Because the use of footnotes or endnotes is rarely recommended for student papers, this style will not be discussed in this chapter. See Chapter 10 (pp. 213–17) for more information on explanatory-type notes. Also see *The Chicago Manual,* Chapter 15, for specific guidelines on the use of note-style documentation. As always, you should check with your instructor regarding which documentation style to follow in your paper.

Understanding Various Styles

The various documentation formats discussed in this chapter and preceding ones provide emphases for writers and readers in what are often specialized fields of study. As bewildering as the variety of styles can often seem, however, try not to be intimidated by their differences. After all, you need only master one documentation style to write your own paper. Familiarity with different documentation styles, on the other hand, can aid you in locating and taking accurate notes from a variety of sources—or even in documenting them in your own paper. If necessary, use your knowledge of a particular documentation style to change your paper's intext citations and References list to conform to any of the formats used by other disciplines. Naturally, which documentation style you follow for your paper will depend upon its subject, the example of a particular journal, or the requirements of your instructor. As you pursue your research and writing, take care not to confuse variant forms appearing among discipline journals with the guidelines given here.

Author-Date Documentation

The author-date style of documentation is so named because it includes an author's last name and the date of publication whenever a writer *cites* a source:

> Hall (1990) points to a lack of adequate research data as the primary hindrance to antidrug legislation. Other writers (Keene & Wilson, 1993), however, stress economic concerns.

Intext citations such as these direct the reader to more complete descriptions of the named authors' works in the paper's References section. Placed at the end of the paper, the References list each source cited in the text alphabetically by the author's last name (or by a work's title when no author is given). In addition to the author's name, each entry also provides the work's title and publication information.

APA Style

Author-date documentation style is the form adapted by the American Psychological Association (APA) and recommended in its guide, *Publication Manual of the American Psychological Association*. Because it provides efficient intext citations of other researchers' work, APA documentation style predominates in papers for the social sciences and several other disciplines, including anthropology, biology, business, education, economics, political science, psychology, and sociology. Though they often practice slight variations, writers and journals in these disciplines follow basic APA style for intext citations and for listing sources in papers' References sections.

Abstracts

Papers written according to APA style or other formats for the sciences or social sciences often include *abstracts,* which are short, 100- to 150-word summaries of the papers. (Abstracts for theoretical papers are usually briefer, 75 to 100 words.) An abstract should state the purpose (thesis), findings, and conclusion of your research without commenting on or evaluating the paper itself. Put the abstract on a separate page, titled Abstract, after the title page. Use lowercase roman numerals for page numbers. The sample abstract for Mark Stevenson's paper in Appendix A provides a model.

Headings

Headings function like brief titles to emphasize certain content and to indicate the main sections of the paper. Like an outline, textual headings indicate the organization of the paper's content and emphasize the importance of each section. Use indentation, upper- or lowercase letters, and underlined, italic, or bold type (depending on whether you are writing on a typewriter or computer) to show the level of importance of each heading (i.e., the hierarchy, as in an outline). Topics with the same level of importance should have the same type of heading throughout the paper.

Many articles in APA journals use standard headings—such as Purpose, Method, Procedure, Results, and Conclusions—to organize the discussion. Most student research papers, however, use headings that reflect their individual subjects, as these sample headings for a paper on *drug testing* illustrate:

1st level—Type the   Rationale for Drug Testing
heading centered,
upper- and lowercase.

    Procedures   **2nd level—Type the heading flush left, upper- and**
                 lowercase, and underlined (or italic).

       Testing methods.
          3rd level—Indent the heading 5 spaces from the left. Capitalize
          the first letter only; underline (or italicize) the heading; end it
          with a period. The text begins on the same line, allowing a
          space after the period.

Although a paper may have as many as five levels of headings, student research papers seldom need more than two or three, if any. Check with your instructor as to the suitability of headings for your paper and his or her requirements for heading levels.

Intext Citation

APA form documents a paper's sources both by citing them in the text and describing them bibliographically in the paper's References list. When the work's author is named in the text, the publication date follows in parentheses:

Ramirez (1994) has pointed out the disadvantages of postponing counseling until depression begins to curtail normal activities.

When the author is not named in the text, cite his or her name parenthetically, *followed by a comma* and the year of the work's publication:

Decorative items found at the Sungir burial sites demonstrate the early existence of social hierarchies (Harlan, 1993).

NOTE: You may find during your research that some journals omit the comma between the author's name and the publication date, such as (*Gross 1988*). APA style, however, requires punctuation. Unless your instructor approves omitting the comma, be sure that you include it.

The following method of citing a source is also acceptable:

Sark's 1993 study has shown that early humans switched to meat eating much earlier than previously thought.

As the above examples demonstrate, intext citation allows acknowledging sources with the least interruption of the reader's attention to the paper's content. You give immediate credit to an authority whose work you have drawn upon and support your own arguments in doing so. Including a work's publication date in the citation is also important. Because information changes rapidly in some disciplines, such dates allow the reader to assess the relevancy of data and to make comparisons.

The guidelines here and on the following pages conform to the *Publication Manual of the American Psychological Association,* 4th ed. (Washington, DC: APA, 1995).

AUTHORS' NAMES

1. CITING AN AUTHOR, EDITOR, GROUP, OR CORPORATE AUTHOR

Treat individuals, editors, corporate authors (e.g., associations, committees, and departments), and others who would normally be considered responsible for producing a work as *authors*. Cite personal authors or editors intext by their surnames only:

Individual author According to Butler (1992), active group participation is another effective route to indirect self-assessment.

Editor The list of recognized AIDS-related infections has grown every year since the disease was first identified (Rossman, 1995).

Spell out the full name of each group or corporate author the first time you cite it parenthetically in text. For subsequent citations, you may cite the full name or a shortened version, depending on whether the name will be readily recognized by the reader and whether the source can be easily found in the References list. For a recognizable, easily located source, give an abbreviated form of the name in brackets within the first intext parenthetical citation (see following example, *World Health Organization*). But if the name is short or would not be readily understood as an abbreviation, spell out the full name each time you cite the source (see *Red Cross,* below):

Group or corporate author	It has been estimated that diarrheal diseases cause the deaths of more than 3.2 million children under the age of 5 (World Health Organization [WHO], 1991). The cost of antibiotics to fight the diseases has led to rationing in some countries (Red Cross, 1995).
Group or corporate author (subsequent citation)	These outbreaks continued even after prolonged attempts to eradicate all known causes of the virus (WHO, 1991). . . . Not until 5 years later did the missing serum arrive, and by that time, most of it was too contaminated to use (Red Cross, 1995).

a. For a Work with Two Authors

Cite both names each time the source is mentioned in text:

First citation	Fuller and Morrison (1995) have interpreted these incidents as memory lapses.
Subsequent citation	. . . although Fuller and Morrison (1995) had different results.

b. For a Work with Three to Five Authors

Name each author the first time the work is cited, but in subsequent citations, give only the first author's last name, followed by a comma and *et al.:*

First citation	Arita, Fenner, Osborn, Purtilo, and Sigal (1993) found no evidence that the drug was harmful.
Subsequent citation	These results were less reliable than those found by Arita et al. (1993).

NOTE: The phrase *et al.* comes from *et alii,* which is Latin for "and others." Since *al.* is an abbreviation for *alii,* it must always be written with a period after it. (Do not underline or italicize *et al.* in your paper.)

c. For a Work with Six or More Authors

Give only the first author's name, followed by a comma and *et al.* Include the date in parentheses:

Source authors   Brunnell, Lemoy, Massey, Freeman, Noser, Siegele, and White (1995)

All text citations   According to Brunnell et al. (1995), such recovery does not last.

If two of your sources with six or more authors happen to have the same first author (or several authors), include as many other names as needed to distinguish between the sources:

Two sources'   Brunnell, Lemoy, Massey, Freeman, Noser, Siegele,
authors   and White (1995)

Brunnell, Lemoy, Ramirez, Noser, Kelly, and White (1995)

Text citations   Research findings vary: Brunnell, Lemoy, and Massey et al. (1995) found that . . . , whereas Brunnell, Lemoy, and Ramirez et al. (1995) found that . . .

NOTE: Be sure to spell out the names of all authors, regardless of how many, when listing a source in the References section of your paper.

2. CITING TWO AUTHORS WITH THE SAME LAST NAME

Differentiate between two authors with the same last name by including their initials in the running text or parenthetic citation. Cite the authors in alphabetical order by their initials:

M. Street (1994) and W. R. Street (1995) identify major lunar provinces yet to be explored by satellite.

At least two experts (Street, M., 1994; Street, W. R., 1995) identify major lunar provinces yet to be explored by satellite.

3. CITING WORKS BY THE SAME AUTHOR, PUBLISHED THE SAME YEAR

Proceeding alphabetically by title, assign each individual work by the same author and published in the same year a lowercase letter (*a, b, c,* and so forth) after the publication date: (*Navarro, 1994a*) or (*Navarro, 1994a, 1994b*). Also add the assigned letter to the publication date of each work as it appears alphabetically by title in the References section of the paper (see Authors section, pp. 290–92).

4. CITING A WORK WITH NO AUTHOR

Cite the work by its title, using the first two or three key words in place of an author's name:

Full title   A Study of Adults Exhibiting Stable Behavioral Patterns
                        over a Twenty-Year Period

Title cited in text One 20-year study found a significant correlation
                        between the way individuals behaved in high school
                        and later as adults (Study of Adults, 1995).

Full title   "Health Cuts Go Deeper"

Title cited in text Cuts in health care funding have forced some hospitals
                        to reduce their staff by as much as a third ("Health,"
                        1995).

List such works alphabetically by full title in the paper's References section.

NOTE: Cite a work's author parenthetically as *Anonymous* only if that is how the author is named in the source. The intext citation will look like this:

The cost of such programs (Anonymous, 1994) may account for . . .

If you do cite an anonymous source, also list the work alphabetically, with *Anonymous* as author, in the References section of the paper.

5. CITING MORE THAN ONE AUTHOR

Separate multiple authors' names with *and* when the names are part of the running text. When you cite names parenthetically, separate them with an ampersand (&), not *and*:

Names in running text Wing and Gould (1993) have shown a correlation
                        between autism and low scores on intelligence tests.

                        Gourdet, Ringly, Howland, and Lin (1994) found that
                        picture dependency decreases as children improve their
                        reading skills.

Names cited parenthetically Other studies (Wing & Gould, 1993) have shown a corre-
                        lation between autism and low scores on intelligence
                        tests.

                        Picture dependency decreases as children improve their
                        reading skills (Gourdet, Ringly, Howland, & Lin, 1994).

NOTE: Do not be confused by journal articles that use other ways to separate authors' names for intext citations. You may also find such parenthetic forms as (*Wells and Shorter, 1990*), (*Behrman; Rankin 1994*) and (*Davis, Graton, 1993; Li, Brennan, Kohler, 1991*) used in journals you research. Unless your instructor tells you otherwise, follow the APA forms shown here.

6. CITING UP TO SIX OR MORE AUTHORS

For works with two authors, use both names in every citation. For works with more than two authors but fewer than six, mention all names in the first reference:

Running text (first citation)	Greggio, Walters, Shore, and Ballen (1993) studied mitochondrial DNA to trace the global divergence of humans back 250,000 years.
Names cited in parentheses	One study (Greggio, Walters, Shore, & Ballen, 1993) used mitochondrial DNA to trace the global divergence of humans back 250,000 years.

After the first citation, give only the first name followed by *et al.* (not italic or underlined) and the year:

Greggio et al. (1993) studied mitochondrial DNA . . .

One study (Greggio et al., 1993) used mitochondrial DNA . . .

All of the authors' names should be spelled out in the References.

When a work has more than six authors, cite only the first author's name, followed by *et al.*, for the first and succeeding intext citations. Spell out the names of all authors when listing them in the References.

7. CITING AUTHORS OF TWO OR MORE SEPARATE WORKS TOGETHER

Only cite such works parenthetically, beginning in alphabetical order with the first author's last name. Separate the citations with semicolons:

The privileged classes, for instance, have the luxury of time for long-term education and career planning (Breit, 1993; Lovett & Anderson, 1990; Wertham, 1994).

Each source should be listed fully in the References section of the paper.

QUOTATIONS AND SPECIFIC PARTS
OF SOURCES

APA documentation style uses the abbreviations *p.* and *pp.* for the words *page* and *pages, ch.* for *chapter,* and *sec.* for *section* (respectively). Use these and other standard abbreviations (see Abbreviations in Chapter 13) when citing specific parts of a work and whenever you use direct quotation or paraphrase. The following examples demonstrate common practices:

> Shepard and Chipman (1995) found that people can rotate mental images but only at a limited rate (cf. Ferguson, 1987, pp. 827-836).
>
> According to Beach (1994, esp. ch. 3), perceptual distortions can be both physiological and cognitive.
>
> Horne (1992) concludes that one primary function of sleep may be "to repair the cerebral cortex from the wear and tear of consciousness" (p. 41).
>
> If we interpret dreaming as "an analogue to our artistic yearnings" (Sheah, 1994, p. 207), we are still left with no explanation of its physiological importance beyond the cases made by Randall (1989, sec. 1) and Horne (1992).

LONG QUOTATIONS

Quotations of 40 words or more should be typed double-spaced and indented five spaces from the left margin. Indent the first line of each quoted paragraph five additional spaces. Place the page number of the source in parentheses after the period ending the quotation:

> Gregory (1992) explains these effects as follows:
>> Sleep-deprivation causes sleepiness. It is difficult to keep awake someone who has been deprived of sleep for 60 hours. Such a person has frequent "microsleeps" and recurrently fails to notice, being unable to sustain a high level of attention. Sometimes visual illusions or hallucinations are experienced or the individual becomes paranoid. (p. 719)

LEGAL REFERENCES

Include the date of a court case in parentheses with the name; if the case is mentioned in the text, put the date in parentheses immediately after the case name:

Fletcher v. Peck (1810) established the right of the U.S. Supreme Court to declare a state law unconstitutional.

The U.S. Supreme Court established its right to declare a state law unconstitutional more than a hundred years ago (*Fletcher v. Peck*, 1810).

Note that the names of court cases are italicized or underlined when cited in text but not when listed in the References section.

To cite a statute, give the name and year. Do not underline or italicize the name in either the text or the References section:

The Securities Exchange Act (1934) was designed to protect the public from fraud or manipulation in the sale of securities.

Federal law requires the regulation and registration of securities exchanges (Securities Exchange Act, 1934).

PERSONAL COMMUNICATIONS

Unpublished letters, memos, telephone conversations, e-mail correspondences, interviews, and such are *personal communications.* Since they are not available to other researchers, you should use them sparingly in your research and only rarely include them in your paper. When you do use such sources, *cite them only in the text,* not in the References for your paper. Give the last name and initials of your personal source as well as the date on which you communicated with him or her (be as accurate as possible):

The institute's chairperson, Dr. A. M. Reyes (personal communication, September 4, 1990), thinks our society celebrates childhood almost effortlessly but has difficulty dealing with the changes that appear in adolescence.

Some forestry personnel are now beginning to regret all the media attention given to the new park proposal (C. May, personal communication, November 4, 1995).

References

Except for personal communications (such as letters, personal interviews, and the like), the References include all of the sources cited in the paper's text. Include no other works, no matter how useful they may have been to you at some point in the research. This means that the References will undoubtedly not include some, perhaps several, works that contributed background information or common knowledge to your research. You may have consulted 50 sources during your research and ended up paraphrasing, quoting, or naming only 10 of them in your paper. Only those 10 should be listed as references.

The following pages provide guidelines and sample entries for works included in the References section of an APA-style research paper. Note that APA form calls for indenting the second and succeeding lines of each entry five to seven spaces. (See the References pages of Mark Stevenson's paper in Appendix A for an example.)

AUTHORS' NAMES

1. LISTING AUTHORS, EDITORS, AND GROUP AUTHORS

Treat the names of editors and group authors (i.e., associations, committees, corporations, councils) and editors the same as authors' names. Cite corporate authors by name, alphabetically. List personal authors and editors alphabetically by surname, followed by the initials of their first and (if given) middle names. For editors, use *Ed.* or *Eds.* in parentheses, followed by a period, after their names. Use an ampersand (&) between names of joint authors; separate the names by commas. Follow these examples:

Single author Atkinson, W. W. (1991). <u>Memory culture: Remembering and recalling.</u> Sante Fe, NM: Sun.

Single editor Bell, William R. (Ed.). (1993). <u>Hematologic and oncologic emergencies.</u> New York: Churchill.

Joint editors Hume, C. A., & Pullen, I. (Eds.). (1993). <u>Rehabilitation for mental health problems: An introduction handbook</u> (2nd ed.). New York: Churchill.

Two authors Selnow, G. W., & Gilbert, R. R. (1993). <u>Society's impact on television: How the viewing public shaped television programming.</u> Westport, CT: Greenwood.

Corporate author Washington State Rehabilitation Board. (1994). <u>Guidelines for mental health facilities funding: 1993-94.</u> Spokane: Author.

Parenthetic citation forms: (Atkinson, 1991); (Bell, 1993); (Hume & Pullen, 1993); (Selnow & Gilbert, 1993); (Washington State Rehabilitation Board, 1994).

There should be a period at the end of the author's name (or the last author's name). If the last part of the name is an initial, as is often the case, do not add a second period (i.e., initial already ends with a period).

NOTE: In the last example, the corporate author is also the publisher. In such a case, the word *Author* should be used in place of the publisher's name.

2. LISTING A WORK WITH NO AUTHOR

Cite a work with no author alphabetically by title (ending with a period). Include the articles *a, an* and *the* at the beginnings of titles, but ignore them when ordering titles alphabetically:

Carnoy, M. (1994). The state and political theory. Princeton, NJ: Princeton University Press.

Book cited by title
A course for the 90s. (1990). Austin, TX: Four Square.

Del Polito, C. M., & Barresi, J. G. (Eds.). (1993). Alliances in health and education: Serving youngsters with special needs. Laurel, MD: Ramsco.

Newspaper article cited by title
Higher health costs hit all sectors, U.S. says. (1995, January 10). Wall Street Journal, p. A2.

Parenthetic citation forms: (Carnoy, 1994); ("Course," 1990); (Del Polito & Barresi, 1993); ("Higher," 1995).

NOTE: When a source provides no author's name, do not use *Anonymous* unless that term is actually given in the source. If the author is named as *Anonymous* in the source, list the work alphabetically under that term.

3. LISTING WORKS PUBLISHED BY THE SAME AUTHOR(S) IN THE SAME YEAR

Proceed alphabetically by title, and assign lowercase letters (*a, b, c,* and so on) after the publication dates. List works in the alphabetical order of the letters assigned:

Searle, J. R. (1990a). Consciousness, explanatory inversion, and cognitive science. Behavioral Brain Science, 13, 385-442.

Searle, J. R. (1990b). Is the brain's mind a computer program? Scientific American, 262, 26-31.

Parenthetic citation forms: (Searle, 1990a); (Searle, 1990b).

4. LISTING MULTIPLE WORKS BY THE SAME AUTHOR(S)

List the works in chronological order of publication. Include each author's last name(s) and first and middle initials (if given) in each entry:

Single author	Neiderman, S. (1993). <u>Taking charge of your life: A guide for women.</u> Boston: Avery.
	Neiderman, S. (1995). <u>How to stay married: Ten simple rules.</u> New York: Engleman.
Joint authors	Leakey, R. E., & Lewin, R. (1977). <u>Origins: The emergence and evolution of our species and its possible future.</u> New York: Dutton.
	- - -. (1979). <u>People of the lake: Mankind and its beginnings.</u> New York: Avon.
	- - -. (1992). <u>Origins reconsidered: In search of what makes us human.</u> New York: Anchor-Doubleday.

Parenthetic citation forms: (Neiderman, 1993); (Neiderman, 1995); (Leakey & Lewin, 1977); (Leakey & Lewin, 1979); (Leakey & Lewin, 1992).

5. ORDERING SINGLE- AND JOINT-AUTHOR ENTRIES

Give the name of the first author in each entry. List personal works before edited works, single-author entries before multiple-author entries. Put joint-author entries in alphabetical order by the second and succeeding authors' names:

Author	Lave, L. B. (1981). <u>The strategy of social regulation: Decision frameworks for policy.</u> Washington, DC: Brookings Institute.
Editor	Lave, L. B. (Ed.). (1983). <u>Quantitative risk assessment regulation.</u> Washington, DC: Brookings Institute.
Joint authors	Lave, L. B., & Omenn, G. S. (1981). <u>Clearing the air: Reforming the Clean Air Act.</u> Washington, DC: Brookings Institute.
	Lave, L. B., & Upton, A. C. (Eds.). (1987). <u>Toxic chemicals, health and the environment.</u> Baltimore, MD: Johns Hopkins University Press.

Parenthetic citation forms: (Lave, 1981); (Lave, 1983); (Lave & Omenn, 1981); (Lave & Upton, 1987).

For ordering multiple works published under the same name(s), follow the guidelines above in section 4.

DATES OF PUBLICATION

Place the work's publication date in parentheses, followed by a period, after the author's name. For magazine or newspaper articles, give the month and date of publication in parentheses after the year, separated by a comma. Do not abbreviate the month. Follow these examples:

Journal article	Merson, M. H. (1993). Slowing the spread of HIV: Agenda for the 1990s. Science, 206, 1266–1268.
Newspaper article	Hoff, G. (1995, November 14). Fat genes may change your life. Los Angeles Times, p. A3.
Magazine article	Raloff, J. (1994, May 7). Cigarettes: Are they doubly addictive? Science News, 14, 294.
Book	Priest, P. J. (1995). Public intimacies: Talk show participants and tell-all TV. Cresskill, NJ: Hampton.

Parenthetic citation forms: (Merson, 1993); (Hoff, 1995); (Raloff, 1994); (Priest, 1995).

TITLES

1. BOOKS

Capitalize only the first word of a work's title, the first word of its subtitle, and all proper nouns within it. Underline or italicize the complete title, and end it with a period:

Herrnstein, R. J., & Murray, C. (1994). The bell curve: Intelligence and class struggle in American life. New York: Free Press.

Parenthetic citation forms: (Herrnstein & Murray, 1994).

Note that APA style uses underlining for titles of published works; however, you may use italics, if your instructor prefers.

2. PERIODICALS

As with a book title, capitalize only the first word of an article title (whether a magazine, journal, or newspaper article), along with the first word of its subtitle and all proper nouns within it. Do not underline or italicize the article title or put it in quotation marks; end it with a period. Type the name of the magazine, journal, or newspaper title in upper- and lower-case letters; underline or italicize it and the comma that follows:

Angrist, J. D. (1991). Does compulsory school attendance affect school-ing and earnings? Quarterly Journal of Economics, 106, 979-1014.

Taubes, G. (1994, December). Surgery in cyberspace. Discover, 15, 85-94.

Parenthetic citation forms: (Angrist, 1991); (Taubes, 1994).

PERIODICAL VOLUME AND ISSUE NUMBERS

For a journal, magazine, or newsletter article, always give the volume number, followed by a comma, after the title of the source. Extend the un-derlining or italics for the title to include the volume number and the comma (see examples below). Add the issue number in parentheses imme-diately after the volume number *only* when each issue of the journal or magazine begins with page 1. (Some periodicals paginate issues continu-ously throughout each year or volume; see Chapter 11, p. 262.) Note that if a parenthetic issue number is given, no space or comma separates it and the volume number. There is, however, a comma following the parenthetic issue number. Follow the punctuation and spacing shown in these exam-ples:

Journal with volume number only   Zollo, P. (1995, November). Talking to teens. American Demographics, 17, 22-28.

Journal with volume and issue numbers   Moore, K. Z. (1995). Eclipsing the commonplace: The logic of alienation in Antonioni. Film Quarterly, 48(4), 22-34.

Magazine article with volume and issue numbers   Shreeve, J. (1995, September). The Neanderthal peace. Discover, 16, 70-81.

Parenthetic citation forms: (Zollo, 1995, pp. 22-24); (Moore, 1995, p. 30); (Shreeve, 1995, p. 80).

PAGE NUMBERS

Use *p.* or *pp.* before the page number(s) for parts of books or articles in newspapers but not for journal, magazine, or newsletter articles. The page numbers for part of a book (such as a chapter) are added in paren-theses following the book's title (see *Heaton & Wilson* example, below). The page numbers for an article in a periodical are added at the end of the entry, following the volume and issue numbers. Give inclusive page num-bers in full: *361–382; 130–133.* Separate discontinuous page numbers with commas: *pp. A5, A12.* Follow these examples:

Magazine article	Bartusiak, M. (1990, August). Mapping the particle universe. <u>Discover, 7,</u> 60-63.
Chapter in book with several volumes	Burke, R. E. (1979). Election of 1940. In A. M. Schlesinger, Jr. (Ed.), <u>History of presidential elections, 1789-1968</u> (Vol. 4, pp. 2917-3006). New York: McGraw-Hill.
Chapter in book	Heaton, J. A., & Wilson, N. L. (1994). Problems for viewers. In <u>Talk TV's destructive impact on mental health</u> (pp. 127-173). San Francisco: Jossey-Bass.
Signed newspaper article	Kelly, J. (1995, April 12). Lawyers ready for battle. <u>Los Angeles Times,</u> pp. A1, A6.
Unsigned newspaper article	Christmas cancelled for these juvenile offenders. (1995, November 19). <u>San Diego Union-Tribune,</u> p. A-24.

Parenthetic citation forms: (Bartusiak, 1990, p. 61); (Burke, 1979, p. 2918); (Heaton & Wilson, 1994, p. 130); (Kelly, 1995, p. A1); (Christmas, 1995).

Note that the period that ends the title goes after the parenthetic information about page numbers, not before it, as shown in these and the following examples (see *Burke* and *Heaton & Wilson* above).

AN EDITION OR REVISION OF A BOOK

Indicate an edition or revision of a book in parentheses after its title:

Stine, G. J. (1996). <u>Acquired immune deficiency syndrome: Biological, medical, social, and legal issues</u> (2nd ed.). Upper Saddle River, NJ: Prentice-Hall.

Taylor, M. J. H. (Ed.). (1995). <u>Jayne's encyclopedia of aviation</u> (Rev. ed.). New York: Crescent.

Parenthetic citation forms: (Stine, 1996, p. 14); (Taylor, 1995, pp. 187-188).

A TRANSLATION OR REPRINT OF A BOOK

Indicate that a book has been translated or reprinted by adding the publication date of the original work in parentheses at the end of the entry (after the end period). For a translation, also include the name of the translator in parentheses after the title:

Lemieux, E. G. (1994). Modern French architecture (S. L. McNally,
  Trans.). Cambridge, MA: Harvard University Press. (Original work
  published 1962)

Ray, I. (1991). Contributions to mental pathology. New York: Scholars'
  Facsimiles and Reprints. (Original work published 1873)

A VOLUME IN A MULTIVOLUME WORK

Give the number of the volume(s) you consulted in parentheses after
the title. Use *Vol.* or *Vols.* before the volume number(s). The number itself
should be an arabic number, not a roman:

Grouws, D. A., & Cooney, T. (1989). Perspectives on research on effective mathematics teaching (Vol. 1.). Hillsdale, NJ: Erlbaum.

Parenthetic citation form   (Grouws & Cooney, 1989).

If particular volumes are published over more than a one-year period,
indicate the span of dates:

Scammon, R. M., & McGillivary, A. V. (Eds.). (1972-1979). America
  votes: A handbook of contemporary American election statistics
  (Vols. 9-13). Washington, DC: Elections Research Center.

Parenthetic citation form: (Scammon & McGillivary, 1972-1979).

A WORK PUBLISHED IN AN EDITED BOOK

List the work by its author's last name, followed by first and (if given)
middle initial(s). Then give the publication date (in parentheses), followed
by the work's title (no underlining or italics). Next, give the editor's initials
and last name, followed by the abbreviation *Ed.* in parentheses (or *Eds.,* if
more than one editor). After a comma, state the title of the book (underlined or italicized). Include the volume number (if applicable), followed by
a comma and the page number(s) for the included piece in parentheses:

Doi, T. (1992). The cultural assumptions of psychoanalysis. In J. W.
  Stigler, R. A. Scweder, & G. Herdt (Eds.), Cultural psychology:
  Essays on comparative human development (pp. 446-453).
  Cambridge, MA: Cambridge University Press.

Parenthetic citation form: (Doi, 1995, p. 448).

A TECHNICAL OR RESEARCH REPORT

List a published report the same as a book. If the issuing agency has
assigned a number to the report, include it in parentheses after the title:

Briggs, D. E. G. (1981). <u>Relationship of arthropods from the Burgess Shale and other Cambrian sequences</u> (Open File Report 81-743). Washington, DC: U.S. Geological Survey.

Petersen, R. O., Shorter, M., & Treat, J. K. (1995). <u>Learning styles among Pueblo children</u> (New Mexico Research Monograph No. 16). Sante Fe: University of New Mexico, Department of Education.

U.S. Congress, Office of Technology Assessment. (1994). <u>Electronic delivery of public assistance benefits: Technology options and policy issues</u> (S/N 052-003-01121-2). Washington, DC: U.S. Government Printing Office.

Parenthetic citations forms: (Briggs, 1981); (Petersen, Shorter, & Treat, 1995); (U.S. Congress, 1994).

THE PROCEEDINGS OF A MEETING

For published proceedings, treat the work the same as a book:

Devorland, J. O., & Kinnerly, M. (Eds.). (1994). <u>Proceedings of the Carmicael Conference on Health and Technology.</u> Lexington: University of Kentucky.

Parenthetic citation form: (Devorland & Kinnerly, 1994).

For unpublished proceedings, cite when and where the meeting was held (as accurately as possible), as no publisher can be cited:

World Food Conference. (1994, May). <u>Proceedings of the World Food Conference.</u> Conference held at University of Virginia, Charlottesville, VA.

Parenthetic citation forms: (World Food Conference, 1994).

LEGAL SOURCES

Give the information needed for a reader to locate the source. Using the source itself or a referent to it as your guide, give the information indicated in the following examples. If you are working on a computer, you should be able to insert the symbol for *section* (§). If you are working on a typewriter or computer that does not have this symbol, use the abbreviation *Sec.* As mentioned earlier, do not underline or italicize the names of court cases in the References, but do underline or italicize them in text citations (see pp. 289–90). Do not underline or italicize the names of laws, acts, codes, or documents in either the text or References (such as the *U.S. Constitution*).

1. A FEDERAL DISTRICT COURT OPINION

Name   Volume   Source   Page   Region   Date

Hazard v. Kinola, 554 F. Supp. 927 (S.W. Ark. 1994).

This 1994 case was tried in federal district court for the Southwestern District of Arkansas. It appears in volume 554, page 927, of the *Federal Supplement*.

Parenthetic citation form: (<u>Hazard v. Kinola,</u> 1994).

2. A CASE APPEALED TO THE U.S. SUPREME COURT

Name   Volume   Source   Page   Date

Baker v. Carr, 369 U.S. 186 (1985).

This case was tried in 1985 before the U.S. Supreme Court. It appears in volume 369 of the *United States Reports*, page 186.

Parenthetic citation form: (<u>Baker v. Carr,</u> 1995).

3. A FEDERAL LAW

Name   Title number   Source   Section   Date

Voting Rights Act, 42 U.S.C. § 1973 (1965).

Passed into law in 1965, this act appears in title 42, section 1973, of the *United States Code*.

Parenthetic citation form: (Voting Rights Act, 1965).

Many federal laws are often cited by title number, rather than by name. Note that the *United States Code* (cited above) may be abbreviated as *U.S.C.:*

15 U.S.C. sec. 221 (1983).

For more information about the forms of legal references, see *The Bluebook: A Uniform System of Citation,* 15th ed. (Cambridge, MA: Harvard Law Review Association, 1991).

NONPRINT SOURCES

1. A FILM OR VIDEO

Give the principal contributors' names, followed by their function(s) in parentheses. Specify the medium in brackets after the title, followed by the location and name of the distributor:

Choate, H. R. (Producer), & Kimbel, M. M. (Director). (1994). <u>Marriage and commitment</u> [Film]. Chicago: Academy Productions.

Intercultural Relations Institute (IRA). (1995). <u>Take two</u> [Video]. Palo Alto, CA: Author.

Parenthetic citation forms: (Choate & Kimbel, 1994); (IRA, 1995).

2. A CASSETTE RECORDING

Give the principal contributors' names, followed by their function(s) in parentheses. Specify the medium in brackets after the title. If a recording number is given on the source, include that information with the medium specification—for example, (*Cassette Recording No. 71*). List the publisher's location and name last:

Peterson, R. T. (Ed.), & Walton, R. K. (Narrator). (1990). <u>Birding by ear</u> [Cassette recording]. Columbus, OH: Ohio State University.

Parenthetic citation form: (Peterson & Walton, 1990).

Sample References List: Psychology

Though variations occur among some journals, the author-date style recommended by the American Psychological Association (APA) predominates in papers in psychology, education, and a number of other fields. The examples shown in Figure 12.1 conform to the guidelines discussed in previous sections and the recommendations of the *Publication Manual of the American Psychological Association,* 4th ed. (Washington, DC: American Psychological Association, 1994).

Discipline Practices: APA Variations

Disciplines that follow APA, author-date documentation cite sources in the text, as described earlier in this chapter. For entries in the References list, however, many of these disciplines employ variations of APA form,

Public Therapy 19

References

Group author/ publisher — American Psychiatric Association. (1994). <u>Diagnostic and statistical manual of mental disorders</u> (4th ed.). Washington, DC: Author.

Banks, J. (1990). Listening to Dr. Ruth: The new sexual primer. In G. Gumpert & S. L. Fish (Eds.), <u>Talking to strangers: Mediated therapeutic communication</u> (pp. 73-86). Norwood, NJ: Ablex. — **Selection included in another work**

Journal article — Carbaugh, D. (1993). "Soul" and "self": Soviet and American cultures in conversation. <u>Quarterly Journal of Speech, 79</u>(5), 182-200.

Didion, J. (1992, July 26). Trouble in Lakewood. <u>New Yorker, 68,</u> 46-50, 60, 62-65. — **Magazine article**

Book/ single author — Holmes, D. (1994). <u>Abnormal psychology.</u> New York: HarperCollins.

McGuire, W. J. (1993). Social psychology. In <u>Academic American Encyclopedia</u> [Online]. Available: CompuServe. — **Encyclopedia article/online source**

Book/joint editors — Morris, A. D., & Mueller, C. M. (Eds.). (1992). <u>Frontiers in social movement theory.</u> New Haven, CT: Yale University Press.

Unsigned newspaper article — "People." (1994, September 30). <u>USA Today,</u> p. D-2.

Priest, P. J. (1992). Self-disclosure on television: The counter-hegemonic struggle of marginalized groups on <u>Donahue</u> [Online]. <u>DAI 53</u>(1993): 2147A. Abstract from: Information Access File: <u>Dissertation Abstracts Online</u> Item: 50-1634. — **Dissertation abstract/ online source**

Report/ corporate author — Psychiatry and the Community Committee. (1995). <u>A family affair: Helping families cope with mental illness</u> (GAP Report: No. 119). New York: Bruner-Mazel.

Stocking, B. (1994, October 1). Confession may be costly. <u>The News and Observer,</u> pp. 1A, 10A. — **Newspaper article**

FIGURE 12.1   Sample References Page: APA Style

modifying punctuation, spacing, capitalization, and other details. You may discover that adapted versions of APA references forms are common in papers or journals written for agriculture, anthropology and archaeology, the biological sciences, business and economics, education, geology, and home economics. Many papers in linguistics follow LSA style, a version of APA recommended by the Linguistics Society of America. In political science and sociology, writers often use APSA style, a variation of APA adopted by the American Political Science Association. (See the section on Discipline Style Manuals near the end of this chapter for guides on LSA and APSA documentation.)

Be alert to modifications of APA style (or any other major documentation style) as you read and record notes from all your research sources. Make sure such notes are accurate and that your own paper follows precisely the documentation style recommended by your instructor.

Number-System Documentation

The majority of authors, editors, and journals in the applied sciences (chemistry, computer sciences, mathematics, and physics) as well as the medical sciences employ the number-system style of documentation. This style uses arabic numerals in the text to cite sources correspondingly numbered and listed in the References section of the paper.

Intext Citation

The intext citation numerals appear in the text either (a) between parentheses, (b) between brackets, or (c) as raised superscript numerals, as shown here:

a. Harland (3) has shown that traditional comparisons of cigarette smoke yields have been reliable. On the other hand, it is important to remember that the chemical composition of nontobacco cigarette smoke is very different from that of ordinary tar (4,5).

b. Despite the endorsement of Nobel laureate Paul Berg [3], some scientists [1,7,12] maintain that the genome project is unnecessary or that it will produce only what Ayala [4, p. 10] calls "indecipherable junk."

c. Oxygen affects yeast viability and is essential to any yeast ethanol production process.[4-6] The Pasteur effect[12] demonstrates the influence of oxygen and respiration on the ability of the cell to produce ethanol.

(See the instructions for typing brackets and superscript numerals in Chapter 13.)

As these example show, it is not unusual for a citation to refer to more than one source at a time with the number-system method. In addition, note that the citation numerals do not necessarily appear in sequential order. The numeral sequence depends upon the method by which each discipline or publishing journal prefers to list and number sources in a paper's References.

References

For ordering sources in the References section, papers that employ the number-system style follow one of two widely used methods:

1. Numbering sources listed in the References section by their order of appearance in the text
2. Numbering sources according to their alphabetized order in the References

Disciplines and journals vary as to their practices. Which numbering method you use will depend upon the discipline or journal you are following or the directions of your instructor.

1. NUMBERING SOURCES BY ORDER OF APPEARANCE IN THE PAPER

In this method, citation numbers proceed sequentially throughout the text (1, 2, 3, and so on) until they are repeated when a source is cited again. Corresponding sources in the References section are listed and numbered in the order they are cited in the paper, rather than alphabetically by author or title:

Parenthetic citation form
While the effects of aging on the brain can differ dramatically among individuals (1), most structural and chemical differences become apparent in late middle life, usually around the fifties and sixties (2,3). Encouragingly, studies have shown that the brain is also capable of dynamic remodeling of its neuronal connections, especially when exposed to new environments (4). Experiments with placing laboratory rats in visually stimulating environments (1) and altering their DNA (5) have produced apparently substantial increases in cognitive function.

References

1. Finch, C. E. Longevity, Senescence, and the Genome. Chicago: U of Chicago P, 1990.
2. Coleman, P. D., Flood, D. G. Neuron numbers and dendritic extent in normal aging and Alzheimer's disease. Neurobiology of Aging 1987;8:521-45.
3. Davis, E. M. Neural Aging and the Brain. New York: Hight, 1992.
4. Weindruch, R., Walford, R. L., The Retardation of Aging and Disease by Dietary Restriction. Springfield, IL: Thomas, 1988.
5. Shule, N., Watts, J. S. Genetics and Cognitive Growth. Chicago: Wayley, 1991.

Given that the order of sources is likely to change as you write the first draft of your paper, using the number-by-appearance method can be troublesome. To avoid numbering and renumbering sources, put each author's name in parentheses as you write the draft. Once you have completed the paper in draft form, with all sources entered and in final order, then substitute numbers for the authors' names. The numbering of citation sources by order of appearance in the References is common for papers written in computer science, engineering, mathematics, and nursing.

NOTE: Titles of sources are not underlined or italicized in number-system style.

2. NUMBERING SOURCES BY ALPHABETIZED ORDER

Begin by alphabetizing all sources for the paper according to the author's last name (or the work's title, if no author is given). Next, number each source sequentially, as shown below:

References

1. Coleman, P. D., Flood, D. G. Neuron numbers and dendritic extent in normal aging and Alzheimer's disease. Neurobiology of Aging 1987;8:521-45.
2. Davis, E. M. Neural Aging and the Brain. New York: Hight, 1992.
3. Finch, C. E. Longevity, Senescence, and the Genome. Chicago: U of Chicago P, 1990.
4. Shule, N., Watts, J. S. Genetics and Cognitive Growth. Chicago: Wayley, 1991.
5. Weindruch, R., Walford, R. L., The Retardation of Aging and Disease by Dietary Restriction. Springfield, IL: Thomas, 1988.

As you write the paper, cite these sources parenthetically by number (or raised superscript) as they appear in the text. Remember that a number should be repeated in the text each time the source it designates is cited:

> While the effects of aging on the brain can differ dramatically among individuals (3), most structural and chemical differences become apparent in late middle life, usually around the fifties and sixties (1,2). Encouragingly, studies have shown that the brain is also capable of dynamic remodeling of its neuronal connections, especially when exposed to new environments (5). Experiments with placing laboratory rats in visually stimulating environments (3) and altering their DNA (4) have produced apparently substantial increases in cognitive function.

Note that sources are *not* cited in numerical order. The citations above for *Finch (3)*, *Coleman (1)*, *Davis (2)*, and *Weindruch (5)*, for example, correspond to the order in which those authors appear in the References section.

Listing sources alphabetically by their authors' last names and then numbering citations accordingly is the usual method for papers in biology, mathematics, and psychology.

Other Features

Abstracts.   A paper following the number-reference style generally includes an *abstract,* or brief summary, of the paper. (Reviews of the literature, however, do not include abstracts.) An abstract informs the reader of the paper's contents and serves as a useful review once the paper has been read. If your instructor wishes you to include an abstract with your paper, see the general discussion in the section Abstracts, earlier in this chapter.

Headings.   Headings serve as short titles for various sections of the paper. They are helpful in organizing the discussion and emphasizing important ideas for the reader. See the section titled Headings earlier in this chapter if you plan to include headings in your paper.

Journal Abbreviations.   Disciplines following the number-system style of documentation consistently abbreviate titles of journals listed in a paper's References section. For example, the *Scandinavian Journal of Clinical Laboratory Investigations* and the *International Journal of Epidemiology* are abbreviated as follows (respectively):

Scand J Clin Lan Invest
Int J Epidemiol

(Remember that titles of works are not underlined or italicized in number-system style references.)

Exceptions to the practice of abbreviating titles are journals whose titles are only single words (e.g., *Biochemistry, Geology, Science*). While such one-word titles should not be abbreviated in your paper, you will need to abbreviate others.

Make certain the abbreviations you use conform to accepted practices for the discipline you are writing about. The major source for all discipline abbreviations is the *American National Standard for Abbreviation of Titles of Periodicals, Z39.5-1969* (New York: American National Standards Institute, 1985). In addition to consulting the discipline style guides listed on page 316, you can find most standard abbreviations for journal titles in the biological and medical sciences in the two following sources:

> *List of Journals Indexed in Index Medicus.* Bethesda, MD: National Library of Medicine (annual).
> *Serial Sources for the BIOSIS Data Base®.* Philadelphia: BIOSIS, 1989–date (annual).

CBE Style

The Council of Biology Editors (CBE) recommends documentation styles for papers in anatomy, genetics, physiology, and zoology. A research article or paper written to conform to CBE standards cites sources in the text and documents them fully in a References section at the end of the work. In its most recent publication, *Scientific Style and Format: The CBE Manual for Authors, Editors, and Publishers,* 6th ed. (Cambridge: Cambridge UP, 1994), the CBE also describes two other acceptable methods of intext documentation: the *citation-sequence* and *name-year* systems. Each of these citation systems is described in a following section; then CBE practices for preparing the References list are summarized and a sample CBE References page is given. Follow your instructor's advice about which CBE recommended style—citation-sequence or name-year—you should use in documenting your research paper.

Name-Year Intext Citation Form

The CBE name-year method is similar to APA style (see the beginning of this chapter) in that each source is cited parenthetically in the text by the author's last name and the work's publication date:

The cost of using solar energy to heat homes has fallen by as much as 65 percent in the last 10 years (Bradshaw and Awerbach 1995).
or

Bradshaw and Awerbach's work (1995) shows that the cost of using solar energy to heat homes has fallen by as much as 65 percent in the last 10 years.

As in APA style, full bibliographic information for all sources cited in-text is provided in the paper's References section. Note, however, that un-like an APA-style intext citation, a CBE citation does not use a comma between the author's name and the publication date (e.g., *Blay 1995*).

Citation-Sequence Intext Citation Form

The citation-sequence system is essentially a number-system style of documentation: Sources are numbered in the order in which they are cited in the text of the paper and listed in the same order in the References section. Subsequent citations of the same source use the same number as its initial citation. Proper CBE style calls for citation numbers to appear as su-perscripts—that is, positioned above the regular line of text and in type one or two sizes smaller than that used for the text. (If your typewriter or computer lacks the ability to do superscripts, you may print the numerals in your paper by hand or use one of the alternate number-citation styles described on pp. 301–2, if your instructor agrees.) As the following ex-ample illustrates, a multiple citation is made by using a dash between three or more sequential numbers; a comma separates nonsequential citation numbers:

It is estimated that by the year 2000, scientists working on the Human Genome Project will have identified more than 99 percent of all active human genes[1] and found ways to use them for medical purposes. Med-ical experts predict, for example, that future advances in gene therapy will allow doctors to inject needed genes directly into the bloodstream. Once there, the genes will seek out targeted cells and unload material that will eventually produce helpful disease-killing proteins.[2-5] Since the majority of diseases originate from gene imperfections,[1,3,5] such therapy will be useful in treating conditions ranging from AIDS to cystic fibrosis and even high cholesterol.

The sources represented by the numeral citations in this paragraph would be correspondingly numbered and listed in the paper's References, as follows:

1. Walters LR. The ethics of human gene therapy. Nature 1986; 320:225-227.
2. Lyon J, Gordon P. Altered fates: Gene therapy and the retooling of human life. New York: Norton; 1995. 245 p.
3. Green RD, Richards MA. Recent gene therapy: Applications and results. J Intl Genet 1994;168:1254-1262.
4. Mason TH. Medical research: practice and promise. Chicago: Hartley; 1993. 285 p.
5. Culver KW. Gene therapy: A handbook for physicians. New York: Liebert; 1994. 361 p.

References Forms

The preceding examples conform to CBE citation-sequence requirements for the most common types of sources (i.e., books and periodicals) appearing in research papers in the sciences. Whether done according to name-year or citation-sequence style, CBE reference entries are precisely stated and punctuated to present only the most essential information about sources. The following sections summarize the major elements of CBE form (including proper punctuation) required for most entries in the References list. To familiarize yourself with CBE references style, study each section carefully and refer to the sample References list (Figure 12.2) for relevant examples of the topics discussed. Review these sections and examples again later, as you write the References section of your paper. Unless specifically stated otherwise, the procedures described apply both to CBE name-year and citation-sequence documentation styles.

1. AUTHORS' NAMES

For name-year style, list authors alphabetically by their last names; for citation-sequence style, list authors in the order in which they are named in the text. For both styles, follow each author's last name with the initials of his or her first and (if given) middle names; there is no comma between the last name and initials and no space and punctuation between initials (*Herrick RW*).

For More Than One Author

For both styles, list two or three authors as just described for a single author, using commas to separate the individual authors' names (*Graham HW, Shaw K*). For more than three authors, list only the first three; then add a comma after the third name, and follow it with the phrase *and others* (*Roberts JD, Brookline AM, Groot ST, and others*). Note that CBE style does not use the Latin phrase *et al.*

For Group or Corporate Authors

Cite a group or corporate author alphabetically by its abbreviated name, which is placed in brackets at the start of the entry (e.g., *[WHO] World Health Organization*).

For an Anonymous Author

For any work not attributed to a specific author, use the term *Anonymous* in brackets at the start of an entry (e.g., *[Anonymous] How Americans can . . .*).

For an Editor

In both the citation-sequence and name-year systems, place the term *editor* or *editors* (lowercase) after the author's name or after the last author's name, if there is more than one (e.g., *Trevitt CK, Hearter LD, editors*). Note that you should not use the abbreviations *Ed.* or *Eds.*

2. TITLES

Capitalize only the first word of a work's title, the first word in its subtitle (i.e., after the colon), as well as all proper nouns within the title and subtitle (*Educational reform: A means of providing for America's children*). Note that CBE style does not underline or italicize titles.

3. PLACE OF PUBLICATION AND PUBLISHER

CBE guidelines for the form and content of publication information for books and similar sources are the same as those for MLA and APA papers (both discussed earlier in this chapter). For a book, give the place of publication following the work's title, followed by a colon. Next, state the publisher's name, shortened to avoid unnecessary details (*Hope for our side. New York: Croft*).

4. DATE OF PUBLICATION

Where the date of publication is placed will depend upon which style of CBE documentation you are using.

For Citation-Sequence Form

For a book, list the publication date following a semicolon after the publisher's name (*New York: Croft; 1995*). For a periodical, give the year after the title of the work, with no punctuation (*Amino acid nomenclature 1995*). For a journal article, follow the year with the abbreviated month (*1994;Mar*), and for a newspaper article, include the day (*1995;Nov 10*).

For Name-Year Form

Place the publication date after the author's name, followed by a period (*Hanes TC. 1995*). For a magazine or newspaper article, include the month (abbreviated, with no period after) and the day, as applicable (*Jones G. 1994 Aug 2*).

5. PAGE NUMBERS

As with the publication date, how you handle the page numbers depends upon which style of CBE documentation you use.

For Citation-Sequence Form

For a book, after the publication date, add a period and two spaces; then state the number of pages the book contains, followed by a space and the letter *p* (*1994. 241 p.*). For a journal article, add a semicolon after the publication date, followed by the volume number (with no space between), the issue number (if included) in parentheses, and a colon; then list the inclusive page numbers (with no space after the colon), like this: *1995 Feb;83(2):455-461*. For a magazine article, give the page numbers after the colon following the date (*1995 July 12:28*). For a newspaper article, give the section number after the date, followed by a colon and then the page number(s) (*1993 May 3;Sec 4:A2*).

For Name-Year Form

Do not give the numbers of pages for books listed in the References section. But if you are citing a source that is included in another work, give the page numbers of where the source appears in that work; to do so, add a period after the date, followed by the letter *p* (with no period) and the inclusive page numbers (*New York: Croft; 1990. p 45–51*). Give the page numbers for a periodical article after the colon following the volume or issue number of a journal (*1993;74:311–2*); after the date and a colon for a magazine article (*1992 Nov:23-29.*); and after the section number (abbreviated *Sec* with no period) and a colon for a newspaper article (*Aug 25;Sec A:2*). If you give the number for the newspaper column (abbreviated *col* with no period) in which a source appears, it should follow the page number, as in *Sect A:2(col 3)*.

6. ELECTRONIC PUBLICATIONS

A references entry for a source published electronically should include the same information usually given for its printed equivalent, plus information relevant to how it was accessed electronically. The latter requirement includes adding a description of the medium (*CD–ROM* or *serial online*) in square brackets following the title of the work as well as a statement of availability, which documents how and when the work was accessed. For an online source lacking a date or page numbers, give as much information as you can, including descriptions of the document number (abbreviated *Doc nr*), the number of words (bracketed) or paragraphs, plus the number of illustrations (if relevant). Use the following examples as models:

> Grieman PT. Biology recycled. Online J Therap [serial article online] 1995 Mar 12; Doc nr 2 [3720 words; 10 paragraphs]. 3 figures; 1 table.

> Rowley LK. Better health gets easier. Time [serial article online] 1994 April 9; 12 paragraphs. Available from: CompuServe. Accessed 1995 Nov 3.

> THE MERCK INDEX ONLINE [monograph online]. 14th ed. Rahway (NJ): Merck; 1992. Adsorption chromatography; monograph nr 87. Available from: Dialog Information Services, Palo Alto, CA. Accessed 1993 Aug 5.

Also refer to Figure 12.2 for additional examples of CBE-style references.

NOTE: Many standard reference works are better known by their titles than their editors' names. In such a case, list the work under its title; if the editor's name is included, place it after the title:

1. Annual review of cell biology. 4th ed. James A. Spudich and others, editors. Palo Alto, CA: Annual Reviews; 1994.
2. Dictionary of genetics. 4th ed. Robert C. King and William D. Stansfield, editors. London: Oxford University Press; 1990. 416 p.

Discipline Practices:
CBE Variations

Like basic author-date (APA) documentation style, number-system style includes varying practices in both citation and references forms. Papers in the applied sciences—chemistry, mathematics, physics, and the medical sciences, for example—often follow documentation styles recommended by discipline associations. (See the list of style manuals for various disciplines near the end of this chapter.) By consciously noting such variations, you should have no trouble understanding the application of number-system documentation to your own research paper.

Advances in Health

References

Abstract   Ainley WM. Genetically altered viruses in controlled temp-
erature conditions [abstract]. In: American Epidem-
iological Association 7th annual meeting program;
1993 Mar 4-11; San Francisco. Chicago (IL):Science
Associates; 1993. p 249. Abstract nr KL116.

[Anonymous]. Counties respond to tuberculosis threat   **Unsigned newspaper editorial**
[editorial]. New York Times 1993 Sept 10:C4+.

Book with editors   Crane FH, Palmer KS, Thurston LD, editors. The phar-
macology of therapeutics. New York: Foundation;
1994. 483 p.

Journal article accessed online   Grieman PT. Biology recycled. Online J Therap [serial
article online] 1995 Mar 12; Doc nr 15[3720 words;
10 paragraphs]. 3 figures; 1 table.

Gross RP, Pennap JD, editors. Community immunization   **Conference proceedings**
programs. Conference on Community Health and
Services; 1994 April 4-7; Chicago. Chicago: West;
1994. 92 p.

Selection included in another work   Hassel HH, Vries ME. Cell biomass yield. In: Campbell KD.
Biothermodynamics. Chicago: Haley; 1993. p 318-25.

Kates RW. Ending death from famine. N Eng J Med   **Journal article**
1993; 328:1055-57.

Magazine article   Mitchison A. Will we survive? Sci Am 1993 Sep 4:136-144.

Watson JD, Hopkins NH, Roberts JW, and others.   **Book with multiple authors**
Molecular biology of the gene. 4th ed. Menlo Park:
Benjamin/Cummings; 1987. 468 p.

Group author   [WHO] World Health Organization. Our planet, our
health. Report to the United Nations Earth Summit.
Rio de Janeiro; 1992 June.

23

FIGURE 12.2   Sample References Page: CBE Citation-Sequence Style

As you take notes during reading or prepare your own paper's references, do not confuse standard CBE documentation form with modified versions. Be certain that your paper follows your instructor's requirements.

Chicago-Style Documentation

As mentioned at the beginning of the chapter, writers in the fine arts (art, music, dance, and philosophy) and in certain areas of the humanities and some sciences follow documentation standards recommended by *The Chicago Manual of Style* (Chicago: The University of Chicago Press, 1993), now in its 14th edition. The style currently recommended by the editors of the *Chicago Manual* for most publications* is essentially author-date, like APA style, in which sources are cited parenthetically in the text by their authors' last names and dates of publication. Sources are then listed alphabetically by authors' last names and described bibliographically in a References section at the end of the paper. There are some relatively minor but distinctive differences between the two styles; nonetheless, students following *Chicago*-style author-date documentation would do well to study the APA practices described earlier in this chapter and apply those practices to the few differences discussed in this section.

Intext Citation

Although *Chicago*-style author-date documentation forms agree in most ways with those recommended for APA-style papers, note the following differences in basic citation elements:

1. AUTHORS: SINGLE AND MULTIPLE

Cite each source parenthetically within text, including the author's last name and the publication year. It is preferable to place these parenthetic citations at the ends of sentences or at natural syntactic breaks near the content being cited. For a work with two or three authors, give all three names in the citation; state only the first author's name, followed by *et al.* or the phrase *and others* for a work with more than three authors. Follow these examples:

---

*See p. 280 for an explanation of which types of documentation *Chicago* recommends for certain subject areas.

(Johnson 1992)

(Parrish and Davidson 1987)

(Wilkins, Nguyen, and McGuire 1994)

(Berzoli et al. 1993)

Note that unlike APA style, *Chicago* style uses the word *and* between authors' names, instead of an ampersand (&), and no comma is used between the last (or only) author's name and the date. Editors are cited by their names only, with no *Ed., Eds., editor,* or other such descriptor included.

Group or corporate authors should be cited by their full names or recognizable shortened versions, which correspond to the alphabetized listing in the References. Cite a work for which no author is named by its title or a similarly recognizable shortened version. Do not use *Anonymous* to cite an unknown author:

(Huntington Library 1991)

(Western Philosophical Society 1995)

(Transitions in Thinking 1990)   *or*   (Transitions 1990)

("Dancing on Air" 1995)   *or*   ("Dancing" 1995)

2. PARTS OF A WORK

When it is necessary to include page numbers or other specific parts of a work in the source citation, add the information (preceded by a comma) after the date. Use a colon between the volume number of a work and the relevant page numbers:

(Bui and Wesson 1994, 46)

(Hassel 1990, 213-20)

(Winter 1990, 3:116)

(Fruehan, King, and Farrar 1991, 2:91)

3. MULTIPLE SOURCES

Separate two or more sources in the same parenthetic citation using a semicolon. Works by the same author or authors should be identified by their publication dates only; add an alphabetical identifier (*a, b, c*) to distinguish works by the same author or authors published in the same year. The page numbers can be included after a comma in entries with multiple sources:

(Crane and Lessing 1991; Stuart and King 1992)

(Jessup 1994a, 1994b)

(Harrison and Waters 1988, 92-97; Cruz and Mitchell 1995)

Notes

A separate section labeled Notes can follow the text of the paper to explain or amplify points made within it. Number each note consecutively to correspond to a superscripted number (one or two types sizes smaller than text type) in the text. In the Notes section, however, the note number should be typed in normal-size type and aligned with the rest of the text:

Citation in text	Russell's objection to Descartes[1] was based on his dislike of ambiguity.
Entry in Notes section	1. Russell describes his objections in his <u>Autobiography</u>, 221-24.

References

The entries for a *Chicago*-style References section are similar in format to those for an APA-style list. One fairly important difference, however, is how authors' first names are cited: While APA style lists authors' first names by their initials only (and their middle initials, too, if available), *Chicago* style prefers that authors be listed by their first names in full, with or without middle initials (although using initials for both names is also acceptable in *Chicago* style):

Maccay, Robert L. 1993. <u>Mind and mind-games: New turns in philosophy</u>. New York: Burton.

or

Maccay, R. L. 1993. <u>Mind and mind-games: New turns in philosophy</u>. New York: Burton.

Figure 12.3 shows a sample *Chicago*-style References page. Use this example as a model for listing various kinds of works in a research paper written according to the author-date documentation standards of *The Chicago Manual of Style*. (See Chapter 16 in *The Chicago Manual* for more information on these standards.)

Discipline Style Manuals

As discussed earlier in this chapter, documentation practices between and among discipline journals vary greatly. The most comprehensive guide is *The Chicago Manual of Style* (14th ed.); however, as previously noted, it is written more for professional writers and editors than for students working on course papers. The style manuals in the following list recommend the

20

References

Book with 2 authors — Clinton, William, and Albert Gore. 1993. Putting people first. New York: Times.

Davies, Peter Ho. 1995. The ugliest house in the world. In Best American short stories, 1995, eds. Jane Smiley and Katrina Kenison, 110–16. Boston: Houghton. — **Work included in another**

Encyclopedia Britannica, 15th ed., s.v. "social justice." — **Encyclopedia article**

Book with single author — Henry, William A. 1994. In defense of elitism. New York: Doubleday.

Kozol, Johnathan. 1993. Rachel and her children: Homeless families in America. New York: Fawcett Columbine. — **Multiple works by same author**

- - -. 1995. Amazing grace: The lives of children and the conscience of a nation. New York: Crown.

Journal article — Lafer, Gordon. 1994. The politics of job training. Politics and Society 22: 349-88.

O'Hare, Grace, Donovan Pollard, and Thomas Moffat. 1991. Ugly Americans in the future. Popular Culture 46: 4-14. — **Journal article with 3 authors**

Volume of book — Mustajuk, Marru, ed. 1993. Law and poverty in the United States. Vol. 2. New York: Greyley.

Planter, Margaret C. 1994. Guidelines for teaching migrant children. (Alabama State Department of Education, September 1991), Dialog, ERIC, ED 18562. — **Online source**

Unsigned journal article — Right and might: Two views. 1994. Journal of Social Thought and Politics 3: 312-23.

U.S. House of Representatives. 1993. Committee on Ways and Means. 1993 greenbook: Background material and data on programs within the jurisdiction of the committee on ways and means. Washington, D.C.: GPO. — **Government document**

Book with more than 3 editors — Weir, Margaret, et al., eds. 1988. The politics of social policy in the United States. Princeton: Princeton University Press.

Will, Marshall, and Martin Schram, eds. 1993. Mandate for change. New York: Berkeley. — **Book with 2 editors**

FIGURE 12.3 Sample References Page: *Chicago* Author-Date Style

basic documentation forms for their respective disciplines. If you need more information than is provided in this text about a particular discipline or journal documentation style, consult one of these sources:

Biological Sciences
Council of Biology Editors. *Scientific Style and Format: The CBE Manual for Authors, Editors, and Publishers.* 6th ed. Bethesda, MD: Council of Biology Editors, 1994.

Chemistry
Dodd, Janet S., ed. *The ACS Style Guide.* Washington, DC: American Chemical Society, 1986.

Geology
United States Geological Survey. *Suggestions for Authors of Reports of the United States Geological Survey.* 6th ed. Washington, DC: GPO, 1990.

Linguistics
Linguistics Society of America. *LSA Bulletin* Dec. issue, annually.

Literature and Languages
Gibaldi, Joseph. *MLA Handbook for Writers of Research Papers.* 4th ed. New York: Modern Language Association of America, 1995.
———. *Style Manual.* New York: Modern Language Association of America, 1988.

Mathematics
American Mathematical Society. *A Manual for Authors of Mathematical Papers.* 8th ed. Providence, RI: American Mathematical Society, 1990.

Medical Sciences
American Medical Association. *American Medical Association Manual of Style.* 8th ed. Baltimore: Williams and Wilkins, 1989. Rev. ed. of *Manual for Authors and Editors,* 7th ed.

Physics
American Institute of Physics. *AIP Style Manual.* 4th ed. New York: American Institute of Physics, 1990.

Political Science
American Political Science Association. *Political Science.* Fall 1985.

W O R K I N G   W I T H   O T H E R S

The complex documentation forms for the various disciplines discussed in this chapter require close attention to details of form, punctuation, and spacing. Review the Notes and References pages of your draft with another person to see that you have handled such details correctly. A close review of the paper's documentation now will help you avoid errors and omissions when you prepare the final copy.

- Begin by asking a classmate or friend to review your paper's author-date or number-system citations for accuracy and correct form. Next, read the notes and the works named in them aloud while your classmate checks to make sure each work named is also included in the References list.

- Point out any unusual or complicated entries included in the References page(s). Ask your reader to verify the form and punctuation for entries such as multiple authors or editors, works included in volumes, and articles in journals. Check such entries together to make sure they appear in correct form.

- Compare your reader's References list with your own. Note any differences in the way you each have listed similar kinds of sources, and discuss reasons for the differences. Make changes as necessary.

- Ask your reader to review the References list for omissions or unwanted inclusions of underlining or italics, quotation marks, colons, or periods. Check to see that you have spaced correctly between volume and issue numbers. Also review any special formats required by your instructor or discipline.

CHAPTER **13**

Preparing the
Final Manuscript

The thoughtful work you have done researching and writing the completed draft of your paper should continue through preparation of the final manuscript. Plan time for production—including revising, editing, typing, and proofreading—of the final copy well in advance of the paper's due date. Your instructor undoubtedly views your taking responsibility for matters of correct formatting and technical details as an important part of the research paper assignment. Careful preparation of the manuscript will enhance its contents and ensure his or her appreciation of your efforts.

Reviewing and Strengthening the Final Draft

Like most writers, you have undoubtedly made changes, additions, and deletions throughout developing several drafts of the research paper. Having now composed a final version, you should carefully review the draft before typing or printing a final copy. As you review, be prepared to (1) *revise* the paper as needed for overall focus and organization; (2) *edit* for style and correctness; and (3) *proofread* for omissions and other small errors.

Revising

Revise by making any necessary changes to the whole paper, taking into account such broad qualities as completeness, organization, unity, and purpose. Expect to add or delete content, but do not interpret *revising* to mean *rewriting* the paper. Your goal in revising is to assess the general flow of ideas and to rearrange content for more effectiveness.

How to Revise

Begin by carefully reading the draft several times to determine if the content flows smoothly and, on the whole, presents a complete discussion. Pay particular attention to and note any areas that appear underdeveloped, out of place, or irrelevant (see following). Mark changes right on the draft itself (see Figure 13.1, p. 321). If you wrote the draft of your paper on a typewriter, use scissors and tape to rearrange sections to achieve the best order for the content. If you wrote the draft on a computer, use its word-processing functions to add content and move or delete whole sections of text as needed. But before making these changes on the computer, mark them on a printed copy to provide a record of your changes. Also make a backup copy of your paper on computer following each work session. It is a good idea to keep a master of the paper on your hard drive and a backup on a disk.

What to Revise

As you review the draft for revision, follow these suggestions:

1. Make sure the paper's content is unified around a clearly stated main idea. The content of Mark Stevenson's paper in Appendix A, for example, develops and supports this thesis:

> With national attention turning to them in judgment, rather than enjoyment, it is likely that television talk shows have taken things too far to survive the backlash by what has been termed "'the revolt of the revolted.'"

Look for content in your draft that strays from the research topic or is not clearly related to the paper's thesis. You may need to change inappropriate content or, if it is a significant amount, revise the thesis statement to include it.

2. Identify the paper's introduction, body, and conclusion. Does the introduction state a thesis and introduce the paper's topic effectively? Do paragraphs in the body of the paper illustrate and support the thesis? Study the conclusion of the paper to be certain that it clearly reasserts your position and has developed logically from the rest of the paper.

3. If you made an outline of the paper during the planning stage, compare the outline with the final draft. Note any differences in content and organization, and determine whether they are appropriate.

4. Consider the flow of content in the paper to determine whether ideas proceed in a logical fashion. Does the content develop and support the

paper's thesis? Look for recognizable patterns of development, such as cause-and-effect, comparison-and-contrast, and chronological order. Are these patterns clear and handled effectively? If the content does not follow any of these patterns, should it be revised to do so?

5. Decide whether the discussion is complete. Do any significant ideas, arguments, supporting examples, or issues seem to be missing? Does the paper answer your original research question? Make any changes or additions necessary to ensure that the paper's discussion is complete.

6. Determine whether your paper has achieved an argumentative or informative purpose (see Chapter 3). Would any changes in content or wording of the thesis accomplish your purpose more effectively?

Editing

Editing focuses upon details that influence the quality of a paper's content and expression. As in revising, the object here is not to rewrite the paper (though some additional writing may be called for). Rather, the goal is to strengthen the paper's argument by sharpening expression and bolstering supporting evidence and documentation.

How to Edit

Work directly on the draft copy with a pen or pencil to add, delete, or modify the content and writing. Keep a dictionary at hand to check spelling. Consult a handbook as necessary for matters of grammar, punctuation, and style. If you write on a computer, use the "spellcheck" and "search" functions to identify errors for editing. Depending on the capabilities of your software, you may be able to check points of style and grammar, as well. In most cases, however, careful reading of the printed draft, with pen or pencil in hand, will produce the best results as well as a permanent record of the changes made.

Edit with an eye to improving the text, rather than recreating it, but do not hesitate to eliminate weaknesses or outright errors. Figure 13.1 demonstrates common techniques as well as the thoroughness that may be required for effective editing.

What to Edit

As Figure 13.1 shows, editing occurs at the paragraph and sentence levels to correct spelling, grammar, and punctuation errors and to strengthen the paper's thesis support and documentation. In general, edit the paper with close attention to these and the following matters of style and correctness:

> *wrote* Ernest Hemingway ~~once wrote that~~ "All modern literature
> comes from one book by Mark Twain called <u>Huckleberry Finn</u>/" ~~He~~
> *most*
> ~~claimed,~~ "It's the best book we've had" (22). Although ~~it appears~~
> ~~that a large number of~~ literary critics and scholars, as well as the
> *general*   *assessment,*
> reading public, would agree with Hemingway's ~~statement;~~
> Mark Twain's <u>The Adventures of Huckleberry Finn</u> is also one of
> the most ~~debated and~~ controversial works on American
> bookshelves ~~today.~~

FIGURE 13.1   An example of editing

1. Edit the paper for redundant, repetitious, or ineffective word choices:

Wordy   Several of the earliest and first settlers in the area made
               immediate friends with the Apaches.

Edited   Several early settlers made friends with the Apaches.

Vague   Some crimes are punished by very long sentences in prison.

Edited   Capital crimes such as murder and kidnapping are
               punishable by life imprisonment or death.

2. Strengthen weak or faulty sentences. Reduce any that are too long to
be effective by eliminating unnecessary words, clauses, and phrases:

Too long   It is people with AIDS who are demanding more and more
               access to new treatments.

Edited   People with AIDS are demanding increased access to new
               treatments.

3. Correct sentences that are incomplete or incorrectly punctuated:

Sentence fragment (bold)   Global warming will have varying effects. **Because of the changes it will create in drought and rainfall frequencies.**

Revised   Global warming will have varying effects because of the
               changes it will create in drought and rainfall frequencies.

Comma splice Most of these ruins have been looted, even the villagers have helped themselves to saleable antiques.

Revised Most of these ruins have been looted. Even the villagers have helped themselves to saleable antiques.

4. Eliminate discriminatory language. Stereotyping individuals by race/ ethnicity, gender, age, exceptionality, or any other characteristic is as inappropriate in a research paper as it is in life. Avoid using language that perpetuates an inaccurate and unfair perception of any person or group of people. Writing a sentence such as *An airline pilot has to be a mechanic as well as a navigator if **he** wants to survive,* for example, implies that only men are airline pilots. Eliminate gender bias by rewriting such sentences:

Make pronoun unnecessary An airline pilot has to be a mechanic as well as a navigator to survive.

Make subject and pronoun plural Airline pilots have to be mechanics as well as navigators if they want to survive.

5. Examine each paragraph for a topic sentence or unifying idea that supports or develops the thesis statement. Check to see that the paragraph includes enough examples, reasons, or facts to support the topic sentence. Make sure that you have integrated your sources into the text in an effective way and that you present ideas of your own in each paragraph.

Technical Editing Guidelines

The following guidelines apply to research papers using the documentation style of the Modern Language Association (MLA). Certain subjects or the requirements of an individual instructor may call for variation. For conventions of manuscript preparation for APA-, CBE-, or *Chicago*-style papers, consult publication guidelines for the particular discipline (e.g., physics, history, or chemistry). (See the list of style manuals in Chapter 12.)

ABBREVIATIONS

The majority of abbreviations should appear in the paper's documentation to save space and add precision to the entries. In the paper's text, generally spell out all words except those commonly abbreviated between parentheses, such as *e.g.* ("for example") and *cf.* ("compare"). Otherwise, use abbreviations for major, recurrent terms in the paper only after first giving the full names in the text, with the abbreviations following in parentheses:

Magnetic resonance imaging (MRI) offers several improvements over x-ray diagnosis. With MRI, for example, doctors can distinguish blood vessels from malignant tissue.

One organization, Mothers Against Drunk Driving (MADD), has been particularly vocal on this issue. According to MADD, . . .

As these examples demonstrate, many abbreviations are written today without periods or other punctuation marks. Use periods or spaces in an abbreviation as common use suggests (in your sources, for example).

Avoid creating your own abbreviation for any term in the paper. When necessary and useful, employ the standard abbreviations listed here for parenthetical comments in the text, for Works Cited (or References) entries, and for content notes, endnotes, or footnotes. Note the punctuation and use indicated for each abbreviation listed.

1. COMMON ABBREVIATIONS AND REFERENCE WORDS

Use the following abbreviations throughout your paper's documentation (Works Cited, References, and any notes), but employ them only parenthetically in the text:

abbr.	abbreviated, abbreviation
abr.	abridged, abridgment
acad.	academy
adapt.	adapted by, adaptation
anon.	anonymous
app.	appendix
assoc.	association
b.	born
bibliog.	bibliography, bibliographer, bibliographic(al)
biog.	biography
bk.	book
bull.	bulletin
c.	*circa* ("about": use with approximate dates: *c. 1492*)
cf.	*confer* ("compare")
ch.	chapter
col.	column
coll.	college
comp.	compiled by, compiler
cond.	conducted by, conductor
Cong.	Congress
Cong. Rec.	*Congressional Record*
Const.	Constitution
(contd.)	continued
d.	died
DA, DAI	*Dissertation Abstracts, Dissertation Abstracts International*
dir.	directed by, director
ed.	edited by, editor

e.g.,	*exempli gratia* ("for example": see also the section on this term later in the chapter)
et al.	*et alli* ("and others")
etc.	*et cetera* ("and so forth")
facsim.	facsimile
fig.	figure
fwd.	foreword, foreword by
GPO	Government Printing Office
HR	House of Representatives
i.e.,	*id est* ("that is")
illus.	illustrated by, illustration, illustrator
intl.	international
introd.	introduction
jour.	journal
LC	Library of Congress
ms., mss.	manuscript, manuscripts
narr.	narrated by, narrator
n.d.	no date of publication
n.p.	no place of publication; no publisher
n. pag.	no pagination
p., pp.	page, pages
perf.	performed by, performer
pref.	preface by, preface
prod.	produced by, producer
pseud.	pseudonym
pt.	part
rept.	reported by, report
rev.	revised by, revision, reviewed by, review
rpt.	reprint
sec.	section
sess.	session
sic	"thus, so" (see the discussion of this term later in the chapter)
trans.	translated by, translator, translation
ts., tss.	typescript, typescripts
UP	University Press
vol., vols.	volume, volumes

2. ABBREVIATIONS OF TIME

Spell out the names of all months in the text. Except for *May, June,* and *July,* abbreviate the names of months in notes and documentation. Abbreviate some standard time designations—*a.m., p.m., BC, AD*—but spell out most other units of time—*minutes, hours, years*—when they appear in the text.

AD	*anno Domini* ("in the year of the Lord": used before year date: *AD 1100*)
Apr.	April
Aug.	August
BC	Before Christ (used after year date: *65 BC*)
BCE	Before the Common Era
cent., cents.	century, centuries
Dec.	December
Feb.	February
hr., hrs.	hour, hours
Jan.	January
Mar.	March
min., mins.	minute, minutes
mo., mos.	month, months
Nov.	November
Oct.	October
sec., secs.	second, seconds
Sept.	September
wk., wks.	week, weeks
yr., yrs.	year, years

3. ABBREVIATIONS OF GEOGRAPHICAL LOCATIONS

Except for common abbreviations of some countries (*USA, UK*), spell out the names of cities, states, territories, provinces, and countries when they appear in the text. Abbreviate such locations in the paper's documentation, however. Designate U.S. states by their ZIP code abbreviations: *AZ* for *Arizona; MA* for *Massachusetts; OH* for *Ohio*. A list of common abbreviations for other geographical locations follows. For places not given here, follow the practice of your research sources, an unabridged dictionary, or a standard atlas:

Aus.	Austria
Austral.	Australia
BC	British Columbia
Braz.	Brazil
Can.	Canada
DC	District of Columbia
Eng.	England
Gt. Brit.	Great Britain
Jap.	Japan
Isr.	Israel
Leb.	Lebanon
Mex.	Mexico
Neth.	Netherlands
Norw.	Norway

NZ	New Zealand
Pan.	Panama
PR	Puerto Rico
S. Afr.	South Africa
Sp.	Spain
Swed.	Sweden
Switz.	Switzerland
UK	United Kingdom
US, USA	United States of America

4. ABBREVIATIONS OF BOOKS OF THE BIBLE

Follow a quotation from a book of the Bible with a parenthetical citation in the text; separate chapter and verse by a period with no space after it: *Acts 16.6* or *2 Kings 4.27*. Except for most one-syllable titles (*Job, Luke, Mark*), abbreviate books of the Bible when citing them in the text: *Eccles. 6.3, Matt. 11.12*. Do not underline or italicize the title of the Bible or place quotation marks around the names of Biblical books (regardless of whether they are abbreviated).

A list of standard abbreviations for books of the Bible follows. For those not given here, devise unambiguous forms of your own, or consult the list of abbreviations found at the fronts of most editions of the Bible:

Old Testament (OT)

1 and 2 Chron.	1 and 2 Chronicles
1 and 2 Sam.	1 and 2 Samuel
Dan.	Daniel
Deut.	Deuteronomy
Eccles.	Ecclesiastes
Esth.	Esther
Exod.	Exodus
Gen.	Genesis
Jer.	Jeremiah
Judg.	Judges
Lev.	Leviticus
Num.	Numbers
Prov.	Proverbs
Ps.	Psalms
Song Sol. (also Cant.)	Song of Solomon (also Canticles)

New Testament (NT)

1 and 2 Cor.	1 and 2 Corinthians
1 and 2 Thess.	1 and 2 Thessalonians
1 and 2 Tim.	1 and 2 Timothy
1 and 2 Pet.	1 and 2 Peter
Eph.	Ephesians
Jas.	James

Gal.	Galatians
Heb.	Hebrews
Matt.	Matthew
Phil.	Philippians
Rev. (also Apoc.)	Revelation (also Apocalypse)
Rom.	Romans

5. ABBREVIATIONS OF WORKS OF LITERATURE

Spell out the names of all sources, including literary works, listed in the Works Cited or References page(s) of your paper. You may abbreviate a work occurring frequently in the text or notes after first using the full title in the text, followed by the abbreviation in parentheses:

The Merchant of Venice (MV) is one of the earliest of Shakespeare's attempts to mix comedy and tragedy.

For well-known authors and their works, use standard abbreviations, such as those in the following list for Shakespeare. For other Shakespearean works or works by other authors, follow the practices of your research sources or devise easily understood abbreviations of your own: *GW* for *The Grapes of Wrath; SL* for *The Scarlet Letter; MD* for *Moby Dick,* and so forth:

Shakespeare

Ant.	*Antony and Cleopatra*
AWW	*All's Well That Ends Well*
F1	First Folio ed. (1623)
F2	Second Folio ed. (1632)
Ham.	*Hamlet*
1H4	*Henry IV, Part 1*
2H4	*Henry IV, Part 2*
H5	*Henry V*
JC	*Julius Caesar*
Lr.	*King Lear*
Mac.	*Macbeth*
MM	*Measure for Measure*
MND	*A Midsummer Night's Dream*
MV	*The Merchant of Venice*
Oth.	*Othello*
R2	*Richard II*
R3	*Richard III*
Rom.	*Romeo and Juliet*
Shr.	*The Taming of the Shrew*
TGV	*The Two Gentlemen of Verona*
TN	*Twelfth Night*
Tro.	*Troilus and Cressida*
WT	*The Winter's Tale*

ABSTRACTS

An abstract is not usually part of an MLA-style paper. Research papers in the sciences and social sciences, however, generally include abstracts as part of the frontmatter (i.e., the preliminary pages before the actual text, including the title page, outline, etc.). (If your instructor requires an abstract with your paper, see the sections on Abstracts and Headings in Chapter 12.)

ACCENT MARKS

For both English and foreign words, include all accent marks necessary for accurate quotation and correct spelling (e.g., *résumé, mañana, tête-à-tête*). If your typewriter or computer does not have the necessary accent marks, print them in neatly by hand.

AMPERSANDS

Do not use the ampersand symbol (&) to replace the word *and* in the text or in MLA-style citations. (Note that the ampersand is correct in APA-style papers only to cite authors parenthetically in the text [*Harriston & Brown, 1989*] and References [*Harriston, R. M., & Brown, L. L.*].)

ANNOTATED BIBLIOGRAPHIES

If your instructor requires, you may annotate the paper's list of references by providing two or three descriptive sentences at the end of each entry in the Works Cited section. Characterize the work's subject, purpose, strengths or weaknesses, and general usefulness to the reader:

> Trenton, Patricia, and Patrick T. Houlihan. <u>Native Americans: Five Centuries of Changing Images</u>. New York: Harry N. Abrams, 1990. This work compares 500 years of historical information and artifacts with drawings, paintings, and photographs depicting Native Americans and their cultures. The historical information provided is useful, but the book provides no art revealing how Native Americans have viewed themselves.

"BARS" (/)

Use a *virgule,* commonly known as a *bar* or *slash,* to indicate division or separation. When quoting up to three lines of poetry in the text, use this mark (with a space on each side) to show the original beginnings and endings of lines:

> William Blake's poem "A Poison Tree" asserts the value of dealing openly with one's feelings: "I told my wrath. / My wrath did end," says the speaker.

Typed without a space before or after, the bar is also used to separate parts of a date expressed in digits (*3/12/95*) and the elements of fractions (*1/2, 1/3*). Avoid using expressions such as *and/or* and *his/her,* which require the bar and are generally too informal for precise writing.

CAPITALIZATION OF TITLES

For papers in MLA form, capitalize the main title and subtitle of all publications such as books, magazines, journals, and newspapers as well as the titles of works published in them (stories, essays, articles, chapters, appendixes, most poems, and plays). Capitalize the first and last words in such titles along with all other words except prepositions, conjunctions, articles, and the word *to* before verbs.

Follow these general examples even if a title's original capitalization differs (as when letters are variously capitalized for visual effect):

Books	A Tale of Two Cities
	Zen and the Art of Motorcycle Maintenance: An Inquiry into Values
Short stories	"A Rose for Emily"
	"I Stand Here Ironing"
Periodicals	Modern Fiction Studies
	New York Daily News
	TV Guide Magazine
Articles and essays	"Clinton Will Try Again"
	"It Is Time to Stop Playing Indians"
	"Motherhood: Who Needs It?"
Short poems	"Theme for English B"
	"The Fish"
Plays	A Midsummer Night's Dream
	Death of a Salesman

When referring in the text to a poem without a title, use the first line as the name of the work. Do not alter the punctuation or capitalization of the original:

The imagery of Dylan Thomas's poem "Do not go gentle into that good night" suggests . . .

The last stanza of Dickinson's "I died for Beauty—but was scarce" compares . . .

The paper's reference list should cite the anthology or other work in which an untitled poem (usually short) appears.

Ordinarily, do not capitalize the initial article in the name of a periodical (the *New York Times*). Nor should you write a title in all capital letters—except for the names of some journals when their titles include capitalized initials (e.g., *PMLA: Publications of the Modern Language Association of America*).

For disciplines following other than MLA style, see the examples in Chapter 12.

CONTENT NOTES

See the discussion and examples of content notes in Chapter 10.

COPYRIGHT LAW

Federal copyright law protects most published works and even unpublished manuscripts from commercial use or reproduction without permission. For the purpose of criticism or research, however, you may reproduce certain amounts of published or unpublished material without permission from the author or copyright holder. The amount you reproduce without permission cannot exceed *fair use*—that is, an amount considered reasonable for your purposes and in fair proportion to the copyrighted work as a whole. As long as your use is noncommercial and in an amount not exceeding fair use, you may copy or quote substantial amounts or even all of a chapter, a short story, article, short essay, short poem, or any drawing or illustration. Naturally, you must give credit in the paper to the source of any ideas or language you include in the text.

DATE OF PUBLICATION

Include the date of publication for each work listed in the Works Cited section of the paper. Dates for articles in magazines or journals usually appear on the cover or table of contents page. Locate the publication date of a book on the title page or the copyright page following it. If no printing date is given, use the latest copyright date. If there is no publication or copyright date given, use the abbreviation *n.d.* ("no date"), as in *New York: Atlas, n.d.*

Whenever possible, get the publication date from the work itself. If you must learn the date of publication from another source, enclose the date in brackets: *[1994]*. Place a *c.* (for *circa*, "around") before a date in brackets if you can only approximate the date: *[c. 1994]*. Follow the date with a question mark if you are not certain of its accuracy: *[1994?]*. (See Chapter 11 for the formats for listing publication dates of revised or reprinted material as well as volumes published over a period of years.)

DATES

Use the same form throughout the paper for dates—that is, writing either *18 July 1992* or *July 18, 1992.* When the month and day precede the year, separate the day and year with a comma, as in the preceding example. An additional comma also follows the year if the date appears other than at the end of the sentence:

On July 7, 1995, Congress again approached the subject of health care
for all Americans.

When the day is not included in the date, do not put a comma between the month and year: *July 1995.* To list daily, weekly, or monthly periodicals in the Works Cited section, abbreviate all months except *May, June,* and *July,* as in *4 Oct. 1995.*

Place the abbreviation *BC* after the year, but use *AD* before it: *450 BC,* but *AD 1100.* Write the names of centuries in lowercase letters—*the nineteenth century*—making certain to hyphenate them when used as adjectives—*nineteenth-century beliefs, seventeenth- and eighteenth-century poetry.* In general, write the names of decades without capitalization—*the sixties*—or use numbers—*the 1960s* or *the '60s.* Indicate a range of years with a hyphen, specifying full dates unless they are within the same century: *1794–1802* or *1951–53.*

DEFINITIONS

Define terms that are central to your topic and may not be familiar to your audience. At the same time, also avoid defining terms that may be unfamiliar only to you. Be consistent in the form for definitions.

Underline or italicize a word you are discussing as a word:

A <u>periodical</u>, as intended here, is a regularly published magazine,
journal, or newspaper.

Set off a technical term the first time you mention it with a definition by underlining or italicizing it; thereafter, use the term without an underline or italics:

An <u>iconic image</u> is a visual pattern that persists in the viewer's experience after the image source terminates. The remarkable completeness of an iconic image suggests . . .

NOTE: In this text, example terms are underlined, rather than italicized, in keeping with the recommended styles of the Modern Language Association (MLA) and American Psychological Association (APA). Although these organizations agree that either form is acceptable, both suggest that students wishing to use italics check first with their instructors and follow their preferences. Regardless of whether you are writing on computer or typewriter, the principles behind highlighting terms are the same as those outlined here. (See also the section on Underlining, later in this chapter.)

If you are translating a foreign term, underline or italicize it and then define it in one of two ways:

1. If the definition follows immediately after the term, with no intervening words or punctuation, put the definition between single quotation marks:

Gorbachev's defense of the new <u>glasnost</u> 'openness' gained wide support in the West.

2. If the definition is separated from the term by words or punctuation, put the definition between double quotation marks:

Gorbachev's defense of the new <u>glasnost</u>, or "openness," gained wide support in the West.

Use accurate terminology as required by your subject, but avoid overloading the paper with terms needing definition. In many instances, the substitution of a more common term or phrase may be just as effective. For example, use *ordered* rather than *enjoined* when describing instructions given by a court of law.

Also see the discussion about defining terms in Chapter 9.

e.g.

Use this abbreviation for *exempli gratia* ("for example") without capital letters and usually in parentheses to introduce an example (*e.g., as shown here*). Use a period after each letter, and do not space between the first period and the second letter. The term is set off by commas, *e.g.,* as here, or set within parentheses. Do not confuse *e.g.* with the abbreviation *i.e.,* which means "that is."

ENDNOTES/FOOTNOTES

As discussed in Chapter 12, the use of endnotes or footnotes for *documentation* is recommended for only a limited selection of topics and papers (i.e., those requiring numerous or extended explanations or definitions apart from the regular text and written for specific, knowledgeable audiences). The use of *content* notes, however, is a separate matter (see Chapter 10). That is, you may use footnotes or endnotes for explanatory information yet cite sources using another form of documentation (e.g., author-date or number-system). In this case, you will have both Notes and Works Cited pages at the end of your paper. Always check with your instructor regarding the use of notes for either content or documentation purposes.

et al.

When referring to a single work by three or more authors, cite all of their names or that of the first author followed by *et al.* ("and others"). An intext citation would follow either of these formats: *(Cage, Andre, and Rothenberg 163)* or *(Cage et al. 163)*. In the Works Cited section, either of the following formats would be correct:

> Cage, John, Michael Andre, and Erika Rothenberg. Poet's
> Encyclopedia. New York: Unmuzzled Ox, 1980.

> Cage, John, et al. Poet's Encyclopedia. New York: Unmuzzled Ox, 1980.

Although either format—citing all authors' names or using *et al.*—is correct according to MLA style, you should select one and use it consistently in your paper. (Papers written according to CBE style should use the phrase *and others* instead of *et al.*)

Note that *al.* is an abbreviation and must be followed by a period. For parenthetic intext citations, no punctuation appears between the author's name and *et al.* Do add a comma before *et al.* in a Works Cited entry, however. (See also Chapter 12 for examples and use of *et al.* in other documentation styles.)

FOREIGN LANGUAGES

Indicate foreign words or phrases with underlining or italics in the text:

> Instead of the Zeitgeist, he discovered only la belle dame sans merci.

For a work published in a foreign language, follow the capitalization, spelling, and punctuation exactly as given in the original. (See also the section on Accent Marks, earlier in this chapter.) If necessary for your particular audience, provide a translation of the title in brackets, along with the place of publication:

> Sand, George. La Petite Fadette [Little Fadette]. Paris: Garnier-Flam-
> marion, 1964.

ITALICS

To avoid misreading, MLA and APA guidelines recommend underlining as preferable to italics for indicating titles and highlighting terms (but allow either, in accordance with instructors' preferences). Consult with your instructor before deciding to use italics, and follow his or her preference. (See Definitions, earlier in this chapter, and Underlining, later.)

NAMES OF PERSONS

State a person's full name the first time you use it in text—*Ernest Hemingway, Joyce Carol Oates, Percy Bysshe Shelley*. Thereafter, refer to the individual by last name only—*Hemingway, Oates, Shelley*—unless your paper mentions more than one person with the same last name, such as *Robert Browning* and *Elizabeth Barrett Browning*. Famous individuals may be referred to by their commonly known names, rather than pseudonyms or seldom-used names—*Voltaire* instead of *Francois-Marie Arouet; Mark Twain* rather than *Samuel Clemens; Vergil* instead of *Publius Vergilius Maro*.

Do not use formal titles when referring to authors or other actual persons. Use *Ernest Hemingway* first, and thereafter *Hemingway*, but not *Mr. Ernest Hemingway* or *Mr. Hemingway*. This also holds true for women: *Emily Dickinson*, then *Dickinson*, but not *Miss Dickinson*. Refer to characters in literary works by their fictional names: *Goodman Brown, Huck, Hester, Gatsby*.

NAMES OF PUBLISHERS

Use shortened forms of publishers' names for sources in the Works Cited or References page(s) and in content notes, footnotes, and endnotes. In general, shorten publishers' names by omitting the following elements:

- Articles (*a, an, the*)
- First names (*Abrams* for *Harry N. Abrams, Inc.*)
- All but the first name listed (*Allyn* for *Allyn and Bacon*)
- Business abbreviations (*Inc., Co., Ltd.*)
- Descriptors (*Publishers, Library, Press, & Sons*)

For a university press, abbreviate *University* as *U* and *Press* as *P*. Do not use a period after either letter.

The following list provides examples of shortened names for many major publishers. For those not listed, devise abbreviated forms of your own following the guidelines and examples given here:

Shortened Form	*Full Publisher's Name*
Abrams	Harry N. Abrams, Inc.
Allyn	Allyn and Bacon
Appleton	Appleton-Century-Crofts
Barnes	Barnes and Noble Books
Bowker	R. R. Bowker Co.
Cambridge UP	Cambridge University Press
Columbia UP	Columbia University Press
Dell	Dell Publishing Co., Inc.
Dutton	E. P. Dutton, Inc.
Feminist	The Feminist Press at the City University of New York

Harcourt	Harcourt Brace Jovanovich, Inc.
Harvard UP	Harvard University Press
Harvard Law Rev. Assoc.	Harvard Law Review Association
Houghton	Houghton Mifflin Co.
Harper	Harper and Row Publishers, Inc.
Holt	Holt, Rinehart and Winston, Inc.
Macmillan	Macmillan Publishing Co., Inc.
McGraw	McGraw-Hill, Inc.
NEA	The National Education Association
Norton	W. W. Norton and Co., Inc.
Oxford UP	Oxford University Press, Inc.
Prentice	Prentice-Hall, Inc.
Putnam's	G. P. Putnam's Sons
Simon	Simon and Schuster, Inc.
UMI	University Microfilms International
U of Chicago P	University of Chicago Press
UP of Florida	The University Presses of Florida

NUMBERS

In most cases and except as described here, use arabic numerals (*1, 2, 3*) rather than roman (*iv, v, vi*) for all numbers in your paper. The following general guidelines apply to most uses of numbers in an MLA-style research paper:

1. Write as words the numbers from *one* to *nine: six people, three restrictions*. Always write any number beginning a sentence as a word: *Nineteen hundred votes* . . . or *Three constellations* . . .
    Use figures to express the numbers *10* and higher: *nearly 300 species, 88 pounds*. Also use figures to express any number requiring more than two words to write: *2¹/₃, 3.477*.

2. To indicate count, place commas between the third and fourth digits from the right or, for larger numbers, between the sixth and seventh, and so on: *4,000; 44,000; 81,723,000*. Do not use commas with figures that indicate line or page numbers, four-digit year numbers, or addresses, including ZIP codes: *lines 1037–67, page 1201, before 1990* (but *50,000 BC*), *25322 Shadywood Rd., Atlanta, GA 30304*.

3. Express related numbers in the same style (i.e., digits or words): *four of the thirty-two students, less than 100 of the 3,000 men and women*. To indicate a range of numbers, give the second number in full when it is *99* or lower: *5–10, 12–21, 75–86*. For a number with three digits or more, give only the last two figures unless the third is needed for clarity: *91–102, 221–31, 998–1007, 5468–71, 5588–600*. Use a combination of words and figures for very large numbers: *2.5 million, 150 billion*.

4. When typing numbers, do not substitute the small letter *l* ("el") for the figure *1* ("one") unless your typewriter lacks the number key. Also, do not type the capital letter *O* for the figure *0* ("zero").

(See related sections for guidelines on uses of numbers: Dates; Percentages and Money; and Roman Numerals.)

PERCENTAGES AND MONEY

If your discussion includes only a few figures and each can be written in no more than two words, spell out numbers to indicate percentages and amounts of money: *six percent, one hundred percent, thirty-five cents, twelve dollars.* It is also acceptable to use numerals and the appropriate symbols to express such amounts: *4%, 85%, 18¢, $45.15, $3,670.* The latter is typical of papers involving many figures, such as those in the applied sciences. (See other guidelines in the section Numbers.)

ROMAN NUMERALS

Use capital roman numerals whenever they are part of established terminology (*a Class III missile*), a name (*Elizabeth I, John Paul II*), or headings in a formal outline (*IV. Major Influences*). Use small roman numerals to cite or to number the frontmatter pages of a book or other printed source (i.e., those pages preceding the regular text): *page vii.* Your instructor may also prefer that you use both capital and small roman numerals to designate acts and scenes of plays: *Hamlet, III.ii.*

Sic

Use the Latin word *sic* (meaning "thus," "so") to indicate that a quotation is accurate, despite an apparent error in spelling, sense, or logic. Place the term, without quotation marks or underlining/italics, between parentheses whenever it follows a quotation (as when included in your own sentence) or between brackets whenever it must be added in the middle of a quotation:

Following a quotation	Rollins considers "the rascal Huckleberry Fin" [sic] too resistant to authority to be an acceptable role model for children (12).
In the middle of a quotation	Rollins insists that "the rascal Huckleberry Fin [sic] is likely to be a bad example for all children" (12).

Note that *sic* is not accompanied by a correction of the quotation. Changes or corrections of quotations should appear in brackets, without *sic*. (See the discussion of *sic* in Using Quotations in Chapter 9.)

SPELLING

Check the accuracy as well as the consistency of spelling throughout the paper. Give extra attention to unfamiliar or complex terms, names of individuals, and foreign words. If you use a computer program to check spelling, do not overlook the need to proofread the manuscript carefully yourself, as well. The "spellcheck" function may register repeated words but not omitted words, misused homonyms (e.g., *it's* vs. *its*), or misspelled words that are still words (e.g., *form* vs. *from*).

As noted earlier, correct spelling means including accents or other marks for some words, such as those from foreign languages. Put the marks in place by hand if your typewriter or computer printer lacks them (see Accents).

Use a complete, college-level dictionary to check words you are unsure about. If more than one spelling is listed for a word, use the first form given or the one with the most complete definition.

SUPERSCRIPTS

Use superscript numbers—like this[2]—for content notes or documentation using footnotes/endnotes or number-system style. Avoid splintering a sentence with numerous superscript numerals or placing numerals where they interfere with reading the text. As with text citations, place the numeral nearest the material to which it refers. Note how the varying placement of superscript numerals in the following examples might direct a reader to different commentary or sources:

Several critics[3] have pointed out that Kaplan's earliest work was realistic, a view that Davidson apparently ignored.

Several critics have pointed out that Kaplan's earliest work was realistic,[3] a view that Davidson apparently ignored.

Several critics have pointed out that Kaplan's earliest work was realistic, a view that Davidson apparently ignored.[3]

Type superscript numerals a half space above the line. If you are writing on a typewriter, turn the roller slightly to move the paper up; type the numeral, and then return the roller to its original position. If you are using a computer, use the formatting function for typing superscripts.

No punctuation or other marks should accompany superscript numerals. Type the numeral so that it follows all punctuation marks, like this.[2] Exceptions include dashes and parentheses when the superscript refers to material inside parentheses (such as here[4]).

TABLES AND ILLUSTRATIONS

Illustrative material included in your research paper should be genuinely helpful and presented as simply as possible. Use tables and illustrations to summarize, illustrate, simplify, or otherwise clarify the paper's content. Place such material as near the text referring to it as possible or in an appendix at the end of the paper.

1. *Tables:* Arrange information for a table in columns, and use the arabic-numbered label *Table 1* as a title (then *Table 2, Table 3,* and so on). Below the title, include a caption explaining the subject of the table. Type the caption and the title both flush left and above the table data. Immediately below the table, list the source and below it, any notes. Identify each note by a superscript letter (to distinguish the note from text). Double-space the title, caption, table data, source information, and notes throughout. Figure 13.2 provides a model for most kinds of tables.

2. *Illustrations:* Nontabular materials—such as drawings, graphs, charts, maps, and photographs—are considered illustrations. Label each illustration as *Fig.* (for *Figure*), and assign it an arabic number, as in *Fig. 3.* Number all illustrations consecutively throughout the text. Place the figure label, *along with a caption or title to explain the material,* below the illustration. Below the caption, give the source of the material. Begin all entries flush left, and double-space throughout the text accompanying the illustration. Figures 13.3 and 13.4 demonstrate models for various kinds of illustrations.

Table 1
4th Week Student Enrollment Profile, 1991-95

Ethnicity	1991	1992	1993	1994	1995
Native					
American	208	209	220	227	233
Asian	2,220	2,245	2,472	2,860	3,164
Black	340	356	390	397	412
White	11,667	11,120	11,131	11,315	11,461
Hispanic	426	451	479	475	494
Filipino	49	58	61	88	99
Other	238	278	345	222	314
Unknown	2,774	2,338	1,463	1,110	901
Total	17,922	17,055	16,561	16,694	17,078

Source: Census System Files, Westfall Community College.

FIGURE 13.2   A sample table

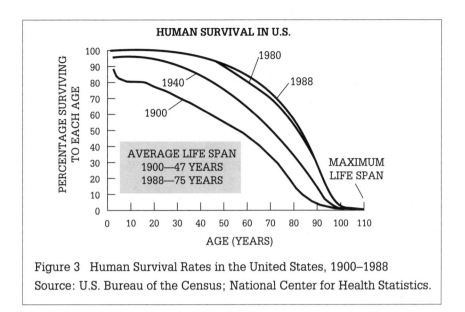

HUMAN SURVIVAL IN U.S.

Figure 3   Human Survival Rates in the United States, 1900–1988
Source: U.S. Bureau of the Census; National Center for Health Statistics.

FIGURE 13.3   A sample illustration

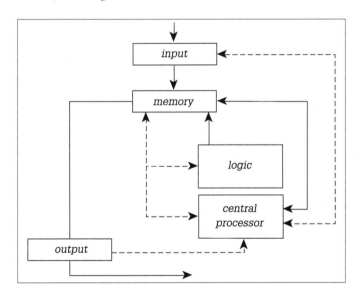

Fig. 2. Schematic diagram of a computer system. Dataflow is indicated by solid lines; signals are indicated by dashed lines.
Source: Judith S. Levey and Agnes Greenhall, "Computer," The Concise Columbia Encyclopedia (New York: Columbia UP, 1983) 188.

FIGURE 13.4   A sample illustration

Always refer to specific tables and illustrations in the text by their labels: *Figure 2, Table 3, col. 1,* or *Fig. 4.* Sources for illustrations should be cited in the text like those for any other works (see Figures 13.2–13.4) as well as fully documented in the Works Cited section of the paper.

TITLES

Other than the exceptions that follow, a title in an MLA-style paper should appear either between quotation marks or underlined/italicized. (See Chapter 12 for various forms for other documentation styles and disciplines.) A general rule is to use quotation marks around the title of a work not published or produced as a whole, such as a short story ("The Tell-Tale Heart") or an essay ("A Defense of Reason"). Also put quotation marks around the titles of chapters, short poems, unpublished works like dissertations or speeches, and individual episodes of radio or television programs.

The titles of works that are published independently should be underlined or italicized, including those of books (*The Heart of Darkness*), plays (*Hamlet*), and long poems (*The Waste Land*), as well as newspapers, magazines, journals, record albums, ballets, operas, films, and radio or television programs. Also underline or italicize the titles of works of art (Rodin's *The Thinker*) and names of ships, aircraft, and space vehicles (*Challenger*). (See also the section on Underlining, following.)

An underlined or italicized title may include the name of a work that should normally be set in quotation marks: *Twain's "Jumping Frog" and American Humor.* Conversely, a work whose name is underlined or italicized may also be part of a title normally set in quotation marks: "The Sea in Virginia Woolf's *To the Lighthouse.*" When a title that is normally set in quotation marks is part of another title in quotation marks, the included title appears within single quotation marks: "Another View of Twain's 'Jumping Frog'." Finally, when one underlined or italicized title includes another, the incorporated title appears without underlining, italicizing, or quotation marks: *Character and Art in Virginia Woolf's To the Lighthouse.*

Do not underline, italicize, or put quotation marks around titles of sacred writings (*the Bible, Genesis, New Testament, Koran, Talmud*) or the names of editions (*Centennial Facsimile Edition, New Revised Edition*), series (*American Poets Series*), societies (*The Thoreau Society*), or academic courses (*philosophy,* or *Philosophy 100*).

UNDERLINING

To avoid misreading, MLA and APA guidelines recommend underlining as preferable to italics for indicating titles and highlighting terms (but allow either in accordance with instructors' preferences). You should use one or the other exclusively in your paper. Note that the same guidelines (as explained throughout this book) apply both to underlining and italicizing.

When typing your paper, keep in mind that a continuous underline is usually easier to read than a broken one and also faster and more accurate to type. Avoid separate underlining of words and punctuation to show titles. That is, avoid this: A Feast of Words: The Triumph of Edith Wharton.

WORD DIVISION

A word divided or hyphenated at the end of a line can make for ambiguous interpretation and interfere with the reader's concentration on the text. Rather than break up such a word at the end of a line, start a new line and leave the preceding one short. If you choose to hyphenate, consult a dictionary and break words syllabically. If your computer has a "hyphenate" function, use it but do so cautiously, verifying the accuracy of word breaks by checking them in a dictionary.

Producing the Final Manuscript

You may elect to type your paper or produce it using a computer and word-processing program. Whichever method you use, print the paper's contents on one side of the paper only. Follow the guidelines given here to prepare the final copy of the paper.

PAPER

Use standard 8½- by 11-inch white paper between 16- and 20-pound weight, or thickness. Do not use onionskin or erasable paper, which often smudges. If you must use either of these for typing or printing the final draft of the paper, submit a photocopy of the finished manuscript on plain, uncoated paper.

TYPE STYLE

Use a common, easily readable type size and style such as 10-point (elite) or 12-point (pica) throughout the manuscript. Use roman type; do not use script, bold, or italic (except for the uses of italic discussed). If your computer or typewriter offers a choice of fonts, Times Roman and Palatino are good options.

TYPE QUALITY

If you are using a typewriter to prepare the final draft of your paper, use a fresh black ribbon to ensure the best results. Watch for smudging or fading, and replace the ribbon if the type becomes difficult to read.

If you are writing the paper on computer, output it using a printer with letter-quality capability. Avoid using a dot-matrix printer (although some 24-pin dot-matrix printers can produce good-quality text). In general, a daisywheel, ink jet, or laser printer will produce the most readable and visually impressive manuscript. Replace the printer's ribbon or cartridge (whether ink or toner) as needed to avoid faint or uneven print quality.

MARGINS

A one-inch margin at the top and bottom, as well as on both sides of the text, is standard for MLA-style papers.

SPACING

Except for footnotes, double-space the paper throughout, including the title, outline, indented quotations, captions, notes, appendixes, and Works Cited entries.

INDENTING

Except for single, quoted paragraphs, indent each paragraph of text five spaces from the left margin. Indent quotations of four or more lines ten spaces from the left margin, but do not indent the first sentence of a single indented paragraph (even if it is indented in the original). When quoting two or more paragraphs, however, indent the first line of each paragraph an additional three spaces (a total of thirteen indented spaces; see Chapter 9, Using Quotations).

To type entries in the Works Cited list, begin each flush left, but indent the second and succeeding lines five spaces. (See Chapter 12 for indentation requirements for APA, CBE, and other styles.)

For typing endnotes and footnotes, indent each first line five spaces, beginning with the raised superscript numeral. Type succeeding lines flush left.

PAGE NUMBERS

Except for the title page, number all pages preceding the first page of text consecutively with lowercase roman numerals (*ii, iii, iv,* and so on). Count but do not put a number on the title page, if it appears as a separate page. If the title page is also the first page of text (as for a short paper), number it as page *1.*

Following the preliminary pages numbered with roman numerals (i.e., the frontmatter), begin on the first page of text to number all pages consecutively with arabic numerals (*1, 2, 3,* and so on) throughout the manuscript. Count and put a number on every page, including the first page of text. Place each page number one-half inch down from the top of the paper and one inch in from the right edge.

RUNNING HEADS

If your paper is in MLA style, begin on page *2* to include your last name, followed by a space, before each page number: *Kramer 2.*

MAKING CORRECTIONS

After carefully proofreading the completely typed or printed paper, make any necessary corrections or revisions. If you are using a typewriter, type in changes or add them by hand in ink. Place all corrections or additions above the text line, never below it or in the margins. Indicate where inserted words or punctuation marks should go in the line of text with a caret (∧). If you are using a computer, make the necessary additions, deletions, or corrections by rewriting and using the "delete" or "cut" and "paste" functions.

You should retype or reprint any page on which numerous revisions or corrections interfere with the readability or neat appearance of the paper. The finished paper should be submitted with as few errors and corrections as possible.

ORGANIZING AND BINDING

Organize the main parts of a completed research paper in this order:

1. Title page
2. Outline*
3. Abstract*
4. Text
5. Content Notes
6. Appendix*
7. Works Cited

Before turning in the finished paper to your instructor, make a photocopy for yourself, in case the original gets lost or damaged. In addition, if you have written the paper on computer, keep a copy of it on your system or a disk. (Actually, making a backup copy is a good idea, too.)

Your paper needs no special cover or binding. Add a blank page at the front and back to help keep it neat. Secure all pages with a paperclip or staple in the upper-left corner. Do not put the paper in a folder or other type of cover unless your instructor approves.

*Not always required

WORKING WITH OTHERS

Many instructors believe students take more responsibility for revising, editing, and proofreading the final drafts of their research papers when they perform these tasks by themselves. Before beginning to work with another person to review your own or each other's final draft, check with your instructor about working cooperatively. If he or she agrees to your sharing the draft with others, use the following suggestions to guide you through this important final process.

- Before typing or printing the final version of your paper, exchange final drafts with another student in your class. Carefully read each other's draft at least twice to share general impressions about the content and writing. Review the suggestions for revision, and offer helpful opinions about organization and unity of content. Check to see that the thesis statement is clearly stated or supported and developed throughout the paper's introduction, body, and conclusion. Is each of these sections effectively handled in the paper?

- Point out parts of your own draft that were improved by editing. Discuss the changes you made with your classmate. Ask his or her opinion about the effectiveness of sentence and paragraph structures and the use of language. If necessary, review the section on editing together.

- Without making corrections on the other person's draft, offer any helpful advice you can about problems in grammar, punctuation, or style. Encourage the author to review the draft to give these matters further attention. Point out any sentences in which the language may be discriminatory, sexist, or otherwise inappropriate. Discuss these problems and ways to resolve them.

- Check general technicalities such as the uses of underlining/italics, numbers, abbreviations, and so forth in each other's draft. Identify anything that you may be unsure about, and discuss its use. Make changes or corrections as necessary.

- After you have printed or typed the final copy of the paper, exchange papers with your partner. Read to catch any glaring omissions or mistakes, and bring any problems to the attention of the author. Before turning the papers in to your instructor, take a few moments to congratulate each other on the work you have done.

Sample Research Papers

APA (Author-Date) and CBE (Citation-Sequence System) Documentation Styles

Sample Paper 1: APA (Author-Date) Documentation Style

The following research paper, Talk Television: Can "Trash TV" Survive? uses the author-date style of documentation recommended by the American Psychological Association (APA). The *Publication Manual of the American Psychological Association* (4th ed., 1994) was written for authors intending to submit their papers for publication; it suggests that students alter guidelines as needed in order to meet the requirements of instructors. In a format consistent with other papers for college courses, for example, the title page of the sample research paper by Mark Stevenson does not include a running head, although APA style calls for one if the paper is intended for publication. All other features of the paper—including the abstract, intext citations, and entries in the References—conform to APA style.

Annotations in the margins of the paper describe important APA style features, which are discussed more fully in Chapter 12. Also consult your instructor regarding any special requirements he or she may have.

Type paper's title and other necessary information double-spaced and centered

Talk Television: Can "Trash TV" Survive?

Mark Stevenson

Bay State College

Professor Margaret Curry

English 102

December 4, 1995

Check with instructor about listing course information

Number all pages consecutively with arabic numerals, beginning with title page

Center heading at page top

Abstract

With national attention turning to them in judgment rather than enjoyment, it is likely that television talk shows have taken things too far to survive the backlash against what critics are calling "trash TV." Fearful of television's power to shape behavior and attitudes, critics charge the shows are corrupting audiences' sensibilities with programs that blur moral distinctions and ultimately erode ethical standards. While the talk shows benefit society by providing a forum for otherwise marginalized individuals and issues, the need for these programs to make titillating entertainment out of serious subjects has begun to worry even those who produce the shows. Criticism and the pressure for change appear to be having an effect, as public interest and advertiser support for talk shows declines. In their desperate pursuit of audiences and higher ratings, television talk shows appear to have succeeded too well in pushing their content up to and beyond the limits of entertainment.

Type abstract as single paragraph, block format

For running head, use short title or your last name, as instructed; first page of text is page 3

Center title at top of page

Talk Television: Can "Trash TV" Survive?

Anyone tuning in to one of America's favorite talk shows recently has very likely witnessed emotionally charged people arguing loudly over such topics as "Women in Love with Gay Men," "What Teens Do When Their Parents Are Not at Home," "Men Obsessed with Their Bodies," and "Committing a Crime for a Mate." Viewed as "frivolous and often inane" (Priest, 1995, p. 140) by some and as "'cultural rot'" (Luscombe, 1995, p. 74) by others, television talk shows have succeeded in capturing the nation's attention to an extent that even those responsible for producing them are concerned. When former Secretary of Education William Bennett recently launched a nationwide campaign against what he termed "'trash TV,'" Gordon Elliott, the host of the Gordon Elliott Show, conceded that Bennett was not at all "'off the mark'" in characterizing the shows (Luscombe, 1995, p. 74). Others defend television talk shows as legitimate and necessary avenues for creating public awareness of important personal and social problems that would otherwise not get the national exposure they deserve. While there is some truth in what the defenders claim, the talk shows may actually have become too successful for their own good. With national attention turning to them in judgment, rather than enjoyment, it is likely that television talk shows have taken things too far to survive the backlash by what has been termed "'the revolt of the revolted'" (Luscombe, 1995, p. 74).

Talk television might not generate the kind of critical scrutiny it does if it were less successful. Though

Single quotation marks within double indicate content appeared in double quotation marks in original

Thesis statement announces paper's main idea

Talk Television 4

talk programs are not all where producers would like
them to be in terms of ratings, Wharton and Flint (1995)
have pointed out that over 30 currently flood the televi-

**Separate
author and
date with
comma**

sion channels every week, with shows like Oprah,
Donahue, Sally Jesse Raphael, and Geraldo reaching, as
Alter (1995) has shown, 3 to 5 million viewers nation-
wide each time they air. So popular have the shows be-

**Underline/
italicize
titles of TV
programs**

come, in fact, that they have spawned Talk Soup, a
"digest" version on cable television's E! channel, where
viewers can get highlights from any talk show they
happen to miss (Anderson, 1993). Online computer ad-
dicts can check out each week's list of topics ahead of
time via the Internet or through any of the nationwide
services, such as CompuServe or Microsoft Network.

It is the popularity of the TV talk shows that concerns critics the most. Despite Fowles's evidence (1992)
that most people tune into television for the purpose of
escaping reality, Leland (1995) has pointed out that
numerous studies show the medium nevertheless has a
profound effect on how we think and live. For this reason, critics are concerned about what kind of impact talk
shows have. Though each has an individual style and
way of doing things, most hosts see their talk shows as
effective in helping people, either those who come on as
guests or those who look on from the audience. According to Heaton and Wilson (1995), the queen of talk hosts,
Oprah Winfrey, for example, views her own show as a
kind of ministry to help people change, while Ricki Lake
compares her role to that of a therapist. Phil Donahue
and Geraldo Rivera tend to focus on helping people
by addressing the problems that afflict them.[1]

**Raised numeral
indicates
content note;
place after final
punctuation**

Talk Television 5

The hosts' instincts may be right, since it is the guests who appear to be the only ones (besides the producers) who actually gain anything from what the shows provide. Many of the people who come on talk shows do so because they are social outcasts, marginalized individuals who feel a need both to defend their ideas or lifestyles as well as to educate the public about them. For such guests, being on television offers what Priest (1995) has described as "the chance to clear up misconceptions and present alternate depictions on the very medium that often propagates damaging stereotypes" about people like themselves (p. 91). Heaton and Wilson (1995) suggested that for one guest, a man who had gone through a sex change, appearing on television was an opportunity to inform society and thereby gain understanding and acceptance of others like himself. Another guest, described by Priest (1995), appeared on a talk show to speak on behalf of herself and other prostitutes so that the public would "start to see us as human beings" (p. 79). Social researchers such as Ehrenreich (1995) and Priest (1995) point out that in providing such opportunities for otherwise silent or misunderstood individuals to be heard, the programs perform a valuable outlet and a needed service to society.

To attract guests and to promote a positive image of talk shows, producers also stress what they claim is the therapeutic effect of public disclosure, whereby individuals gain both validation and, according to Morse (1994), a sense of release by sharing their views of themselves and others in public. Episodes such as "A Confrontation between Jilted Lovers and the People

Writer incorporates quoted material into own sentence

Use ampersand (&) between names of two authors

Cite multiple sources alphabetically by authors' last names; separate with semicolons

Examples provide convincing details

Talk Television 6

Who Rejected Them" (<u>Carnie</u>), "Family Members Inter-
fering with Relationships" (<u>Jerry Springer</u>), or "Get Bigger Breasts- -Or Else" (<u>Rolonda</u>) have been indicated by
Priest (1995) as providing opportunities for guests and
audiences to begin to address problems by first getting
them out into the open. Thus, when Ricki Lake interviewed and then convinced several severely overweight
women to cease denying their obesity and seek professional help, Heaton and Wilson (1995) have argued that
she is seen as fulfilling the potential of the talk show
format to engage people with their problems and
expose important problems to public discussion.

Guests may also benefit from the criticism expressed against their ideas or behavior when they appear on the shows. As Ehrenreich (1995) explained,
appearing on a television talk show may be the only opportunity many have had for any hard-hitting exposure
to external standards of morality. It is routine, for example, for the hosts and audiences of most shows to scold
and jeer loudly at any guests who deny responsibility
for their own immoral or aberrant behavior. Hosts quiz,
scold, lecture, and contradict guests in an effort to get
them to recognize their own shortcomings- -and often,
apparently, to good effect. It is not uncommon for the
shows to feature returning guests who, months after
their first appearance, return completely changed for
the better, apparently due to "the rough-and-ready
therapy dispensed on the show" (Ehrenreich, 1995, p.
92).[2]

Such therapy may not always be appropriate, however. Mental health professionals are concerned about

the shows' uses of "experts," some of whom do not always possess the qualifications their roles suggest. As Heaton and Wilson (1995) have shown, even when guest experts are qualified psychologists, doctors, lawyers, or other professionals, their own input averages less than 13 seconds of a show's usual one-hour length, hardly enough to gain adequate understanding of the individuals onstage or their generally complex and serious problems. The importance of professional insight into the psychological ramifications of the shows' dynamics was tragically underscored earlier this year when, just three days after appearing on <u>Jenny Jones,</u> a guest named Scott Amedure was shot and killed, allegedly by another male guest on the same show. As recounted by Bellafante (1995), Amedure had appeared as a surprise " secret admirer" of the other man, who became so upset by the revelation of Amedure's homosexual feelings for him that he apparently tracked down Amedure after the show and killed him. Although the producers of the show denied any responsibility for what happened, critics point to the tragedy as an example of talk television's "increasingly desperate quest for confrontation" spinning out of control (p. 86).

The shows' continual quests for higher ratings certainly appear to be pushing them beyond other limits of acceptability. Producers use everything from titillating titles such as "Get Bigger Breasts- -or Else" (<u>Rolonda</u>) to "You're Too Old to Be Dating a Teen" (<u>Maury Povich</u>) and "I Won't Wait for the Wedding Day, I Want to Sleep with You First" (<u>Ricki Lake</u>) to near strip shows to hook viewers' attention. Partially nude men and

Talk Television 8

women--ranging from strippers to prostitutes and
cross-dressers and wearing everything from thong biki-
nis to miniskirts and wet T-shirts--are regular attrac-
tions on the shows. A recent "Wild Teens" program on
Jerry Springer used the excuse of showing teenage female guests what they should not become to bring out
a scantily-dressed porno film actress, wearing only high
heels, a satin G-string, and matching barely-enough-to-
cover satin strips over her breasts. As the woman strut-
ted and posed her way across the stage to rounds of ap-
plause and admiring whistles from the men in the
audience, however, the lesson appeared to be predictably lost on the girls (Springer, 1995).

Such scenes are not lost upon the shows' critics,
however, who say such raunchiness only masks the far
more serious issue of what the overall content of the
shows is doing to Americans' values and sense of
morality. Critics charge that television talks shows de-
sensitize their audiences and blur moral distinctions by
what Bellafante (1995, p. 86) has termed an "Oprahiza-
tion" of their sensibilities. Rather than accurately inform the audience about a subject or treat it with the respect it might deserve, the shows tend to trivialize
topics by turning serious, real-life concerns into mere
television spectacles. Psychologists Jeanne A. Heaton   **Authors can be**
and Nona L. Wilson (1995) have pointed out that the   **named in text**
shows use a standard, attention-absorbing format that
has the effect of transforming all problems and issues
into entertainment:

Bullets
appeared in
source and
are retained
to provide
clarity

- Present all problems (from dealing with a questionable date to the murder of a family member) as

equally urgent. Create an air of expectancy, a sense that a secret is going to be revealed.

- Highlight pain and conflict, underscoring the idea that something "real" and of consequence is happening.

- After spending the better part of the show establishing that the issue of the day is damaging and life-altering, shift gears and provide a solution. End on a positive note and reinforce the idea that useful information has been provided. (p. 3)

According to Heaton and Wilson, the result of such formatting is that it distorts real problems, magnifying simple ones and often abbreviating those that are actually complex:

Format quotation of 40 words or more as double-spaced block; indent 5 to 7 spaces from left margin (but not right); no quotation marks

> For example, we can tune in and watch as a young girl describes in lurid detail how she was neglected by her alcoholic mother whom she has not seen for several years. In response to a truly traumatic childhood, the girl's pain appears great. Then the host tells her, and us, that the mother is in the studio. The mother walks on stage and says, "I'm sorry" and the daughter replies, "I love you."
>
> That's it. That's the resolution. (pp. 3-4)

Cite source of quote in parentheses after end punctuation; if authors are named in text, as here, cite only page numbers; use *p.* or *pp.* before page number(s)

The danger in such scenarios is that they trivialize significant problems and suggest that they can be resolved by a brief discussion, confrontation, simple meeting, or the "quick-fix" of a psychologist's two-minutes of analysis (Heaton & Wilson, 1995, pp. 3-4).

Talk show formats also trivialize serious problems by putting them in the same contexts as lighter and more commonplace events. One typical procedure on

Talk Television 10

several shows, for example, is to surprise guests with
unexpected revelations by friends or family members.
While these surprises are sometimes positive and light
hearted- -such as marriage proposals or revelations of
secret crushes- -many are more serious: "daughters
confront fathers with sexual abuse; husbands reveal affairs; children tell their parents they are taking guns to
school, dancing in a strip joint, . . . lovers reveal that
they have had a sex change operation" (Heaton & Wilson, 1995, p. 189). Treating such subjects as "surprises"
has the effect of undermining the seriousness of their
consequences for the individuals involved and trivial-
izes their significance. Confronting fathers with sexual
abuse is presented, as well as seen by viewers, as no
more serious and consequential, for example, than a
surprise reunion of high school sweethearts.

Use ellipsis
to indicate
omitted
content in
quotation

 Trivialization of significant problems also occurs
when a show encourages the audience to offer advice
or pass judgment. Although the audience jeers and
shouts its condemnation of "Married Men Who Have
Relationships with Their Next-Door Neighbors" (<u>Montel
Williams</u>), for example, these are the same rowdy responses they may earlier have given to "Men Who Forget Birthdays," as if the moral level of responsibility involved in both cases were of the same degree.

 Such game show leveling of moral judgment is also
reinforced by the reporting and constantly updating
viewer opinion polls taken while the shows are in
progress. Most of the shows invite viewers to call in
their opinions during the program, with the tallies constantly being flashed on the screen to reveal what

people think about the day's topic. Thus, viewers were encouraged on a recent <u>Jerry Springer</u> episode to call a special "9-Line" to answer the question "Would you accept the fact that your 13-year-old was having sex?" The percentage of viewers who responded "yes" or "no" was flashed on the screen throughout the show's discussion of the topic (Springer, 1995). Although such surveys are, as Tichi (1991) has shown, intended to involve the audiences more and provide a basis for reflection of community standards, the game show atmosphere they create oversimplifies and detracts from the real seriousness of the issues. The result is that whether or not 13-year-olds should be engaging in sex becomes more a matter of popular opinion- -"phone in your vote"- -than one of personal values.

Type long dash as two unspaced hyphens

Critics charge that the result of these and other ways problems are treated on talk shows teaches viewers that there are multiple, equally compelling and equally correct sides to every issue. Critics such as Heaton and Wilson (1995) have claimed that shows often elevate personal beliefs to the level of personal rights and then afford those rights "infinitely more attention than their accompanying responsibilities" (p. 136). The guests on a recent <u>Ricki Lake</u> show, for example, were young men and women who routinely killed or mistreated animals but felt no remorse over doing so (Lake, 1995). One guest was a young man who had shot and killed a pet cat belonging to a friend who paid him to get rid of the animal. When told by others on the show that he should feel more guilt about what he had done, the young man shouted back, "That's your

Talk Television 12

belief, not mine!" (Lake, 1995). Despite the criticism offered by the psychologist on the show, by the host, and
by other guests and the audience, the young man held
firm in his insistence that he had a right to do what he
did and to feel no remorse.

The concern of critics is that discussions such as
this present values and personal opinions about behavior as being wholly subjective, with one point of view
presented as really no more imperative or important
than another. Indeed, there is a danger that the moral
ambiguity and television validation of talk show subjects can lead viewers, children as well as adults, to become less certain about their own values or to adopt an
"anything goes" ethic about behavior (Alter, 1995,
p. 47). Experts agree that allowing people with questionable or ambiguous values to articulate and argue
them on television has the effect of validating those
values and consequently blurring or eroding moral
distinctions. Communications researcher Cecelia Tichi,
for example, has pointed out that those appearing on
talk shows gain a certain level of validity in American
culture because of an "as seen on TV" type of verifica-
tion, whereby they are "elevated out of the banal realm
of the off-screen and repositioned in the privileged onscreen world" (qtd. in Priest, 1995, p. 167). When products or ideas so validated include a moral dimension,
their influence gains momentous significance. Noting
correlations between juror television viewing habits
and the way they vote on juries, for example, legal authorities point to recent acquittals of O. J. Simpson,
Lorena and John Bobbitt, and the Menendez brothers[3]

Use *qtd. in*
to indicate
indirect
source

Talk Television 13

as evidence that people are bringing ambiguous, talk-
show-derived concepts about right and wrong with
them into the jury box (Bellafante, 1995).

Talk shows have come to the nation's attention at
a time when parents are expressing serious concern
about their children's moral and cultural futures. Gen-
der- and ethnic-sensitive books for children fill every
bookstore, and high-minded texts like William Bennett's
<u>The Book of Virtues</u> and E. D. Hirsch's <u>Cultural Literacy</u>
lead the best-seller lists for adults as well as children.
As Cashmore (1994) has pointed out, because television
is "qualitatively different from many other forms of
leisure" and because it is seen as more influential in
conveying ideas and culture than other forms of information (p. 4), parents and others are increasingly concerned about its influence on children. According to
Gabriel (1995), studies show that baby-boomer parents
(those between the ages of 35 and 50) have stricter
ideas about television viewing, homework, and bedtime
than they had or their parents had a generation ago. It
is these same parents who recently pushed Congress to
prohibit making pornography available over the Internet
as well to consider legislating the "V-chip" to regulate
the amount of prime-time television violence children
are exposed to and who also helped pressure Time-
Warner to sell off its holdings in "gangsta' rap" productions (Gabriel, 1995, p. 140). Estimates are that "more
than 650,000 American children, ages 2 to 11 are watching" talk show programs, "with viewership even heav-
ier among teenagers" (Alter, 1995, p. 47). As a result,
Heaton and Wilson (1995) have described our children

(margin note) Underline/
italicize titles
of books;
capitalize
significant
words

Talk Television 14

as "soaking up the same doses of pathology, perversity,
and interpersonal aggravation" that adults do (p. 169),
and argued that for every problem the shows create for
adult viewers, there are more serious ones created for
children who watch.

The most recent and possibly most definitive pres-
sures to clean up talk television came in two significant events in November 1995. The first was a so-called
talk summit in New York, a meeting between talk
show producers and social science professionals who
wanted the shows to take more responsibility for
what they presented. According to Luscombe
(1995), Donna Shalala, one of the summit leaders,
reminded television executives that they were
very good at getting young people's attention. "'The
question is,'" she challenged, "'what are you going
to tell them?'" (p. 74).

Almost at the same time, television executives
were also busy responding to a letter sent by ex-Secre-
tary of Education William Bennett and Connecticut
Senator Joseph Lieberman. Sent on behalf of Empower
America, a nationwide reform organization of which
Bennett and Lieberman are co-directors, the letter
asked the producers to reconsider their support for
"trash TV." As described by Wharton and Flint (1995,
p. 62), the letter pointed out that, with the exception of
Oprah (which stopped using controversial and raunchy
material several years ago), current talk shows "'cele-
brate indecent exposure as a virtue, and distort perceptions of what is acceptable behavior in a civil society.'"
The letter asked, "'Would you want your young children

**Use
parentheses
for less
important
information**

to view a program showcasing the sexual adventures of a
14-year-old girl who married her 71-year-old foster father?'"

Talk show producers, hosts, and others in the television industry responded immediately, often with a
flow of what appeared to be stored-up admissions of
agreement and guilt. Several production representatives
announced that the talk shows had indeed gone too far
and that they expected to see changes coming soon.
King World Productions, producers of Rolonda, took
issue with criticism of its own show but agreed with
Bennett and Lieberman that "'some shows have gone
too far. . . . A lot of companies have gone over the line'"
(Wharton & Flint, 1995, p. 61). Larry Pollock, president of
the Capital Cities/ABC television, said his stations had
already told producers that "'more attention has to be
paid to the sleaze factor'" and that low ratings and lack
of support from advertisers were sure to eliminate some
shows (Wharton & Flint, 1995, p. 61). According to Flint
and Levin (1995), the biggest news came when major
television advertiser Procter & Gamble announced it was
pulling out of much daytime television because of the
"'parade of pathologies and dysfunctions that trash TV
continues to thrust into the public square'" (p. 50).

The letter's importance was not lost upon talk
show hosts themselves. Alter (1995, p. 46) quotes
Geraldo Rivera, of the Geraldo show, as saying that
"'these shows have great relevance to millions, but
sometimes the moral message is obscured by a bur-
lesque theater. . . . What comes next? Fornication on
the air?'" Said Gordon Elliott, host of Gordon Elliott,
"I don't think Bennett is off the mark. The concerns he

Talk Television 16

has, every family man and woman would have" (Luscombe, 1995, p. 74). Perhaps predictably, not all hosts
agreed with Bennett and Lieberman's letter. According
to Luscombe (1995), talk show host Jerry Springer down-
played the seriousness of the shows' impact on viewers
by claiming that his own guests were simply "'entertaining'" and the show intentionally "'silly'" (p. 74). But by
that time, it was becoming clear to everyone that the
time for change was on the horizon for the talk shows.

   If the summit talks and Bennett's letter had not
clearly signaled a coming change for the talk shows,
current ratings certainly have. Recent Nielsen reports
show that audiences are turning away form this sea-
son's syndicated talk shows. Even the long-time queen
of talk shows, <u>Oprah,</u> is down slightly in viewers
(though still out in front of every other show by a huge
margin). All the others- -including <u>Ricki Lake, George
and Alana, Gabrielle, Donahue, Tempestt, Danny Bona-
duce, Carnie Wilson, Charles Perez, Mark Walberg, Sally
Jesse Raphael, Jenny Jones, Maury Povich, Montel
Williams, Jerry Springer, Gordon Elliott,</u> and even
<u>Geraldo</u>- -have lost viewers, in some cases to each other
(Benson, 1995). Television experts agree that talk
shows will undoubtedly tone down their content as the
combined effects of political pressure, advertiser interests, and what Benson (1995, p. 104) has dubbed "the
ultimate taste arbiter," Nielsen ratings, decide who
stays and who goes. "Many of the shows will undoubtedly go away," says one television executive. "But with
thirty-two talk shows out there, who's going to miss
them?" (Wharton & Flint, 1995, p. 61).

Indeed, one wonders how many more examples of the lurid and bizarre Americans need. An announcement between segments of a recent <u>Montel</u> show said the program is looking for "pregnant women who sell their bodies to make ends meet." As one writer asks, "What's next? . . . 'Homeless people who eat their own scabs?'" (Ehrenreich, 1995, p. 92). There seems little doubt that television talk shows have gone too far to sustain their current direction and even their popularity. Yet it would be rash to dismiss them as merely "trash" events without meaning. If we look past the sensationalism of the talk shows, what confronts us are the sad realities of lives caught up, burdened, and even crushed by conditions from which they cannot escape. Children abused by parents, adults confused about their own genders, women who hate their bodies, men obsessed with themselves- -all these and more seek their so-called "fifteen minutes of fame" as perhaps their one opportunity for relief or justification. In providing such opportunity, talk shows have indeed gone too far, for they have moved into realities which, once examined, cannot remain entertaining. As we watch people's lives held up for examination and exposed on TV screens, our better judgment tells us they deserve another kind of forum than <u>Geraldo</u> or <u>Ricki Lake</u> can provide. It is for this reason that as the talk shows change, as they surely must to survive, their alteration will result less from mere matters of taste than from an overruling, collective conscience as to what is fair and decent.

Begin section on new page after regular text; center title

Notes

[1]Oprah herself made talk show history in 1985 when she disclosed on her program that she had experienced repeated acquaintance rapes throughout her life (Priest, 1995, p. 3). The disclosure was hailed by thousands of women who needed Oprah's example to confront their own victimization and to begin to heal their pain from it.

Provides additional information not immediately relevant to text discussion; source cited parenthetically

Offers extended example

[2]One 12-year-old girl, for example, made a return appearance on a recent Jerry Springer show, beaming with smiles and contentment, to explain that since first appearing months earlier as an angry and uncontrollable teenager, she had since stopped hating her mother and was now getting good grades in school. The girl claimed that after watching herself on television when the show aired, she had felt like "an idiot" and, as a result of the audience's criticism, thereafter began working with her mother to better their relationship (Springer, 1995).

Explains references in text to well-known court cases

[3]After a long and sensational trial, O. J. Simpson was declared innocent of the 1994 murder of his wife, Nicole Brown Simpson, and her friend Ron Goldman. Although Lorena Bobbitt admitted cutting off her husband's penis, a jury found that she acted out of fear and found her not guilty. In their first trial, Eric and Lyle Menendez were declared not guilty after claiming they had murdered their parents out of fear of being further abused by them. They were later retried, found guilty, and sentenced to life imprisonment.

Talk Television 19

Begin section on new page after Notes (or regular text, if no notes); center title

References

Alter, J. (1995, November 6). Next: "The Revolt of the Revolted." Newsweek, 124, 46-47.

Weekly periodical; original title included in double quotation marks

Anderson, K. (1993, October 12). Oprah and Jo-Jo the Dog-Faced Boy. Time, 143, 64-66.

Bellafante, G. (1995, March 24). Playing "Get the Guest." Time, 145, 86.

Benson, J. (1995, November 20). Ratings are in. Variety, 352(2), 103-104.

Periodical with volume issue numbers; no quotation marks around article title; underline/italicize journal title and volume number

Ellipsis included in original title

Cashmore, E. (1994). . . . And then there was television. London: Routledge.

Ehrenreich, B. (1995, December 4). In defense of talk shows. Time, 146, 92.

Flint, J., & Levin, G. (1995, November 14). Advertisers reduce spending on talk shows. Variety, 352(2), 50.

Book with 1 author; capitalize first words of title and subtitle and all proper nouns

Fowles, J. (1992). Why viewers watch: A reappraisal of television's effects. New York: Sage.

Gabriel, R. (1995). Kids in the '90s. New York: Grafton.

Heaton, J. A., & Wilson, N. W. (1995). Tuning in trouble: Talk TV's destructive impact on mental health. San Francisco: Jossey-Bass.

Book with 2 authors; separate names with comma; use ampersand (&) before last name

TV program

Lake, R. (Host). (1995, November 12). People who kill animals. Ricki Lake. KCET.

Leland, J. (1995, December 11). Violence, reel to real. Newsweek, 124, 46-48.

Luscombe, B. (1995, November 6). Target: Trash. Time, 145, 74.

Journal abstract on CD–ROM; capitalize all significant words in journal titles

Morse, R. (1994). Affective communication [CD-ROM]. Advances in Psychology, 20, 349-351. Abstract from: SilverPlatter File: PsycLIT Item: 6216743.

Talk Television 20

Priest, P. J. (1995). Public intimacies: Talk show participants and tell-all TV. Cresskill, NJ: Hampton.

Springer, J. (Host). (1995, October 28). Wild teens. Jerry
Springer. KCAL.

Tichi, C. (1991). Electronic hearth: The acculturation of
television in the United States. New York: Oxford
University Press.

Wharton, D., & Flint, J. (November 10, 1995). Bennett
hits producers on "trash TV." Variety, 352(2),
61-62.

Cite author
by last
name; use
initials for
first and
middle
names

After first line
of entry, indent
remaining lines
5 to 7 spaces

Sample Paper 2:
CBE (Citation-Sequence System)
Documentation Style

The following sample paper presents a selected review of literature published during 1994–96 about AIDS and the virus that causes it, HIV (human immunodeficiency virus). The intext citations and References section of the paper follow the citation-sequence system of documentation recommended by the Council of Biology Editors (CBE) (see Chapter 12) and described in its publication *Scientific Style and Format: The CBE Manual for Authors, Editors, and Publishers* (6th ed., 1994).

Note that sources in the References section are listed and numbered in their order of appearance in the text. Each author's last name is followed by a space and then his or her initials, with no intervening periods or spaces between the initials. There is no comma between the author's last name and initials, but commas are used to separate individual authors' names. Titles of sources are not underlined or italicized; titles of journals may be abbreviated. The publication date, journal and issue numbers, and page numbers are added at the end of each entry, separated with punctuation marks but no spaces.

Sources are cited in the text by corresponding superscripted numbers, following the content they reference. Intext citations include page numbers after quotations or whenever sources are lengthy. (See also discussion of CBE style in Chapter 12).

Annotations in the margin explain certain stylistic and documentation features of the CBE citation system. You should also consult your instructor regarding any special requirements he or she may have.

1

Research on HIV:

A Selective Review of Literature for 1994-96

Center title, your name, and other relevant information

Daniel Nguyen

Psychology 202

May 10, 1996

Abstract
defines
paper's
focus and
summarizes
content

Abstract

A selected review of literature published during 1994-96 about AIDS-causing HIV demonstrates greater understanding of the interaction of the immune system's CD4 T cells and their responses to the human body's invasion by HIV. Studies of cases involving individuals infected with HIV but able to resist it over long periods of time or even to ultimately reject HIV infection provided insight about the nature of the virus and the immune system. Several new drug therapies promise wide application for use in establishing future models for research and for administering to people with HIV or AIDS. The understanding of and new techniques for dealing with HIV that were reported in the literature offer hope for more improved means of preventing and treating the disease in the future.

Running
head is
optional,
unless
paper to be
submitted
for
publication
use short
title or
your last
name (as
instructed),
plus page
number

No title on
first page
of text

3

A selected review of research reported during 1994-
96 demonstrates increased understanding of the means
by which the human immunodeficiency virus, or HIV, at-
tacks human cells, as well as the identification of promising new drugs and techniques for the prevention and
treatment of AIDS (acquired immunodeficiency syndrome). While researchers continued to encounter further evidence of the powerful, devastating effects of HIV
and AIDS upon infected individuals, they also reported
several new insights into ways the human body fights
off and, in some cases, successfully rejects HIV infection,
resulting in treating AIDS through natural resistances.
Studies are guardedly optimistic about the eventual application of the results they describe, and all conclude
that full understanding and use of most findings in the
fight against AIDS will require further research.

POTENCY OF HIV

Cell Destruction

Several research studies in 1994-96 detailed new insight about the overpowering, lethal effects of HIV invasion upon the human immune system. One study,[1] for
example, described the powerful struggle between the
immune system and the invading HIV, with the body
producing and ultimately losing over 1 billion of the
white, antiviral CD4 T cells a day in the struggle to ward
off HIV infection. This description of the potency of the
HIV echoed another study, which found that HIV suc-
ceeds by rapidly overwhelming the immune system
through sudden attack and destruction of "naive" CD4
T cells that have not yet had a chance to gain information about the invading virus.[2] Another study found that

---

Marginal notes (left):

No title on
first page
of text

Define key
terms and
abbreviations
used

Headings and
subheadings
indicated by
different
placements
and type
styles

Cite sources
by number
in order they
appear in
text

Marginal notes (right):

Count title
and abstract
as pages 1
and 2; text
begins on 3;
use arabic
numbers

First-level
heading
centered, all
capital letters;
second-level
heading flush
left, with
significant
words
capitalized

Superscript
citation
numbers
should be 1
or 2 type
sizes
smaller
than text

Research on HIV

4

smokers infected with HIV-1 tended to develop AIDS at significantly faster rates than others because of the ability of HIV-1 to bind rapidly with cellular protein and then suddenly enter and destroy the nuclei of gene cells.[3] Research by Raloff and others[4] described their research on the insidious attack on the vital organs when, instead of destroying fat tissue (as in other wasting diseases), HIV that had moved into the AIDS stages decimated the essential protein cells of vital organs.

Authors may be named in text; give number for locating source in References

Cell Resistance

More positive news about the ability of the immune system to fight HIV came with research concerning HIV-2, a less virulent form of HIV, or HIV-1 (as it has been called since the second type was discovered in 1985). Marlink and his co-researchers have described CD4 T cell counts that have remained less affected by HIV-2 over longer periods of time than was previously known. The research showed a mere 1% drop in T cell numbers faced with HIV-2 infection, versus an approximate 10% drop and accompanying infections in cases with HIV-1.[5]

Third-level heading indented, followed by period; significant words capitalized

Applications of Results. Studies reporting on the swift potency of HIV in attacking the immune system also indicated useful applications of their findings. For example, a study by Shiramizu and his colleagues of delayed AIDS-related cancer has lent strong support to other findings that HIV may evolve and change the way it infects individuals.[6] The work of Roederer and others[2] on naive CD4 T cells suggests that keeping an accurate and ongoing count of such cells may help doctors measure the level of the immune system's resources for fighting HIV infection. The study reported by Yao and colleagues

Research on HIV

5

on smokers with HIV-1 infections[3] provides insights to
monitoring the likelihood of infection when the right combination of HIV and reduced CD4 T cells are present.

COUNTERACTING HIV

Natural Resistances

Several studies described research into apparent
cases of HIV resistance and the factors contributing to
such resistance. Reporting at the Tenth International
AIDS Conference in Japan, Fauci and others described
preliminary results from their research on people who
had remained healthy despite being infected with HIV
for a decade or longer.[7] Similar outcomes were reported
from research on numerous infants who showed signs
of HIV at birth but, when tested a few months later,
seemed to have cleared the infection from their systems
entirely.[8] Shiramizu and colleagues reported evidence of
individuals who were infected with HIV but remained
symptom free for years, until the virus altered their DNA
sufficiently enough to cause a rare and lethal cancer.[6]

Drug Research

In contrast to these studies of apparent natural resistance to HIV, other researchers reported on the effectiveness of several new drugs. A group led by Belshe reported on the use of a genetically engineered vaccine
that successfully spurs the production of antibodies that
attack several strains of HIV,[9] and Lasch and others described their success in producing a significant, long-
term boost in the production of infection-fighting white
cells through a regular regimen of interleukin-2, a naturally produced protein.[10] Although the results from both
groups were promising, further research will be required

Research on HIV

6

to tell whether the increase in cells they report can have a lasting impact on HIV infections and AIDS survival.

Reporting from the University of Washington, Tsai reported success with a new drug that seems capable of stopping SIV, the animal equivalent of AIDS-causing HIV. Unlike AZT and other anti-AIDS drugs now given to humans, the new drug, PMPA, seems to have no ill effects upon the animals that receive it. Further research will determine its long-term effects and possible uses for humans.[11] Barnett and her colleagues reported optimism that their work studying baboons injected with varying strains of HIV will eventually establish a primate model for AIDS and a way to fight the disease.[12]

Application of Results. The research reviewed demonstrated increased support for earlier findings that some individuals' immune systems can inhibit or even ultimately throw off the HIV.[7,8,9] Such findings may lead to naturally resistant, immunologically based approaches to fighting HIV without the use of toxic or otherwise endangering effects of drug therapies. Drug therapies such as those that stop SIV, the simian form of AIDS, or that developed from interleukin-2 promise potential for treating HIV or AIDS.

Form for citing multiple sources at same time

Conclusion summarizes paper's major findings

Conclusion

The important research reviewed in this selective study of the literature for 1994-96 demonstrates the wide-ranging aspects of AIDS research and current promising results. Successful results of several types of drugs, together with the natural resistance to HIV exhibited by some individuals, provides tantalizing evidence of the potential for immunological models upon which to base future, more permanent prevention and treatment strategies.

References section
begins new page;
center title at top

References

Sources listed
in order of
appearance
in text

1. Wain-Hobson S. AIDS: Virological mayhem. Nature 1995;373(6510):117-22.

2. Roederer M, Dubs JG, Anderson MT, Raju P, Herzenberg LA, Herzenberg LA. CD8 naive T cell counts decrease progressively in HIV-infected adults. J Cli Invest 1995;95(5):2061-80.

3. Yao Y, Hoffer A, Chang CY, Puga A. Dioxin activates HIV-1 gene expression by an oxidative stress pathway requiring a functional cytochrome P450 CYP1A1 enzyme. Environ Health Prob 1995; 103(4): 366-71.

Use authors' initials instead of first names, with no spaces or periods

Capitalize
first words
and all
proper
nouns in
book and
article titles;
capitalize all
significant
words in
journal titles

4. Raloff J. Troubling insights into AIDS wasting. Sci News 1995 April:254.

5. Marlink R, Cather ND, Foster KL, Chang CC. Long-term survival evidence in HIV-2 patients. J Health 1995;167(4):341-2.

6. Shiramizu B, Herndier BG, McGrath MS. Identification of a common clonal human immunodeficiency virus integration site in human immunodeficiency virus-associated lymphomas. Cancer Res 1994;54(8): 20-72.

Article in monthly magazine

7. Fauci AS, Martin LJ, Veer H. Preliminary results of a study of apparently healthy individuals with HIV infection. Tenth International AIDS Conference, Yokohama, Japan. August 10, 1995.

Material presented at conference

Do not
underline/
italicize
journal titles
or volume
numbers

8. Bryson YJ, Pang S, Wei LS, Dickover R, Diagne A, Chen IS. Clearance of HIV infection in a perinatally infected infant. New Eng J Med 1995;332(13):833-8.

Research on HIV

8

9. Belshe BB, Bolognessi DP, Clements ML,
Corey L, Dolin R, Mestecky J, Mulligan M, Satblein D,
Wright P. HIV infection in vaccinated volunteers. JAMA
1994;272(6):431.

10. Lasch PR, Hainey KH, Jones LB. Variables in
HIV levels in a study of combinant drug applications.
J Pub Health 1995;83(6):578-82.

Article in
journal

11. Tsai C-C, Follis KE, Sabo A, Beck TW, Grant RF,
Bischogberger N, Beneviste RE, Black R. Prevention of
SIV infection in macques by (r)-9-(2-phosphonylmeth-
oxypropyl) adenine. Sci 1995;270(5239):1121-2.

12. Barnett SW, Murthy KK, Herndier BG, Levy JA.
An AIDS-like condition induced in baboons by HIV-2.
Sci 1994;269(51017):642-6.

Journal
titles are
abbreviated
according to
standard
practice

APPENDIX B

Reference Sources for Selected Subjects

This appendix is comprised of lists of commonly found reference sources, first, by subject and next, within each subject, by type. Use these resources and others located near them in the library to find materials for general reading about a subject and for establishing a preliminary bibliography for research. Also consult the general reference sources listed throughout Chapter 4.

Index to Subjects

Anthropology and Archaeology, p. 376
Art and Architecture, pp. 376–77
Biological Sciences, pp. 377–78
Business, pp. 378–79
Chemistry and Chemical Engineering, p. 379
Computer Science, p. 380
Ecology, pp. 380–81
Education, pp. 381–82
Ethnic Studies, pp. 382–83
    Asian American Studies, p. 382
    Black Studies, pp. 382–83
    Hispanic American Studies, p. 383
    Native American Studies, p. 383
Film, p. 384
Geography, p. 384

Geology, p. 385
Health and Physical Education, pp. 385–86
History, p. 386
Journalism and Mass Communications, p. 387
Language, pp. 387–88
Literature, pp. 388–89
Mathematics, p. 390
Medical Sciences, pp. 390–91
Music, p. 391
Philosophy and Religion, pp. 391–92
Physics, pp. 392–93
Political Science, p. 393
Psychology, p. 394
Sociology and Social Work, pp. 394–95
Speech, p. 395
Women's Studies, pp. 395–96

Reference Sources by Subject

Anthropology and Archaeology

Bibliographies, Guides, and Indexes
International Bibliography of the Social Sciences: Anthropology, 1990. Comp. International Committee for Social Science Information and Documentation Staff. New York: Routledge, 1990.

Encyclopedias, Dictionaries, and Handbooks
The Cambridge Encyclopedia of Archaeology. Ed. Andrew Sherratt. New York: Cambridge UP, 1980.
Encyclopedia of Anthropology. Ed. David E. Hunter and Phillip Whitten. New York: Harper, 1976.
Heizer, Robert F., et al. *Archaeology: A Bibliographical Guide to the Basic Literature.* New York: Garland, 1980.
Student Anthropologist's Handbook: A Guide to Research, Training and Careers. Cambridge, MA: Schenkman, 1972.

Abstracts and Digests
Abstracts in Anthropology. Farmingdale, NY: Baywood, 1970–date. Quarterly.

Art and Architecture

Bibliographies, Guides, and Indexes
American Art Directory. New York: Bowker, 1952–date.
Applied and Decorative Arts: A Bibliographic Guide. Ed. Donald L. Ehresmann. 2nd ed. Littleton: Libraries Unlimited, 1993.
Art Index. New York: Wilson, 1929–date. Quarterly.
Art Research Methods and Resources: A Guide to Finding Art Information. Ed. L. S. Jones. Dubuque, IA: Kendall, 1985.
Bibliographic Guide to Art and Architecture, 1991. Boston: Hall, 1992.
Contemporary Architects. 2nd ed. Chicago: St. James, 1987.
Fine Arts: A Bibliographic Guide to Basic Reference Works, Histories, and Handbooks. Ed. D. L. Ehresmann. 3rd ed. Littleton: Libraries Unlimited, 1990.
Guide to the Literature of Art History. Comp. Etta Arntzen and Robert Rainwater. Chicago: ALA, 1981.
Illustration Index. Ed. Marsha Appel. 4th ed. Metuchen, NJ: Scarecrow, 1980.
Index to Art Periodicals. 11 vols. Boston: Hall, 1962. With supplements.

Encyclopedias, Dictionaries, and Handbooks
Dictionary of American Art. Ed. Matthew Baigell. New York: Harper, 1980.
Dictionary of American Painters, Sculptors, and Engravers. Ed. Mantle Fielding. New York: Editions, 1986.
Encyclopedia of American Architecture. Eds. Robert T. Packard and Balthazar Korab. 2nd ed. New York: McGraw, 1994.
Encyclopedia of American Art. New York: Dutton, 1981.
Encyclopedia of Twentieth-Century Architecture. Ed. Vittorio M. Lampugnani. Rev. ed. New York: Abrams, 1986.
Encyclopedia of Visual Art. 10 vols. Chicago: Encyclopaedia Britannica, 1989.
Encyclopedia of World Art. 15 vols. New York: McGraw, 1959–68.

Handbook of Architectural Technology. Ed. Henry J. Cowans. New York: Van Nostrand, 1991.
McGraw-Hill Dictionary of Art. 5 vols. New York: McGraw, 1969.
Oxford Companion to Twentieth-Century Art. Ed. Harold Osborne. Oxford, Eng.: Clarendon, 1982.
Oxford Dictionary of Art. Ed. Ian Chilvers. Oxford, Eng.: Oxford UP, 1988.
Praeger Encyclopedia of Art. 15 vols. New York: Praeger, 1971.

Biographical Dictionaries and Directories
American Art Directory. 49th ed. New York: Bowker, 1982.
Afro-American Artists: A Bibliographical Directory. Ed. and comp. Theresa Cederholm. Boston: Boston Public Library, 1973.
Cumming, Paul. *A Dictionary of Contemporary American Artists.* 5th ed. New York: St. Martin's, 1988.
Marks, Claude. *World Artists 1950–1980.* 4 vols. New York: Wilson, 1982.
Who's Who in American Art. Ed. Jacques Cattell Press. 17th ed. New York: Bowker, 1986.

Databases
ARCHITECTURE DATABASE (RILA)
ART BIBLIOGRAPHIES MODERN
ART LITERATURE INTERNATIONAL

Biological Sciences

Bibliographies, Guides, and Indexes
Agriculture Index. New York: Wilson, 1916–63.
Bibliography of Bioethics. 8 vols. Detroit: Gale, 1975–date.
Biological Abstracts. Philadelphia: Biological Abstracts, 1926–date.
Biological and Agricultural Index. New York: Wilson, 1947–date. Monthly except August.
Botanical Bibliographies: A Guide to Bibliographical Materials Applicable to Botany. Monticello: Lubrecht, 1974.
General Science Index. New York: Wilson, 1978–date.
Guide to the Literature of the Life Sciences. Ed. R. C. Smith and W. M. Reid. 9th ed. Minneapolis, MN: Burgess, 1980.
Information Sources in the Life Sciences. Ed. H. V. Wyatt. Stoneham, MA: Butterworth, 1987.
Library Research Guide to Biology: Illustrated Search Strategy and Sources. Ann Arbor, MI: Pierian, 1978.

Encyclopedias, Dictionaries, and Handbooks
American Men and Women of Science: Physical and Biological Sciences. Ed. Jacques Cattell Press. 16th ed. 8 vols. New York: Bowker, 1968.
Cambridge Encyclopedia of Life Sciences. E. Adrian Faraday and David S. Ingram. Cambridge: Cambridge UP, 1985.
CRC Handbook of Agricultural Productivity. 2 vols. Boca Raton, FL: CRC, 1981.
Dictionary of Botany. Ed. John R. Little and Eugene C. Jones. New York: Van Nostrand Reinhold, 1980.
Dictionary of the History Science. Ed. William F. Bynum et al. Princeton, NJ: Princeton UP, 1985.

Dictionary of Zoology. Ed. A. W. A. Leftwich. Princeton, NJ: Van Nostrand Reinhold, 1973.

Encyclopedia of Bioethics. Ed. Warren T. Reich. 2 vols. New York: Macmillan, 1982.

Encyclopedia of the Biological Sciences. Ed. Peter Gray. 2nd ed. New York: Van Nostrand Reinhold, 1981.

Hammond Barnhart Dictionary of Science. Ed. Robert Barnhart. Maplewood, NJ: C. S. Hammond, 1986.

Larousse Encyclopedia of Animal Life. New York: McGraw, 1967.

McGraw-Hill Dictionary of the Life Sciences. Ed. Daniel N. Lapedes. New York: McGraw, 1984.

United States Department of Agriculture. *Yearbook of Agriculture.* Washington, DC: GPO, 1894–date.

Van Nostrand's Scientific Encyclopedia. Ed. Douglas M. Considine. 6th ed. New York: Van Nostrand Reinhold, 1982.

Abstracts and Digests

Biological Abstracts. Philadelphia: Biological Abstracts, 1926–date.

Databases

AGRICOLA
AGRIS INTERNATIONAL
AQUACULTURE
BIOSIS
LIFE SCIENCES COLLECTION
SCISEARCH
ZOOLOGICAL RECORD

Business

Bibliographies, Guides, and Indexes

Accountant's Index. New York: American Institute of Certified Public Accountants, 1921–date.

Brownstone, David, and Gorton Carruth. *Where to Find Business Information.* 2nd ed. New York: Wiley, 1982.

Business Index. New York: Wilson, 1958–date. Microfilm.

Business Periodicals Index. New York: Wilson, 1958–date. Monthly except August.

Daniells, Lorna M. *Business Information Sources.* Rev. ed. Berkeley: U of California P, 1985.

Encyclopedias, Dictionaries, and Handbooks

Ammer, Christine, and Dean Ammer. *Dictionary of Business and Economics.* Rev. ed. New York: Free Press, 1984.

Encyclopedia of Business Information Sources. Ed. James B. Woy. 11th ed. Detroit: Gale, 1996.

Rosenberg, Jerry M. *Dictionary of Business and Management.* New York: Wiley, 1978.

Databases

ABI/INFORM
ACCOUNTANTS INDEX
D&B DUN'S FINANCIAL RECORD

D&B ELECTRONIC YELLOW PAGES
DISCLOSURE
ECONOMIC LITERATURE INDEX
LABORLAW
MANAGEMENT CONTENTS
MOODY'S CORPORATE NEWS
PTS F&S INDEXES
PTS PROMPT
STANDARD & POOR'S NEWS
TRADE AND INDUSTRY INDEX

Chemistry and Chemical Engineering

Bibliographies, Guides, and Indexes

Applied Science and Technology Index. New York: Wilson, 1958–date.
Chemical Industries Information Services. Ed. T. P. Peck. Detroit: Gale, 1979.
Chemical Publications. Ed. M. G. Mellon. 5th ed. New York: McGraw, 1982.
Chemical Titles. Easton: ACS, 1960. Biweekly.
Guide to Basic Information Sources in Chemistry. Ed. Arthur Antony. New York: Wiley, 1979.
How to Find Chemical Information: A Guide for Practicing Chemists, Teachers, and Students. Ed. Robert E. Maizell. 2nd ed. New York: Wiley, 1987.
Selected Titles in Chemistry. 4th ed. Washington, DC: ACS, 1977.

Encyclopedias, Dictionaries, and Handbooks

Chemical Engineer's Handbook. 6th ed. New York: McGraw, 1984.
Condensed Chemical Dictionary. 10th ed. New York: Van Nostrand Reinhold, 1981.
CRC Handbook of Chemistry and Physics. Ed. Robert C. Weast. 75th ed. Boca Raton, FL: CRC, 1994.
Kirk-Othmer Encyclopedia of Chemical Technology. 3rd ed. 24 vols. New York: Wiley, 1978. Supplements.
Riegel's Handbook of Industrial Chemistry. 8th ed. New York: Van Nostrand Reinhold, 1983.

Abstracts and Digests

Annual Reviews of Industrial and Engineering Chemistry. Washington, DC: ACS, 1972–date.
Chemical Abstracts. Washington, DC: ACS, 1907–date.
General Science Index. New York: Wilson, 1978–date.

Databases

CA SEARCH
CHEMICAL ABSTRACTS
CHEMICAL INDUSTRY NOTES
CHEMIS
CHEMNAME
COMPENDEX
INSPEC
NTIS
SCISEARCH

Computer Science

Bibliographies, Guides, and Indexes

AMC Guide to Computing Literature. 1978–date. Annually.

Annotated Bibliography on the History of Data Processing. Ed. James W. Cortada. Westport, CT: Greenwood, 1983.

Applied Science and Technology Index. New York: Wilson, 1958–date.

Computer Literature Index. Phoenix, AZ: ACR, 1971–date.

Computer-Readable Bibliographic Data Bases: A Directory and Data Sourcebook. Washington, DC: ASIS, 1976–date.

Scientific and Technical Information Sources. Ed. C. Chen. Boston: MIT, 1987.

Zorkocsy, Peter. *Information Technology: An Introduction*. New York: Knowledge, 1983.

Encyclopedias, Dictionaries, and Handbooks

Computer Dictionary and Handbook. 4th ed. Indianapolis, IN: Sams, 1985.

Dictionary of Computer Terms. Ed. Douglas Downing and Michael Covington. 2nd ed. New York: Barron, 1992.

Encyclopedia of Computer Science and Engineering. Ed. Anthony Ralston. 3rd ed. New York: Van Nostrand Reinhold, 1993.

Encyclopedia of Computer Science and Technology. Ed. Jack Belzer. 20 vols. New York: Dekker, 1975–date.

McGraw-Hill Illustrated Dictionary of Microcomputers. Ed. Michael F. Hordeski. New York: McGraw, 1994.

Abstracts and Digests

Artificial Intelligence Abstracts. New York: Bowker, 1983–date. Annually.

Databases

BUSINESS SOFTWARE DATABASE
COMPUTER DATABASE
INSPEC
MICROCOMPUTER INDEX

Ecology

Bibliographies, Guides, and Indexes

Energy Information Guide. Ed. David R. Weber. Santa Barbara, CA: ABC-Clio, 1982–83.

Environment Index. Ed. M. Pronin. New York: Environment Information. Annual.

Environment Information Access. New York: EIC, 1971–date.

Environmental Periodicals Bibliography. Santa Barbara, CA: Environmental Studies Institute, 1972–date .

Encyclopedias, Dictionaries, and Handbooks

Encyclopedia of Community Planning and Environmental Protection. Ed. Marilyn S. Schultz and Vivian L. Kasen. Ann Arbor, MI: Books on Demand, 1995.

General Science Index. New York: Wilson, 1978–date.

Grzimek's Encyclopedia of Mammals. Ed. Bernhard Grzimek. 2nd ed. 5 vols. New York: McGraw, 1990.

McGraw-Hill Encyclopedia of Environmental Science. Ed. S. R. Parker. 2nd ed. New York: McGraw, 1980.

Abstracts and Digests
Biological Abstracts. Philadelphia: Biological Abstracts, 1926–date.
Ecology Abstracts. Bethesda, MD: Cambridge Scientific Abstracts, 1975–date. Monthly.
Energy Abstracts for Policy Analysis. Oak Ridge, TN: TIC, 1975–date.
Environment Abstracts. New York: Environment Information Center, 1971–date.
Pollution Abstracts. Bethesda, MD: Cambridge Scientific Abstracts, 1970–date.

Databases
APTIC
BIOSIS PREVIEWS
COMPENDEX
ENVIRONLINE
ENVIRONMENTAL PERIODICALS BIBLIOGRAPHY
POLLUTION ABSTRACTS
WATER RESOURCES ABSTRACTS

Education

Bibliographies, Guides, and Indexes
Berry, Dorothea. *A Bibliographic Guide to Educational Research.* 2nd ed. Metuchen, NJ: Scarecrow, 1980.
Bibliographic Guide to Education. Boston: Hall, 1978–date.
Bibliographic Guide to Educational Research. Ed. D. M. Berry. 2nd ed. Metuchen, NJ: Scarecrow, 1980.
Current Index to Journals in Education. Phoenix, AZ: Oryx, 1969–date.
Education Index. New York: Wilson, 1929–date. Ten times a year with annual cumulations.
Education Journals and Serials. Ed. Mary E. Collins. Metuchen, NJ: Scarecrow, 1988.
Exceptional Child Education Resources. Reston, VA: CEC, 1968–date.
Philosophy of Education: A Guide to Information Sources. Ed. Charles A. Baatz. Detroit: Gale, 1980.
Resources in Education [formerly *Research in Education*]. Washington, DC: ERIC, 1956–date.
Subject Bibliography of the History of American Higher Education. Westport, CT: Greenwood, 1984.

Encyclopedias, Dictionaries, and Handbooks
Dictionary of Education. Ed. Derek Roundtree. New York: Barnes and Noble, 1982.
Encyclopedia of Educational Evaluation. Ed. Scarvia B. Anderson et al. Ann Arbor, MI: Books on Demand, 1995.
Encyclopedia of Educational Research. Ed. Marvin C. Alkin. New York: Macmillan, 1992.
Handbook of Research on Teaching. Ed. Merlin C. Wittrock. 3rd ed. New York: Macmillan, 1986.
Handbook of Research on Teacher Education. Ed. Robert Houston. New York: Macmillan, 1990.
Library Research Guide to Education. Ed. James R. Kennedy, Jr. Ann Arbor, MI: Pierian, 1979.

Abstracts and Digests
Digest of Educational Statistics. Washington, DC: United Sates Department of Education, National Center for Educational Statistics, 1962–date.
Education Abstracts. Paris: UNESCO, 1949–date.
Educational Documents Abstracts. New York: Macmillan, 1966–date.

Databases
AIM/ARM
A-V ONLINE
ERIC
EXCEPTIONAL CHILD EDUCATIONAL RESOURCES

Ethnic Studies

Bibliographies, Guides, and Indexes
Comprehensive Bibliography for the Study of American Minorities. Comp. Wayne C. Miller. 2 vols. New York: New York UP, 1976.
Ethnic Information Sources of the United States. Ed. Paul Wasserman. 3rd ed. 2 vols. Detroit: Gale, 1995.
Harvard Encyclopedia of American Ethnic Groups. Ed. Stephan Thernstrom et al. Cambridge, MA: Harvard UP, 1980.
MLA International Bibliography. New York: MLA, 1921–date.
Social Sciences Index. New York: Wilson, 1974–date.

Abstracts and Digests
Sage Race Relations Abstracts. San Mateo, CA: 1976–date.
Sociological Abstracts. La Jolla, CA: Sociological Abstracts, 1952–date.

Asian American Studies
Bibliographies, Guides, and Indexes
Chen, Jack. *The Chinese of America.* New York: Harper, 1982.
Immigration and Emigration: Index of Modern Authors and Subjects with Guide for Rapid Research. Ed. Darrow R. Davidson. Washington, DC: ABBE, 1991.
Melendy, Henry Brett. *Asians in America: Filipinos, Koreans, and East Indians.* New York: Hippocrene, 1981.
Wong, James I. *A Selected Bibliography on the Asians in America.* Palo Alto, CA: R and E, 1981.

Black Studies
Bibliographies, Guides, and Indexes
Afro-American Reference: An Annotated Bibliography of Selected Sources. Ed. N. Davis. Westport, CT: Greenwood, 1985.
Bibliographic Guide to Black Studies: 1987. Boston: Hall, 1988.
Black Access: A Bibliography of Afro-American Bibliographies. Comp. R. Newman. Westport, CT: Greenwood, 1984.
Black Resource Guide, 1990. Washington, DC: Black Resource, 1990.
Blacks in Selected Newspapers, Censuses and Other Sources: An Index to Names and Subjects. Ed. James de T. Abajian. 3 vols. Boston: Hall, 1977. First supplement 2 vols., 1985.
Fisher, Mary L. *The Negro in America: A Bibliography.* 2nd ed. Cambridge, MA: Harvard UP, 1970.
Index to Afro-American Reference Resources. Comp. Rosemary Stevenson. Westport, CT: Greenwood, 1988.

Index to Periodical Articles by and about Blacks. Boston: Hall, 1983–date. Annually.
The Negro in the United States: A Selected Bibliography. Comp. Dorothy B. Porter. Washington, DC: Library of Congress, 1970.
The Progress of Afro-American Women: A Selected Bibliography and Resource Guide. Comp. Janet Sims. Westport, CT: Greenwood, 1980.

Encyclopedias, Dictionaries, and Handbooks
Black American Information Directory. 3rd ed. Detroit: Gale, 1993.
Dictionary of American Negro Biography. Ed. Rayford W. Logan and Michael R. Winston. New York: Norton, 1983.
Encyclopedia of Black America. Ed. W. Augustus Low. New York: McGraw, 1981.
Negro Almanac. Ed. H. A. Ploski and James Williams. 4th ed. New York: Wiley, 1983.
Who's Who Among Black Americans. Northbrook: WWABA, 1976–date.

Hispanic American Studies
Bibliographies, Guides, and Indexes
A Bibliography of Criticism of Contemporary Chicano Literature. Comp. Ernestina N. Eger. Berkeley, CA: Chicano Studies Library Publications, U of California, 1982.
Dictionary of Mexican American History. Ed. Matt S. Meier and Feliciano Rivera. Westport, CT: Greenwood, 1981.
Hispanic American Periodicals Index. Los Angeles: UCLA Latin American Center, 1974–date.
Mexican Americans: An Annotated Bibliography of Bibliographies. Comp. Julio A. Martinez and Ada Burns. Saratoga, CA: R and E, 1984.
Selected and Annotated Bibliography for Chicano Studies. Comp. Charles M. Tatum. 2nd ed. Lincoln, NE: Society of Spanish and Spanish-American Studies, 1979.

Native American Studies
Bibliographies, Guides, and Indexes
American Indian Novelists: An Annotated Critical Bibliography. New York: Garland, 1982.
Guide to Research on the North American Indians. Ed. Arlene Hirschfelder. Chicago: ALA, 1893.
Indians of North America: Methods and Sources for Library Research. Hamden, CT: Library Professional, 1983.

Encyclopedias, Dictionaries, and Handbooks
Encyclopedia of North American Indian Tribes. Ed. Bill Yenne. New York: Random, 1988.
Handbook of North American Indians. Ed. W. C. Sturtevant. 15 vols. Washington, DC: Smithsonian, 1978–in progress.
Reference Encyclopedia of the American Indian. Ed. T. M. Inge. 4th ed. Santa Barbara, CA: ABC-Clio, 1986.

Databases for All Ethnic Studies
AMERICA: HISTORY AND LIFE
ERIC
PAIS
SOCIAL SCISEARCH
SOCIOLOGICAL ABSTRACTS

Film

Bibliographies, Guides, and Indexes

Armour, Robert A. *Film: A Reference Guide*. Westport, CT: Greenwood, 1980.
Film Literature Index. New York: Film and Television Documentation Center, 1973–date. Quarterly with annual indexes.
Halliwell, Leslie. *Halliwell's Film Guide*. 4th ed. New York: Scribner's, 1983.
International Index of Film Periodicals. New York: Bowker, 1975–date.
Oxford Companion to Film. Ed. Liz-Anne Bawden. New York: Oxford UP, 1976.
Performing Arts Research: A Guide to Information Sources. Detroit: Gale, 1976.
Ross, Harris. *Film as Literature, Literature as Film: An Introduction to and Bibliography of Film's Relationship to Literature*. Westport, CT: Greenwood, 1987.
Whalon, Marion K. *Performing Arts Research: A Guide to Information Sources*. Detroit: Gale, 1976.

Encyclopedias, Dictionaries, and Handbooks

Film and Television Handbook, 1994. Ed. David Leafe. Bloomington: Indiana UP, 1994.
Film Encyclopedia. Ed. Phil Hardy. New York: Morrow, 1983–84.

Abstracts and Digests

New York Times Film Reviews. New York: Times Books, 1970–date.

Geography

Bibliographies, Guides, and Indexes

Geographers: Bio-Bibliographical Studies. Ed. T. W. Freeman et al. London, Eng.: Mansell, 1977–date. Annually.
Geography and Local Administration: A Bibliography. Ed. Keith Hoggart. Monticello, IL: Vancy, 1980.
Geologic Reference Sources: A Subject and Regional Bibliography. Ed. Dedrick C. Ward, Marjorie Wheeler, and Robert A. Bier. 2nd ed. Metuchen, NJ: Scarecrow, 1980.
Guide to Information Sources in the Geographical Sciences. London, Eng.: Croom Helm, 1983.
International List of Geographical Serials. 4th ed. Chicago: U of Chicago, 1995.
Social Sciences Index. New York: Wilson, 1974–date.

Encyclopedias, Dictionaries, and Handbooks

Encyclopedia of Geographic Information Sources. Ed. J. Mossman. 4th ed. Detroit: Gale, 1986.
Encyclopedia of World Geography. North Bellmore, NY: Marshal Cavendish, 1993.
Longman Dictionary of Geography. Ed. Audrey N. Clark. London, Eng.: Longman, 1989.

Abstracts and Digests

Geo Abstracts, A–G. Norwich, Eng.: Geo Abstracts, 1972–date. Bimonthly.

Databases

GEOBASE
SOCIAL SCISEARCH

Geology

Bibliographies, Guides, and Indexes
Bibliography and Index of Geology. Boulder, CO: American Geological Institute, 1933–date. Monthly with annual indexes.
Bibliography of North American Geology. 49 vols. Washington, DC: Geological Survey, 1923–71.
General Science Index. New York: Wilson, 1978–date.
Geological Reference Sources: A Subject and Regional Bibliography. Ed. Dedrick C. Ward, Marjorie W. Wheeler, and Robert A. Bier. Metuchen, NJ: Scarecrow, 1981.
Publications of the Geological Survey. Washington, DC: GPO, 1979.

Encyclopedias, Dictionaries, and Handbooks
Challinor's Dictionary of Geology. 6th ed. New York: Oxford, 1986.
Encyclopedia of Field and General Geology. Ed. C. W. Finkle. New York: Van Nostrand Reinhold, 1988.
Glossary of Geology. Ed. R. L. Bates and J. A. Jackson. 3rd ed. Falls Church, VA: AGI, 1987.
McGraw-Hill Encyclopedia of the Geological Sciences. 2nd ed. New York: McGraw, 1988.

Databases
COMPENDEX
GEOARCHIVE
GEOBASE
GEOREF

Health and Physical Education

Bibliographies, Guides, and Indexes
Consumer Health Information Source Book. Ed. Alan M. Rees. 4th ed. New York: Bowker, 1994.
Current Index to Journals in Education. Phoenix, AZ: Oryx, 1969–date.
Education Index. New York: Wilson, 1929–date.
Food and Nutrition Information Guide. Englewood, CO: Libraries Unlimited, 1988.
Foundations of Physical Education and Sport. Ed. C. A. Bucher. St. Louis, MO: Mosby, 1986.
Health Services Research. Ed. G. N. Fracchia and M. Theofilatou. Wooster, OH: IOS, 1993.
Health Statistics: A Guide to Information Sources. Detroit: Gale, 1980.
Physical Education Index. Cape Giradeau, MO: Oak, 1978–date.
Physical Fitness and Sports Medicine. Washington, DC: GPO, 1978–date.
Sports and Physical Education: A Guide to the Reference Sources. Ed. Bonnie Gratcher et al. Westport, CT: Greenwood, 1983.

Encyclopedias, Dictionaries, and Handbooks
Columbia Encyclopedia of Nutrition. New York: Putnam, 1988.
Dictionary of Nutrition and Food Technology. Ed. Arnold E. Bender. 6th ed. Newton, MA: Butterworth-Heinemann, 1990.
Encyclopedia of Nutrition Science. Ed. [sic] Rollinson. New York: Wiley, 1988.

Encyclopedia of Physical Education, Fitness and Sport. Ed. Thomas K. Cureton, Jr. 3 vols. Salt Lake City, UT: Brighton, 1980.

Encyclopedia of Sports Contacts: The Sports Networking Reference Guide. Santa Monica, CA: Global Sports, 1994.

Abstracts and Digests

Nutrition Abstracts and Reviews. New York: Wiley, 1931–date.

Databases

ERIC

MEDLINE

MEDOC

SOCIAL SCISEARCH

SPORT AND RECREATION INDEX

History

Bibliographies, Guides, and Indexes

Arts and Humanities Citation Index. Philadelphia: Institute for Scientific Information, 1976–date. Annually.

Combined Retrospective Index to Journals in History, 1838–1974. 11 vols. Arlington: Carrollton, 1977–78.

Guide to Historical Method. Ed. Robert J. Shafer. 3rd ed. Belmont, CA: Wadsworth, 1980.

Harzfeld, Lois. *Periodical Indexes in the Social Sciences and Humanities: A Subject Guide.* Metuchen, NJ: Scarecrow, 1978.

Kaplan, Louis. *A Bibliography of American Autobiographies.* Madison: U of Wisconsin P, 1961.

Prucha, Francis Paul. *Handbook for Research in History.* Lincoln: U of Nebraska P, 1987.

Social Sciences Citation Index. Philadelphia: Institute for Scientific Information, 1979–date. Annual supplements.

Wars of the United States. New York: Garland, 1984–date.

Encyclopedias, Dictionaries, and Handbooks

Dictionary of American History. Ed. Michael Martin and Leonard Gelber. New York: Dorset, 1990.

Encyclopedia of American History. Ed. Richard B. Morris and Jeffrey B. Morris. 6th ed. New York: Harper, 1982.

Encyclopedia of World History. 5th ed. Boston: Houghton, 1972.

Abstracts and Digests

Recently Published Articles. Washington, DC: American Historical Association, 1976–date.

Writings on American History. Washington, DC: American Historical Association, 1903–date.

Databases

AMERICA: HISTORY AND LIFE

HISTORICAL ABSTRACTS

SOCIAL SCIENCES CITATION INDEX

Journalism and Mass Communications

Bibliographies, Guides, and Indexes

Annotated Media Bibliography. Ed. Brenda Congdon. Washington, DC: ACC, 1985.

Black Media Directory. Ed. Martin Pollack. Fort Lauderdale, FL: Alliance, 1990.

Black Media in America: A Resource Guide. Ed. G. H. Hill. Boston: Hall, 1984.

Blum, Eleanor. *Basic Books in Mass Media.* 2nd ed. Urbana: U of Illinois P, 1980.

Broadcast Television: A Research Guide. Ed. F. C. Schreibman. Los Angeles: AFI Education Services, 1983.

Business Periodicals Index. New York: Wilson, 1958–date.

Humanities Index. New York: Wilson, 1974–date.

Journalism Bibliographies: Master Index. Detroit: Gale, 1979. Supplements.

Media Research: An Introduction. Ed. R. D. Wimmer and J. R. Dominick. Belmont, CA: Wadsworth, 1982.

Radio and Television: A Selected Annotated Bibliography. Metuchen, NJ: Scarecrow, 1978. Supplements to 1982.

Encyclopedias, Dictionaries, and Handbooks

Paneth, Daniel. *Encyclopedia of American Journalism.* New York: Facts on File, 1983.

Taft, William H. *Encyclopedia of Twentieth Century Journalists.* New York: Garland, 1986.

Abstracts and Digests

Communications Abstracts. San Mateo, CA: Sage, 1978–date.

Databases

AP NEWS
MAGAZINE INDEX
NATIONAL NEWSPAPER INDEX
NEWSEARCH
REUTERS
SOCSCI SEARCH
UPI NEWS

Language

Bibliographies, Guides, and Indexes

American Literature and Language: A Guide to Information Sources. Detroit: Gale, 1982.

Annual Bibliography of English Language and Literature. Cambridge, Eng.: Cambridge UP, 1921–date. Annual.

Cambridge Encyclopedia of Language. Ed. David Crystal. New York: Cambridge UP, 1987.

A Concise Bibliography for Students of English. 5th ed. Stanford, CA: Stanford UP, 1972.

McCrum, Robert, William Cran, and Robert MacNeil. *The Story of English.* New York: Viking, 1986.

The World's Major Languages. Ed. Bernard Comrie. New York: Oxford UP, 1987.

Encyclopedias, Dictionaries, and Handbooks
Barnhart, Robert K. *The Barnhart Dictionary of Etymology.* New York: Wilson, 1987.
Mathews, Mitford M. *Americanisms: A Dictionary of Selected Americanisms on Historical Principles.* Chicago: Chicago UP, 1966.
Oxford English Dictionary. Ed. James A. H. Murray et al. 13 vols. New York: Oxford UP, 1933. Supplements.
Skeat, Walter W. *An Etymological Dictionary of the English Language.* New ed. rev. Oxford, Eng.: Clarendon, 1910.
Webster's Dictionary of English Usage, 1989 ed.

Abstracts and Digests
Language and Language Behavior Abstracts. Chicago: Sociological Abstracts, 1967–date.

Databases
LANGUAGE AND LANGUAGE BEHAVIOR ABSTRACTS
MODERN LANGUAGE ASSOCIATION BIBLIOGRAPHY

Literature

Bibliographies
Bibliographic Guide to Black Studies: 1987. The Schomburg Center for Research in Black Culture. Boston, MA: Hall, 1988. Supplements.
Bibliographical Guide to the Study of Literature of the USA. Ed. Clarence L. Gohdes. 5th ed. Durham, NC: Duke UP, 1984.
Bibliography of American Literature. New Haven: Yale UP, 1955–date.
Bibliography of Criticism of Contemporary Chicano Literature. Comp. Ernestina N. Eger. Berkeley, CA: Chicano Studies Library Publications, U of California, 1982.
Black American Fiction: A Bibliography. Ed. Carol Fairbanks and Eugene E. Engeldinger. Metuchen, NJ: Scarecrow, 1978.
Black Americans in Autobiography: An Annotated Bibliography of Autobiographies and Autobiographical Books Written Since the Civil War. Durham, NC: Duke UP, 1984.
A Decade of Chicano Literature (1970–1979): Critical Essays and Bibliography. Ed. Luis Leal et al. Santa Barbara, CA: Editorial La Causa, 1982.
Garland Shakespeare Bibliographies. 18 vols. New York: Garland, 1980–date.
MLA International Bibliography of Books and Articles on the Modern Languages and Literatures. New York: MLA, 1921–date.
New Cambridge Bibliography of English Literature. Ed. George Watson. 5 vols. Cambridge, Eng.: Cambridge UP, 1974.
Poetry Explication: A Checklist of Interpretations Since 1925 of British and American Poems Past and Present. Boston: Hall, 1980.

Guides
American and British Poetry: A Guide to the Criticism. Athens, OH: Swallow, 1984.
Cambridge Guide to Literature in English. Ed. Ian Ousby. New York: Cambridge UP, 1988.
Contemporary Literary Criticism. Detroit: Gale, 1973–date.

English Romantic Poets: A Review of Research and Criticism. 4th ed. New York: MLA, 1985.

Literary Research Guide. Ed. Margaret Patterson. 2nd ed. New York: MLA, 1983.

McGraw-Hill Guide to English Literature. Ed. K. Lawrence, B. Seifter, and I. Ratner. New York: McGraw, 1985.

Reader's Guide to Contemporary Literary Theory. Ed. Raman Selden and Peter Widdowson. 3rd ed. Lexington, KY: UP of Kentucky, 1993.

Research Guide for Undergraduate Students: English and American Literature. Ed. Nancy L. Baker. 3rd ed. New York: MLA, 1985.

Histories

Literary History of the United States. Ed. Robert E. Spiller et al. 4th ed. 2 vols. New York: Macmillan, 1974.

Oxford History of English Literature. Oxford, Eng.: Clarendon, 1945–date.

Indexes

Book Review Index. Detroit: Gale, 1965–date.

Essay and General Literature Index. New York: Wilson, 1934–date.

Granger's Index to Poetry. Ed. William J. Smith and William F. Bernhardt. 7th ed. New York: Columbia UP. 1982.

Humanities Index. New York: Wilson, 1974–date.

Index to Black American Writers in Collective Biographies. Dorothy W. Campbell. Littleton, CO: Libraries Unlimited, 1983.

Index to Book Reviews in the Humanities. Detroit: Thompson, 1960–date.

Index to Full-Length Plays: 1895–1964. 3 vols. Westwood, MA: Faxon, 1956–1965.

Literary Criticism Index. Ed. A. R. Weiner and S. Means. Metuchen, NJ: Scarecrow, 1984.

Play Index. 6 vols. New York: Wilson, 1953–date.

Short Story Index: Collections Indexed 1900–1978. New York: Wilson, 1979.

Encyclopedias

Benet's Reader's Encyclopedia. 3rd ed. New York: Harper, 1987.

Encyclopedia of World Literature in the Twentieth Century. Ed. Leonard S. Klein. 2nd ed. 5 vols. New York: Ungar, 1983. Supplement 1993.

Dictionaries

Dictionary of Classical Mythology. Ed. Pierre Grimal. Cambridge, MA: Basil Blackwell, 1985.

Oxford Companion to American Literature. Ed. James D. Hart. New York: Oxford UP, 1983.

Handbooks

Cambridge Handbook of American Literature. Ed. Jack Salzman. New York: Cambridge UP, 1986.

Abstracts and Digests

Abstracts of English Studies. Urbana IL: NCTE, 1958–date.

Book Review Digest. New York: Wilson, 1905–date.

Databases

BOOK REVIEW INDEX

MLA BIBLIOGRAPHY

Mathematics

Bibliographies, Guides, and Indexes

Annotated Bibliography of Expository Writing in the Mathematical Sciences. Ed. M. P. Gaffney and L. A. Steen. Washington, DC: Mathematics Association, 1976.

Bibliography of Mathematical Works Printed in America through 1850. Ed. I. Bernard Cohen. Repr. of 1940 ed. Salem, NH: Ayer, 1980.

Index of Mathematical Papers. Vols. 9 & 10. Providence, RI: American Mathematical Society, 1979.

Encyclopedias, Dictionaries, and Handbooks

CRC Handbook of Mathematical Sciences. Ed. William Beyer. 5th ed. West Palm, FL: CRC. 1978.

Encyclopedic Dictionary of Mathematics. Ed. Kiyoshi Ito. 2nd ed. 2 vols. Cambridge, MA: MIT P, 1993.

Facts on File Dictionary of Mathematics. Ed. Carol Gibson. Rev. ed. New York: Facts on File, 1988.

Gellert, W., et al., eds. *The VNR Concise Encyclopedia of Mathematics.* Florence, KY: Reinhold, 1977.

Prentice Hall Encyclopedia of Mathematics. Ed. Barry Henderson West et al. Englewood Cliffs, NJ: Prentice Hall, 1982.

Abstracts and Digests

General Science Index. New York: Wilson, 1978–date.

Mathematical Reviews. Providence, RI: American Mathematical Society, 1940–date. Monthly.

Databases

MATHSCI

Medical Sciences

Bibliographies, Guides, and Indexes

Cumulative Index to Nursing and Allied Health Literature. Glendale, CA: Glendale Adventist Medical Center, 1977–date. [Formerly *Cumulative Index to Nursing Literature,* 1956–1976.]

Guide to Library Resources for Nursing. Ed. K. P. Strauch and D. J. Brundage. New York: Appleton, 1980.

Health Statistics: A Guide to Information Sources. Detroit: Gale, 1980.

Hospital Literature Index. Chicago: American Hospital, 1945–date.

Index Medicus. Washington, DC: National Library of Medicine, 1960–date.

Information Sources in the Medical Sciences. Ed. L. T. Morton and S. Godbolt. 3rd ed. London, Eng.: Butterworths, 1984.

Introduction to Reference Sources in Health Sciences. Ed. F. Roper and J. Boorkman. 2nd ed. Chicago: Medical Library, 1984.

Library Research Guide to Nursing. E. Katina Strauch et al. Ann Arbor, MI: Pierian, 1989.

Medical Reference Works, 1679–1966: A Selected Bibliography. Ed. John B. Blake and Charles Roos. Chicago: Medical Library, 1967. Supplements 1970–date.

Morton, Leslie, and Robert J. Moore. *A Bibliography of Medical and Biomedical Biography.* Gower, Eng.: Gower, 1989.

Polit, Denise, and Bernadette Hungler. *Nursing Research: Principles and Methods.* 3rd ed. Philadelphia: Lippincott, 1987.

Encyclopedias, Dictionaries, and Handbooks
Black's Medical Dictionary. Ed. W. A. R. Thompson. London, Eng.: Black, 1984.
Dorland's Illustrated Medical Dictionary. 26th ed. Philadelphia: Saunders, 1985.
Encyclopedia of Medical History. Ed. Roderick McGrew. New York: McGraw, 1985.

Databases
BIOSIS PREVIEWS
EMBASE
MEDLINE
NURSING AND ALLIED HEALTH
SCISEARCH

Music

Bibliographies, Guides, and Indexes
Bibliographic Guide to Music. Boston: Hall, 1976–date.
Cohn, Arthur. *Recorded Classical Music: A Critical Guide to Compositions and Performances.* New York: Macmillan, 1981.
Horn, David. *The Literature of American Music in Books and Folk Music Collections: A Fully Annotated Bibliography.* Metuchen, NJ: Scarecrow, 1977.
Music Article Guide. Philadelphia: Information Services, 1966–date.
Music Index. Warren, MI: Information Coordinators, 1949–date.
Music Reference and Research Materials: An Annotated Bibliography. Ed. Vincent Duckles. 3rd ed. New York: Free Press/Macmillan, 1974.
Popular Music: An Annotated Index to American Popular Songs. 10 vols. New York: Adrian, 1964–85.
RILM (Repertoire Internationale de Litterature Musicale). New York: City U of New York, 1967–date.

Encyclopedias, Dictionaries, and Handbooks
Baker's Biographical Dictionary of Musicians. 7th ed. New York: Schirmer, 1984.
International Cyclopedia of Music and Musicians. Ed. Oscar Thompson. New York: Dodd, 1985.
International Encyclopedia of Hard Rock and Heavy Metal. Ed. Tony Jasper and Derek Oliver. 2nd ed. New York: Facts on File, 1991.
New College Encyclopedia of Music. New York: Norton, 1981.
New Grove Dictionary of Music and Musicians. Ed. H. Wylie Hitchcock and Stanley Sadie. 4 vols. New York: Grove, 1986.
New Oxford Companion to Music. Ed. Denis Arnold. 11th ed. 2 vols. Oxford, Eng.: Oxford UP, 1983.

Databases
RILM ABSTRACTS (Repertoire Internationale de Litterature Musicale)

Philosophy and Religion

Bibliographies, Guides, and Indexes
Bynagle, Hans E. *Philosophy: A Guide to the Reference Literature.* Littleton, CO: Libraries Unlimited, 1986.
The Philosopher's Guide: To Sources, Research Tools, Professional Life, and Related Fields. Ed. R. T. DeGeorge. Lawrence, KS: Regents, 1980.

The Philosopher's Index: An International Index to Philosophical Periodicals and Books. Bowling Green, OH: Bowling Green University, 1967–date.
A Reader's Guide to the Great Religions. Ed. Charles J. Adams. 2nd ed. New York: Free Press, 1977.
Religion Index One: Periodicals. Chicago: American Theologian, 1978–date.
Religious Periodicals Directory. Ed. Graham Cornish. Santa Barbara, CA: ABC-Clio. 1986.
Research Guide to Philosophy. Ed. Terence Tice and Thomas Slavens. (Sources of Information in the Humanities, No. 3.) Chicago: ALA, 1983.
Social and Historical Sciences, Philosophy and Religion. Vol. 2 of *Guide to Reference Material.* Ed. A. J. Walford. 4th ed. London, Eng.: Library Association, 1982.

Encyclopedias, Dictionaries, and Handbooks
Dictionary of American Religious Biography. Westport, CT: Greenwood, 1977.
A Dictionary of Philosophy. Ed. P. A. Angeles. New York: Harper, 1981.
Dictionary of Philosophy. Ed. A. R. Lacey. New York: Paul/Methuen, 1987.
Dictionary of the History of Ideas. Ed. P. Winer. 5 vols. New York: Scribner's, 1974.
Handbook of World Philosophy: Contemporary Developments Since 1945. Ed. John R. Burr. Westport, CT: Greenwood, 1980.
Harper's Bible Dictionary. Ed. Paul Achteimer. New York: Harper, 1985.
Melton, J. Gordon. *Encyclopedia of American Religions.* 2nd. ed. Detroit: Gale, 1986.
Parrinder, Geoffrey. *A Dictionary of Non-Christian Religions.* Philadelphia: Westminster, 1971.
Who's Who in Religion. Chicago: Marquis, 1985.

Abstracts and Digests
World Philosophy: Essay Reviews of 225 Major Works. Ed. Frank Magill. 5 vols. Englewood Cliffs: Salem, 1982.

Databases
PHILOSOPHER'S INDEX

Physics

Bibliographies, Guides, and Indexes
Applied Science and Technology Index. New York: Wilson, 1958–date.
Current Papers in Physics. London, Eng.: IEE, 1966–date.
Sources of History of Quantum Physics. Ed. T. S. Kuhn et al. Philadelphia: APS, 1967.
Use of Physics Literature. Ed. H. Coblans. Woburn, MA: Butterworth, 1975.

Encyclopedias, Dictionaries, and Handbooks
Encyclopedia of Physics. Ed. Robert Besancon. 3rd ed. New York: Chapman and Hall, 1990.
McGraw-Hill Encyclopedia of Physics. 2nd ed. New York: McGraw, 1991.
McGraw-Hill Encyclopedia of Science and Technology. 20 vols. 6th ed. New York: McGraw, 1987.

Abstracts and Digests
Owen, Dolores B. *Abstracts and Indexes in the Sciences and Technology.* 2nd ed. Metuchen, NJ: Scarecrow, 1985.
Physics Abstracts. Surrey, Eng.: IEE, 1898–date.
Science Abstracts. London, Eng.: IEE, 1898–date.

Databases
SCISEARCH
SPIN

Political Science

Bibliographies, Guides, and Indexes

ABC: Pol Sci. Santa Barbara, CA: ABC-Clio, 1969–date.
Combined Retrospective Index to Journals in Political Science, 1886–1974. 8 vols. New York: Carrollton, 1977–78.
Foreign Affairs Bibliography. New York: Council on Foreign Relations, 1933–date. Published every 10 years.
Hall, K. L. *Bibliography of American Constitutional and Legal History, 1896–1979.* 5 vols. Millwood, NY: Kraus, 1984.
Information Sources in Politics and Political Science: A Survey Worldwide. Ed. D. Englefield and G. Drewry. London, Eng.: Butterworth, 1984.
International Bibliography of Political Science. Paris, France: UNESCO, 1953–date. Annually.
Political Science: A Bibliographic Guide to the Literature. Metuchen, NJ: Scarecrow, 1965. Supplements 1966–date.
Public Affairs Information Service. *Bulletin.* New York: PAIS, 1915–date. Semimonthly.
Social Sciences Citation Index. New York: Wilson, 1973–date.
Social Sciences Index. New York: Wilson, 1974–date.

Encyclopedias, Dictionaries, and Handbooks

American Political Dictionary. Ed. Jack C. Plano and Milton Greenberg. 7th ed. New York: Holt, 1985.
Blackwell Encyclopedia of Political Institutions. Ed. Vernon Bogdanor. Cambridge, MA: Blackwell, 1987.
Encyclopedia of the Third World. Ed. George Thomas Kurian. 3 vols. New York: Facts on File, 1987.
Handbook of Latin American Studies. Gainesville: U of Florida P, 1936–date.
World Encyclopedia of Peace. Ed. Ervin Lazlo et al. 4 vols. New York: Pergamon, 1986.

Abstracts and Digests

International Political Science Abstracts. Oxford, Eng.: Blackwell, 1951–date.
Political Science Abstracts. New York: Plenum, 1967–date.
Sage Urban Studies Abstracts. San Mateo, CA: Sage, 1973–date.
United States Political Science Documents (USPSD). Pittsburgh: U of Pittsburgh P, 1975.

Databases

ASI
CIS
CONGRESSIONAL RECORD ABSTRACTS
GPO MONTHLY CATALOG
NATIONAL NEWSPAPER INDEX
PAIS
U.S. POLITICAL SCIENCE DOCUMENTS
WASHINGTON PRESSTEXT
WORLD AFFAIRS REPORT

Psychology

Bibliographies, Guides, and Indexes

Bibliographical Guide to Psychology. Boston: Hall, 1982.

Bibliography of Aggressive Behavior: A Reader's Guide to the Research Literature. Ed. J. Michael Crabtree and Kenneth E. Moyer. New York: Liss, 1977.

McInnis, Raymond G. *Research Guide for Psychology.* Westport, CT: Greenwood, 1982.

Marken, Richard. *Introduction to Psychological Research.* Monterey, CA: Brooks, 1981.

Mental Health Book Review Index. New York: Research Center for Mental Health, 1956–72.

Psychoanalysis, Psychology, and Literature: A Bibliography. Ed. Norman Kiell. 2nd ed. 2 vols. Metuchen, NJ: Scarecrow, 1982.

Psychological Index. 42 vols. Princeton: Psychological Review, 1895–1936. Succeeded by *Psychological Abstracts* (see below).

Reed, Jeffery J., and Pam M. Baxter. *Library Use: A Handbook for Psychology.* Washington, DC: APA, 1983.

Science Citation Index. Philadelphia: Institute for Scientific Information, 1961–date. Annually.

Social Sciences Citation Index. Philadelphia, PA: Institute for Scientific Information, 1969–date. Annually.

Encyclopedias, Dictionaries, and Handbooks

Encyclopedia of Psychology. Ed. Raymond J. Corsini. 2nd ed. 4 vols. New York: Wiley, 1994.

Encyclopedic Dictionary of Psychology. Ed. Terry F. Pettijohn. 4th ed. Guilford, CT: Duskin, 1991.

Oxford Companion to the Mind. Ed. Richard L. Gregory. Oxford, Eng.: Oxford UP, 1987.

Abstracts and Digests

Annual Review of Psychology. Palo Alto, CA: Annual Review, 1950–date.

Child Development Abstracts and Bibliography. Chicago: U of Chicago P, 1927–date.

Psychological Abstracts. Washington, DC: APA, 1927–date.

Sage Family Studies Abstracts. San Mateo, CA: Sage, 1979–date.

Databases

CHILD ABUSE AND NEGLECT
ERIC
MENTAL HEALTH ABSTRACTS
PSYCHOLOGICAL ABSTRACTS
SOCIAL SCISEARCH
SOCIOLOGICAL ABSTRACTS

Sociology and Social Work

Bibliographies, Guides, and Indexes

Combined Retrospective Index to Journals in Sociology, 1895–1974. 6 vols. Woodbridge, CT: Research Publications, 1978.

Humanities Index. New York: Wilson, 1974–date.

Library Research Guide to Sociology: Illustrated Search Strategy and Sources. Ed. Patricia Macmillan and James R. Kennedy. Ann Arbor, MI: Pierian, 1981.

Reference Sources in Social Work: An Annotated Bibliography. Ed. James H. Conrad. Metuchen, NJ: Scarecrow, 1982.
Social Science Index. New York: Wilson, 1974–date.

Encyclopedias, Dictionaries, and Handbooks
A Dictionary of Social Science Methods. Comp. P. M. Miller and M. J. Wilson. New York: Wiley, 1983.
Encyclopedia of Social Work. Ed. Anne Minahan. 18th ed. 3 vols. Silver Spring, MD: National Association of Social Workers, 1987.
Encyclopedia of Sociology. Ed. Edgar F. Borgatta and Marie L. Borgatta. New York: Macmillan, 1991.
Student Sociologist's Handbook. Ed. P. B. Bart and L. Frankel. 3rd ed. Glenview, IL: Scott, 1981.

Abstracts and Digests
Social Work Research and Abstracts. New York: NASW, 1964–date.
Sociological Abstracts. New York: Sociological Abstracts, 1953–date.

Databases
CHILD ABUSE AND NEGLECT
FAMILY RESOURCES
NCJRS (National Criminal Justice Reference Service)
SOCIAL SCISEARCH
SOCIOLOGICAL ABSTRACTS

Speech

Bibliographies, Guides, and Indexes
Bibliography of Speech and Allied Areas, 1950–1960. Westport, CT: Greenwood, 1972.
Humanities Index. New York: Wilson, 1974–date.
Index to American Women Speakers, 1828–1978. Metuchen, NJ: Scarecrow, 1980.
Index to Speech, Language, and Hearing: Journal Titles, 1954–78. San Diego, CA: College Hill, n.d.
Radio and Television: A Selected Annotated Bibliography. Metuchen, NJ: Scarecrow, 1978.
Speech Index: An Index to Collections of World Famous Orations and Speeches for Various Occasions, 1935–65. Metuchen, NJ: Scarecrow, 1965–date.

Databases
ERIC
LLBA (Language and Language Behavior Abstracts)
MLA BIBLIOGRAPHIES
SOCIAL SCISEARCH

Women's Studies

Bibliographies, Guides, and Indexes
American Women and Politics: A Selected Bibliography and Research Guide. New York: Garland, 1984.
Ballou, Patricia. *Women: A Bibliography.* 2nd ed. Boston: Hall, 1986.
Bibliographic Guide to Studies on the Status of Women: Development and Population Trends. Paris, France: UNESCO, 1983.

Feminist Library Criticism: A Bibliography of Journal Articles. Ed. Wendy Frost and Michelle Valiquette. New York: Garland, 1988.
Feminist Resources for Schools and Colleges: A Guide. Ed. Anne Chapman. New York: Feminist, 1979.
Fishburn, Katherine. *Women in Popular Culture: A Reference Guide.* Westport, CT: Greenwood, 1982.
Index-Directory of Women's Media. Washington, DC: Women's Institute for Freedom of the Press, 1975–date.
The Progress of Afro-American Women: A Selected Bibliography and Resource Guide. Comp. Janet Sims. Westport, CT: Greenwood, 1980.
Shepard, Bruce D., and Carroll A. Shepard. *Complete Guide to Women's Health.* Tampa, FL: Mariner, 1982.
Social Sciences Index. New York: Wilson, 1974–date.
Women: A Bibliography. Ed. Patricia Ballou. 2nd ed. Boston: Hall, 1986.
Women Helping Women. New York: Women's Action Alliance, 1981.
Women in America: A Guide to Information Sources. Ed. V. R. Terris. Detroit: Gale, 1980.
Women's History Sources: A Guide to Archives and Manuscript Collections in the U.S. 2 vols. New York: Bowker, 1979.

Encyclopedias, Dictionaries, and Handbooks
Dictionary of Feminist Theory. Ed. Maggie Humm. Columbus, OH: Ohio State UP, 1990.
Encyclopedia of Feminism. Ed. Lisa Tuttle. New York: Facts on File, 1986.

Abstracts and Digests
Women Studies Abstracts. New York: Rush, 1972–date.

Databases
ERIC
SOCIAL SCISEARCH
SOCIOLOGICAL ABSTRACTS

INDEX

Abbreviations (of),
  books of the Bible, 326–27
  common scholarly, 288, 323–24
  dates, 324–25, 331
  geographical locations, 325–26
  government/legal publications, 259,
    260–61
  journal titles, 304–05
  literature titles, 327
  MLA guidelines for, 322–27
  pages/chapters/sections, 288, 294
  publishers' names, 245, 334–35
  time, 324–25
Abstracts
  in research papers, 281, 304, 328,
    343, 347, 368
  of journal articles, 76–77, 265
  of newspaper articles, 78–79
Accent marks, 328, 337
Access, 66–67, 68
Acknowledging sources. *See* Documentation
America Online, 67, 79, 96, 112, 118,
  120. *See also* Internet
American Library Directory, 17, 18, 95,
  96
American Psychological Association
  (APA)
  documentation style of. *See* APA doc-
    umentation style
  publication guidelines of, 134, 177,
    281–82, 283, 322, 345
Ampersands, 328
Analysis (as critical thinking technique),
  1, 5, 51
Anonymous authors, 60, 249, 308
Anthologies/Collections, 254–55
APA documentation style, 279, 281–301
  abstracts, 281, 347
  Chicago style vs., 314
  content notes with, 363
  disciplines using, 279, 281, 300–01

intext citation, 279, 282–89
References list, 279, 281, 282,
  289–99, 364–65
sample paper, 345–65
variations of, 299–301, 310, 345
Appendices, 3, 134, 343
Archie, 123–24, 125, 128. *See also* Internet, search tools
Argumentation (as pattern of development), 174–75
Argumentative papers, 53–54, 162–64,
  320
Artworks/Photographs, 275–76
Audience (of research paper), 49, 52,
  182–84, 201
Audio recordings, 277, 299
Author-date documentation, 279, 281.
  See also APA documentation style;
  Chicago documentation style
Authorities (on subjects)
  evaluating credibility of, 154–58
  notetaking and, 139
  quoting, 148, 185–86
Authors
  anonymous, 60, 249
  corporate/group, 252
  documenting. *See specific documen-
    tation styles*
  evaluating credibility of, 154–58
  pseudonyms of, 249

Bars (virgules), 328–29
Biased language, 202, 322
Bible, 258–59, 326–27
Bibliographies, 61–66. *See also* Refer-
  ences list; Working bibliography;
  Works Cited list
Bibliography cards, 58–60, 103–04,
  109–10, 111, 113, 114, 116, 153.
  See also Working bibliography
Block quotations, 196, 288. *See also*
  Quotation(s)

397

Body (of research paper), 4, 187–96, 200, 319
Book area (of library), 19
Book catalogs, 22, 26
Book reviews, 154–55
Books
anthologies/collections, 254–55
authors of. *See* Authors
bibliographies of, 61, 134
documenting. *See specific documentation styles*
editions of, 255–57, 295–96
editors of, 243, 251–52
features of, 132–34
multivolume, 253–54, 296
selecting subjects using, 35–37
series of, 254
skimming, 132–34
Books in Print, 64–65
Brackets, 192–93, 336

Call numbers, 19, 20, 21–22, 85. *See also* Classification systems, library
Capitalization, 329–30
Card catalog, 22–24,
Catalogs (library), 22–27
Cause-and-effect, 176–77, 320
CBE. *See* Council of Biology Editors
CBE documentation style, 280, 305–12. *See also* Number-system documentation
disciplines using, 280, 305, 310–12
intext citation, 280, 305–07, 366
References list, 280, 306–11, 366, 373–74
sample paper, 366–74
variations of, 310–12
CD–ROM (compact disk–read-only memory), 22, 26–27, 67
Chicago documentation style, 279, 380, 312–14
APA style vs., 314
content notes with, 280, 314
disciplines using, 279, 280, 312
intext citation, 279, 312–14
References list, 279, 314, 315
use of endnotes/footnotes, 280
Chicago Manual of Style, The (14th ed., 1993), 279, 280, 314, 322
Citation indexes, 155–56
Citation-sequence intext citation form, 305–09, 311. *See also* CBE documentation style
Claim, 160–61. *See also* Thesis statement

Classification (as pattern of development), 176
Classification systems (library), 19–22
Close reading, 135–36. *See also* Reading
Clustering, 45
Common knowledge, 152–53. *See also* Documentation; Plagiarism
Compact discs. *See* CD–ROM
Comparison-and-contrast, 175–76, 320
CompuServe, 67, 79, 112, 118, 120, 155. *See also* Internet
Computers. *See also* Internet; online access
home use of, 29, 67, 118, 120
library use of, 29, 118, 120, 125–26
recording notes/sources on, 58, 143–44
writing on. *See* Word processing
Conclusion (of research paper), 4, 196–99, 200, 319
Conference/Meeting proceedings, 252–53, 274, 297
Content notes (MLA style), 3, 199, 205, 213–17, 235, 330, 343. *See also* APA documentation style, content notes with; *Chicago* documentation style, content notes with; Endnotes/Footnotes
Continuous vs. discontinuous pagination, 261–62
Copyright law, 28, 330. *See also* Plagiarism
Council of Biology Editors (CBE), 280, 305, 322, 366. *See also* CBE documentation style
publication guidelines of, 305, 316, 366
Critical thinking, 1–14
definition of, 1
learning skills for, 2, 154
research question and, 50–52
source evaluation and, 153–56
techniques of, 1–2, 50–52

Databases, 5, 20, 118–20. *See also* online access
Dates, 293, 324–25, 330–31
Definitions
form for, 331–32
in content notes, 217
in introductions, 187
of unfamiliar/special terms, 182–84, 187, 201
Dewey Decimal (DD) system, 19–21

DIALOG, 69, 79, 88, 116, 119, 155
Dictionaries, 202, 320, 337, 341
Directory of Special Libraries and Information Centers, 9, 95, 96
Discovery techniques. *See* Clustering; Freewriting
Dissertations, 259, 265
Documentation (of research paper)
   APA style. *See* APA documentation style
   author-date. *See* Author-date documentation
   CBE style. *See* CBE documentation style
   Chicago style. *See Chicago* documentation style
   common knowledge, 152–53
   definition of, 4, 5
   discipline guides for, 281, 314–16. *See also specific documentation styles*
   intext citation. *See* Intext citation
   MLA style. *See* MLA documentation style
   notetaking. *See* Notes/Notetaking
   number-system. *See* Number-system documentation
   overview of, 151–53, 205–06, 279–81
   plagiarism. *See* Plagiarism
   purpose of, 205
   References list. *See* References list
   subject/type of paper and, 279–81
   Working bibliography. *See* Working bibliography
   Works Cited list. *See* Works Cited list
Drafts (of research paper), 181, 200–03, 318, 341–43. *See also* Editing; Proofreading; Revising; Writing

Editing (the research paper), 6, 201–02, 320–41
   for style, 320–22. *See also* Style
   methods of, 320
   MLA guidelines for, 322–41
   rewriting vs., 320
   sample of, 321
Editions, 255–57, 295–96
Editors, 243, 251–52
e.g., 322, 324, 332
Ellipses, 192, 194–96
Encyclopedias, 5, 34–35
Endnotes/Footnotes, 3, 5, 280, 332. *See also* Content notes

et al., 284–85, 324, 333
Evaluation (as critical thinking technique), 1, 5, 50–51

File transfer protocol. *See* FTP
Footnotes. *See* Content notes; Endnotes/Footnotes
Foreign languages
   books in, 257
   words from, 332, 333, 337
Formal outlines, 164, 165–73, 220. *See also* Outlines/Outlining
Freewriting, 43–44, 45
FTP (file transfer protocol), 122–24, 125, 127. *See also* Internet, search tools

Gale Directory of Publications and Broadcast Media, 80, 113–14
Gopher, 41–42, 121, 123, 124, 125, 127. *See also* Internet, search tools
Government publications/documents, 5, 84–89, 115–16

Headings
   in notes, 139, 145, 159
   in outlines, 165–73
   in research notebooks, 9, 42, 50
   in research papers, 134, 282, 304
   parallelism in, 173
Home page, 121–22. *See also* World Wide Web
Humanities Index, 74–76
Hypertext, 40, 121–22

Illustrations, 275–76, 338–40
Indexes, 66–89
   citation, 155–56
   definition of, 66
   locating sources using, 66–89
   on CD–ROM, 67
   online, 67, 78–79, 81, 82
   selecting subjects using, 36–37
   skimming, 133–34
   to books, 36–37, 133–34
   to government publications, 84–89
   to journals, 69–77
   to literature, 8, 80–83
   to magazines, 66–69
   to newspapers, 77–80
   to pamphlets, 83–84
   to periodicals, 66–77

Informal outlines, 164, 165. *See also*
    Outlines/Outlining
Informative research papers, 54,
    163–64, 320
Interlibrary loan, 28, 84
Internet, 118–30. *See also* online access;
    World Wide Web
    addresses, 120–21, 274
    commercial providers, 67, 118, 120.
        See also specific providers
    database searches via, 119–20
    definition of, 120
    hypertext, 40, 121–22
    research via, 120–30
    search tools, 121–25, 127–29. *See also*
        specific search tools
    selecting topics using, 40–42
Interviews, 5, 97–104, 263–64
Intext citation
    APA style, 279, 282–89
    CBE style, 280, 305–07, 366
    Chicago style, 279, 312–14
    definition of, 206
    MLA style, 206–13
    number-system style, 280, 301–02
Introduction (of research paper), 4,
    184–87, 200, 319
Italics
    of definitions, 331–32
    of foreign words, 333
    of titles. *See specific documentation*
        styles
    underlining vs., 209, 214, 244, 282,
        333, 340–41. *See also* Underlining

Journals (professional). *See also* Maga-
        zines; Periodicals
    abbreviations of titles, 304–05
    abstracts of articles, 76–77, 265
    definition of, 69
    documenting. *See specific documen-*
        tation styles
    electronic, 77, 274
    indexes to, 69–77
    pagination of, 261–62

Lectures. *See* Speeches/Lectures/Ad-
        dresses
Legal sources/citations, 149, 260–61,
        288–89, 297–98
Letters, 5, 264, 268, 289
Libraries, 15–29
    academic, 15–17
    assessing, 16–17

catalogs of, 22–27
classification systems of, 19–22
computer facilities of, 29, 118, 120,
    125–26
locating, 17–18
museum, 94, 95–96
online accessibility to. *See* online
    access, libraries
organization of, 18–19
public, 15, 17–18
Regional Depository, 84, 115
resources of, 27–29
selecting subjects using, 34–38
services provided by, 27–29
society, 94, 95–96
special emphasis, 16
Library catalogs, 22–27
Library of Congress (LC) classification
    system, 19–20, 21–22
Library of Congress Subject Headings,
    23
Literature
    abbreviations of titles of, 327
    indexes to, 8, 80–83
    summarizing, 186

Magazines. *See also* Journals; Periodi-
        cals
    documenting. *See specific documen-*
        tation styles
    electronic, 67–69, 274
    indexes to, 66–69
    pagination of, 261–62
Margins, 342
Microform catalogs, 22, 26
Microsoft Network, 118. *See also*
    Internet
MLA. *See* Modern Language Association
MLA documentation style, 205–37
    content notes, 213–17
    intext citation, 206–13
    sample paper, 217–37
    working bibliography, 59–60
    Works Cited. *See* Works Cited list
Modern Language Association (MLA),
    205–06
    Handbook for Writers of Research
        Papers (4th ed., 1995), 239, 316
    publication guidelines of, 239, 316,
        322. *See also* MLA documentation
        style; Works Cited list
Monthly Catalog (MC) of United States
    Government Publications, 84,
    85–86, 116

Name-year intext citation form, 305–06, 309. *See also* CBE documentation style

Names
of persons, 334
of publishers, 245, 334–35

NETCOM, 41, 124. *See also* Internet

New Riders' Official Internet Yellow Pages, 17, 89, 126

Newspapers
abstracts of articles, 78–79
documenting. *See specific documentation styles*
indexes to, 77–80
online access to, 78–80

NEXIS, 79, 80

Notecards, 9, 58, 138, 140–41, 142. *See also* Bibliography cards

Notes (page). *See* Content notes; Endnotes/Footnotes

Notes/Notetaking, 3, 6, 136–53
content notes. *See* Content notes
content of, 136–41
documentation. *See* Documentation; *specific documentation styles*
endnotes/footnotes. *See* Endnotes/Footnotes
format of, 137
headings in, 139, 145, 159
outlining from. *See* Outlines/ Outlining, creating
recording methods, 12, 141–44
reviewing, 158–59
types of, 144–50. *See also* Quotation; Paraphrase; Summary
writing from, 140–41. *See also* Writing

Number-system documentation, 280, 301–05. *See also* CBE documentation style

Numbers/Numerals, 335–36. *See also* Page numbers

Observation (onsite), 51, 92–94

Online access (to)
abstracts, 77
book reviews, 155
databases, 20, 118–20
documenting. *See specific documentation styles*
encyclopedias, 35
finding topics via, 40–42
government publications, 87–89
indexes, 67, 78–79, 81, 82

interviewing via, 103
journals, 77, 274
libraries, 17, 24–26, 28, 29, 96
magazines, 67–69, 274
museums, 96
newspapers, 78–80
resources about, 125–26
Social Issues Resources Series, 38
speeches, 111–12

Outlines/Outlining, 3, 6, 164–77
creating, 170–72
definition of, 164
guidelines for, 164
patterns of development and, 174–77
purpose of, 164
samples of, 166–77, 220
types of, 164, 165–70
writing from, 319

Page numbers
abbreviations for, 288, 294
in References/Works Cited lists. *See specific documentation styles*
of periodicals, 261–62
of research papers, 220, 238, 342–43, 347, 368, 369

PAIS. *See* Public Affairs Information Service

Pamphlets, 5, 83–84, 268–69

Paper, 341

Paragraph outlines, 169–70

Paragraphs
concluding. *See* Conclusion
developing, 187–88
editing, 201, 322
introductory. *See* Introduction
revising, 200–01
topic sentences of. *See* Topic sentences

Paraphrase, 144, 146–48

Parenthetical citation. *See* Intext citation

Patterns of development (in writing), 174–77, 320

Periodicals. *See also* Journals; Magazines; Newspapers
area in library, 19
bibliographies of, 61
definition of, 60, 66
documenting. *See specific documentation styles*
files and serials lists, 80
indexes to, 66–77
skimming, 134

Photocopying
as library service, 29
notetaking and, 28, 142–43
of final paper, 343
Plagiarism, 28, 150–53
Poetry, 196
Population (of survey), 108–09. *See also*
Surveys
Prefaces, 134, 257–58
Primary sources, 4–5, 91–92
Prodigy, 67, 79, 88, 118. *See also* Internet
Proofreading (the research paper),
202–03
Public Affairs Information Service
(PAIS)
Bulletin, 111–12, 116
publications of, 86
Publication information
dates, 244, 293, 308–09, 330
publishers' names/locations, 245,
308, 334–35
Punctuation
editing for, 320, 321–22
of quotations, 190–96
proofreading for, 202
Purpose (of research paper), 2, 13,
52–54, 162–64, 320

Questionnaires. *See* Surveys
Quotation marks, 190–91
Quotation(s), 190–96
altering, 191–96
block, 196, 288
documenting. *See specific documentation styles*
errors in, 336
in conclusion, 197–98
in introduction, 185–86
integrating, 190–96
notetaking for, 144, 148–50
purposes of using, 148–50, 185–86,
191

Radio programs, 112–13, 277
Reader's Guide to Periodical Literature
locating magazines using, 60, 66, 67
selecting subjects using, 32, 37
Reading (sources), 131–36
Reference sources. *See also specific
types of sources*
for selected subjects, 375–96
location in library, 18
References list, 3, 4. *See also* Works
Cited list

APA style, 279, 281, 282, 289–99,
364–65
CBE style, 280, 306–11, 366, 373–74
Chicago style, 279, 314, 315
number-system, 280, 302–04
samples of, 299, 300, 311, 315
Regional Depository Library, 84, 115
Research
critical thinking and, 2, 50–52
definition of, 4
focus of, 6–8, 25
library. *See* Libraries
organizing, 5–13
patterns of, 8
purpose of, 2
via the Internet. *See* Internet,
research via; online access
Research notebook, 8–13
headings in, 9, 42, 50
recording notes in, 142. *See also*
Notes/Notetaking
recording research questions in, 50
recording research subjects in, 11,
33–34
recording research topics in, 42–43,
46
sample of, 10–11, 42, 51
Research paper
audience of, 49, 52, 182–84, 201
definition of, 2
drafts of, 181, 200–03, 318, 341–43
organization of, 3–4, 174–77, 199,
343. *See also* Body; Conclusion;
Content notes; Introduction; References list; Works Cited list
proofreading. *See* Proofreading
purpose of, 2, 13, 52–54, 162–64, 320
revising. *See* Revising
samples of, 163–64, 217–37, 345–74
tables/illustrations in, 338–40
title of, 177–78, 340
typing. *See* Typing; Word processing
writing. *See* Writing
Research paper schedule, 6–8, 12
Research question, 49–52. *See also*
Thesis statement
audience and, 52
critical thinking techniques and,
50–52
formulating, 2, 3, 6, 15, 49–52
recording, 9, 11, 12, 30, 50
reviewing, 159, 320
Research subject. *See* Subject
Research topic. *See* Topic

Revising (the research paper), 200–01, 318–20
Running heads, 343, 348, 368. *See also* Page numbers

Sampling (survey population), 108–09
Scientific patterns (of development), 177
"Search engines." *See* Internet, search tools
Secondary sources, 5, 91–92
Sentence outlines, 169
Sentences, 201, 321–22. *See also* Topic sentences
Sexist language, 202, 322
sic, 193, 324, 336
Skimming, 35, 132–34
Sources (for research paper)
  documenting. *See* Documentation; *specific documentation styles*
  evaluating credibility of, 153–56
  finding, 4–5, 12, 96–97. *See also* Libraries; Research; *specific types of sources*
  integrating in writing, 189–90, 201
  storing, 58–60. *See also* Working bibliography
  taking notes from. *See* Notes/ Notetaking
  types of, 4–5, 91–92
Speeches/Lectures/Addresses, 110–12, 267–68
Spelling, 202–03, 320, 337
Style (of writing)
  audience and, 181–82
  coherence and unity, 188
  editing to improve, 320–22
  integrating information, 189–96, 201
  paragraphing, 187–88, 201, 322
  punctuation, 190–96, 202, 320, 321–22
  sentence structure, 201, 321–22
  tense, 188–89, 201–02
  tone, 181, 182
  transitions, 188
  vocabulary, 201–02, 321
  voice, 181–82
Subject (of research paper), 30–40
  assigned, 32
  free-choice, 32–33
  narrowing for topic, 39–40
  personal interests as, 2, 13, 33, 46
  recording, 11, 33–34
  selecting, 6, 30–38
  topic vs., 31. *See also* Topic

Subject cards, 22–23
Summary
  as critical thinking technique, 1, 5, 50
  as notetaking method, 144, 145–46
Superscript numerals, 214, 280, 301–02, 306, 337. *See also* Content notes; Number-system documentation
Surveys, 104–10
Synthesis (as critical thinking technique), 1, 5, 52

Table of contents
  of book, 35, 36, 132–33
  of magazine, 69
  samples of, 36, 133
  skimming, 35, 132–33
Tables, 338, 340
Television programs, 112–14, 277
Telnet, 122, 123, 125, 127. *See also* Internet, search tools
Tense (of writing), 188–89, 201–02
Text (of research paper), 3–4. *See also* Body; Conclusion; Introduction
Thesis statement, 160–64
  claims, 160–61
  final, 160–64, 319
  placement of, 162–63, 184, 197
  preliminary, 6, 30, 55, 139, 159
  purpose of paper and, 162–64
  qualities of effective, 160–61
  reading for, 135
  statement in conclusion, 197
  statement in introduction, 184
Title cards, 23, 24
Title page, 3, 343, 346, 367
Titles
  abbreviations of, 327, 334–34
  documenting. *See specific documentation styles*
  of research papers, 177–78, 340, 343, 346, 367
  skimming, 132
Tone (of writing), 181, 182
Topic (of research paper)
  audience and, 49, 52
  back-up, 43, 47–48
  definition of, 3
  evaluating, 61
  narrowing focus of, 43–46, 47
  online resources for, 40
  recording, 42–43
  selecting, 2, 6, 11, 12, 15, 30–32, 39–42, 48–49
  subject vs., 3. *See also* Subject

Topic outlines, 168
Topic sentences, 135–36, 187–88, 201, 322
TV. *See* Television
Type quality/style, 341–42
Typing (the research paper)
  accent marks, 328, 337
  APA guidelines for, 281–82, 288
  binding, 343
  correcting errors, 202–03, 319, 343
  final draft, 202–03, 318
  headings, 282
  indenting/spacing, 195–96, 288, 290, 342
  length, 3
  margins, 342
  MLA guidelines for, 341–43
  numbers, 336
  page numbers, 342
  paper, 341
  running heads, 343
  superscripts, 214, 306, 337
  type quality/style, 341–42
  underlining. *See* Underlining
  Works Cited page, 239, 240

Underlining
  continuous, 341
  italics vs., 209, 241, 244, 282, 331–32, 333, 340–41
  of definitions, 331–32
  of foreign words, 333
  of titles. *See specific documentation styles*
Uniform resource locator (URL), 120–21, 274

Veronica, 123–24. *See also* Internet, search tools
Vertical file, 83–84, 115
Video recordings, 276–77
Virgules, 328–29
Vocabulary, 182–84, 187, 201–02, 321
Voice (of writing), 181–82

WAIS (wide area information service), 124–25, 129
Word division, 341
Word processing. *See also* Typing
  accent marks, 337
  backing up files, 343
  correcting errors, 202–3, 343

editing/proofreading tools, 201, 202–03, 319, 320, 337, 341, 343
  headings, 282
  library facilities for, 29
  superscripts, 214, 306, 337
  type quality/style, 341–42
  use of italics vs. underlining, 209, 241, 244, 282, 331–32, 333, 340–41. *See also* Underlining
Working bibliography, 57–61
  definition of, 57
  evaluating topic using, 61
  information needed, 59–60
  recording sources, 58, 97, 110, 113, 114
  reviewing, 89, 131
Works Cited list (MLA style), 3, 4, 6, 199, 206, 208, 238–78
  alphabetization of, 239
  authors'/editors' names in, 242–43
  basic information in, 238–42
  bibliography vs., 238
  content notes vs., 213, 215
  general guidelines for, 239–46
  index to specific forms, 246–47
  page numbers in, 245–46
  pagination of, 238
  placement of, 238, 343
  publication information in, 244–45
  samples of, 236–37, 240
  titles in, 244
  typing, 239, 240
World Wide Web (WWW), 96, 121–22, 125, 128. *See also* Internet, search tools; online access
Writing (the research paper), 180–204
  final draft, 200–03
  integrating quotes, 190–96
  integrating sources, 189–90
  notes used in, 140–41
  on computer. *See* Word processing
  on typewriter. *See* Typing
  patterns of development, 174–77
  preparing for, 180–84
  stages of, 180–81. *See also* Editing; Proofreading; Revising
  style of writing. *See* Style
Writing style. *See* Style
WWW. *See* World Wide Web

Yahoo, 122. *See also* Internet, search tools